KW-278-558

GENDER IDENTITY

DISORDERS, DEVELOPMENTAL PERSPECTIVES AND SOCIAL IMPLICATIONS

SOCIAL ISSUES, JUSTICE AND STATUS

Additional books in this series can be found on Nova's website
under the Series tab.

Additional e-books in this series can be found on Nova's website
under the e-book tab.

SOCIAL ISSUES, JUSTICE AND STATUS

GENDER IDENTITY

DISORDERS, DEVELOPMENTAL PERSPECTIVES AND SOCIAL IMPLICATIONS

BEVERLY L. MILLER
EDITOR

nova publishers

New York

Library of Congress Cataloging-in-Publication Data

Gender identity : disorders, developmental perspectives and social implications / editor, Beverly L. Miller.
   pages cm. -- (Social issues, justice and status)
 Includes index.
 ISBN: 978-1-63321-488-0 (hardcover)
 1. Gender identity. 2. Gender identity disorders. 3. Sex role. I. Miller, Beverly L.
 BF692.2.G4673 2014
 155.3'3--dc23
                     2014025208

Published by Nova Science Publishers, Inc. † *New York*

CONTENTS

PREFACE

In this book, gender identity is examined as a disorder, along with developmental perspectives and social implications. Some of the topics discussed include gender identity as a personality process; the intersection of gender and sexual identity development in a sample of transgender individuals; gender dysphoria; representations of teachers about the relation between physical education contents and gender identities; and common hypothetical etiology of excess androgen exposure in female-to-male transsexualism and polycystic ovary syndrome.

Chapter 1 – Within psychology and psychiatry, *gender identity* has developed at least two distinguishable meanings: awareness of anatomy and endorsing specific traits that are stereotypical of different gender groups. However, neither existing approach has considered gender identity to be a self-categorization process that exists within personality science. In this chapter, the author develops the argument that gender identity can be fruitfully explored as a personality process. The author use both classic and modern personality process approaches to demonstrate that theorizing about gender identity from the personality perspective clarifies and complements—rather than eclipses—prior theorizing. Additionally, several unique insights are available to researchers when gender identity is approached as a personality process, and some of these insights are identified within this chapter.

Chapter 2 – This study investigated relationships among the experience of trauma, identity development, distress, and positive change among 908 emerging adults with a mean age of 19.99 (SD = 1.97) years. Greater identity exploration was associated with more distress, whereas greater identity commitment was associated with positive change after the trauma. Participants with a PTSD diagnosis reported more distress and identity exploration as compared to participants without PTSD who reported more positive change and identity commitments. Regression analyses found the centrality of the trauma event to one's identity predicted identity distress above and beyond the experience of trauma. Identity distress and the centrality of the trauma together predicted identity exploration, while only identity distress predicted identity commitments. Identity development predicted positive change above and beyond identity distress, centrality of the trauma event, and the experience of trauma. Collectively, these results indicate that aspects of distress and growth occur after traumatic events.

Chapter 3 – Studies of gender identity development in transgender individuals suggest that for these individuals an awareness of their non-heteronormative gender identity typically occurs in early childhood, with awareness and self-definitions of sexual identity typically occurring later on in puberty and young adulthood. In this chapter the authors describe the findings from eleven self-identified transgender individuals (4 MTF, 6 FTM, 1 intersex) who were interviewed about the age at which they became aware of their non-heteronormative gender identity and about whether they recalled specific life events associated with their awareness of their gender identity. Consistent with the previous literature, seven of the participants gave specific early childhood ages at which they became aware of their non-heteronormative gender identity. Most of these transgender individuals did not cite any specific event that made them aware of their non-heteronormative gender identity, instead recalling that they just knew they were different. The four other transgender participants (all FTMs), however, reported that their non-heteronormative gender identity awareness did not become solidified until their teen years and beyond and that this gender identity awareness occurred in the context of their sexual identity. These findings are discussed in terms of the intersectionality of gender and sexual identity in the development of non-heteronormative gender/sexual identities.

Chapter 4 – Since the origins of humanity the possibility of an area existing beyond the binary subdivision of sexual genders has been incorporated into myth and symbolic representations as expressed through rite, from Plato's Androgyne to Hermaphrodite, from the myth of Attis and Cybele to the figure of Venus Castina. At the same time different cultures have envisaged, and in some cases continue to envisage, outside any "pathologized" category, the possibility of there being a non-correspondence between an individual's biological sex and their subjective experience of belonging to a given sexual gender: for example, the Neapolitan *Femminiello*, the *"two-spirits"* among American natives, and the *Hijras*, who still exist on the Indian sub-continent. Nevertheless, in the West today this existential condition is to some extent shaped, and somehow even produced, by a series of *discourses*, which are first and foremost medical/psychiatric and define and mold its very nature. *Gender Dysphoria*, the clinical taxonomic category which the American Psychiatric Association has recently adopted to replace the existing *Gender Identity Disorder*, refers to an individual's affective/cognitive discontent with the assigned gender and the distress that may accompany the incongruence between one's experienced or expressed gender and one's assigned gender, which in many, but not all, cases also involves a somatic transition by cross-sex hormone treatment and genital surgery (*Sex Reassignment Surgery*). As Michel Foucault would have it, psychiatric knowledge molds bodies. In any case, the work of preparation and drafting of the recent edition of the DSM, the Diagnostic and Statistical Manual of Mental Disorders has been accompanied by a lively debate on whether or not it is legal to include the condition within the ranks of Mental Disorders. The result of this debate was to keep the condition in the manual, therefore interpreting it as a manifestation of a Mental Disorder. In the present paper, the authors will analyze the main historical stages of the process of inclusion of this condition within psychiatric knowledge. The authors will, therefore, discuss the main problems that this inclusion produces, questioning the very foundations of psychiatric knowledge. Moreover, the authors will consider the exact nature of this condition within the framework of a phenomenological/existential approach, beyond the simplistic diagnostic criteria proposed by the American manual.

Chapter 5 – Gender Dysphoria (GD) is a complex and most probably multifactorially caused condition and it is increasingly a matter of interest in the media and scientific literature. In particular, it is expressed by a significant discomfort that is usually associated with the incongruence between natal sex and gender identity and it represents a dimensional phenomenon that can occur with different degrees of intensity. The most extreme form of GD is usually accompanied by a desire for gender reassignment (GR). GD can have an early onset, since preschool age, with extremely variable and hard to predict clinical outcomes. Etiopathogenic theories are still uncertain and no specific etiological factor determining atypical gender development has been found to date, but there seems to be an increasing evidence of a biologic and/or genetic component involved. Professionals that deal with this kind of issues need to be able to recognize gender variant youth in order to perform an early assessment, to support awareness and structuring of sexual identity dimensions, to prevent associated psychopathology (if present), and consequently to improve the quality of life. Despite international guidelines being available, treatment of gender dysphoric children and adolescents is still controversial and there is currently poor consensus on psychological and medical intervention. Specialized GD services appear to be important in order to prevent suffering and distress and ensure psychosocial wellbeing of gender variant children/adolescents and their families. Aim of this chapter is to deal with psychological, medical and ethic aspects related to GD in children and adolescents, and to provide an overview of current debates and clinical options available internationally.

Chapter 6 – Transsexualism is a gender identity disorder with a multifactorial etiology. Neurodevelopmental processes and genetic factors seem to be implicated.

The aim of this study was to investigate the association between the genotype and female-to-male (FtM) and male-to-female (MtF) transsexualism by performing a karyotype and molecular analysis of three variable regions of the genes *ERβ* (estrogen receptor β), *AR* (androgen receptor) and *CYP19A1* (aromatase).

Methods: The authors carried out a cytogenetic and molecular analysis in 273 FtMs, 442 MtFs, 371 control females and 473 control males. The control groups were healthy, age- and geographical origin-matched. The karyotype was investigated by G-banding and by high-density (HD) array in the transsexual group. The molecular analysis involved three tandem variable regions of genes *ERβ* (CA repeats in intron 5), *AR* (CAG repeats in exon 1) and *CYP19A1* (TTTA repeats in intron 4). The allele and genotype frequencies, after division into short (S) and long (L) alleles, were obtained.

Results: No karyotype aberration has been linked to transsexualism (FtM or MtF), and prevalence of aneuploidy (3%) appears to be slightly higher than in the general population (0.53%). Concerning the molecular study, FtMs differed significantly from control females with respect to the median repeat length polymorphism *ERβ* ($P = 0.002$) but not to the length of the other two studied polymorphisms. The repeat numbers in *ERβ* were significantly higher in FtMs than in the female control group, and the likelihood of developing transsexualism was higher (odds ratio: 2.001 [1.15–3.46]) in the subjects with the genotype homozygous for long alleles.

No significant difference in allelic or genotypic distribution of any gene examined was found between MtFs and control males. Moreover, molecular findings presented no evidence of an association between the sex hormone-related genes (*ERβ*, *AR*, and *CYP19A1*) and MtF transsexualism.

Chapter 7 – Gender violence is a social problem that has a great impact in Spain. This complex process has also personal implications in women's health (physical and mental health) and social implications (laws or cultural constrains, among others) that affect interpersonal relationships. To analyze this phenomenon a wide range of variables should be taken into account. Two of these important variables are cultural level (culture of honor) and individual level (gender identity). Their studies show that there is a relationship between gender identity and culture of honor. Specifically, individuals high in masculine gender identity give more importance to culture of honor whereas high feminine gender identity relates with a lower concern to honor affairs. In this book chapter for *Gender Identity: Disorders, Developmental Perspectives and Social Implications*, the authors analyze the role that this relation has on gender violence and their consequences and social implications. Specifically, the authors summarize a series of studies that examine gender identity, culture of honor and gender violence both in prisoners and in non prisoners' men and in general population. Their results would help to better understand gender violence and the role that gender identity has in this complex, personal and social, phenomenon.

Chapter 8 – Gender Identity Disorder (GID) is included in the ICD-10 among the Mental and Behavioural Disorders (so called F-Codes) (F64). The World Health Organization is currently preparing the eleventh version of the ICD, to be published in 2015 or 2017. Members of the WHO Working Group on the Classification of Sexual Disorders and Sexual Health propose the removal of GID from the Mental and Behavioural Disorders and its inclusion in a non-psychiatric category. One motion is to rename the condition 'Gender Incongruence', and place it within a new category called 'Certain conditions related to sexual health', thereby formalising the idea that whatever the condition is, it is not a disorder.

Retaining GID within the ICD is thought to facilitate access to publicly funded or otherwise subsidised medical treatment. Whereas removing GID from mental illnesses is certainly a step forward in the recognition of the diversity of individual gender and sexual orientations, it may be asked whether it is still too small a step. Why should gender differences be included at all in diagnostic manuals? On what grounds? This chapter explores the reasons for and against retention of the diagnostic category of GID in the ICD, and it discusses where it should eventually be placed.

It will conclude that, as proposed by some LGBT groups, gender variance could be enclosed within the so-called Z coded of the ICD. These are non-pathologising codes, currently listed under the "Factors influencing health status and contact with health services".

Chapter 9 – In the past few decades, the literature has addressed transsexual patients' quality of life, satisfaction and various other outcomes such as sexual functioning after sex reassignment surgery. Instead, the role of the cross-sex hormonal treatment alone in the well-being of transsexual patients has been the subject of very little differentiated investigation. Moreover, due to their cross-sectional design, previous studies did not demonstrate a direct effect of hormonal treatment in transsexual patients' distress. To their knowledge only three recent researches studied the transsexual patients' distress related to the hormonal treatment in a longitudinal study. In light of the importance of this information, this chapter discusses a review of these three perspective studies, two of whom were performed in partially overlapping samples from the same gender unit. Although transsexualism has been described as a diagnostic entity in its own right, not necessarily associated with severe comorbid psychiatric findings, for most patients transsexualism may be a stressful situation and may cause clinical distress or impairment in important areas of functioning. This review provides information on the prevalence and/or severity of psychobiological distress, mental distress and functional impairment in untreated transsexual patients. One of these three studies revealed that, despite the majority of transsexual patients do not suffer of a psychiatric disorder, the condition is associated with subthreshold anxiety/depression, psychological distress and functional impairment. Another of these three studies achieved the same results on the psychological distress in untreated transsexual patients, using part of the methodology of the previous study in a different sample. The last study added information about the untreated transsexual patients' stress system dysregulation, revealing that these patients show hypothalamic-pituitary-adrenal (HPA) system dysregulation and appear to notably differ from normative samples in terms of mean levels of perceived stress. In particular, untreated transsexual patients showed elevated cortisol awakening response (CAR), with cortisol levels above the normal range, and elevated perceived stress. Moreover, this review reports the role of the hormonal treatment in reducing psychobiological and mental distress in transsexualism. Specifically, when treated with hormonal treatment transsexual patients reported less anxiety, depression, psychological distress and functional impairment. Also transsexual patients showed reduced cortisol awakening response (CAR) and perceived stress levels after the beginning of the cross-sex hormonal treatment. It should be added that in all the three studies the psychobiological and mental distress scores resembled those of a general population after cross-sex hormonal treatment was initiated. Finally, the review discusses the hypothesis of a direct relation versus an indirect relation between the hormone therapy itself and the patients' well-being, supporting a psycho-social meaning of the hormonal treatment (indirect relation) rather than a biological effect of sex hormones (direct relation).

Chapter 10 − The demands of gender dysphoria (GD) in children and adolescents are increasing in recent years in the Spanish public health system. The complexity of the process and its clinical approach requires providing treatment by specialized units with multidisciplinary teams. The legislation relating to children with GD is not homogeneous in Spain. It currently provides health care for this population in gender teams with a non-interventionist attitude in children, and recommending pubertal suppression for adolescents in Tanner Stage above 2, in most units. Integral care of the GD begins in the Spanish public health system in Andalusia (southern region) in 1999 (Andalusian-Gender-Team, AGT). The demand for minors has grown dramatically in recent years, having a fivefold increase in the number of applications since 2007, especially in the group of natal boys.

From 1999 through 2013, 165 subjects with a range of age (5 to 17 years) have been evaluated. 74,5% were natal males (male-to-female, MtF) and 25,5% female-to-male (FtM). 12%, were ≤ 12 years (childhood group), the rest had 12 to 17 years (adolescent group). 4 cases were excluded and 22 dropped out from the AGT. 3 boys regreted the GD in this period. Currently 136 subjetcs maintain follow up (42% in psychogical-evaluation-phase and 58% in cross-hormone-treatment, CHT). In 10 adolescents the puberty has been blocked. No alterations in the karyotype, ultrasound or analytical tests were found but basal bone mineral mass is decreased, especially in the group of MtF. During this period, at the legal age (18 years), sex-reassignment-surgeries have been indicated in 16% of the patients (female genitoplasty in 21 MtF and hysterooforectomies in 5 FtM). 24 cases have had breast surgeries (13 mamoplasties and 10 mastectomies). Most of the adolescents, or their parents, asked for intervention (psychological, endocrine, or surgical) at the first visit. Parents of children also requested intervention in most cases. The request at first visits in their Unit is significatively associated to the age group.

In recent years there has been an associative movement of patients and their families around social groups, which has led to increased demand for therapeutic procedures or deadlines that do not always agree with the recommendations of scientific societies. In the case of minors, sometimes these demands include not only early medical intervention, but full integration in schools according to their sexual identity. Therefore, it is essential to organize care with transgender population through specialized interdisciplinary teams, in close collaboration with the family and educational environment.

Chapter 11 – Objective: The authors aim to study the relation between exposure to violence during childhood and adolescence and substance consumption in adulthood in a population of transsexuals.

Material and Methods: Descriptive study of 209 transsexual subjects, based on the ICD-10 diagnostic criteria (109 male-to-female, and 100 female-to-male), followed at the Transsexuality and Gender Identity Unit of the General University Hospital of Malaga (Spain). The Social-demographic structured questionnaire and Exposure to Violence Questionnaire (EVQ) were used during the psychological evaluation phase of the gender reassignment process.

Results: The highest score of direct violence experienced in childhood and adolescence was obtained from when the subjects were at school, the lowest score was obtained at home, and direct violence in the neighbourhood came second. The average score of the EVQ questionnaire (Violence in the neighbourhood) was significantly higher in those who had consumed cannabis in the past compared to those who hadn't ($p<0.05$). Differences were not observed either in the total direct score of EVQ nor in the other EVQ scores for active *cannabis* consumers. The average of the EVQ direct score in those who had consumed cocaine in the past ($p<0.05$) were higher. Specifically, higher scores of violence were experienced at home, both among current and past consumers of cocaine. The differences between consumers and non-consumers of designer drugs in the past were significant within the scores of exposure to violence at home ($p<0.05$) but not on the total questionnaire score.

Conclusions: In accordance with the data, violence experienced during childhood and adolescence may play a role in substance abuse in adult transsexuals. In addition, some characteristic patterns are observed between exposure to violence and the type of drug consumed. In an attempt to prevent early exposure to violence and its consequences on mental health and influence the psychosocial adjustment in transsexuals, early interventions are imperative.

Chapter 12 – This study aims to investigate how Physical Education (P.E.) teachers of elementary/middle schools from Municipal Education Foundation of Niterói (FME) represent the relationship between course content and the construction of gender identities. The study was developed in three stages: i) document research on the FME Curriculum; ii) a structured questionnaire with all 55 P.E. teachers from FME-Niterói to analyze their professional profiles; iii) ten structured interviews with teachers who have five or more years of experience in teaching P.E. in elementary/middle school. After documental analysis, general questions of gender were identified in the P.E. Curriculum of FME, leading us to the conclusion that FME teachers should be knowledgeable about this subject. Literature Research on the subject of gender was completed about gender identities, co-education and course content. The group of teachers interviewed was composed of 59% women, and 41% men, and the average age was 40 years old. Most of them (86%) were born in Rio de Janeiro. Regarding their higher education background, 79% came from public universities and 24% from private institutions. The average time experience teaching P.E. was 14 years. All teachers work in public schools, and four of them also teach in private schools. The Content Analysis of interviews resulted in six categories: "misunderstanding about the concept of gender identity"; "teacher's program versus FME curriculum"; "students' resistance to mixed gender classes"; "lack of knowledge about Co-Education"; "sports as a factor for gender exclusion"; and "course content and identity". The authors concluded that most of the teachers don't know concepts about gender and Co-education, and don't follow the learning objectives related to the gender issues presented in the curriculum orientation of FME. The teachers interviewed have a tendency to teach the P.E. content in a gendered way, reproducing gender stereotypes and/or separating students by gender during the class activities. The authors believe that P.E. class is a moment of learning relevant questions related to diversity and gender, creating a sense of inclusion for every student. Teachers need to select their content that encourages gender-related discussions, allowing students to question their gender representations. In this way, they could recreate themselves in a non-stereotypical way, being free to construct their identities and participate in any activities in P.E. classes. To achieve this objective, teachers must be better prepared by the universities to face this important question. Unfortunately, in Brazil, universities rarely or poorly discuss gender topics in P.E. undergraduate courses.

Chapter 13 – Gender identity disorder is recognized as a rare disease. The prevalence of this disorder is different among regions and races. In Japan, the prevalence of female-to-male transsexual (FTM-TS) patients is estimated to be 1 in 12,500 women, which is approximately twice as many as male-to-female transsexual patients.

There are two interesting facts in association with FTM-TS: 1) the complication rate of polycystic ovary syndrome (PCOS) is high among FTM-TS patients; and 2) natal female patients with congenital adrenal hyperplasia (CAH) tend to have gender identity problems more often than the normal population. PCOS is a common disease and it affects 5–10% of women of reproductive age. PCOS is characterized by ovulation disorder, hyperandrogenism, and polycystic ovarian morphology. Additionally, PCOS is correlated with insulin resistance, and predisposes to type 2 diabetes mellitus, atherosclerosis, and metabolic syndrome. The etiology of PCOS is still obscure, but excess androgen exposure during the fetal period is considered to be a dominant hypothesis. CAH is an autosomal recessive disorder impairing adrenal steroid metabolism, which causes excess androgenemia from the fetal period. A review on 250 natal female cases with CAH showed that 13 (5.2%) of the patients had serious gender identity problems. Surprisingly, the occurrence of FTM-TS in CAH is extremely high. The pathogenesis of FTM-TS is still uncertain. However, excess androgen exposure may be related to FTM-TS according to the above-mentioned findings.

In humans, experimental androgen administration to women is impossible. However, cross-sex hormone administration to FTM-TS patients is not associated with any problems because it is a standard tactic for treatment. If excess androgen exposure is a cause of PCOS, androgen-treated FTM-TS patients may be a disease model of PCOS. Assessment of the effects of androgen administration on metabolic parameters is informative because FTM-TS patients with PCOS may have potent insulin resistance.

In this chapter, the authors discuss endocrinological aspects of FTM-TS, the effect of cross-sex hormones, and the hypothetical etiology in FTM and PCOS.

Chapter 14 – Transgender (TG) individuals who believe in the God of the three major faith traditions, Judiasm, Islam, and Christianity, and have an internal conflict surrounding their gender identity often say to themselves, "Where is God in all of this?" For the many people who wonder, "Why do I have these experiences?" there is no consensus for how to best answer that question. Experiencing these questions or conflicts and not having many solid answers may make lead TG persons of faith to feel confusion, frustration, or anger—this negative affect can be directed inward (toward themselves) or outward (toward their parents, their religious institutions and leaders, and even to God). In this chapter the authors present some questions and results from preliminary research with TG persons of faith that might help clinicians and religious persons explore this area and find their own answers. Topics that are explored include the etiology of Gender Dysphoria and the potential conflict with any of the three major Abrahamic religions (Judaism, Christianity, and Islam), the pursuit of God for meaning and purpose for the TG individual, how TG persons of faith can live in the tension, and lastly, the authors give specific recommendations for both clinicians and TG individuals based on the limited existing research in this area.

Chapter 15 – This report presents the findings from an exploratory study of the experiences of 34 male-to-female transgender persons of faith. These findings are from a larger study on the experiences of transgender (TG) Christian. Some of the items discussed are ages/timeframes in which people begin to acknowledge for themselves that there is an apparent conflict between their birth sex and their sense of gender; when and what types of attributions are made to these experiences; when and with whom they disclosed their inner conflict; and if/when they began to transition. Additionally, questions are asked about the participants' experiences within their faith traditions, including such areas as church life, relationship with God, and understanding of Scripture. Granted this study is retrospective and subject to all the limitations of recall, but prior research on children whose gender dysphoria persists and desists, as well as milestone events in identify formation in other areas of study warrants some examination of typical timelines in which some of common life events generally occur.

In: Gender Identity
Editor: Beverly L. Miller

ISBN: 978-1-63321-488-0
© 2014 Nova Science Publishers, Inc.

Chapter 1

GENDER IDENTITY AS A PERSONALITY PROCESS

Charlotte Tate

Department of Psychology, San Francisco State University, US

ABSTRACT

Within psychology and psychiatry, *gender identity* has developed at least two distinguishable meanings: awareness of anatomy (e.g., Stoller, 1974) and endorsing specific traits that are stereotypical of different gender groups (e.g., Bem, 1974; Wood & Eagly, 2010). However, neither existing approach has considered gender identity to be a self-categorization process that exists within personality science. In this chapter, I develop the argument that gender identity can be fruitfully explored as a personality process. I use both classic and modern personality process approaches to demonstrate that theorizing about gender identity from the personality perspective clarifies and complements—rather than eclipses—prior theorizing. Additionally, several unique insights are available to researchers when gender identity is approached as a personality process, and some of these insights are identified within this chapter.

GENDER IDENTITY AS A PERSONALITY PROCESS

Over the past 50 years in psychology and psychiatry, *gender identity* has developed at least two distinguishable meanings. One meaning is the sense of self that is little more than a person's anatomical awareness. This meaning is seen in Stoller's (1968/1974) original ideas about *core gender identity*. With modification through the years, Stoller's view has remained part of both the psychiatric and clinical psychology understanding of gender identity to the present. The other meaning of gender identity is the sense of self as endorsing specific traits that are stereotypical of different gender groups. This meaning is seen in Bem's (1974, 1981a) *gender schema theory*, Spence and colleagues (1975) *personal attributes* approach, and to the present in Eagly and Wood's (2010) approach to gender identity—all of which are found under the purview of social psychology. Yet, none of the current understandings has considered gender identity to be a self-categorization process that exists within modern personality psychology (also called personality science). The goal of this chapter is therefore to detail an argument for gender identity as a personality process that is inclusive of all gender identity experiences and developmental profiles. Using classic personality process approaches (e.g., Kluckhohn & Murray, 1948), this chapter starts from the premise that gender identity, like any other personality process, at the broadest level covers all people in some way, at a second level constitutes the traditional individual difference (i.e., applies to some people differently than others), and, at a third level, becomes idiosyncratic for a specific person.

Using modern personality process approaches (e.g., Caspi, Roberts, & Shiner, 2005; Revelle, 1995), this chapter also starts from the premise that gender identity involves both self-perception and other-perception components as well as biological and social influences. The chapter then develops the case for measuring gender identity as self-categorization consistent with the personality trait approaches. Specifically, one part of the argumentation within this chapter is to show that the study of gender self-categorization would benefit from making explicit the supposition that one's internal sense of self is likely a process different from genital anatomy awareness—substantially revising the Stollerian view. With this supposition in mind one can unite the descriptive experiences of *cisgender individuals* (i.e., those whose current gender identity labels are the same as their birth-assigned category labels) and *transgender spectrum individuals* (i.e., those whose current gender identity labels are different from their birth-assigned category labels) to argue that each is emanating from a common source that is not awareness of genitals as ultimate or core identity. Additionally, one can view transgender spectrum experiences as providing an extremely useful and necessary lens on this common source of gender identity experience because these experiences are not as easily confused with additional information sources—namely, other people's perceptions of the self—as happens with cisgender experiences. I also argue that much of the social psychological view starts from a cisgender bias that focuses research attention primarily on the perception of the self by others, and only secondarily (if at all) on self-perception and self-categorization (see also Ansara & Hegarty, 2012). While also important, this social psychological view is not the whole of the story for gender identity.

Another part of the specific argumentation in this chapter is to show that gender self-categorization can be measured at different levels—not just the broadest level of checking a box that corresponds to one's current gender identity label. Self-categorization itself may imply a sense of strong overlap with, affinity to, or subsumption within any or none of the available gender categories in one's culture. Importantly, the argument for gender identity as a personality process does not eclipse prior theorizing about gender identity as involving a person's consideration of anatomy (at some level) and social schemas (at another level); instead, this new argument clarifies and complements the previous arguments. I argue that gender identity as a personality process exists within a bundle of gender-related constructs, and that specifying focus on this aspect allows researchers to more completely characterize the others.

In order to develop the arguments as clearly as possible, this chapter first details the early and current approaches to gender identity within various disciplines of psychology and psychiatry and then makes the argument for gender identity as a personality process within the context of the historical and current theorizing. Finally, the new insights that accompany theorizing about gender identity as a personality process are enumerated.

THE EARLY PERSONALITY APPROACHES TO GENDER IDENTITY

Among the earliest personality and psychiatric approaches to gender identity was Sigmund Freud's psychoanalytic theory, which emphasized biological differences between sex-assigned categories (viz. men and women), and spelled out the implications of these differences for psychological development (Eagly, Beall, & Sternberg, 2004). Notably, Freud argued that gender is different from biological sex (i.e., the presence of vagina-vulva or penis-scrotum genital structures [viz. sex assignment]) (Eagly et al., 2004). In doing so, Freud was implicitly arguing that parts of gender—namely, psychological identity experiences—are crafted or develop, and are not fixed from birth. This thinking was not unique to Freud (cf., Ellis, 1905; Hirschfeld, 1919/2000); however, the whole perspective of starting with biological differences between men and women and using those as the scaffolding on which to build theories of individual differences was coming into vogue at that time and persists to the present (see, e.g., Penke, 2010).

In the 1920s and 1930s, Lewis Terman and Catherine Cox Miles approached gender theory via the measurement perspective to create the Terman and Miles Attitude-Interest Analysis Test (Terman & Miles, 1936). Terman and Miles believed that organizing their data by participants who self-categorized as female or male would allow researchers to empirically determine the important aspects of gender identity by examining differential response patterns to research questions. In brief, the Terman and Miles approach was that women and men differ from each other on certain psychological phenomena and not on others. Accordingly, to determine that gender influenced female and male psychologies, one simply needed to find the types of differences via response patterns. This approach might be construed as atheoretical, insofar as Terman and Miles used an ostensibly inductive approach to determining how women and men differed from each other. Yet, with the benefit of a historical perspective, Terman and Miles (1936) had one fundamental assumption that is worth noting because it limits the kinds of conclusions that may be drawn from this approach. The assumption is that the kinds of questions asked were a sampling from the universe of all possible similarities and differences that these gender groups could have one from the other. Nonetheless, many of the items used by Terman and Miles (1936) reflected intergroup dynamics that a scholar today might classify as sexism or gender bias—even if in its benevolent form (see Glick & Fiske, 2001, for a discussion of benevolent bias). For example, summarizing responses to some of their items concerning affinity for celebrities of the time and literary characters, Terman and Miles (1936) wrote "[f]emales show a distinctive preference for women, unfortunate people, and philanthropists; males for successful generals, sports heroes, and defiers of convention" (p. 446). Since at that time women and men were sociologically differentiated on a variety of dimensions, including women having fewer rights and privileges and less social mobility at the time, any psychological differences may have been a conflation of the realities of intergroup social conflict being measured at a psychological level (cf. Eagly, 1987; Eagly & Wood, 1999; Eagly, Wood, & Diekman, 2000). Thus, Terman and Miles (1936) may have revealed more about intergroup evaluations than other constructs related to gender, such as self-categorization or other identity processes.

Items from the Terman and Miles (1936) Attitude-Interest Analysis Test would later be adapted for use in the Minnesota Multiphasic Personality Inventory (MMPI) (Hathaway & McKinley, 1940) to measure sexual inversion in males, which was an early name for homosexuality (see summaries within Constantinople, 1973; Dahlstrom, Welsh, & Dahlstrom, 1972; Hoffman, 2001; Nichols, 2011). The same conceptual analysis can be seen in the Strong (1935) Vocational Interest Blank that was designed to measure vocational interests with the rationale that men and women will choose different careers (Strong, 1936). Thus, from the 1900s into the 1940s, gender identity was being theorized about and measured as the differences between self-identified women and men with the conceptual anchors of heterosexual socialization (Freud) and intergroup evaluations (Terman, Miles, Strong, Hathaway and McKinley).

Freud's ideas about gender identity development (and the similar ideas on which his were based; see Ellis, 1905; Hirschfeld, 1919/2000) appear to have infiltrated both developmental psychology and psychiatry. It seems that the former focused on the acquisition of gender identity and its constancy, while the latter focused on the mechanisms by which one acquires a gender identity in normative and non-normative ways. Lawrence Kohlberg's (1966) cognitive-developmental theory of gender identity development recapitulated part of the Freudian psychoanalytic theory with a focus on the internal factors of gender identity (Bussey & Bandura, 1999). Additionally, cognitive-developmental theory is a stage model of gender identity that reveals different layers of gender experience over time. Unlike the Freudian model, Kohlberg's (1966) theory did not emphasize heterosexual socialization or imply that such a sexual orientation was indicative of successful psychological adjustment to one's gender category assignment. Instead, Kolhberg's theory focused on the child's self-labeling in reference to the labels provided at birth by others in the child's life as the first stage of gender development. This stage occurs around three years of age and can be seen when the child begins to "correctly" self-label using the birth-assigned sex category (see Bussey & Bandura, 1999; Kohlberg, 1966). Kohlberg (1966) also argued that children begin to develop the next stage, *gender constancy*, between the ages of three to seven years. At this stage, children begin to realize that their sex—and thus gender identity in this theory—will remain permanent (Kohlberg, 1996; Stangor & Ruble, 1987). In this way, Kolhberg's theory created a strong connection between birth-assigned category and self-experienced gender categorization as appropriately cisgender (viz., the same label for each). Thus, it is unclear how Kohlberg's (1966) approach might account for children who have transgender spectrum experiences of identity development (viz., the self-categorization being different from the birth-assigned category label).

Kohlberg's (1966) theory of gender constancy and the well-documented anatomical (and physiological) differences between men and women—as medically defined—led to discussions of any differences between these two groups being referred to as *sex differences*. However, the more modern term *gender differences* is an even better characterization of the psychological information discussed at this time in history. Nonetheless, using the notion of sex difference and that language, Maccoby and Jacklin (1974) reviewed the psychology of gender differences at that time and extracted two important insights. One, the theory of gender development grew to include two main socialization processes of gender identity development—namely, social learning theory and social exchange theory—creating some controversy among gender theorists who were mainly concerned with cognitive processes (see also Martin, Ruble, & Szkrybalo, 2002). Both socialization processes were derived from the behaviorist approach to psychology and assume that people will repeat rewarded behaviors and abandon those behaviors that are followed by negative reinforcement or punishment (see Howard & Hollander, 1997). In particular, social learning theory focuses on individual behaviors, whereas social exchange theory is an application of social learning theory to social relationships (Howard & Hollander, 1997). In either case, little room was made for cognitive appraisals or more interesting psychological dynamics between the person and their reinforcement environment and reinforcement schedules at this time. In any event, the discussion of gender differences as sex differences reinforced a marginalization of transgender spectrum experiences and, as I develop below, masked some of the interesting insights about gender identity as a personality variable while over-emphasizing gender identity as a social psychological phenomenon.

For psychiatry in the same time period (i.e., the 1960s and 1970s), the conceptual issues centered on gender identity development in relation to one's awareness of genital anatomy, the putative power of attendant physiological differences that create genital structures to influence psychological processes, and the presumed genetic underpinnings of those genital structures. The psychiatric line of thinking on gender identity might be most clearly expressed in the writing of Robert Stoller's (1968/1974) *Sex and Gender*. Stoller's influential view of gender identity can be succinctly stated by quoting his definition of *core gender identity*: "This aspect of one's over-all sense of identity can be conceptualized as a *core gender identity* [italics in original], produced by the infant-parents relationship, by the child's perception of its external genitalia, and by a biologic force that springs from the biologic variables of sex" (Stoller, 1974, pp. 29-30). Stoller's original formulation of *core gender identity* was no more than a psychological representation of one's genital anatomy, the social labeling of that anatomy as female or male, and the expectation that one should, based on these two pieces of information, label oneself according to the term that described the anatomy. Additionally, Stoller (1968/1974) believed that the social stereotypes associated with gender groups were somehow part and parcel of the experience of being assigned to a particular genital anatomy category. In effect, Stoller asserted that gender identity was only a specific outgrowth of the biology associated with the development of one's genitals. This general assertion with slight, but important, modification would also be seen in the social psychological approach to gender of the 1970s—one which also extends to the present. Moreover, based on these beliefs, Stoller (1968/1974) explicitly characterized transgender spectrum experiences as forms of mental disorder—a conception that has, with some revision, continued to the present (Dresher, 2010).

THE SOCIAL PSYCHOLOGY APPROACH TO GENDER IDENTITY

While the developmental and psychiatric perspectives provided their somewhat separate views of the development of gender identity, clinical, social, and personality psychology researchers started to deal with and respond to the Terman and Miles approach (see Hegarty & Coyle, 2005). In the 1970s, these disciplines grappled with the internalization of gender stereotypes for adults and how these stereotypes might affect healthy and normative functioning. Ann Constantinople (1973) questioned the usefulness of treating gender identity as a single continuum from *masculinity* on one end to *femininity* on the other end. This conceptual practice appears to be a holdover from or further specification of the general Terman and Miles approach. Bem (1974) put Constantinople's ideas about measuring femininity and masculinity as separate dimensions into practice with the Bem-Sex Role

Inventory (BSRI). The name of the scale still reflected the supposition that one's birth-assigned sex category was eventually the same as one's gender self-label; yet, it also focused researchers on the idea that gender category stereotypes were not actually bipolar and opposing. Instead, to some extent, masculinity and femininity were accessible to all people. Gender socialization and internalization processes created psychological dynamics in which men, for example, might be encouraged to internalize more traits associated with masculinity and simultaneously fewer traits associated with femininity. Similarly, women might be encouraged to internalize more traits associated with femininity and simultaneously fewer traits associated with masculinity. However, for Bem (1974, 1981a, b), there was an appropriate proportion of internalizing these traits to increase psychological well-being: men and women separately should internalize both masculine and feminine traits—an experience referred to as *psychological androgyny*. If men were too masculine and not feminine enough in terms of gender stereotype endorsement, then they would be hypermasculine and not experience the best psychological well-being outcomes. Likewise, if women were too feminine and not masculine enough in terms of gender stereotype trait endorsement, then they would be hyperfeminine and thereby not experience the best psychological well-being outcomes. The arc of Bem's (1974, 1981a,b) theorizing was that men and women should strive for moderation in terms of internalizing both masculine and feminine traits—and this activity toward the psychologically androgynous state became another meaning of gender identity. The BSRI was developed as a way to test this psychological androgyny hypothesis, as well as the implications of hypermasculinity and hyperfemininity.

In parallel to Bem's work, Spence, Helmreich, and Stapp (1975) developed the Personal Attributes Questionnaire (PAQ) to also separately measure masculinity and femininity as gender stereotype endorsement within the same individual. Though importantly distinct in terms of the kinds of traits used, how these traits were derived, and the fact that Spence et al. used traits that were meant to be androgynous on their own (whereas Bem used separate masculine and feminine traits whose aggregation was considered androgyny), the Spence et al. and Bem approaches are united in the fact that they allowed researchers to create at least a two-dimensional understanding of gender identity as stereotype endorsement, rather than the single-dimensional understanding provided by the Terman and Miles approach. Considering the separability of the femininity and masculinity constructs theoretically and empirically, Bem (1974, 1981a) outlined four major ways by which data could be organized. Participants could be located into quadrants that represented (a) mostly masculine and not very feminine (masculine-typed), (b) mostly feminine and not very masculine (feminine-typed), (c) both masculine and feminine (psychologically androgynous), or (d) neither masculine nor feminine (undifferentiated). These four types were Bem's gender identities. The early Spence et al. (1975) approach allowed for a similar data organization using different methods owing to the explicit androgyny items (see also Spence, 1991). In any case, the social psychological approach focused on a definition of gender identity that was overtly concerned with the extent to which people internalized the social meanings of gender categories via the endorsement of various traits or behaviors that were organized by researchers as stereotypically associated with gender groups. This meaning of gender identity as stereotype endorsement or gender role adherence is the most common and influential in social psychology to the present (see Wood & Eagly, 2010).

While more theoretically sophisticated than the Terman and Miles approach, both the Bem and Spence approaches might be seen as a continuation of the Terman and Miles thinking. Instead of focusing on the differences between respondent groups, Bem and Spence made the "differences" the gender stereotypes themselves, with the explicit statement in the theorizing that people should strive to internalize what appeared to be expected social differences between men and women. Extending this theorizing, Spence (1991) and other scholars have since argued that masculinity approximates an *agency* or *instrumentality* dimension of personality—indicating self-reliance, assertiveness and related constructs—and that femininity approximates a *communion* or *expressiveness* dimension of personality—indicating other-orientedness, emotional focus and related constructs (see Laurent & Hodges, 2008; Spence & Helmreich, 1980; Witt & Wood, 2010); yet, both are still supposed to index something about socially expected gender differences. Even while Bakan (1966) had argued for agency and communality as fundamental aspects of human experience that were not tied to gender (see Helgeson, 1994), the approaches of Bem and Spence did not appear to take this into account in their early formulations, and many psychologists remain unaware of Bakan's theorizing to the present. Thus, the method of asking about social stereotypes allowed for more than two possible outcomes, but importantly focused on personal adherence to social stereotypes associated with gender groups—not one's sense of being categorizable as a man or a woman (see Tate, 2012).

The approach ushered in by Bem and Spence was completely amenable to a social psychological approach that was becoming increasingly cognitively oriented (e.g., Markus, 1977). Summarizing her approach to gender stereotype endorsement, Bem (1981a) coined *gender schema theory*. Schema theories were developed within cognitive psychology and generally posit that people organize social information into mental templates or knowledge structures (schemas). Schemas aid in information processing by filtering incoming information, directing future behavior, and making sense of past behavior. In the case of gender schemas, these knowledge structures focus attention on self-relevant information and allow people to categorize gender relevant information faster than gender irrelevant information, based on the individualized content of their own schemas (Bem, 1981a). Gender schema theory assumes that any individual can actively process and represent information from socialization (and other sources) and build and refine one's self-schema in terms of gender stereotypes and other gender-related information. Importantly, men and women could vary along the quadrants of possible schema organizations from masculine-typed, feminine-typed, psychologically androgynous, and undifferentiated as defined above (Bem, 1981a).

Bem's gender schema approach was picked up and built upon by many researchers in social psychology, and chief among them were Alice Eagly and Wendy Wood. Eagly and Wood's theory of sex differences changed the names of Bem's terms to the ones that Spence preferred and placed focus on *agency* (male-stereotypical traits) and *communion* (female-stereotypical traits) as the central trait clusters that differentiate men and women, on average (Eagly & Wood, 1999, 2011; Eagly et al. 2000; Wood & Eagly, 2000). It is no accident that Eagly and Wood named this approach *sex differences*. For Eagly and Wood, social psychology had to acknowledge the demonstrable anatomical differences between men and women (evident in the medical designations at birth) and the chromosomal differences that were assumed to produce these anatomical differences in a uniform manner. Yet, the existence of gender stereotypes, gender socialization, and how these two connected at the levels of self-schemas and social schemas became the dominant understanding of gender difference in social psychology propounded by Eagly and Wood. Herein, the biology of sex is a scaffold on which gender differences (and, conceptually, similarities) might develop.

However, the development of these differences might have more to do with socialization processes, and less to do with genetic predilections toward behaviors than other theorists might assume—though, admittedly, both are important (see Eagly & Wood, 1999, 2011 for excellent discussions). Several theorists have followed this manner of thinking about gender identity, which, given its focus on stereotypy, is also easily amenable to the study of gender bias as gender prejudice, gender discrimination, and sexism in social psychology. Note, however, that gender identity for Eagly and Wood and most of social psychology has little to do with the definitions of Stoller or Kohlberg or the idea of developmentally acquiring self-knowledge that translates into self-categorization as *female*, *male*, or some other gender category.

THE NEWEST APPROACH TO GENDER: A MULTIDIMENSIONAL SOCIAL PSYCHOLOGICAL UNDERSTANDING

In what can be construed as an integration of the perspectives above, in 2001, Susan Egan and David Perry developed what they termed a multidimensional approach to studying gender with children. Egan and Perry (2001) argued that five dimensions are important to characterize how children experience gender: (a) membership knowledge (awareness that the self is categorized into a specific gender group); (b) contentment with one's gender assignment; (c) gender typicality (a sense of being similar to other children with the same gender label); (d) pressure to conform to gender stereotypes or expectations; and, (e) intergroup bias (feeling superior to gender outgroups). This multidimensional approach shows a layered understanding of gender experience, and integrates many of the historical insights into a decidedly social psychological approach. By identifying specific psychological processes associated with *interpersonal evaluations*, Egan and Perry created a nuance not seen in the Kohlberg, Bem, and Spence approaches, and a perspective that is more consistent with Eagly and Wood. Yet, even Egan and Perry's multidimensional understanding does not showcase a personality approach to gender identity. Rather, each dimension of Egan and Perry's framework is either a judgment of self in relation to others or an attitude about information provided by others. For instance, estimates of gender typicality and intergroup bias are two different ways to consider interpersonal dynamics—that is, the self in relation to others. The typicality dimension is self as compared to the ingroup while the intergroup bias dimension is self as compared to an outgroup. The remaining dimensions can be construed as *intrapersonal* attitudes.

Membership knowledge is one's recognition of the category to which one was birth-assigned, and, though not explicitly valenced, it does fit into the cognitive component of attitude structure (cf. Zanna & Reppel, 1988). Contentment with gender assignment is prototypically an attitude insofar as it requires a perceiver to place valence on the assignment to a gender category by someone else in the generic evaluative forms of positive, negative, neutral, or ambivalent. Pressure to conform to stereotypes is both an affective and cognitive statement regarding how other people treat the self. Thus, even while nuanced, Egan and Perry's multidimensional understanding of gender experience does not approach any aspect of gender as a personality process.

THE MISSING LINK: GENDER IDENTITY AS A PERSONALITY PROCESS

Since the days of Terman and Miles, personality psychologists have routinely overlooked the idea that gender identity could be a personality process. Instead, to the present, personality theorizing has focused on factor models of personality (e.g., Caspi et al., 2005; Srivastava, John, Gosling, & Potter, 2003), dimensions of personality that might exist outside the basic factors (e.g., coping) (Bolger, 1990), on the distinction between attributes as traits and the expression of them as cognition (Cantor, 1990), and on the link between temperament and personality (Rothbart, Ahadi, & Evans, 1999; Caspi et al., 2005)—to name a fraction of the pursuits in personality science over the past 50 years. In the cases where gender does appear, it is often as a moderator of the stability of another trait (e.g., Srivastava et al., 2003) or as a way to test evolutionary and social role hypotheses about the putative origins of gender differences (e.g., Costa, Terracciano, & McCrae, 2001). While interesting and worthwhile, these approaches to gender individually and collectively only serve to recapitulate the Terman and Miles (1936) reasoning. Common practices notwithstanding, below I develop the case for treating gender identity as a personality process in its own right. I use classic and modern personality process insights to demonstrate that gender identity as self-categorization is completely amenable to being theorized about and modeled as a personality trait.

Classic Personality Process Thinking and Gender Identity

Kluckhohn and Murray (1948) introduced what has come to be known as the classic personality process approach (see Revelle, 1995). As a summary, Kluckhohn and Murray (1948) argued that any personality process, at the broadest level covers all people in some way, at a second level constitutes the traditional individual difference (i.e., applies to some people differently than others), and, at a third level, becomes idiosyncratic for a specific person. Revelle (1995) has shown that this construal of personality processes has remained a common thread through the personality theorizing of the 1920s to the 1990s with additional insights and perspectives growing up around it. I would argue that the theme continues to the present, and this statement is supported by a more recent review of personality processes focusing on stability and change (Caspi, Roberts, & Shiner, 2005). With this classic perspective in mind, let us consider whether gender identity could be characterized as a personality process. At the broadest level, there appears to be little disagreement among psychologists that every person has a self-categorization that considers gender in some way. While it is most common in the United States and other industrialized cultures to think of *female* and *male* as being the exhaustive categories (e.g., Wood & Eagly, 2010), empirical research has shown that there are additional categories. In particular, in the U.S. and Canada, at least, individuals identify as *female, male, trans female, trans male, intersex,* and *nonbinary/ genderqueer* (Factor & Rothblum, 2008; Kuper, Nussbaum, & Mustanski, 2012; Scheim & Bauer, 2014; Tate, Ledbetter, & Youssef, 2013). The nonbinary or genderqueer category can be further specified into the broad concepts of *genderblended* (i.e., a combined sense of being self-categorizable as female and male) and *post-gender* (i.e., a sense of being self-categorizable as neither female nor male) (Tate et al., 2013). Importantly, having a gender identity for oneself outside of the traditional, binary understanding of gender can still be viewed as having gender apply to one's self-concept, and the words *nonbinary* and *genderqueer* convey this through language. In this way, the first aspect of the classic personality process perspective appears to be met. While it is true that the examples given focus on the U.S. and Canada, most psychological researchers presume that gender identity (defined as self-categorization) applies to all humans irrespective of culture (cf. Wood & Eagly, 2010).

Considering the second aspect of the classic personality process perspective (i.e., individual differences), gender identity also meets this standard. While gender identity appears to characterize all people (as argued above), it is experienced as an individual difference such that some people experience their gender identity as *female*, others as *male*, still others as *genderblended*, and yet more as *post-gender* (Tate et al., 2013). It should be noted that these are scholarly summaries of the natural language terms that exist in English to describe these identities. Though it is likely familiar to readers that *female* has associated terms such as *woman* and *girl* and that *male* has associated terms such as *man* and *boy*, what might be less familiar are the other terms associated with *genderblended* (e.g., "pangender," "bigender") and *post-gender* (e.g., "agender," "non-gendered"). Also, as developed in detail below and in other publications (e.g., Tate, 2012; Tate et al., 2013), these four labels appear to be the most parsimonious individual difference labels because they include profiles or trajectories of gender identity experience. Transgender women and cisgender women are two different developmental profiles of the same category: women. In this case, some researchers use the terms *trans women* and *cis women* to emphasize the self-categorization similarity (women) while acknowledging the developmental trajectory as the different modifiers (trans or cis) (Tate et al., 2013). In parallel, transgender men and cisgender men are two different developmental profiles of the same category: men. In this case, some researchers use the terms *trans men* and *cis men* to emphasize the self-categorization similarity (men) while acknowledging the developmental trajectory as the different modifiers (trans or cis) (Tate et al., 2013). In any event, the gender identity experience appears to apply differently to different groups of people—thereby qualifying as an individual difference in the second aspect of classic personality process theory (Kluckhohn & Murray, 1948; Revelle, 1995).

Considering the third and final aspect of classic personality process theory (i.e., idiosyncrasy at the level of each individual), it appears that even within the four broadest individual difference labels (i.e., female, male, genderblended, post-gender), individuals vary from each other. Though virtually no research has yet examined the nonbinary gender identities, a number of studies have examined how women are different from each other and how men are different from each other. It should be acknowledged that, at the broadest level of analysis, these idiosyncrasies can be identified whenever variability is shown within women as a grouping variable or within men as a grouping variable. Although the specific focus may not be on a life story approach to gender identity (see McAdams, 1990, 1993; Ruynan, 1990, for the life stories approaches), the fact that the variance is above zero for any set of women or men on any set of life outcomes (e.g., Newton & Stewart, 2013) or personality variables (e.g., Srivastava et al., 2003; Costa et al., 2001) shows that it is possible to explore how individual women differ from each other on their experiences of having a female gender identity and how individual men differ from each other on their experiences of having a male gender identity. Additionally, it should be possible to discuss even how one's self-categorization as *female, male, genderblended* or *post-gender* differs between individual people within those categories. Thus, it appears that gender is experienced idiosyncratically at the level of each person.

Inclusivity of All Gender Experiences Is Necessary to Focus on Gender Identity As a Personality Process

With the three levels of classic personality theory rhetorically demonstrated, I now specify the argument for including all gender experience as a necessary scholarly activity to maintain the focus on gender identity as a personality process. Although developmental and social psychology has largely ignored transgender spectrum experiences, they are actually integral to understanding gender identity as a personality process. Moreover, given that classic personality theory holds that any personality process applies to all people at some level, it seems necessary to include all experiences of gender identity in order to make this statement true. While it appears that the numerical majority of people experience their gender identity within a cisgender profile (see Tate et al., 2013), cisgender experience is not exhaustive across people (Ansara & Hegarty, 2012; Factor & Rothblum, 2008, Kuper et al., 2012; Scheim & Bauer, 2014; Tate et al., 2013). In fact, transgender spectrum experiences may actually provide the clearest illustration that gender identity is a personality process, while considering cisgender experience alone biases researchers to consider the aspects of gender identity that are largely interpersonal phenomena. For instance, Fleming, Jenkins, and Bugarin (1980) were among the first researchers to examine transgender participants using the BSRI. Fleming et al. (1980) recruited a group of adult trans women and trans men (at the time, the term *transsexuals* was used) who were all seeking counseling through a non-profit organization that specialized in assisting clients in their emotional and medical transitions. Fleming et al. found that 24% of the transgender participants were considered psychologically androgynous according to the BSRI scoring methods, which was a similar finding to Bem's (1974) study (with cis women and cis men—even though those terms were not used at the time). Fleming et al. (1980) suggested that transgender people are not seeking genital surgery because their gender role endorsement differs from the expectations based on their birth-assigned sex category, and this could be seen in the fact that the psychologically androgynous transgender participants seemed comfortable with flexibility in their behavior concerning gender stereotypes. Fleming et al. (1980) instead proposed that internal gender identity (or what I call *gender self-categorization*) and stereotypic gender roles are independent of each other, which is one of the first appearances of this argument within literature relevant to social/personality psychology.

Additionally, the suggestions that gender identity as self-categorization derive from social learning, behaviorist, or cognitive accounts (see Bussey & Bandura, 1999; Howard & Hollander, 1997; Maccoby & Jacklin, 1974; Martin et al., 2002) benefit from considering the perspectives of individuals with transgender spectrum identities. If it were truly the case that gender self-categorization was nothing more than an elaborated calculation of external inputs from society and one's genital anatomy, then it would be extremely difficult to generate transgender spectrum experiences. While Stoller (1968/1974) attempted to explain the experiences via a notion of clinical disorder, this proposition is ultimately unconvincing because it does not detail a process by which transgender spectrum experience arises—aside from vague, untestable assumptions based on neo-Freudian psychodynamic postulates. Even if these untestable claims were true, it would mean that those with transgender spectrum experiences were virtually immune to the well-demonstrated social-cognitive processes of learning and development, but only for gender identity and not any other learning or developmental outcome. Using a principle of parsimony, it is more likely that transgender spectrum experiences are subject to the same kinds of well-documented social-cognitive processes as everyone else for the learning and development of gender identity. At the same time, transgender spectrum experiences should provide a useful lens on the underpinning process of gender identity as self-categorization for everyone—especially the unique part of this process that is not reducible to learning via external inputs. This unique underpinning process might be characterized as an internal sense of self or *felt-sense of gender identity*. At present, no one understands from where this felt-sense might originate or the specific biological mechanisms that convey or support gender self-categorization. Nonetheless, researchers might infer the existence of such an internal experience and the biology that supports it in order to posit a conceptual interplay between the social-cognitive processes and this felt-sense variable in the following manner. When the felt-sense of gender identity and the gender label used for the self by others are the same, then there is still psychological activity—namely, a person identifies with the label that matches the internal sense of self— but this activity might appear *as though it is being generated by others* since the perceptions of others are visible to observers, but internal self-dynamics are comparatively opaque to observers. To make this insight concrete, consider an individual whose internal sense of self is FEMALE and who is also assigned to the medical category *female* at birth based on the presence of a prototypical vaginal-vulval structure. Under the model being proposed, this individual will continue to have access to the felt-sense of self as FEMALE even while other people use the cultural terms "girl" (and later "woman") and "female" through this person's life course. In this case, it only appears as though other people are influencing this individual's sense of self; instead, there is simply a convergence between self and other perception using very different sources of information. The self uses this internal sense of identity while others use the social meaning of and cues associated with being medically assigned to an anatomy category. This woman would be described as a cis woman because the gender identity profile is calculated across these two perspectives (self and medical) (Tate et al., 2013). Importantly (and developed more fully in the next example), the private, internal information to which the self has access is likely not accessible to others unless the self discloses it (e.g., "I am a woman"). Nonetheless, in this example, since others already *assumed* the self's same category membership (e.g., "she is a woman") based on the social cues that normatively indicate gender category membership in that culture, it appears as though the self might be using information from others. Yet, I argue that the separate sources of information remain separate and either converge or diverge almost incidentally in interpersonal interactions. Now, consider another case. Consider an individual whose internal sense of self is FEMALE and who is assigned to the medical category *male* at birth based on the presence of a prototypical penile-scrotal structure. Under the model being proposed, this individual will continue to have access to the felt-sense of self as FEMALE even while other people use the cultural terms "boy" (and possibly later "man") and "male" through some part of this person's life course. In this case, it appears as though other people are not influencing this individual's sense of self, and this is likely true. In this situation, one's self-assigned gender identity diverges from other people's perceptions of this individual's gender category. And, as described in the previous example, each actor is using a very different source of information. Other people use the medical category designation based on anatomy and the normative social cues that signal gender category membership within that culture, while the self uses another, private source that is likely not accessible to other people unless the self discloses it (e.g., "I am a woman, despite what you might think"). This woman would be described as a trans woman because the gender identity profile is calculated across these two perspectives (self and medical) (Tate et al., 2013). With the balance of these examples, it appears that scholars have a conceptual space that features two information sources working in the same location. One source being the individual's felt-sense of gender identity and the other source being the social perception of that individual depending on normative social cues. Consequently, any individual's gender identity experience in the world appears to be the convergence or divergence of the intrapersonal and interpersonal perceptions.

In fact, there is support for this modeling from different scholarly sources. One source is the narrative reports of trans men and women who argue that they had access to an internal sense of self long before they disclosed this internal identity to other people (e.g., Bornstein, 1998; Devor, 1997; Green, 2004, 2005; Mock, 2014; Morris, 1974; Serano, 2007). Prejudice and fear of discrimination appear to be major reasons why trans men and women delay disclosing their authentic identities (Factor & Rothblum, 2008; Grant et al., 2011). Although memoirs of cis men and women rarely invoke the same narrative structure, it is likely that they too had access to an internal sense of self long before they disclosed this internal identity to other people. For cis women and men, however, the need to disclose their internal identities might not be perceived as strongly because this self-disclosure converged rather early with other-perception on the same label. In effect, cis men and women might not notice as easily that they are disclosing an internal sense of self because other people arrive at that categorization via another route. The other source of support is admittedly indirect and comes from brain anatomy research. Rametti and colleagues argue that trans men (before any hormone treatment) and cis men show similar white matter microstructures in the same area of the brain when both are compared to cis women (Rametti, Carrillo, Gómez-Gil, Junque, Segovia, Gomez, & Guillamon, 2011a). Likewise, these researchers argue that trans women (before any hormone treatment) and cis women have more similarity in the white matter structures at the same locus when both groups are compared to cis men (Rametti, Carrillo, Gómez-Gil, Junque, Zubiarre-Elorza, Segovia, Gomez, & Guillamon, 2011b). My discussion of the Rametti and colleagues is not meant to suggest that these brain fiber differences reflect a particular direction of causality relative to genetic, physiological, or experiential sources (see Tate, 2013a, for detailed discussions of the differences among these sources and particularities of causal inferences from them). Nonetheless, the organization of the Rametti and colleagues' data and the findings presented by that group illustrate that exploring similarities between cis men and trans men and, separately, similarities between cis women and trans women can provide interesting results that point toward the commonalities within men and within women—irrespective of developmental profiles and the ultimate causal origins of these commonalities.

Treating Gender Identity As a Trait and Measuring It Like a Trait

Treating gender self-categorization as a personality process might provide a useful inroad to studying gender identity as the felt-sense of gender categorization because treating it in this way allows psychological researchers to keep social meanings of gender separable from the personal meaning of gender. There appears little dispute within the psychology literature that gender categorization by others (e.g., "you are a girl") exists and is information to which the self has to respond on some intrapsychic level. Yet, the contours of this response at the intrapsychic level (e.g., "yes, I am a girl" or "no, I am not a girl") are poorly understood within children and adults. Nevertheless, personality theory allows for such contours to be explored and examined via psychological research, especially using the methodology of joint self-report and informant-report to assess personality traits. As the dominant model of developmental psychology suggests, gender *self-categorization* happens at an early age (i.e., individual respondents can tell another person about their gender identity as self-disclosure). However, only in some cases does the *self-categorization* appear to coincide with *others-categorization* of that person. That is, informants (others categorizing the self) sometimes use the same label as the self and other times do not. As one can easily imagine, informants' reports are largely tethered to the birth-assigned category, especially when the focal individual is a child, and then later uses normative social cues for gender groups when the focal individual is an adult. Thus, informants are one source of information about an individual's self-categorization, but they might not be the most reliable source. Thus, the personality approach to gender identity as self-categorization may be more useful when researchers assign greater weight to self-report and less weight to informant-reports throughout the lifespan.

The personality approach to gender identity also invites researchers to explore the current unknowns for gender self-categorization by focusing on the research topic of stability and change for personality traits (see Caspi et al., 2005). One current unknown is the stability of gender self-categorization from childhood to (early and late) adulthood. Using the personality approach, the tools of trait change become available for studying gender self-categorization. As Roberts and DelVecchio (2000) note, questions of personality trait change can be approached from at least four perspectives on consistency over time: *intraindividual* (same individual across time), *ipsative* (salience of attributes within persons over time), *mean-level* (average increase or decrease across persons over time), and *rank-order* (ordinal positions across persons over time). Taking the *intraindividual differences* perspective (see also Nesselroade, 1991), as an example, it is unknown at present whether there is variability for gender self-categorization within the same individual from childhood to adulthood. Because historical perspectives (e.g., Kohlberg, 1966) have assumed that once a child consistently uses the same label as the one used by others that gender identity is solidified, researchers have routinely missed the precise measurement of self-assigned identity that comes from the felt-sense, internal source. Focusing on convergence between self-labeling and other-labeling largely ignores or marginalizes transgender spectrum experiences. As noted above, many trans men, trans women, and nonbinary individuals disclose their self-categorization as such between 18 to 24 years old in the U.S. (Factor & Rothblum, 2008), likely because of fear of prejudice and discrimination or to avoid interpersonal difficulties at younger ages (cf. Bornstein, 1998; Devor, 1997; Green, 2004, 2005; Mock, 2014; Morris, 1974; Serano, 2007). Thus, it is possible that there is an internal, felt-sense of self that is solidified early in development—possibly around 3 years old for everyone—and that the field's current emphasis on convergence of self and social labels (and particularly others' perceptions of the self) creates imprecision for measuring this aspect of trait consistency at the intraindividual level. In fact, virtually no information is known about any of the four perspectives on trait consistency that could be usefully applied to gender self-categorization. Nonetheless, the measurement concepts already exist within personality science to provide this information.

Measuring the Specific Dynamics of Gender Self-Categorization As the Lower-Order Personality Process of Gender Identity

Caspi et al. (2005) summarize personality process thinking as involving taxonomies that include higher-order and lower-order traits. Caspi et al. (2005) describe extraversion, for instance, as being the highest-order trait descriptor, indicating that "successively lower levels are more specific traits (e.g., sociability, dominance) that, in turn, are composed of more specific responses (e.g., talkative, good at leading others)" (p. 456). If one applies this approach to gender identity, the self-categorization as *female, male,* or *nonbinary* might be viewed as the highest-order trait. The more specific traits and responses, as Caspi et al. (2005) described them, could begin with the idea that any gender self-categorization might be modeled by focusing on constructs such as overlap with, affinity toward, or subsumption within any available gender category within one's culture. For example, part of the female experiences of identity (cis or trans) may be overlapping *more* with a female gender category than with a male gender category. In fact, the two categories may be experienced intrapsychically as linearly separable to achieve a female self-categorization. That is, to categorize oneself as female one's felt-sense of self might overlap completely or almost completely with this category while simultaneously showing no overlap with the category male. Likewise, part of the male experiences of identity (cis or trans) may be having a sense of self that overlaps almost completely with a male gender category and simultaneously shows no overlap with the category female. Again, this felt-sense of self is independent of gender role endorsement or other social psychological approaches to gender; instead, it is a sense of belonging to an abstract category of persons in the world irrespective of social similarities to them that is likely difficult to articulate because most lay and scholarly language around gender focuses on interpersonal rather than intrapersonal dynamics.

The personality approach is useful for describing such intrapersonal dynamics. If one takes extraversion as an example, what is the intrapersonal sense of being extraverted? This might be very difficult to describe, other than to say, "I really like being around other people and socializing." Notice two points. One, the foregoing quote is a description that is easy for another person to access. Two, the internal experience that generates the statement might have contours that could be usefully described as the self overlapping more with sociability and less with seclusion. Given this second point, researchers ask questions to assess extraversion such as "I am the kind of person who is reserved" (to index overlap with seclusion) and "I am the kind of person who is outgoing, sociable" (to index overlap with sociability) (Rammestadt & John, 2007, p. 210). The former item negatively correlates with the latter item and thus a respondent receives a high extraversion score if they report high overlap between self and sociability and simultaneously low overlap with self and seclusion. Likewise, a person receives a low extraversion score (and might be considered introverted) if they report high overlap between self and seclusion and simultaneously low overlap between self and sociability.

In parallel fashion, the reasoning about overlap with dichotomous gender categories can and should be tested empirically. Furthermore, this method of asking about overlap with two gender categories can be usefully applied to nonbinary experiences of gender identity as well. In particular, researchers could determine whether genderblended individuals report similarly high overlap with both female and male gender categories and whether post-gender individuals report similarly low overlap with both female and male gender categories. The two hypothetical patterns appear to be consistent with the definitions of these experiences provided above. This new method therefore has the possibility to showcase both measurement precision and parsimony for the felt-sense of gender identity that is inclusive of all experiences. Also, the approach of examining comparative self-gender category overlap with at least two gender categories would allow for the eventual investigation of the four kinds of personality trait stability (i.e., intraindividual, ipsative, mean-level, and rank-order) in the following ways. The intraindividual consistency would be either test-retest reliability (at the shortest time interval) or longitudinal collection (at the longest time interval) for overlap ratings with either gender category. If a respondent for instance, overlaps highly with the female category at time-1, this result should remain at time-2. Likewise, if that same participant overlaps at near zero with the male category at time-1, this result should be similar at time-2. Ipsative consistency can be examined by comparing the relative extremities of endorsing each of the self-gender overlap categories within the same people across time. For example, it is possible that before the age of 4 years, children are relatively low and undifferentiated in their felt-sense of overlap with both the female and male gender categories. Yet, soon after age 4 years, many children may start to experience more overlap with one gender category, while overlap with the other remains low. The foregoing example assumes a binary experience of gender self-categorization, but the same reasoning would be applicable to nonbinary experiences, as either experience of high overlap with both female and male categories concurrently (genderblended) or as continued low overlap with both female and male categories (post-gender). The main point for the ipsative consistency would be to show a saliency change in self-category overlap (or lack thereof) over time within the same person. Mean-level consistency might be indexed by comparing those who self-categorize as either female or male to show that female respondents' overlap with the self and the female gender category is always higher (on average) than male respondents' overlap with the self and the female category. Likewise, the inverse should also be true: male respondents' overlap with the self and the male gender category may always be higher (on average) than the female respondents' rated overlap for self and the male category. Finally, rank order consistency might be indexed by showing that over time, self-categorized women and men (cis and trans) should show a greater discrepancy (i.e., larger absolute difference) between their self and female overlap ratings and their self and male overlap ratings compared to self-categorized genderblended or post-gender individuals. To see the specific mechanisms of this comparison strategy, one needs to conceptualize self-category overlap as both an extent (e.g., high, low) and target (e.g., female, male) combination. In this conceptualization some respondents (nonbinary experiences) are high-high (genderblended) or low-low (post-gender), but the absolute difference between these ratings within each group should be small. On the other hand, some respondents (binary experiences) are high-low (female) and low-high (male) combinations, and the absolute difference between these ratings of self and category overlap within each group should be large. A researcher could then compare the sizes of the absolute differences *across the groups* to determine rank order consistency. In this comparison and over time, binary experiences should show a larger absolute difference between their ratings of overlap as compared to nonbinary experiences. Thus, with a measurement tool of the kind describe here, personality approaches to gender identity are both possible and illuminating.

GENERAL DISCUSSION

In this chapter, I have attempted to demonstrate that there are compelling reasons to begin an investigation of gender identity as a personality process. While the dominant social psychological perspective has been useful and informative, it does not and cannot provide a complete picture of a life science understanding of gender. Instead, the social psychological perspective (like all perspectives) caters to its strengths as a discipline of psychological science—namely, focusing the field's attention on attitudes toward self and others and the social expectations and pressures that largely affect the aspects of self that require social coordination between and among people. The personality process approach complements the social psychological one in that the intrapsychic dynamics that are relatively opaque to interpersonal language can be detailed and modeled using the techniques that have largely been the domain of individual difference thinking and modeling. The tension between the social psychology and personality perspectives is well known to those within either of these fields even though a small and tenuous nexus exists between them (see, e.g., Funder & Fast, 2010). Consequently, it is not my intention to create further controversy or acrimony. Rather, this chapter has tried to unite the two perspectives. Gender, in its totality, is a set of psychological constructs that people experience in a manner that requires both a personality approach and a social psychological approach to fully characterize. Social psychology excels at modeling what Egan and Perry have termed constructs such as: (a) membership knowledge, (b) contentment with one's gender assignment, (c) gender typicality, (d) pressure to conform to gender stereotypes, and (e) intergroup bias. The social psychological perspective is also excellent at modeling large-scale societal gender roles, socially derived gender expectations, as well as individual-level variability around them, and the intrapsychic and interpersonal dynamics of *genderhoods* (e.g., manhood, womanhood) and their consequences for cognition, affect, and behavior. Each of the research topics listed above, however, requires an individual social perceiver's self-categorization into a gender group *before* any of these processes are meaningfully described or modeled by researchers. In this manner, personality science on self-categorization appears to be requisite for the social psychological dynamics to commence and be meaningful. As a result, only when the perspectives work together and explicitly acknowledge this nexus point—at gender identity specifically—can psychological science on gender be comprehensive.

As noted above, the dynamics of self-categorization as gender identity can and should be modeled at all levels of the personality process framing: self-report, informant report, physiological, and genetic. Of course, the biological approach to gender self-categorization requires researchers to avoid conflating or confounding the existing discussions of *gender difference* in medicine, biology, psychiatry, or psychology. Self-categorization is not tantamount to the fact that genders differ; it is a requirement for researchers to have gender groupings in the first place (rather than simple genital anatomy groupings). Related to this point, researchers should endeavor to theorize about gender self-categorization at the most inclusive level possible. The history of psychiatry and clinical psychology, for instance, shows the glaring misstep of categorizing homosexuality as a mental disorder from 1900 until 1973 (see Drescher, 2010), which led to a marginalization of theorizing on sexual orientation that could have been more inclusive and more informative earlier in the history of these fields. One consequence of that style of thinking was and continues to be subtle and overt prejudice and discrimination toward lesbians and gay men (e.g Herek, 1988, 2000; Kite & Deaux, 1986), as well as bisexual individuals (e.g., Ben-Zeev, Dennehy, & Kaufman, 2012; Mohr & Rochlen, 1999), that may be perceived as justified by the "scientific" thinking at the turn of the last century. Another consequence is that evolutionary psychology approaches to the origins of sexual orientations have underestimated how inclusive theorizing about sexual orientation (that treats all experiences of sexual orientation as valid) would strengthen the field's understanding of sexual orientation overall (Tate, 2013b). Instead, the current approaches lurch between uncovering conceptual insights and falling into so-called paradoxes because the collective thinking is heteronormative rather than inclusive (Tate, 2013b; Tate & Ledbetter, 2010). The missed opportunities for sexual orientation theorizing and the difficulty of current work to capture new insights in the face of lingering prejudices and other academic resistance should be a cautionary tale for a personality approach to gender identity. Personality researchers should approach gender identity by including all profiles of gender self-categorizations—cisgender and transgender spectrum—from the outset to avoid missed opportunities, marginalization, and the ultimate delaying of theoretical advancement. Tate et al. (2013) have already provided researchers with a demographic method that simultaneously captures cisgender and transgender spectrum experiences for U.S. populations, and this work should be expanded for both cross-cultural use and as the basis for pursuing basic personality science questions about gender identity as self-categorization.

In the final analysis, the scientific approaches to gender across the life and behavioral sciences find themselves at the precipice of a new age of discovery. As developed in this chapter, personality science can offer a crucial nexus between the popular and ever-expanding social psychological insights and the need to focus specific attention on self-categorization processes. Only then can researchers develop solid theories about the origin and intrapersonal function of gender identity and connect these to the interpersonal meanings of gender identity. It is my hope that the relevant fields of study use these insights to create a better, more inclusive science of gender identity sooner rather than later.

AUTHOR NOTE

A special thanks to Ryan Howell for encouraging some of these ideas in their most nascent form and pointing me in useful directions regarding personality theorizing. Also, I thank Cris Youssef and Jay Ledbetter for their feedback on many of the ideas presented. No funding source aided in the completion of this chapter.

REFERENCES

Ansara, Y., & Hegarty, P. (2012). Cisgenderism in psychology: pathologising and misgendering children from 1999 to 2008. *Psychology & Sexuality, 3(2)*, 137-160.

Bakan, D. (1966). *The duality of human existence*. Chicago, IL: Rand McNally.

Bem, S. L. (1974). The measurement of psychological androgyny. *Journal of Counseling and Clinical Psychology, 42,* 155-162.

Bem, S. L. (1981a). Gender schema theory: A cognitive account of sex typing. *Psychological Review, 88,* 354-364.

Bem, S. L. (1981b). The BSRI and gender schema theory: A reply to Spence and Helmreich. *Psychological Review, 88*(4), 369-371.

Ben-Zeev, A., Dennehy, T. C., & Kaufman, J. C. (2012). Blurring boundaries: Bisexual versus lesbian and heterosexual women's self-assessed creativity. *Journal of Bisexuality, 12,* 1-13.

Bolger, N. (1990). Coping as a personality process: A prospective study. *Journal of Personality and Social Psychology, 59,* 525-537.

Bornstein, K. (1998). *My gender workbook*. New York: Routledge.

Cantor, N. (1990). From though to behavior: "Having" and "doing" in the study of personality and cognition. *American Psychologist, 45,* 735-750.

Caspi, A., & Roberts, B. W. (2001). Personality development across the life course: The argument for change and continuity. *Psychological Inquiry, 12,* 49-66.

Caspi, A., Roberts, B. W., & Shiner, R. L. (2005). Personality development: Stability and change. *Annual Reviews of Psychology, 56,* 453-484.

Constantinople, A. (1973). Masculinity-femininity: An exception to a famous dictum? *Psychological Bulletin, 80*(5), 389-407.

Dahlstrom, W. G., Welsh, G. S., & Dahlstrom, L. E. (1972). *An MMPI handbook: Volume I: Clinical interpretation* (2nd ed.). Minneapolis, MN: University of Minnesota Press.

Costa, P. T., Terracciano, A., & McCrae, R. R. (2001). Gender differences in personality traits across cultures: Robust and surprising findings. *Journal of Personality and Social Psychology, 81,* 322-331.

Devor, H. (1997). *FTM: Female-to-Male transsexuals in society*. Bloomington, IN: Indiana University Press.

Drescher, J. (2010). Queer diagnoses: Parallels and contrasts in the history of homosexuality, gender variances, and the *Diagnostic and Statistical Manual. Archives of Sexual Behavior, 39,* 427–460.

Eagly, A. H. (1987). *Sex differences in social behavior: A social-role interpretation.* Hillsdale, NJ: Erlbaum.

Eagly, A. H., Beall, A. L., & Sternberg, R. J. (2004). *The psychology of gender* (2nd ed.). New York: Guilford.

Eagly, A. H., & Wood, W. (1999). The origins of sex differences in human behavior: Evolved dispositions versus social roles. *American Psychologist, 54,* 408-423.

Eagly, A. H., & Wood, W. (2011). Feminism and the evolution of sex differences and similarities. *Sex Roles, 64,* 758-767.

Eagly, A. H., Wood, W., & Diekman, A. (2000). Social role theory of sex differences and similarities: A current appraisal. In T. Eckes & H. M. Tautner (Eds.), *The developmental social psychology of gender* (pp. 123-174). Mahwah, NJ: Erlbaum.

Egan, S. K., & Perry, D. G. (2001). Gender identity: A multidimensional analysis with implications for psychosocial adjustment. *Developmental Psychology*, 37, 451-463. doi:10.1037/0012-1649.37.4.451

Ellis, H. (1905). *Studies in the psychology of sex* (vol. 1). New York, NY: Random House.

Factor, R., & Rothblum, E. (2008). Exploring gender identity and community among three groups of transgender individuals in the United States: MTFs, FTMs, and genderqueers. *Health Sociology Review*, *17*, 235-253.

Fleming, M. Z., Jenkins, S. R., & Bugarin, C. (1980). Questioning current definitions of gender identity: Implications of the Bem Sex-Role Inventory for transsexuals. *Archives of Sexual Behavior, 9*(1), 13-26.

Glick, P., & Fiske, S. T. (2001). An ambivalent alliance: Hostile and benevolent sexism as complementary justifications for gender inequality. *American Psychologist, 56*, 109-118.

Grant, J. M., Mottet, L. A., Tanis, J., Harrison, J., Herman, J. L., & Keisling, M. (2011). *Injustice at every turn: A report of the national transgender discrimination survey.* Washington, DC: National Center for Transgender Equality and National Gay and Lesbian Task Force.

Green, J. (2004). *Becoming a visible man.* Nashville, TN: Vanderbilt University Press.

Green, J. (2005). Part of the package: Ideas of masculinity among male-identified transpeople. *Men and Masculinities, 7(3)*, 291-299.

Hathaway, S. R., & McKinley, J. C. (1940). A multiphasic personality schedule (Minnesota): I. Construction of the schedule. *Journal of Psychology, 10*, 249-254.

Hegarty, P., & Coyle, A. (2005). Editor's introduction: An undervalued part of the psychology gender canon? Reappraising Anne Constantinople's (1973) 'Masculinity-feminity: An exception to the famous dictum?'. *Feminism & Psychology, 15*, 379-383.

Helgeson, V. S. (1994). Relation of agency and communion to well-being: Evidence and potential explanations. *Psychological Bulletin, 116*, 412-428.

Herek, G. M. (1988). Heterosexuals' attitudes towards Lesbians and Gay Men: Correlates and gender differences. *Journal of Sex Research, 25*, 451-477.

Herek, G. M. (2000). Sexual prejudice and gender: Do heterosexuals' attitudes toward lesbians and gay men differ? *Journal of Social Issues, 56*, 251-266.

Hirschfeld, M. (1919/2000). *The homosexuality of men and women.* (M. A. Lombardi-Nash, trans.). Amherst, NY, USA: Prometheus Books.

Hoffman, R. M. (2001). The measurement of masculinity and femininity: Historical perspective and implications for counseling. *Journal of Counseling & Development, 79*(4), 472-485.

Howard, J. A., & Hollander, J. A. (1997). *Gendered situations, gendered selves: A gender lens on social psychology.* Thousand Oaks, CA, US: Sage.

Kite, M. E., & Deaux, K. (1987). Gender belief systems: Homosexuality and the implicit inversion theory. *Psychology of Women Quarterly, 11*, 83-96.

Kuper, L. E., Nussbaum, R., & Mustanski, B. (2012). Exploring the diversity of gender and sexual orientation identities in an online sample of transgender individuals. *Journal of Sex Research, 49*, 244-254

Laurent, S. M., & Hodges, S. D. (2009). Gender and empathic accuracy: The role of communion in reading minds. *Sex Roles, 60*, 387-398.

Maccoby, E. E., & Jacklin, C. N. (1974). *The psychology of sex differences.* Standford, CA: Stanford University Press.

Markus, H. (1977). Self-schemata and processing information about the self. *Journal of Personality and Social Psychology, 35*, 63-78.

Martin, C. L., Ruble, D. N., & Szkrybalo, J. (2002). Cognitive theories of early gender development. *Psychological Bulletin, 128*(6), 903-933.

McAdams, D. P. (1990). Unity and purpose in human lives: The emergence of identity as a life story. In A. I. Rabin, R. A. Zucker, R. A. Emmons, & S. Frank (Eds.), *Studying persons and lives* (pp. 148-200). New York: Springer-Verlag.

McAdams, D. P. (1993). *The stories we live by: Personal myths and the making of self.* New York: Morrow.

McCrae, R. R., & Costa, P. T. (1994). The stability of personality: Observations and evaluations. *Current Directions in Psychological Science, 3,* 173-175.

Mock, J. (2014). *Redefining realness: My path to womanhood, identity, love, and so much more.* New York, NY: Atria Books. Mohr & Rochlen, 1999

Morris, J. (1974). *Conundrum.* New York: Harcourt Brace Jovanovich.

Nasselroade, J. R. (1991). Interindividual differences in intraindividual change. In L. M. Collins & J. L. Horn (Eds.), *Best methods for the analysis of change* (pp. 92-105). Washington, D. C.: American Psychological Association.

Newton, N. J., & Stewart, A. J. (2013). The road not taken: Women's life paths and gender-linked personality traits. *Journal of Research in Personality, 47,* 306-316.

Nichols, D. S. (2011). *Essentials of MMPI®-2 assessment* (2nd ed.). Hoboken, NJ: Wiley.

Penke, L. (2010). Bridging the gap between modern evolutionary psychology and the study of individual differences. In D. M. Buss & P. H. Hawley (Eds.): *The evolution of personality and individual differences* (pp. 243-279). New York: Oxford University Press.

Rametti, G., Carrillo, B., Gómez-Gil, E., Junque, C., Segovia, S., Gomez, Á., & Guillamon, A. (2011a). White matter microstructure in female to male transsexuals before cross-sex hormonal treatment: A diffusion tensor imaging study. *Psychiatric Research, 45,* 199-204.

Rametti, G., Carrillo, B., Gómez-Gil, E., Junque, C., Zubiarre-Elorza, L., Segovia, S., Gomez, Á., & Guillamon, A. (2011b). White matter microstructure in male to female transsexuals before cross-sex hormonal treatment: A DTI study. *Psychiatric Research, 45,* 949-954.

Rammstedt, B. & John, O. P. (2007). Measuring personality in one minute or less: A 10-item short version of the Big Five Inventory in English and German. *Journal of Research in Personality, 41,* 203-212.

Revelle, W. (1995). Personality processes. *Annual Reviews of Psychology, 46,* 295- 328.

Roberts, B. W., & DelVecchio, W. (2000). The rank-order consistency of personality traits from childhood to old age: A quantitative review of longitudinal studies. *Psychological Bulletin, 126,* 3-25.

Roberts, B. W., Walton, K. E., & Viechtbauer, W. (2006). Patterns of mean-level change in personality traits across the life course: A meta-analysis of longitudinal studies. *Psychological Bulletin, 132,* 1-25.

Rothbart, M. K., Ahadi, S. A., & Evans, D. E. (1999). Temperament and personality: Origins and outcomes. *Journal of Personality and Social Psychology, 78,* 122-135.

Runyan, W. M. (1990). Individual lives and the structure of personality. In A. I.

Rabin, R. A. Zucker, R. A. Emmons, & S. Frank (Eds.), *Studying persons and lives* (pp. 148-200). New York: Springer-Verlag.

Scheim, A. I., & Bauer, G R. (2014). Sex and gender diversity among transgender persons in Ontario, Canada: Results from a respondent-driven sampling survey. *Journal of Sex Research.* Advance online publication.

Serano, J. (2007). *Whipping girl: A transsexual woman on sexism and the scapegoating of femininity.* Berkeley, CA: Seal Press.

Spence, J. T. (1991). Do the BSRI and PAQ measure the same or different concepts? *Psychology of Women Quarterly, 15*(1), 141-165.

Spence, J. T., & Helmreich, R. L. (1980). Masculine instrumentality and feminine expressiveness: Their relationships with sex role attitudes and behaviors. *Psychology of Women Quarterly, 5*(2), 147-163.

Spence, J. T., Helmreich, R. L., & Stapp, J. (1975). Ratings of self and peers on sex-role attributes and their relation to self-esteem and conceptions of masculinity and femininity. *Journal of Personality and Social Psychology, 32*, 29-39.

Srivastava, S., John, O. P., Gosling, S. D., & Potter, J. (2003). Development of personality in early and middle adulthood: Set like plaster or persistent change? *Journal of Personality and Social Psychology, 84*, 1014-1053.

Stangor, C., & Ruble, D. N. (1987). Development of gender role knowledge and gender constancy. *New Directions for Child Development, 38*, 5-22.

Stoller, R. J. (1968/1974) *Sex and gender: Volume I the development of masculinity and femininity*. New York: Jason Aronson.

Strong, E. R., Jr. (1935). *Manual for the Vocational Interest Blank*. Stanford, CA, USA: Stanford University Press.

Strong, E. R. (1936). Interests of men and women. *The Journal of Social Psychology*. 749-767.

Tate, C. C. (2012). Considering lesbian identity from a social-cognitive vantage: Two models of "being a lesbian." *Journal of Lesbian Studies, 16*, 17-29.

Tate, C. C. (2013a). Addressing conceptual confusions regarding evolutionary theorizing: How and why evolutionary psychology and feminism do not oppose each other. *Sex Roles, 69*, 491-502.

Tate, C. C. (2013b.). Another meaning of Darwinian feminism: Toward inclusive evolutionary accounts of sexual orientations. *Journal of Social, Cultural, and Evolutionary Psychology, 7*, 344-353.

Tate, C., & Ledbetter, J. N. (2010). Oversimplifying evolutionary psychology leads to explanatory gaps. *American Psychologist, 65*, 929–930.

Tate, C. C., Ledbetter, J. N., & Youssef, C. P. (2013). A two-question method for assessing gender categories in the social and medical sciences. *Journal of Sex Research*, 50, 767-776.

Terman, L. M., & Miles, C. C. (1936). *Sex and personality: Studies in masculinity and femininity* (1st ed.). New York: McGraw-Hill.

Witt, M. G., & Wood, W. (2010). Self-regulation of gendered behavior in everyday life. *Sex Roles, 62*, 635-646.

Wood, W. & Eagly, A. H. (2000). Once again, the origins of sex differences. *American Psychologist, 55*, 1062-1063.

Wood, W., & Eagly, A. H. (2010). Gender. In S. T. Fiske, Gilbert, D. T., & Lindzey, G. (Eds.), *Handbook of Social Psychology* (5th ed., vol. 1), pp. 629-667. Hoboken, NJ: Wiley.

Zanna, M. P., & Rempel, J. K. (1988). Attitudes: A new look at an old concept. In D. Bar-Tal & A. W. Kruglanski (Eds.), *The social psychology of knowledge* (pp. 315-334). New York: Cambridge University Press.

In: Gender Identity
Editor: Beverly L. Miller

ISBN: 978-1-63321-488-0
© 2014 Nova Science Publishers, Inc.

Chapter 2

"WHO AM I NOW?"
DISTRESS AND GROWTH AFTER TRAUMA

Rachel E. Wiley[*] and Sharon E. Robinson-Kurpius
Counseling Psychology, School of Letters and Sciences,
Arizona State University, Tempe, AZ

ABSTRACT

This study investigated relationships among the experience of trauma, identity development, distress, and positive change among 908 emerging adults with a mean age of 19.99 (SD = 1.97) years. Greater identity exploration was associated with more distress, whereas greater identity commitment was associated with positive change after the trauma. Participants with a PTSD diagnosis reported more distress and identity exploration as compared to participants without PTSD who reported more positive change and identity commitments. Regression analyses found the centrality of the trauma event to one's identity predicted identity distress above and beyond the experience of trauma. Identity distress and the centrality of the trauma together predicted identity exploration, while only identity distress predicted identity commitments. Identity development predicted positive change above and beyond identity distress, centrality of the trauma event, and the experience of trauma. Collectively, these results indicate that aspects of distress and growth occur after traumatic events.

INTRODUCTION

It is well-known that trauma can lead to posttraumatic stress (PTS), depression, physical health problems, and/or behavioral dysfunctions (e.g., D'Andrea, Sharma, Zelechoski & Spinazzola, 2011; Edwards, Holden, Felitti, & Anda, 2003; Felitti & Anda, 2008). The current literature on trauma exposure, however, has tended to minimize the psychosocial

---

[*] Please address correspondence concerning this manuscript to: Rachel Wiley, Counseling Psychology, School of Letters and Science, Arizona State University, Tempe, AZ 85287-0811; E-mail: Rachel.Wiley@asu.edu; Phone Number: 480-965-6104.

scope and healthy adaptations and to overestimate the psychological impact (Bonanno, Brewin, Kaniasty, & La Greca, 2010). Studying the psychosocial stage of identity development in the aftermath of trauma is important because difficulties within this stage may hinder healthy development in later stages (Deeny & McFetridge, 2005). Additionally, the perspective of resilience and posttraumatic growth (PTG) needs further study that is informed by developmental principles (Aldwin & Levenson, 2004). For example, there are positive aspects of exposure to trauma, including the ability to adapt and grow from these experiences (Bonanno, 2005; Tedeschi & Calhoun, 2004). It is expected that understanding these relationships can increase prevention of mental health problems and difficulties resolving developmental stages (Parker, Buckmaster, Schatzberg, & Lyons, 2004).

Identity Development

Developing a personal identity is considered a lengthy process, with few young people forming a sense of who they are and what path they will follow until later adulthood (Côté, 2006; Kroger, 2006; Santrock, 1996). Emerging adulthood is a "crucial time for the development of a world view" (p. 166, Arnett, 2004) and the advanced pursuits for education bring with it a transition period between adolescence and adulthood (Berger, 2008). The ages of 18 to 25 incorporate this stage of life in which the process of identity development primarily occurs.

Identity has been defined as "an internal, self-constructed, dynamic organization of drives, abilities, beliefs and individual history" (Marcia, 1980, p. 159). Marcia (1966) described self-exploration and commitment as key dimensions of identity development. Individuals in the exploration dimension are actively seeking, questioning, and weighing various identity alternatives before resolving issues about their life's direction and purpose. Committed individuals have resolved their identity issues, are more secure in their choices, and engage in activities to implement these choices.

Marcia (1966) combined dimensions of high or low levels of identity exploration and commitment to create four identity statuses: Diffusion; foreclosure; moratorium; and achievement. Diffused individuals are not actively seeking or exploring different alternatives and have not committed to any particular goals, roles, or beliefs (Berger, 2008; Marcia, 1966). Individuals in the foreclosed status do not question or analyze their values and goals but instead, adopt their parents', friends', or society's values. Foreclosure is often a comfortable status where individuals can avoid the anxiety of forging their own path (Berger, 2008; Marcia, 1966).

Moratorium is the identity status in which individuals postpone making decisions that lead to identity achievement. This stage is often related to a time of crisis in which active exploration of different options, and desperate searching for a decision occurs (Berger, 2008; Marcia, 1966). According to Erikson (1968), the ultimate psychosocial goal is identity achievement or the point when an individual understands who he or she is as a unique person. Having explored various alternatives, these individuals are able to make a commitment that they currently implement and desire to continue in the future.

Longitudinal and cross-sectional studies have revealed a hierarchy of identity statuses from diffused and foreclosed levels to statuses of moratorium and achievement (Kroger &

Haslett, 1988; Marcia, 1976). According to Kroger, Martinussen, and Marcia (2010), during the college years there are more transitions through moratorium status than at other ages.

Identity Development, Identity Distress, and Trauma

As young adults explore different elements of their lives, some distress related to their identity is normal and expected (Erikson, 1963); however, some individuals experience a significant identity crisis (Waterman, 1988). Adolescents and emerging adults who experience trauma may be prone to impaired identity formation including premature closure of identity formation and early entrance to adulthood (Pynoos & Eth, 1985). Thus, traumatic experiences may be damaging to a person's sense of identity (Mancini & Bonanno, 2006).

Identity distress can be described as having exceptional difficulties in the process of identity development and has been related to poorer psychological adjustment (Berman, Kennerly, & Kennerly, 2009; Hernandez, Montgomery, & Kurtines, 2006; Wiley & Berman, 2013). Although identity distress decreases with age from late adolescence/emerging adulthood into middle age and beyond (Waterman, 1993; Wiley et al., 2011), research has found the experience of trauma in childhood and adolescence can have a negative impact on adult development and functioning (Briere, Kaltman, & Green, 2008; Cook et al., 2005).

Identity distress and PTSD have been linked empirically. For example, during crisis intervention training for humanitarian aid workers, Spiers (1997) found that the trauma of the war exacerbated an identity crisis. Studying sexually assaulted women, Ehlers et al., (1998) found that the perception of loss of autonomy, choice, and free will, and the perception that one's identity cannot be maintained were predictive of PTSD and symptom severity. Wiley et al. (2011) found that Hurricane Katrina survivor's trauma exposure was related to identity distress ratings and suggested that this association was a function of PTS symptoms. Similar results were reported by Brewin, Garnett, and Andrews (2011) who found PTSD was related to perceiving more negative changes about themselves and the world.

That traumatic memories form a central component of one's personal identity is evidenced by several empirical investigations. In an early study by McNally, Lasko, Macklin, and Pitman (1995), veterans with PTSD reported that their identity and personal memories had become centered around their trauma. Indeed, individuals with a PTSD diagnosis agreed that the trauma was more central to their identity than did individuals without a PTSD diagnosis (Berntsen & Rubin, 2006) and those with PTSD tended to identify themselves as defined by the trauma (Sutherland & Bryant, 2005). Webb and Jobson (2011) also found trauma-centered identity to be related to PTS symptomatology, which supports the theory that individuals are more likely to suffer from symptoms of PTSD when the trauma memory is more central to their identity. In their 2007 study, Berntsen and Rubin had reported that one's cognitive organization of traumatic memories and identity may be a part of the development and/or maintenance of PTSD symptoms. It appears that individuals with PTSD often must struggle to reconcile the new, trauma-acquired identity with their old identity.

A trauma can become a turning point in identity as survivors reflect on their stressful experience and recognize a discrepancy between their unattained goals or schemas (McAdams, Reynolds, Lewis, Patten, & Bowman, 2001). Tedeschi and Calhoun (2004) noted that these survivors may try formulating new goals and worldviews to help them move forward and establish who they are after the trauma. For example, some survivors of partner violence report a negative impact on their identity, while other survivors report their experience having a positive impact. Describing themselves as survivors reflects a sense of resilience (Weaver, Turner, Schwarze, Thayer, & Carter-Sand, 2007). Conway (2005) suggested that incongruence between the trauma event and existing self-definition or identity can be a catalyst for change.

Trauma, Resilience and Posttraumatic Growth

While trauma can be quite debilitating, both physically and psychologically, some individuals show an ability to move beyond the traumatic stressor with little or no distress (Bonanno, 2004; Mancini & Bonannno, 2006; Parker et al., 2004). Bonanno (2004) also defined resilience as adults' ability to maintain relatively stable, healthy levels of psychological and physical functioning and positive emotions after life-threatening situations. Thus, the construct of resilience provides a framework for understanding healthy development in the face of risk and trauma. Fonagy, Steele, Steele, Higgitt, and Target (1994) described resilience as "normal development under difficult conditions" (p. 233); therefore, individuals who report experiencing traumatic events and are resilient may also report healthy identity formation.

In contrast to resilience, posttraumatic growth (PTG) refers to reports of positive changes that occur as a result of individual's cognitions about and ability to cope with trauma. Those who are resilient have adjusted to adversity, while those experiencing PTG have been transformed by their struggles. Tedeschi and Calhoun (2004) provided examples of growth such as perceiving greater meaning in relationships or spirituality, embarking on a new life path, or having a newfound sense of competence. PTG is not superior to resilience (Westphal & Bonanno, 2007); however, resilient individuals may not need or have opportunities to experience PTG.

Although PTG does not lessen the trauma survivor's emotional distress, it may trigger a reconsideration of one's life, purpose, and meaning (Calhoun, Cann, Tedeschi, & McMillan, 2000; Tedeschi & Calhoun, 2004). Trauma survivors may recognize having grown from the trauma but continue to experience distress, which produces a paradoxical outlook. While PTG may come from great distress and may be maintained through continued distress, it is the struggle during the aftermath of the trauma and not the trauma itself that produces PTG (Tedeschi & Kilmer, 2005). The challenge of experiencing traumatic events can lead to PTG and identity development.

The Current Study

Although there is a paucity of research examining the relations among identity, PTSD, resilience, and PTG, what is known is that individuals who have resolved their identity issues report better psychological well-being, adjustment, and emotional stability (e.g., Crocetti et al., 2008; Kroger, 2007; Luyckx, Goossens, Soenens, & Beyers, 2006). In the current study, multiple constructs were investigated simultaneously. The first construct was the experience of trauma, consisting of trauma exposure, trauma severity, time since the most recent trauma, and PTS symptoms. The second construct was identity development, which consisted of identity exploration and identity commitment. Also of interest were the centrality of the trauma event to one's identity and identity distress. The third construct was positive change, which consisted of resilience and PTG.

The current study specifically examined whether there were differences among identity status groups and PTSD diagnostic status in identity distress, centrality of the trauma event, PTS symptoms, positive change, and identity development. It was hypothesized that participants in the diffused and moratorium identity statuses would report more identity distress, centrality of the trauma event, and PTS symptoms, and less positive change than participants in the foreclosed and achieved identity status groups. Participants with a PTSD diagnosis were expected to report greater centrality of the trauma event, more identity exploration, more identity distress, more PTG, and less resilience and identity commitment than were participants without a PTSD diagnosis. In addition, centrality of the trauma event was hypothesized to predict identity distress above and beyond the experience of trauma. Identity distress and the centrality of the trauma event were hypothesized to predict identity development above and beyond the experience of trauma. And finally, identity development, identity distress, centrality of the trauma event, and the experience of trauma was hypothesized to predict positive change.

METHOD

Recruitment

After Institutional Review Board approval was obtained, community advocates and class instructors were contacted and invited to give the participant recruitment script to their clients or students. Participants were recruited from undergraduate courses at a large southwestern university, websites that serve trauma and abuse survivors, psychological listservs, national Reserve Officers' Training Corps (ROTC), and community mental health centers. The consent form and study measures were provided using surveygizmo.com, an online survey program.

Participants

There were 908 participants (41.3% male, 58.5% female, .1% transgender, and .1% missing) with a mean age of 19.99 ($SD = 1.97$) years. Of those who reported race/ethnicity, most were Caucasian ($n = 592$; 65.2%), while 124 (13.7%) were Hispanic American, 94 (10.4%) other/multi-racial, 53 (5.8%) Asian American, 28 (3.1%) African American, and 14 (1.5%) Native American/Alaskan Native. Educational status included: Less than high school diploma ($n = 1$; .1%), high school diploma ($n = 38$; 4.2%), an associate's degree ($n = 36$; 4.0%), current undergraduate student ($n = 791$; 87.1%), bachelor's degree ($n = 18$; 2.0%), current master's student ($n = 7$; .8%), and master's degree ($n = 1$; .1%). Yearly household income (including income for everyone living with the participant) varied, with 141(15.5%) under $9,999, 164 (18.0%) with $10,000 to $29,999, 131 (14.5%) with $30,000 to $49,999, 141 (15.5%) with $50,000 to $69,999, and approximately a third of the participants reporting

$70,000 or more ($n$ = 319; 35.1%). Three fourths of the sample (n = 687; 75.4%) reported living in the Southwest.

Measures

The Life Stressor Checklist-Revised (LSC-R; Wolfe & Kimerling, 1997) is a measure of lifetime exposure to potentially traumatic events. Respondents answered yes/no to a list of events including natural disasters, physical or sexual assault, and death of a relative. Items that asked about the effect on their life and how upsetting the event was at the time were rated on a 5-point intensity scale (1 = "not at all" to 5 = "extremely"). Higher scores were reflective of more subjective ratings of severity for the traumas endorsed. An indirect exposure item "No, but I have witnessed this" was added to the modified LSC-R used in this study. Items from the LEC (Gray, Litz, Hsu, & Lombardo 2004) were also added that ask about: toxic substances, assault with a weapon, combat or a war-zone, held captive, and fired or unemployed for a long time. In addition, the question "How many times did this happen?" was added to each item in order to assess multiple traumas experienced by respondents. A total score for traumatic stressor indirect exposures had a possible range of 0 to 13 and total direct exposures scores ranged from 0 to 32 with higher scores reflecting more trauma exposure. The original LSC-R has demonstrated good test-retest reliability and good criterion-related validity with diverse populations (Brown, Stout, & Mueller, 1999; Kimerling et al., 1999).

Current posttraumatic stress (PTS) symptomatology, using DSM-IV criteria, was assessed by the 17-item, self-report Posttraumatic Stress Disorder Checklist-Civilian Version (PCL-C; Weathers, Litz, Huska, & Keane, 1994). For the PCL-C, the items are worded generically to refer to "stressful experiences in the past." The symptoms endorsed are not specific to just one event. For the symptom indicated in each item, respondents rate their degree of distress over the previous month on a 5-point Likert-type scale ranging from 1 ("not at all") to 5 ("extremely"). Items included symptoms such as, "Feeling jumpy or easily startled?" A continuous severity score for PTS symptoms is obtained by summing responses across items. Possible scores range from 17 to 85 with higher scores reflecting greater severity of PTS symptoms. Additionally, a total score of 44 is considered to be PTSD positive for the general population. The PCL has demonstrated excellent psychometric properties with a reported Cronbach's alpha of .97 and test-retest reliability of .96 (Weathers et al., 1994). In this study, the Cronbach's alpha was .93.

The construct, identity development, was comprised of identity exploration and identity commitment and was measured by two subscales of the 32-item Ego Identity Process Questionnaire (EIPQ; Balistreri, Busch-Rossnagel, & Geisinger, 1995). Participants rated items such as: "My beliefs about dating are firmly held" from "1 = strongly disagree" to "5 = strongly agree." Two subscales are included in the EIPQ, identity exploration and identity commitment. The authors reported Cronbach's alpha for the exploration subscale to be .86 with a test-retest reliability of .76. For the commitment subscale the Cronbach's alpha was .80 and the test-retest reliability was .90 (Balistreri et al., 1995). In this study, the Cronbach's alphas were .71 for the exploration subscale and .67 for the commitment subscale.

Balistreri et al., (1995) used median splits on the two subscales to assign one of four identity statuses to the participants. Since each item is answered on a scale of 1 to 5, a cut off score of 3.5 is used to classify individuals who report having explored or committed to their identity. According to Lee and MacLean (2006), this method may have slightly superior predictive utility for differences on psychological adjustment variables. As was previously used by Berman et al., (2009), participants in the current study who scored low on exploration and commitment were classified as diffused, those low in exploration but high in commitment were classified as foreclosed, high scores in exploration but low in commitment were classified as moratorium, and those high in both exploration and commitment were classified as achieved. Balistreri et al., (1995) reported the Cronbach's alpha for the exploration subscale as .86 with a test-retest reliability of .76. For the commitment subscale the Cronbach's alpha was .80, and the test-retest reliability was .90. In this study, the Cronbach's alphas were .71 for the exploration subscale and .67 for the commitment subscale.

The Centrality of Events Scale (CES; Berntsen & Rubin, 2006) is a 7-item scale that measures how central a traumatic stressor is to a person's identity and life story. Participants were asked to think about the most stressful or traumatic event in their life and to answer questions using a 5 point Likert-type response scale ranging from "1 = totally disagree" to "5 = totally agree." A sample item is "I feel that this event has become part of my identity." A total centrality of the trauma event score was derived by summing the responses across items, with total scores ranging from 7 to 35 with higher scores reflecting greater centrality of the event to one's identity. This measure has a reported internal consistency of .88 (Berntsen & Rubin, 2006). The Cronbach alpha for the current study sample was .88.

The Identity Distress Survey (IDS; Berman, Montgomery, & Kurtines, 2004) is a 10-item brief self-report measure that assesses distress associated with unresolved identity issues. Items such as "To what degree have you recently been upset, distressed, or worried over the following issues in your life" are rated on a scale from 1 (Not at all) to 5 (Very severely). Issues include long-term goals, career choice, friendships, sexual orientation and behavior, religion, values and beliefs, and group loyalties. Three additional items assess the participant's level of discomfort about the seven issues, how much uncertainty they have regarding these issues as a whole, how they have interfered with their life, and how long they have felt distressed. Total identity distress scores are averaged, with a possible range from 1 to 5 with higher scores indicating more identity distress. Internal consistency has been reported as .84 with test-retest reliability of .82 (Berman et al., 2004). The Cronbach's alpha for this study was .86.

The construct of positive change was comprised of resilience and PTG. The Connor-Davidson Resilience Scale (CD-RISC; Connor & Davidson, 2003) is a 25-item, self-rated measure of respondent's ability to adapt well and overcome adversity. The items were designed to reflect content related to well-established sources and theories of resilience (Lyons, 1991; Kobasa's, 1979; Rutter's, 1985). In response to items such as "I am able to adapt to change," participants rate each item on a five-point Likert-type scale ranging from "0 = not true at all" to "4 = true nearly all of the time." Total scores range from 0 to 100, with higher scores indicating greater resilience. An internal consistency of .89 and a test-retest reliability of .87 have been reported by Connor and Davidson (2003). In this study, the Cronbach's alpha was .92.

The 10-item Posttraumatic Growth Inventory (PTGI-SF; Cann et al., 2010) measures significant positive changes and growth that occur after the experience of highly challenging life circumstances. The original inventory (Tedeschi & Calhoun, 1996) included 21-items. A 6-point Likert-type response scale ranging from 0 ("no change") to 5 ("great change") was used for items such as "I discovered that I'm stronger than I thought I was." Responses to all items were summed to produce a total score that could range from 0 to 50, with higher scores indicating greater levels of PTG. This brief inventory has internal reliability that is only slightly lower than the full PTGI (α = .90) across samples of bereaved parents, intimate partner violence victims, and acute leukemia patients. In this study, the Cronbach's alpha was .92.

RESULTS

Based on the participants' responses to the EIPQ (Balistreri et al., 1995), they were classified into one of four categories. This identity status classification procedure resulted in 36.0% (n = 327) being placed in the diffused status, 28.9% (n = 262) in the moratorium status, 24.2% (n = 220) in the foreclosed status, and 10.9% (n = 99) in the achieved status. To examine differences among identity status groups and PTSD diagnostic status in identity distress, centrality of the trauma event, PTS symptoms, positive change, and identity development, multivariate analysis of variance (MANOVA) was used. Follow-up univariate analyses of variances (ANOVA), with a Bonferroni correction to control for Type I error, were examined when the MANOVA was significant. The identity status groups were significantly different, Wilks's Λ = .78, $F(15, 890)$ = 16.03, p < .001, η^2 = .08. Examination of the ANOVAs revealed differences in identity distress [$F(3, 892)$ = 29.16, p< .001], centrality of the trauma event [$F(3, 892)$ = 10.00, p< .001], PTS symptoms [$F(3, 892)$ = 16.72, p< .001], resilience [$F(3, 892)$ = 46.75, p< .001], and PTG [$F(3, 892)$ = 12.92, p< .001]. Multiple comparisons examining the specific hypothesized group differences indicated that the moratorium identity status group reported more identity distress than did the foreclosed and achieved groups. The diffused group reported more identity distress than did both the foreclosed and achieved groups. When centrality of the trauma event served as the dependent variable, the diffused group reported less centrality than did the achieved group. In contrast, the moratorium group reported more centrality than did the achieved group and the foreclosed group. When PTS was the outcome variable, the diffused and moratorium groups reported more symptoms than did the foreclosed group, but not the achieved group.

When resilience was examined, as hypothesized, the achieved group reported more resilience than did the diffused and moratorium groups. Additionally, the foreclosed group reported more resilience than did the moratorium and diffused groups. Examination of the multiple comparisons for PTG indicated that the achieved group reported more PTG than did the diffused group but not more than the moratorium group. The foreclosed identity status group reported less PTG than did the moratorium group. There were no differences between the foreclosed and diffused identity groups (See Table 1 for means and standard deviations).

There were 242 (26.7%) participants who met criteria for PTSD using the PCL-C cut-off score of 44 (Weathers et al., 1993). The PTSD groups differed on the linear combination of these variables, Wilks's Λ = .76, $F(6, 889)$ = 46.99, p < .001, η^2 = .24. Examination of the ANOVAs, revealed group differences in centrality of the trauma event [$F(1, 894)$ = 111.41, p < .001], in identity exploration [$F(1, 894)$ = 41.07, p< .001], in identity distress [$F(1, 894)$ = 146.80, p< .001], in resilience [$F(1, 894)$ = 36.42, p< .001], in identity commitment [$F(1, 894)$ = 21.13, p< .001], and in PTG [$F(1, 894)$ = 76.55, p< .001].

Table 1. Means and Standard Deviations for Identity Status Differences

Variables	Diffused		Foreclosed		Moratorium		Achieved	
	M	SD	M	SD	M	SD	M	SD
Identity distress	2.25	.67	1.95	.64	2.55	.77	2.23	.74
Centrality	22.50	6.60	22.70	6.75	25.10	5.72	24.58	6.80
PTS symptoms	34.16	13.07	29.87	12.14	38.48	15.17	37.65	16.28
Resilience	67.96	13.77	79.19	11.13	70.08	13.56	80.14	12.39
PTG	18.99	12.10	19.90	13.51	23.44	11.59	26.72	14.93

Table 2. Means and Standard Deviations for PTSD Group Differences

Independent Variables PTSD	No PTSD
M SD	M SD
Centrality 27.11 5.74	22.21 6.29
Id. Exp. 56.29 7.62	52.76 7.18
Identity distress 2.72 .75	2.10 .65
PTG 27.32 11.08	19.14 12.83
Resilience 68.05 15.39	74.27 12.97
Id Com. 51.08 7.40	53.51 6.83

Investigation of the group means revealed that participants who met criteria for PTSD diagnosis reported greater centrality of the trauma event, more identity exploration, more identity distress, more PTG, less resilience, and less identity commitment than did those without a PTSD diagnosis (See Table 2).

To examine whether the centrality of the trauma event would predict identity distress above and beyond the experience of trauma, a hierarchical multiple regression analysis was conducted. The experience of trauma (trauma exposure, trauma severity, PTS symptoms, and time since the most recent trauma) was entered as step one and the centrality of the event was entered as step two to predict identity distress. The full model was significant [$F(5, 868) = 49.11$, $p < .001$]. The cluster of predictors entered in step one was significant, $R^2 = .22$ and adjusted $R^2 = .21$, $F (4, 869) = 60.07$, $p < .001$, with significant standardized beta coefficients for trauma severity ($\beta = .14$, $t = 1.94$, $p = .05$) and for PTS symptoms ($\beta = .43$, $t = 12.35$, $p < .001$). Centrality of the trauma event to one's identity above and beyond the experience of trauma was also statistically significant, [$\Delta R^2 = .004$, $\Delta F(1, 868) = 4.34$, $p = .04$] with standardized beta coefficients for PTS symptoms ($\beta = .40$, $t = 11.25$, $p < .001$) and for centrality of the trauma event ($\beta = .07$, $t = 2.08$, $p = .04$) reaching significance. In step two, trauma severity was no longer a significant predictor of identity distress.

To examine whether identity distress and the centrality of the trauma event would predict identity development above and beyond the experience of trauma, two hierarchical regression analyses were calculated, the first with identity exploration as the dependent variable and the second with identity commitment as the dependent variable. When trauma exposure, trauma severity, PTS symptoms, the centrality of the trauma event, and identity distress were entered in the regression to predict identity exploration, the full model was significant, $R^2 = .16$ and adjusted R^2 = .15, F (6, 867) = 27.24, $p <$ .001, with trauma exposure (β = .22, t = 2.98, p = .003) and PTS symptoms (β = .13, t = 3.67, $p <$ .001) the significant predictors. The contribution of identity distress and the centrality of the trauma event above and beyond the experience of trauma variables was statistically significant at model two, accounting for an additional 5% of the variance [ΔF(2, 867) = 24.28, $p <$ .001]. Trauma exposure (β = .26, t = 3.52, $p <$ .001), centrality of the trauma events (β = .07, t = 1.95, $p <$ .05) and identity distress (β = .23, t = 6.54, $p <$ .001) were significant predictors. PTS symptoms did not remain a significant predictor.

When identity commitment was the dependent variable, the full model was again significant, R^2 and adjusted R^2 = .13, F (6, 867) = 21.90, $p <$ .001, with trauma exposure (β = -.19, t = -2.48, p = .01), trauma severity (β = .19, t = -2.44, p = .01), PTS symptoms (β = -.23, t = 6.10, $p <$ .001), and time since the trauma (β = -.09, t = -2.53, p = .01) having predictive power. The contribution of the centrality of the trauma event and identity distress above and beyond trauma exposure was significant for model two, ΔR^2 = .08, ΔF(2, 867) = 41.14, $p <$ .001, with trauma exposure (β = -.22, t = -3.00, p = .003), trauma severity (β = .24, t= 3.11, p = .002), PTS symptoms (β = -.09, t = -2.26, p = .02), time since the most recent trauma (β = -.09, t = -2.68, p = .007), and identity distress (β = -.32, t = -9.03, $p <$ .001) the significant predictors of identity commitment.

To examine whether identity development, identity distress, centrality of the trauma events, and the experience of trauma would predict positive change, identity exploration and identity commitment were added as step three to the above multiple regression, with resilience as the dependent variable. The overall model was significant, R^2 and adjusted R^2 = .25, F (8, 861) = 36.58, $p <$ .001. Significant standardized beta coefficients were found for trauma exposure (β = .15, t = 1.99, p = .05) and PTS symptoms (β = -.30, t = -7.91, $p <$ .001). The contribution of the centrality of the trauma event and identity distress above and beyond the trauma variables was significant [ΔR^2 = .05, ΔF(2, 863) = 24.34, $p <$ .001], with significant standardized beta coefficients for PTS symptoms (β = -.20, t = -4.84, $p <$ .001) and identity distress (β = -.25, t = 6.97, $p <$ .001). Identity exploration and identity commitment significantly predicted resilience above and beyond the trauma and other identity variables [ΔR^2 = .13, ΔF(2, 861) = 72.67, $p <$ .001], with trauma exposure (β = .17, t = 2.49, p = .01), PTS symptoms (β = -.17, t = -4.37, $p <$ .001), identity distress (β = -.17, t = -4.78, $p <$ .001), identity exploration (β = .18, t = 5.42, $p <$ .001), and identity commitment (β = .38, t = 11.76, $p <$ .001) the significant predictors.

A second hierarchical regression analysis was conducted to determine whether identity development, identity distress, centrality of the trauma events, and the experience of trauma would predict PTG. Trauma exposure, trauma severity, PTS symptoms, and time since the most recent trauma variables (step one), centrality of the trauma event and identity distress (step two), and identity exploration and identity commitment (step three) were entered in the regression, with PTG as the dependent variable. The full model was significant, R^2 = .22 and adjusted R^2 = .21, F (8, 859) = 29.76, $p <$ .001. For step one [F (4, 863) = 33.54, $p <$ .001], significant standardized beta coefficients were found for PTS symptoms (β = .32, t = 9.58, $p <$ .001) and time since the most recent trauma (β = -.07, t = -2.13, p = .03). For step two [ΔR^2 = .18, ΔF(2, 861) = 25.27, $p <$ .001], significant standardized beta coefficients were found for PTS symptoms (β = .20, t = 5.26, $p <$ .001) and the centrality of the trauma event (β = .23, t =

6.69, $p < .001$). The third model significantly predicted PTG above and beyond the trauma and other identity variables [$\Delta R^2 = .03$, $\Delta F(2, 859) = 18.93$, $p < .001$], with significant standardized beta coefficients for PTS symptoms ($\beta = .21$, $t = 5.47$, $p < .001$), centrality of the trauma event ($\beta = .21$, $t = 6.23$, $p < .001$), identity distress ($\beta = .08$, $t = 2.18$, $p = .03$), identity exploration ($\beta = .16$, $t = 4.74$, $p < .001$), and identity commitment ($\beta = .16$, $t = 4.03$, $p < .001$).

CONCLUSION

The primary goal of this study was to examine the psychosocial stage of identity development in the aftermath of trauma. In this study, the participants were more likely to be in the identity statuses comprised of identity exploration (diffused and moratorium) than those comprised of identity commitments (foreclosed and achieved). The transitional period of emerging adulthood provides an extension of the moratorium status in which young adults continue the exploration stage of developing their identity before making concrete commitments to their many potential choices (Arnett, 2004; Waterman, 1999). Keeping this in mind, it is not surprising that the achieved identity status group had the fewest number of participants. The findings of this study add to the increasing evidence (Arnett, 2000; Santrock, 1996) that identity development is an extensive process that continues beyond adolescence.

Examination of the identity status comparisons revealed that participants in the diffused and moratorium statuses experienced more identity distress as compared to participants in the foreclosed and achieved status groups. Moratorium is considered the status in which an identity crisis occurs due to active exploration of different options, desperate searching for choices, and having not yet chosen from alternatives (Erikson, 1968; Marcia, 1966). Studies have also found the diffused status to be related to psychological dysfunctions and more distress (e.g., Luyckx et al., 2006; Vleioras & Bosma, 2005; White, 2000; Wiley & Berman, 2012). In contrast, the foreclosed and achieved identity statuses, which are associated with greater identity commitments, have been linked to greater well-being (Vleioras & Bosma, 2005).

Compared to individuals who had already made identity commitments (foreclosed and achieved), participants who were exploring more areas of their identity without having made any concrete commitments (moratorium) reported not only experiencing more distress in their identity but also experiencing trauma as a central component of their personal identity. Those in identity statuses low in commitment (moratorium and diffused) also reported more PTS symptoms than did those in the foreclosed identity status. Furthermore, participants who met criteria for PTSD diagnosis reported less identity commitment and more identity exploration. Given that traumatic events have the potential of disrupting developmental trajectories, it is reasonable to conclude that trauma exposure may be related to changes in identity development and, in turn, to changes in how confident individuals feel about their identity choices.

This study also found that exposure to trauma and PTS symptoms predicted identity exploration; however, further examination of these relations revealed that identity distress and centrality of the trauma event were the only significant predictors of identity exploration above and beyond trauma exposure and PTS symptoms. When identity distress and the centrality of the trauma event to one's identity were added to the equation, PTS symptoms no longer accounted for a significant portion of the variance in identity exploration. Therefore, it may not be trauma exposure, in and of itself, that is associated with exploration of one's identity but rather how central the trauma event is to one's identity and how much distress the individual is experiencing in his or her identity. Emerging adults who experience trauma may perceive more negative personal changes and experience more difficulties in developing a healthy sense of identity. They may be vulnerable to developmental disruptions in which their ability to move through the task of identity construction is delayed, and they are less able to make identity commitments.

It is also possible that identity distress may be temporary and alleviated when identity commitments are made (Crocetti et al., 2008; Schwartz et al., 2009, 2010). This study found that fewer trauma exposures, fewer PTS symptoms, less trauma severity, and more time since the trauma were significant predictors of identity commitments. When the centrality of the trauma and identity distress were added as predictors of identity commitment, only identity distress predicted of identity commitments above and beyond the experience of trauma. Therefore, individuals who have had fewer exposures to trauma and are not experiencing distress in their identity are more likely to develop a stable, cohesive, sense of self by making commitments to identity-related issues. The predictions of identity development suggest that trauma may be related to difficulties resolving the psychosocial developmental task of emerging adulthood. However, identity-related distress and the centrality of the trauma to one's identity predicted identity exploration, while less identity distress predicted identity commitments above and beyond the experience of trauma. It is possible that issues related to identity after traumas may be more important to identity development than the experience of trauma alone.

Not surprisingly, participants who met criteria for PTSD diagnosis reported more identity distress. This finding supports the idea that the elaboration and consolidation of a sense of identity may be more difficult after having experienced psychological effects from traumas (Wiley et al., 2011). It is important for an individual to have an average, predictable environment in order to construct a stable identity (Erikson's, 1968), and this environment may be disrupted when a traumatic event occurs. Individuals with a PTSD diagnosis also reported the trauma as being more central to their identity. As noted by Hollon and Garber (1988), individuals who experience distress after traumatic exposure may have more difficulties accommodating the new trauma-acquired identity with their pre-trauma identity in comparison to individuals who do not experience distress after trauma.

Centrality of the trauma event also predicted identity distress above and beyond the experience of trauma. Trauma severity no longer predicted identity distress when the centrality of the trauma event was added to the regression, which suggests that the centrality of the trauma event to one's identity is more important to the experience of identity distress than is how severe the trauma experience is perceived to be. As trauma survivors reflect on their stressful experience, they may begin to recognize the discrepancy between their unattained goals or schemas, and the trauma may become a turning point in their identity (McAdams, 1993; McAdams et al., 2001), contributing to more identity distress.

While trauma is related to symptoms of PTS and identity distress, it is possible that the experience of distress can either serve as a growth point or instead contribute to further psychopathology (Dugan, 2007). It is not presumed that these issues are mutually exclusive, but rather, survivors of trauma might experience both a time of distress and a period of growth. Having made identity commitments, participants in the foreclosed status reported more resilience than did those in the identity status groups (diffused and moratorium) without identity commitments. Making identity commitments may serve a protective function for individuals who have experienced traumatic stressors (Madan-Swain et al., 2000).

Since the committed statuses of diffusion and achievement are congruent with less distress and more resilience, psychologists can help trauma survivors who are emerging adults by providing opportunities for proactive identity exploration and by facilitating commitment making (Berman et al., 2009; Kurtines et al., 2009; Montgomery & Côté, 2003; Montgomery, Hernandez, & Ferrer-Wreder, 2008). For PTG, participants in the achieved status reported more growth than did those in the diffused status; however, participants in the moratorium status reported more growth than did participants in the foreclosed status. Therefore, exploration within one's identity may be a necessary part of being able to experience growth after trauma. The findings that identity development predicted resilience and PTG above and beyond the experience of trauma, identity distress, and the centrality of the trauma event further support the importance of identity on the ability to adapt and grow after trauma.

As predicted, participants who met criteria for PTSD reported more PTG than did participants without a PTSD diagnosis. PTG may result from great distress while also being maintained through continued distress (Calhoun & Tedeschi 1998; Tedeschi & Kilmer, 2005). Trauma survivors may not only experience psychological distress by the threats or challenges to the core beliefs they hold, but they may also experience the potential consequence of PTG through their cognitive efforts to redefine those beliefs and rebuild their assumptive world (Calhoun & Tedeschi, 2006; Tedeschi & Calhoun, 2004).

Individuals with a PTSD diagnosis also reported less resilience. Experiencing a negative psychological state may motivate people to search for and create positive psychological states in order to gain relief from distress (Folkman, 1997). Resilient individuals are able to move beyond a traumatic stressor with little or no distress (Bonanno, 2004; Parker et al., 2004). These current results do not suggest that resilience is superior to PTG or vice versa, but rather that resilient individuals may not have the desire, need, or opportunity to experience PTG (Westphal & Bonanno, 2007). PTG may not lessen the trauma survivor's emotional distress but, instead, may trigger a reconsideration of their life, purpose, and meaning (Tedeschi & Calhoun, 2004).

While centrality of the trauma event did not predict resilience, it did predict PTG. This finding may be related to the higher persistence of cognitive processing that occurs with PTG in comparison to resilience (Tedeschi & Calhoun, 2004). The centrality of the event to one's identity may not only serve a role in the development and /or maintenance of PTS symptoms (Berntsen & Rubin, 2007), but it may also increase an ability to experience growth. As suggested by Conway (2005), incongruence between the traumatic stressors and the existing self-definition or identity can motivate change, which may be seen here through PTG.

While the current study has many strengths, there are also limitations that are important to discuss. The sample was non-representative of the general population as it consisted mostly of Caucasian, undergraduate students in the emerging adult age group of 18 to 24. The data were collected using an online survey and the sample self-selected into the study. Thus, random sampling was not conducted. While the use of a web-based data collection and self-report measure, rather than an interview or hand-written response, may provide participants with more confidentiality and result in more honest responses (e.g., Krantz & Dalal, 2000;

Reips, 2000; Schlenger & Silver, 2006), it also limits participation to only those individuals with a computer and/or internet access.

Since the cross-sectional data were only obtained at one point in time, lifetime estimates of trauma exposure were based on participant recall. The cross-sectional analyses also make it difficult to understand how patterns in identity formation emerge over time. The stability of the variables over time was not assessed, and the reciprocal nature of the variables in question is unknown. Furthermore, the retrospective accounts of traumatic experiences are subject to recall biases. Researchers cannot attribute causality when discussing historical events and pre-exposure factors such as underlying psychopathology (El-Sayed, & Galea, 2011).

Another limitation to this study is the use of a modified traumatic stressor checklist. Although the standard practice for measuring traumatic stressors is to provide a list of events, there are still limitations to the current methodology. The modified LSC-R extended the number of traumatic stressors assessed by combining those provided with the LEC (Gray et al., 2004) and reorganized items on the current LSC-R (Wolfe & Kimerling, 1997). These changes allowed for the assessment of both indirect and direct exposures; however, analyses to assess the reliability and validity of the modified LSC-R are needed.

In conclusion, the findings of this study can help inform public policy and prevention and intervention programs designed to improve the mental health for emerging adults who have experienced trauma. Current interventions for helping people to deal with the emotional and behavioral problems related to trauma often include promotion of a sense of self, identity, collective efficacy, a sense of safety and connectedness, instillation of hope, and self-soothing and relaxation skills (Hobfoll et al., 2007). Future intervention programs designed specifically to help trauma survivors who seek therapeutic services would benefit from the inclusion of skill development in exploring identity-related issues and facilitating identity commitments.

Psychologists can help emerging adult trauma survivors learn to reconcile "who they are now" and move towards PTG after the trauma by assimilating the new trauma-acquired identity with their old identity or a revision of existing schemas to accommodate the new information (Joseph & Linley, 2006). In therapy, the trauma survivor can be encouraged to explore, clarify, explain, and expand their understanding of their sense of identity. When these efforts are deliberately practiced and supported by therapists, trauma survivors may gain insights and begin to understand better the challenges and choices they have in their lives. When this is successful, the trauma survivor may experience a new sense of how to identify, address, and overcome distressful symptoms. Consequently, the better one knows one's self, the more influence one has toward finding meaning and purpose in life.

Since the trauma may have changed the reality of their life and their identity commitments, trauma survivors can work toward making meaning out of trauma through cognitive processing and restructuring their identity. Topics can include not only the symptoms associated with posttraumatic stress but also the potential for change. These changes may occur in the perceptions of intimacy, closeness, and meaning in relationships, or increased compassion for other trauma survivors. Trauma survivors might also discuss growth regarding the discovery of potential possibilities for their life now in comparison to before the trauma. They may experience more confidence, feel a greater sense of purpose, understand better the meaning of life, and discover a renewed sense of spirituality (Tedeschi & Calhoun, 1996, 2004). Assessment of these growth areas and how they may be met through therapy to help trauma survivors reach a positive change after trauma exposure is an important next step for future research studies.

REFERENCES

Aldwin, C. M., & Levenson, M. R. (2004). Commentaries on posttraumatic growth: A developmental perspective. *Psychological Inquiry, 15,* 19–22. doi:10.1207/s15327965 pli1501_02.

Arnett, J. J. (2000). Emerging adulthood: A theory of development from the late teens through the twenties. *American Psychologist, 55,* 469-480. doi: 10.1037/0003-066X. 55.5.469.

Arnett, J. J. (2004). *Emerging adulthood: The winding road from the late teens through the twenties.* New York: Oxford University Press.

Balistreri, E., Busch-Rossnagel, N. A., & Geisinger, K. F. (1995). Development and preliminary validation of the Ego Identity Process Questionnaire. *Journal of Adolescence, 18,* 179-192. doi: 10.1006/jado.1995.1012.

Berger, K. S. (2008). *The developing person through the life span* (7th ed.). New York: Worth Publishers.

Berman, S. L., Kennerly, R. J., & Kennerly, M. A. (2009). Promoting adult identity development: A feasibility study of a university-based identity intervention program. *Identity: An International Journal of Theory and Research, 8,* 139-150. doi: 10.1080/15283480801940024.

Berman, S. L., Montgomery, M. J., & Kurtines, W. M. (2004).The development and validation of a measure of identity distress. *Identity: An International Journal of Theory and Research, 4,* 1-8. doi: 10.1207/S1532706XID0401_1.

Berman, S. L., Weems, C. F., & Petkus, V. F. (2009). The prevalence and incremental validity of identity problem symptoms in a high school sample. *Child Psychiatry and Human Development, 40,* 183-195. doi: 10.1007/s10578-008-0117-6.

Berntsen, D., & Rubin, D. C. (2006). The centrality of event scale: A measure of integrating a trauma into one's identity and its relation to post-traumatic stress disorder symptoms. *Behaviour Research and Therapy, 44,* 219-231. doi: 10.1016/j.brat.2005.01.009.

Berntsen, D., & Rubin, D. C. (2007). When a trauma becomes a key to identity: Enhanced integration of trauma memories predicts posttraumatic stress disorder symptoms. *Applied Cognitive Psychology, 21,* 417-431.doi: 10.1002/acp.1290.

Bonanno, G. A. (2004). Loss, trauma, and human resilience: Have we underestimated the human capacity to thrive after extremely aversive events? *American Psychologist, 59,* 20 –28.doi:10.1037/0003-066X.59.1.20.

Bonanno, G. A. (2005). Resilience in the face of potential trauma. *Current Directions in Psychological Science, 14,* 135-138. doi: 10.1111/j.0963-7214.2005.00347.x.

Bonanno, G. A., Brewin, C. R., Kaniasty, K., & La Greca, A. M. (2010).Weighing the costs of disaster: Consequences, risks, and resilience in individuals, families, and communities. *Psychological Science in the Public Interest, 11*(1), 1-49. doi: 10.1177/ 1529100610387086.

Brewin, C. R., Garnett, R., & Andrews, B. (2011). Trauma, identity and mental health in UK military veterans. *Psychological Medicine, 41,* 1733-1740. doi: 10.1017/ S003329171000231X.

Briere, J., Kaltman, S., & Green, B. L. (2008). Accumulated childhood trauma and symptom complexity. *Journal of Traumatic Stress, 21,* 223–226. doi: 10.1002/jts.20317.

Brown, P. J., Stout, R. L., & Mueller, T. (1999). Substance use disorder and posttraumatic stress disorder comorbidity: Addiction and psychiatric treatment rates. *Psychology of Addictive Behaviors, 13*, 115–122. doi: 10.1037/0893-164X.13.2.115.

Calhoun, L. G., Cann, A., Tedeschi, R. G., & McMillan, J. (2000). A correlational test of the relationship between posttraumatic growth, religion, and cognitive processing. *Journal of Traumatic Stress, 13*, 521-527. doi: 10.1023/A:1007745627077.

Calhoun, L. G., & Tedeschi, R. G. (1998). Posttraumatic growth: Future directions. In R. G. Tedeschi, C. L. Park, & L. G. Calhoun (Eds.), *Posttraumatic growth: Positive change in the aftermath of crisis.* (pp. 215-238). Mahwah, NJ: Lawrence Erlbaum Associates, Inc.

Calhoun, L. G., & Tedeshi, R. G. (2006). (Eds).*Handbook of posttraumatic growth: Research & practice.* Mahwah, NJ: Lawrence Erlbaum Associates, Inc.

Cann, A., Calhoun, L. G., Tedeschi, R. G., Taku, K., Vishnevsky, T., Triplett, K. N., &Danhauer, S. C. (2010). A short form of the Posttraumatic Growth Inventory. *Anxiety, Stress, & Coping: An International Journal, 23*, 127-137. doi: 10.1080/10615800903094273.

Connor, K. M. & Davidson, J. R. T. (2003). Development of a new resilience scale: The Connor-Davidson Resilience Scale (CD-RISC). *Depression and Anxiety, 18*, 76-82. doi: 10.1002/da.10113.

Conway, M. A. (2005). Memory and the self. *Journal of Memory and Language, 53*, 594–628. doi: 10.1016/j.jml.2005.08.005.

Cook, A., Spinazzola, J., Ford, J., Lanktree, C., Blaustein, M., Cloitre, M.,… DeRosa, R., (2005). Complex trauma in children and adolescents. *Psychiatric Annals, 35*(5)*, 390-398.*

Côté, J. E. (2006). Emerging adulthood as an institutional moratorium: Risks and benefits to identity formation. In J. J. Arnett & J. L. Tanner (Eds.), *Emerging adults in America: Coming of age in the 21st century* (pp. 85-116). Washington, DC: American Psychological Association. doi: 10.1037/11381-004.

Crocetti, E., Rubini, M., & Meeus, W. (2008). Capturing the dynamics of identity formation in various ethnic groups: Development and validation of a three-dimensional model. *Journal of Adolescence, 31*, 207-222. doi: 10.1016/j.adolescence.2007.09.002.

D'Andrea, W., Sharma, R., Zelechoski A. D., & Spinazzola, J. (2011). Physical Health Problems After Single Trauma Exposure : When Stress Takes Root in the Body, *Journal of the American Psychiatric Nurses Association,* 17: 378-392. doi: 10.1177/1078390311425187.

Deeny, P., & McFetridge, B. (2005). The impact of disaster on culture, self, and identity: Increased awareness by health care professionals is needed. *Nursing Clinics of North America, 40*, 431-440.doi: 10.1016/j.cnur.2005.04.012.

Dugan, B. (2007). Loss of identity in disaster: How do you say goodbye to home. *Perspectives in Psychiatric Care, 43*, 41-46. doi: 10.1111/j.1744-6163.2007.00105.x.

Edwards, V. J., Holden, G. W., Felitti, V. J., & Anda, R. F. (2003). Relationship between multiple forms of childhood maltreatment and adult mental health in community respondents: Results from the Adverse Childhood Experiences study. *The American Journal of Psychiatry, 160*, 1453-1460. doi: 10.1176/appi.ajp.160.8.1453.

Ehlers, A., Clark, D. M., Dunmore, E., Jaycox, L., Meadows, E., & Foa, E. B. (1998). Predicting response to exposure treatment in PTSD: The role of mental defeat and alienation. *Journal of Traumatic Stress, 11*, 457-471. doi: 10.1023/A:1024448511504.

El-Sayed, A. M. & Galea, S. (2011). Challenges and future horizons in epidemiological research into PTSD. In: D. Stein, M. Friedman, & C. Blanco (Eds). *Post-traumatic Stress Disorder, First Edition.* (pp. 75-84).Chichester, West Sussex, UK: John Wiley & Sons, Ltd. doi: 10.1002/9781119998471.

Erikson, E. H. (1963). *Youth: Change and challenge.* New York, NY: Basic Books.

Erikson, E. H. (1968). *Identity, youth, and crisis.* New York, NY: Norton.

Felitti, V. J., & Anda, R. F. (2008). The relationship of adverse childhood experiences to adult health, well-being, social function, and healthcare. In L. Vermetten. *The Hidden Epidemic: The Impact of Early Life Trauma on Health and Disease.* Cambridge University Press.

Fonagy, P., Steele, M., Steele, H., Higgitt, A., & Target, M. (1994). The Emanuel Miller Memorial Lecture 1992: The theory and practice of resilience. *Journal of Child Psychology and Psychiatry, 35,* 231–257. doi: 10.1111/j.1469-7610.1994.tb01160.x.

Gray, M. J., Litz, B. T., Hsu, J. L., & Lombardo, T. W. (2004). Psychometric properties of the Life Events Checklist. *Assessment, 11,* 330-341. doi: 10.1177/1073191104269954.

Hernandez, L., Montgomery, M. J., & Kurtines, W. K. (2006).Identity distress and adjustment problems in at-risk adolescents. *Identity: An International Journal of Theory and Research, 6,* 27-33. doi: 10.1207/s1532706xid0601_3.

Hobfoll, S. E., Watson, P., Bell, C. C., Bryant, R. A., Brymer, M. J., Friedman, M. J.,...Ursano, R. J. (2007b). Five essential elements of immediate and mid-term trauma intervention: Empirical evidence. *Psychiatry: Interpersonal, and Biological Processes, 70,* 283-315. doi: 10.1521/psyc.2007.70.4.283.

Hollon, S. D., & Garber, J. (1988). *Cognitive therapy.* In L. Y. Abramson (Ed.), Social cognition and clinical psychology: A synthesis (pp. 204–253). New York: Guilford Press.

Joseph, S., & Linley, P. A. (2006). Growth following adversity: Theoretical perspectives and implications for clinical practice. *Clinical Psychology Review, 26,* 1041–1053. doi: 10.1016/j.cpr.2005.12.006.

Kimerling, R., Calhoun, K. S., Forehand, R., Armistead, L., Morse, E., Morse, P.,... Clark, L. (1999). Traumatic stress in HIV-infected women. *AIDS Education and Prevention, 11*(4), 321–330.

Kobasa, S. C. (1979). Stressful life events, personality and health: An inquiry into hardiness. *Journal of Personality and Social Psychology, 37,* 1-11. doi: 10.1037/0022-3514.37.1.1.

Krantz, J. H., & Dalal, R. (2000).Validity of web-based psychological research. In: Birnbaum, M. H., ed. *Psychological Experiments on the Internet.* San Diego, CA: Academic Press, 35-60.

Kroger, R. O. (2006). Review of the development of a postmodern self: A computer-assisted comparative analysis of personal documents. *Psyc. CRITIQUES, 34,* 1-84. doi: 10.1037/027599.

Kroger, J. (2007). *Identity development: Adolescence through adulthood* (2ⁿᵈed.). Thousand Oaks, CA: Sage.

Kroger, J., & Haslett, S. J. (1988). Separation–individuation and ego identity status in late adolescents: A two-year longitudinal study. *Journal of Youth and Adolescence, 17,* 59–81. doi: 10.1007/BF01538724.

Kroger, J., Martinussen, M., & Marcia, J. E. (2010). Identity status change during adolescence and young adulthood: A meta-analysis. *Journal of Adolescence, 33,* 683-698. doi: 10.1016/j.adolescence.2009.11.002.

Kurtines, W. M., Montgomery, M. J., Eichas, K., Ritchie, R., Garcia, A., Albrecht, R.,... Lorente, C. C. (2009). Promoting positive identity development in troubled youth: A developmental intervention science outreach research approach. *Identity: An International Journal of Theory and Research, 8*, 125-138. doi: 10.1080/ 15283480801938515.

Lee, M. R. & MacLean, M. G. (2006, March). *Evaluation of alternative methods of identity status classification using the ego identity process questionnaire.* Poster presented at the meeting of the Society for Research on Adolescence, San Francisco, CA.

Luyckx, K., Goossens, L., Soenens, B., & Beyers, W. (2006). Unpacking commitment and exploration: Preliminary validation of an integrative model of late adolescent identity formation. *Journal of Adolescence, 29*, 361-378. doi: 10.1016/j.adolescence.2005.03.008.

Lyons, J. A. (1991). Strategies for assessing the potential for positive adjustment following trauma. *Journal of Traumatic Stress, 4*, 93-111. doi: 10.1002/jts.2490040108.

Madan-Swain, A., Brown, R. T., Foster, M. A., Vega, R., Byars, K., Rodenberger, W.,... Lambert, R. (2000). Identity in adolescent survivors of childhood cancer. *Journal of Pediatric Psychology, 25*, 105-115. doi: 10.1093/jpepsy/25.2.105.

Mancini, A. D., & Bonanno, G. A. (2006). Resilience in the face of potential trauma: Clinical practices and illustrations. *Journal of Clinical Psychology: In Session, 62*, 971-985. doi: 10.1002/jclp.20283.

Marcia, J. E. (1966). Development and validation of ego-identity status. *Journal of Personality & Social Psychology, 3,* 551-558. doi: 10.1037/h0023281.

Marcia, J. E. (1976). Identity six years after: a follow-up study. *Journal of Youth and Adolescence, 5*, 145–160.

Marcia, J. E. (1980). Identity in adolescence. In J. Adelson (Ed.), *Handbook of adolescent psychology* (pp. 159-187). New York, NY: Wiley.

McAdams, D. P., Reynolds, J., Lewis, M., Patten, A. H., & Bowman, P. J. (2001). When bad things turn good and good things turn bad: Sequences of redemption and contamination in life narrative and their relation to psychosocial adaptation in midlife adults and in students. *Personality and Social Psychology Bulletin, 27*, 474-485. doi: 10.1177/ 0146167201274008.

McNally, R. J., Lasko, N. B., Macklin, M. L., & Pitman, R. K. (1995). Autobiographical memory disturbance in combat-related posttraumatic stress disorder. *BehaviourResearch and Therapy, 33*, 619–630. doi: 10.1016/0005-7967(95)00007-K.

Montgomery, M. J., & Côté, J. (2003).College as a transition to adulthood. In G. R. Adams & M. D. Berzonsky (Eds.), *Blackwell handbook of adolescence* (pp. 149–172). Malden, MA: Blackwell.

Montgomery, M. J., Hernandez, L., & Ferrer-Wreder, L. (2008). Identity development and intervention studies: The right time for a marriage? *Identity: An International Journal of Therapy and Research, 8*, 173-182. doi: 10.1080/15283480801940115.

Parker, K. J., Buckmaster, C. L., Schatzberg, A. F., & Lyons, D. M. (2004). Prospective investigation of stress inoculation in young monkeys. *Archives of General Psychiatry, 61,* 933–941. doi:10.1001/archpsyc.61.9.933.

Pynoos, R. S., & Eth, S. (1985). Developmental perspective on psychic trauma in childhood. In C.R. Figley (Ed.) *Trauma and its Wake* (pp. 640-666). New York: Brunner/Mazel.

Reips, U. D. (2000). The web experiment method: Advantages, disadvantages, and solutions. In: M. H. Binbaum (Ed.), *Psychological Experiments on the Internet* (pp. 89-117). San Diego, CA: Academic Press.

Rutter, M. (1985). Resilience in the face of adversity: Protective factors and resistance to psychiatric disorder. *British Journal of Psychiatry, 147*, 598-611. doi: 10.1192/bjp.147.6.598.

Rutter, M. (1993). Resilience: Some conceptual considerations. *Journal of Adolescent Health, 14*, 626-631. doi: 10.1016/1054-139X(93)90196-V.

Santrock, J. W. (1996). *Adolescence: An Introduction* (6[th]ed.). Madison, WI: Brown & Benchmark Publishers.

Schwartz, S. J., Forthun, L. F., Ravert, R. D., Zamboanga, B. L., Rodriguez, L., Uman͂a-Taylor, A. J.,…Hudson, M. (2010). The protective role of identity consolidation against health-compromising behaviors in college-attending emerging adults. *American Journal of Health Behavior, 34*, 214–224. doi: 10.5993/AJHB.34.2.9.

Schwartz, S. J., Zamboanga, B. L., Weisskirch, R. S., & Rodriguez, L. (2009). The relationships of personal and ethnic identity exploration to indices of adaptive and maladaptive psychosocial functioning. *International Journal of Behavioral Development, 33*, 131–144. doi: 10.1177/0165025408098018.

Spiers, C., (1997). Counselling and crisis intervention training for humanitarian aid workers. *International Journal of Stress Management, 4*, 309-313. doi: 10.1023/B:IJSM.0000009335.47755.da.

Sutherland, K., & Bryant, R. A. (2005). Self-defining memories in post-traumatic stress disorder. *British Journal of Clinical Psychology, 44*, 591–598. doi: 10.1348/014466505X64081.

Tedeschi, R. G., & Calhoun, L. G. (2004). Posttraumatic growth: Conceptual foundations and empirical evidence. *Psychological Inquiry, 15,* 1–18. doi:10.1207/s15327965pli1501_01

Tedeschi, R. G., & Calhoun, L. G. (1996). The Posttraumatic Growth Inventory: Measuring the positive legacy of trauma. *Journal of Traumatic Stress, 9,* 455-471. doi: 10.1002/jts.2490090305.

Tedeschi, R. G., & Kilmer, R. P. (2005). Assessing strengths, resilience, and growth to guide clinical interventions. *Professional Psychology: Research and Practice, 36*, 230-237. doi: 10.1037/0735-7028.36.3.230.

Vleioras, G., & Bosma, H. A. (2005). Are identity styles important for psychological well-being?. *Journal of Adolescence, 28*, 397-409. doi: 10.1016/j.adolescence.2004.09.001.

Waterman, A. S. (1988). Identity status theory and Erikson's theory: Communalities and differences. *Developmental Review, 8,* 185–208. doi: 10.1016/0273-2297(88)90003-2.

Waterman, A. S. (1993). Developmental perspectives on identity formation: From adolescence to adulthood. In J. E. Marcia, A. S. Waterman, D. R. Matteson, S. L. Archer, & J. L. Orlofsky (Eds.), *Ego identity: A handbook for psychosocial research* (pp. 22-41). New York: Springer-Verlag.

Waterman, A. S. (1999). Issues of identity formation revisited: United States and the Netherlands. *Developmental Review, 19*, 462-479. doi: 10.1006/drev.1999.0488.

Weathers, F. W., Litz, B. T., Huska, J. A., & Keane, T. M. (1994). *PCL-C for DSM-IV.* Boston: National Center for PTSD: Behavioral Science Division.

Weaver, T. L., Turner, P. K., Schwarze, N. N., Thayer, C. A., & Carter-Sand, S. (2007). An exploratory examination of the meanings of residual injuries from intimate partner violence. *Women & Health, 45*, 85-102. doi: 10.1300/J013v45n03_06.

Webb, H., & Jobson, L. (2011). Relationships between self-consistency, trauma-centered identity, and post-traumatic adjustment. *Clinical Psychologist, 15*, 103-111. doi: 10.1111/j.1742-9552.2011.00028.x.

Westphal, M., & Bonanno, G. A. (2007). Posttraumatic growth and resilience to trauma: Different sides of the same coin or different coins? *Applied Psychology: An International Review, 56*, 417-427.doi: 10.1111/j.1464-0597.2007.00298.x.

White, J. M. (2000). Alcoholism and identity development: a theoretical integration of the least mature status with the typologies of alcoholism. *Alcoholism Treatment Quarterly, 18*, 43-59.doi: 10.1300/J020v18n01_03.

Wiley, R. E., & Berman, S. L., (2013). The relationships among caregiver and adolescent identity status, identity distress and psychological adjustment, *Journal of Adolescence*, doi:10.1016/j.adolescence.2012.04.001.

Wiley, R. E., Berman, S. L., Marsee, M. A., Taylor, L. K., Cannon, M. F., & Weems, C. F. (2011). Age differences and similarities in identity distress following the Katrina disaster: Theoretical and applied implications of Erickson's theory, *Journal of Adult Development, 18*, 184-191. doi: 10.1007/s10804-011-9130-2.

Wolfe, J., & Kimerling, R. (1997). Gender issues in the assessment of posttraumatic stress disorder. In J. P. Wilson & T. M. Keane (Eds.), *Assessing psychological trauma and PTSD* (pp. 192-238). New York: Guilford.

In: Gender Identity
Editor: Beverly L. Miller

ISBN: 978-1-63321-488-0
© 2014 Nova Science Publishers, Inc.

Chapter 3

THE INTERSECTION OF GENDER AND SEXUAL IDENTITY DEVELOPMENT IN A SAMPLE OF TRANSGENDER INDIVIDUALS

Craig T. Nagoshi[1],*, Ph.D., Julie L. Nagoshi[2], Ph.D., Heather L. Peterson[2], MSW and Heather K. Terrell[3], Ph.D.
[1]Department of Psychology and School of Social Work, University of Texas at Arlington, US
[2]School of Social Work, University of Texas at Arlington, US
[3]Department of Psychology, University of North Dakota, US

ABSTRACT

Studies of gender identity development in transgender individuals suggest that for these individuals an awareness of their non-heteronormative gender identity typically occurs in early childhood, with awareness and self-definitions of sexual identity typically occurring later on in puberty and young adulthood. In this chapter we describe the findings from eleven self-identified transgender individuals (4 MTF, 6 FTM, 1 intersex) who were interviewed about the age at which they became aware of their non-heteronormative gender identity and about whether they recalled specific life events associated with their awareness of their gender identity. Consistent with the previous literature, seven of the participants gave specific early childhood ages at which they became aware of their non-heteronormative gender identity. Most of these transgender individuals did not cite any specific event that made them aware of their non-heteronormative gender identity, instead recalling that they just knew they were different. The four other transgender participants (all FTMs), however, reported that their non-heteronormative gender identity awareness did not become solidified until their teen years and beyond and that this gender identity awareness occurred in the context of their sexual identity. These findings are discussed in terms of the intersectionality of gender and sexual identity in the development of non-heteronormative gender/sexual identities.

* Address all correspondence to: Julie L. Nagoshi, Ph.D., School of Social Work, University of Texas at Arlington, 211 South Cooper St., Box 19129, Arlington, TX 76019. Email: julienagoshi@uta.edu.

Four recent, large-sample, cross-sectional studies (Factor & Rothblum, 2008; Kuper, Nussbaum, & Mustanski, 2012; Nuttbrock et al., 2009; Rankin & Beemyn, 2012) have assessed aspects of gender and sexual identity in transgender/transsexual individuals. Factor and Rothblum's (2008) interview study of 50 male-to-female (MTF), 52 female-to-male (FTM), and 64 genderqueers (neither completely female nor completely male) individuals focused on transgender identity development, levels of disclosure of transgender status, and relationship to community. While MTFs first identified as other than their assigned sex earlier than FTMs, they did not present themselves to others in a gender-congruent way until much later than FTMs. MTFs were less likely to disclose their gender identity to their parents than were FTMs. Disclosure of assigned birth sex was more common among younger participants. Genderqueers felt more connected to the lesbian, gay, and bisexual community than did MTFs or FTMs.

Nuttbrock et al.'s (2009) interview study of 571 MTF transgender individuals from New York City focused on disclosures of transgender identity to others and responses from others allowing for desired gender role behavior as important aspects of the development of transgender identity. Gender identity affirmation was found to be more likely with friends than with parents, with younger participants more likely to report gender identity disclosure and desired gender role casting than older participants. Interestingly, the sexual orientation of these MTF participants was predictive of likelihood of transgender identity disclosure, with disclosure more likely for participants exclusively attracted to biological males.

Kuper et al.'s (2012) online survey of 292 individuals who identified with a gender identity different than or in addition to the gender identity associated with their birth found that these individuals had a range of and often more than one self-identified gender identity, with gender queer and transgender being the most commonly endorsed. These individuals also had a range of and often more than one self-identified sexual orientation, with pansexual and queer being the most commonly endorsed. Those in the oldest age group were less likely to identify as gender queer. Birth sex females (FTM) were more likely than birth sex males (MTF) to retain their birth sex as their gender identity and to self-identify as genderqueer rather than transsexual.

Rankin and Beemyn's (2012) findings, based on 3,500 surveys and 400 interviews with trans-masculine, trans-feminine, and gender-nonconforming people in the United States, focused on transgender identity development in terms of awareness of gender identity non-conformity, deliberately presenting or repressing one's non-conforming gender identity, self-identification in terms of a non-heteronormative gender and/or sexual identity, learning about and meeting other similarly transgender individuals, overcoming internalized genderism, physical transitioning, and disclosure of transgender identity to others. While most participants reported being aware of their gender non-conformity at an early age (mean = 5.4 years), many did not report such an awareness until their teenage years, and age variations were also found for other aspects of trangender identity development. While FTM individuals often felt that they could openly display gender non-conforming dress and behaviors and were often allowed to be tomboys without concerns being raised initially, all of the MTF individuals did so secretly, fearing punishment from their families for gender-inappropriate behavior. For many FTM individuals, self-identification as being lesbian was a step toward transgender identity, while self-identification as a gay male was not typical for MTF transgender identity development.

Several themes emerge from these studies of transgender identity development. Transgender individuals vary in the ages at which important identity events occur, and these age differences may reflect different developmental courses or historical cohort effects. The transgender identity development experiences of FTM individuals differ from those of MTF individuals due to the greater pressure on born-male individuals to conform to masculine gender role norms. Sexual orientation/identity development may be an integral part of transgender identity development.

While it would seem inevitable that the transgender experience includes the intersectionality of gender and sexual identity, such that changes in one identity affect changes in the other (Diamond & Butterworth, 2008; Nagoshi & Brzuzy, 2010; Nagoshi, Nagoshi, & Brzuzy, 2014; Shields, 2008), interview studies of transgender individuals often find differences in how these individuals perceive the relationships between gender and sexual identity. Rubin's (2003) FTM transsexual participants rejected any connection between their gender identity and their sexual orientation, but nevertheless, Rubin found that becoming a lesbian was part of the developmental process for over half of the transsexuals interviewed. Most of these individuals nevertheless did not feel that being a lesbian was consistent with their gender identity, i.e., that having a lesbian sexual orientation was not the same as being male. When the female would transition to becoming a male, s/he would then see his or her orientation as being different. Prior to the surgery, s/he would be viewed by society as being a lesbian, yet s/he would identify him/herself as being heterosexual. After the surgery, he would see himself as being male and would continue to see himself as being heterosexual.

On the other hand, Dozier's (2005) interviews with trans-identified individuals found that sexual orientation was not only based on the object of attraction, but also on the gendered meanings created in sexual and romantic interactions. In contrast to traditional theories that assume that gender is the behavioral, socially constructed correlate of one's physical sex (i.e., that gender is "written on the body"), Dozier (2005) argued for the opposite relationship, in which sexuality is one important basis for defining gender identity. Devor's (1997) findings were also interpreted in terms of FTM transsexuals' sexual attractions changing in accordance with their changes in gender identity. Many of the interviewees reported changing their sexual orientation after transitioning to have a more physically male identity, in terms of genitalia and/or other readily visible physical characteristics, and that changing their sexual orientation, in turn, reinforced their transformed gender identity. Williams et al. (2013) examined the experiences of 25 persons who were assigned female status at birth, but did not wish to live as women and instead took on a masculine or queer gender identity. These researchers explored how experiencing gender identity was tied to sexuality and the ways in which these two embodiments were tightly, moderately, or loosely coupled.

Our own interview study of transgender individuals (Nagoshi, Brzuzy, & Terrell, 2012; Nagoshi et al., 2014) found that some participants described their sexual orientation as changing with changes in their manifested gender identity, which in turn reinforced those changes in gender identity. Consistent with this, many of the interviewees reported changing their sexual orientation after transitioning to a more physically male identity, in terms of genitalia and/or other readily visible physical characteristics, and that changing their sexual orientation, in turn, reinforced their transformed gender identity. On the other hand, half of our transgender participants categorically rejected any relationship between gender identity and sexual orientation. Bockting, Benner, and Coleman's (2009) questionnaire study of FTM transsexual individuals also found differences in these individuals' perceptions of the relationships between gender identity and sexual orientation, with some participants reporting that sexual attractions and experiences with men affirmed their gender identity, while for others, self-acceptance of a transgender identity facilitated actualization of their attractions toward men.

Based on the responses of the transgender participants in our interview study of perceptions of gender roles, gender identity, and sexual orientation (Nagoshi et al., 2012, 2014), the research presented here focuses on whether there are systematic differences in the age (early childhood vs. adolescence and later) at which our participants reported being first aware of their gender identity. It was expected that these age differences would related to different experiences of transgender identity formation, particularly with regard to sexual orientation, which should be more salient for transgender individuals experiencing the salience of their gender identity in adolescence. Analyses also focused on how these developmental processes may differ for FTM vs. MTF transgender individuals.

METHOD

Participants

As described previously (Nagoshi et al., 2012, 2014), half of the transgender participants were recruited through community contacts, who asked prospective participants if they were willing to be contacted by the principal investigator for a possible interview about issues of gender identity. Other participants were recruited through a posting on the Ubiquity bulletin board for GLBTQ students and staff at Arizona State University. This posting for LGBTQ participants described the interview as an exploration of the nature of gender identity and left a phone number and email address of the second author (JLN). The second author then contacted the prospective participant via phone, briefly explained the nature of the interview, and set up a time for a meeting at the participant's place of residence, on campus, or at a public location.

Table 1. Participant demographics: Transgender individuals

Initials	Self-identification	Age range	Race-ethnicity	Occupation	Age of gender awareness
TAF	FTM transgender	25-35	White	College staff/employee	4th grade
TBL	MTF transsexual	35-45	White	College staff/employee	4, 5, or 6
TCP	Intersex	25-35	White	College staff/employee	3 or 4
TDN	MTF transsexual	35-45	White	College student	7
TEV	FTM transgender	25-35	White	College staff/employee	1st or 2nd grade
TFD	MTF transgender	18-25	White	College student	4 or 5
TGR	FTM transgender	18-25	Hispanic	College staff/employee	15 queer, 19 trans
THW	FTM transgender	18-25	White	College staff/employee	high school
TJT	FTM transsexual	45-55	White	College staff/employee	as a child
TKS	FTM transsexual	35-45	White	College staff/employee	20 to 40
TLK	MTF transgender	18-25	White	College student	between 6 and 8

All interviews were conducted by the second author from October 2005 through December of 2005. The transgender participant sample (Table 1) included 11 self-identified transgender individuals, 6 stating on the demographic forms that they were "born female," 4 "born male," and 1 "born intersex." All of the participants stated that they were transgender but did not necessarily distinguish themselves as transsexual, except for one individual. Participants ranged in age from 19 to 43 years. Among the participants, 5 indicated having had postgraduate education or having earned a postgraduate degree, while the remaining participant indicated having had some college education. All transgender participants were White, except for one Hispanic.

Procedures

At the beginning of the interview session, the nature of the interview questions was briefly described to the participant, who then read and signed an informed consent form. This consent form assured participants that no data obtained for the research would have any identifying information attached and that participants were free to withdraw from participation in the research at any time without penalty. Interviews were recorded on a microcassette audio recorder and took between 40 and 60 minutes to complete. The interview questions, discussed below, were set up to include prompts in places to encourage participants to stay on the relevant topic, and the interviewer was free to deviate from the scripted questions to pose follow-up questions to participant responses. The Institutional Review Board-approved procedures included protections of participant data confidentiality and contingencies for dealing with participant distress.

Measures

The overall intent of the project was to capture the unique perspective on the bases of gender identity of a transgender individual and to then try to link the interviews to transgender theory (Nagoshi et al., 2012, 2014). The resulting interview questions focused on issues of maleness-femaleness vs. masculinity-femininity as they related to biological sex, physical appearance and function, social norms and privileges, and sexual orientation, as well as experiences of discrimination. The present report focuses on the responses toward the end of the interview to the following questions: At what age did your gender identity become salient and/or apparent? Are there any particular events that made that time period, transition, salient to you?

Analyses

The identification of themes was guided by the research literature and was driven by a thematic analysis (Braun & Clarke, 2006) in which the researchers' interest in and knowledge of the research literature on the development of gender and sexual identities in LGBT individuals informed the analyses. The first thematic analyses focused on whether there were distinct differences in the age at which transgender participants became aware of their gender identity. The second thematic analysis focused on whether this awareness of gender identity was associated with a specific event. The final analyses focused on the relationships between awareness of gender vs. sexual identity in participants' narratives of the development of their gender identities.

RESULTS

Table 1 presents the ages that participants reported for when they first became aware of their gender identity. For 7 of these transgender participants (TAF, TBL, TCP, TDN, TEV, TFD, TLK), there was a clear age or grade in early childhood when their gender identity became salient, whereas 3 of the remaining participants (TGR, THW, TKS) gave ages that were in adolescence or later and/or gave more general older age ranges ("high school"). The remaining participant (TJT), like TGR, gave two ages when awareness changed ("as a child" and "as a teenager"). As will be discussed below, TJT's experiences were similar to those of TGR in first understanding sexual identity as related to gender identity then transgender identity.

For all of the 7 transgender participants who remembered being aware of their gender identity during early childhood, the awareness was about their in some way not conforming to some aspect of the gender role associated with the sex they were born as. For FTM TAF, it was about "always wanting to wear dress pants and more masculine shirts, and I never wanted to wear jeans, and I wanted to look very, very good. Which I look at now, and, like, oh my God, I was such a gay guy." For MTFs TBL and TFD, it was about knowing at an early age that there was something "wrong" about their preferences for female playmates. As TBL put it, "I was very effeminate. I didn't do very well with the boys, I played better with the girls." MTF TLK talked about how "whenever I would dream I appeared I was never male, I was always a female, and that's where I mostly noticed it, 'cause you know it was kinda odd."

TCP, TDN, and TEV reported specific incidents in early childhood that solidified their awareness of their gender identity, but in all cases, the awareness of gender nonconformity was already there. For intersex TCP, "my grandmother or my aunt, said, 'No, you're a little boy,' because we had been fighting about clothes or something. And I remember being in a bathroom, and standing there, and I'm just mad as all get-out that this person is telling me I'm a boy, and I'm like, 'No, I'm not, I'm a girl.' And I got upset, and I walked out of the room, and went down the hallway, and that's all I remember. But that really solidified for me who I was." For MTF TDN it was about:

> Walking down Bourbon Street with my stepfather and my mother, we passed a bar called Papa John's, which is a drag bar, a trannie bar, a strip club, in New Orleans. And my stepfather leans over—it's Mardi Gras—like it's a dirty little secret, he leans down and says, "See those women over there?" And I said, "Yeah." A little seven year-old "yeah." He says, "They're not really women, those are guys.' "What?" And he went into some elaborate detail to explain it, as though it were a dirty little thing. And I looked over, it was through a child's eyes. I didn't see the fact that they were heroin addicts and, you know, whatever. They were having a great time, and it just looked absolutely normal to me. It was, like, "Oh, okay, yeah, it makes sense to me. I don't know what your fucking problem is, Dad, but why are you whispering?" So that kind of put it all together.

FTM TEV remembered, "I knocked the TV over on purpose, took a screwdriver, took the entire TV apart, inventoried everything it takes to make a TV, put the entire TV back together, and made it work. I was in, like, second grade maybe. First grade. And, the response of my family was, 'Oh, I didn't know you had two sons.'"

For the 4 transgender participants who reported their awareness of their gender identity occurring during adolescence and later, there was more of an interaction between sexual orientation and gender. For FTMs TGR, THW, and TJT, there were similar narratives of having an awareness in childhood of being gender non-conforming, but transgender awareness only came after an identification as being non-heteronormative in sexual orientation/identity. TGR described:

> When I was younger, I always had like this feeling that I was very masculine, I was a very masculine child, and I was like "oh, ok, well, that's why I kind of strutted around with my dad" when I was five years old in front of the girl next door, and like you know things that are just "like wow this is really weird." Because, I mean, for people, for the queer community and for transgender community, which aren't always necessarily the same, if you identify yourself as queer first, you have to come out once, and then if you identify yourself as trans, you have to come out another time. Most of the time it's the second time that's more difficult.

THW discussed:

> Younger I was always a tomboy. I always played football with the kids on the block. In high school, my junior year, somewhere after my junior year, I got my hair cut. It used to be really long. It was all cut off. I had an inch and half or two inches left of it. And maybe a month or so after that I came out to a friend, no, it was a little longer than that, because this was when I was just first realizing it. And she goes, it's the hair, look how you cut your hair. So it stand out and it's a little weird but she was a lesbian so it's nothing like she was playing stereotypes. If a girl has short hair, short hair is considered more masculine, so therefore she must be gay because she looks like a man.

TJT remembered:

> As a child I recognized that I identified more with my nephew than with my female friends at school. I didn't know that was gender identity at the time. I was too young to understand that, and I didn't know that there was such as thing as a transsexual at that age. But I always felt kind of odd, I identified with my brother who was older than me, my nephew that was younger than me. Again I had to interpret that in some way, and for a while I thought that I just wasn't mature yet, I am just immature and I will get out of it or it will go away. But when I was a teenager I began to develop a certain pride in it, even though it was frustrating. I didn't see any way out of it. I discovered people like me in the world, not in my life, but for example, watching Lily on Masterpiece Theater in the 70's which was about Lily Langtree, and she was friends with Oscar Wilde, and so they had an actor named Peter Eagen play Oscar Wilde on that series, and he just took my breath away. So I kind of internally developed this kind of gay pride that I could not talk about. And I got on the Pride committee in my 20's, and I didn't explain it because I thought they would all think I was nuts. So apparently they thought of me as a straight woman who cared about the gay community, but I did work for them, and it was hard to get volunteers. I was treated just fine but I think that they all wondered why is she here? But

I knew if I tried to explain, I identify with the gay men here, I would be crazy because that wasn't talked about yet.

For FTM TKS, lesbian self-identity was explicitly the precursor to transgender identity:

It was a long time before I knew there was such thing as gender identity. I think, most of my life I didn't think about it a whole lot. Even though I was attracted to girls at a very young age, and so I thought, "Oh, I'm a lesbian." Because I have the parts of a girl or a woman. So I must be a lesbian. So I was able to express my gender identity in a great way in that social context. But then, in the last few years, when I thought more about transitioning, then I had to think more about why there's this, like, discordance between my mentally and my...something. And then, that something is normally identified as gender identity. So then, that's really when I had to think more about it.

In our previous work (Nagoshi et al., 2012; 2014), we have reported that in our sample of transgender participants, when asked whether one's sexual orientation defined one's gender identity, some were adamant that there was no relationship between sexual orientation and gender identity, while others noted the dynamic negotiations between sexual orientation and gender identity through the transition process and in the lived experiences of being transgender. In fact, most of the transgender participants who asserted no relationship between sexual orientation and gender identity were also those who reported an awareness of their gender identity in early childhood (TAF, TBL, TCP, TDN, TLK), with MTF TLK explicitly stating that gender identity defines sexual orientation. Of the remaining two transgender participants who reported an awareness of their gender identity during early childhood, FTM TEV did describe a dynamic interaction between their sexual and gender behaviors, "When I'm in relationships, depending on what roles I'm in and who I'm dating, there are times when I feel significantly more masculine than the person that I'm dating, and there's times when I feel significantly more feminine than the person I'm dating." Such an active negotiation was also reported by MTF TFD, "It happens by accident when you discover your sexual orientation, because you change."

Of the four FTM transgender participants that reported their gender awareness as having occurred during adolescence or later, two (THW and TKS) said that sexual orientation was not related to gender identity, but both of their responses were qualified. THW discussed that, "I don't think people identify themselves anymore as being male or female through their orientation, for the most part. But I think other people do. That can play a role in how you feel about yourself. If people keep telling you you're butch, you're butch. Eventually you are going to go, 'Oh I'm butch.'" TKS first said no and then reconsidered, "I'm attracted to women, but it's possible that I could be attracted to men, too. Because there are transgender individuals who are gay, so.... Well, no, I never thought of it like that. It's more, probably, the other way around." For FTMs TGR and TJT, there was explicit acknowledgment that sexual orientation interacted with gender identity, with TGR defining themselves as "omni-sexual," while TJT discussed:

The idea that they are the same thing but joined together. Because I was obviously able to live a life in a relationship with a man in the role of the women, but that had nothing to do with my identity which was male. There is a certain community aspect, too, that I would really rather be in the gay community than in the straight community but they are really two different things. Because if I didn't need to be male and interact with people as male, I wouldn't have needed to do this and would have been able to be in a relationship with a man as a woman with no discrimination, that is the easier road, societally speaking. So obviously I didn't do this because of orientation. I did it because of gender reasons.

DISCUSSION

Consistent with Rankin and Beemyn (2012), while most of the transgender participants reported an early childhood age at which they "just knew" that their gender identity did not conform to what was expected based on their birth sex, a minority of participants reported that such awareness occurred in adolescence and even adulthood. This latter group is notable in two respects. These individuals who reported an awareness of gender identity in adolescence and later were all FTM transgender individuals, and their narratives reflected the findings from Rankin and Beemyn (2012) that FTMs generally experience more freedom to express masculine gender appearance and behaviors in early childhood, compared to the more strict enforcement of masculine gender role norms experienced by MTF transgender individuals. For these FTM individuals, the latitude to manifest gender non-conformative appearances and behaviors in early childhood allowed for a gender non-heteronormative sexual orientation to become part of their transgender identity process in adolescence. The self-identification of these FTM individuals with being lesbian as a step toward a transgender identity is also consistent with the findings of Rankin and Beemyn (2012). All of these FTM transgender individuals either explicitly accepted the intersectionality of gender and sexual identity or implied that there were reasons for why such a connection might exist, including constructing narratives of their lived experiences that reflected the dynamic developmental interactions between gender and sexuality.

For those mostly MTF transgender individuals in the present study who reported becoming aware of their gender identity in early childhood, it can be argued that this awareness was particularly salient because of the more strict enforcement of masculine gender role appearances and behaviors for boys than the comparable enforcement of feminine gender roles for girls. Many of these transgender individuals then categorically rejected any connection between their gender identity and their sexual orientation, and it would be interesting to explore the developmental and psychological adjustment implications of having such beliefs in the separation of these seemingly inevitably intersectional identities.

As noted previously, all of the participants stated that they were transgender but did not necessarily distinguish themselves as transsexual, except for one individual. This may have been problematic for a transsexual individual who has assumed an identity that is the opposite of their born gender identity. The performance (Butler, 1990) of the new gender, enacting and embodying the new gender identity and physical body, also offers an alternative paradigm that future research should consider. While one's born gender may continue to be written on one's body, even after the sex reassignment surgery (Johnson, 2012), the inherent belief of the individual that they are now the opposite sex and their lived experience as the opposite sex offers a counterpoint to the idea that embodiment cannot be overcome. The studies by Kuper et al. (2012) and Rankin and Beemyn (2012) also explored the desire for hormonal treatment and sex reassignment surgery among transgender individuals, finding large individual differences in this desire, as well as differences in this desire between FTM and MTF individuals. The narratives presented here suggest that some of these differences may be driven by differences in experiences of being forced to conform to the gender binary and of becoming empowered to resist this oppression (Nagoshi et al., 2014).

The present findings are limited in their generalizability by the small, mostly White, college-based sample used. There is clearly a need for longitudinal studies to more validly assess the developmental processes suggested by this and previous studies of gender and sexual identity development in transgender/transsexual individuals. It would have been desirable to have asked a comparable question about when sexual orientation/identity awareness first became salient to participants and to explore this development, particularly for those transgender participants who reported an early childhood gender awareness. It is apparent that there are important individual differences in the intersectionality of gender and sexual identity development in transgender individuals, and it is likely that such differences would also be found in other gender non-heteronormative individuals.

REFERENCES

Bockting, W., Benner, A., & Coleman, E. (2009). Gay and bisexual identity *Archives of Sexual Behavior, 38,* 688-701.

Butler J. (1990). *Gender trouble: Feminism and the subversion of Identity.* New York: Routledge.

Devor, H. (1989). *Gender blending: Confronting the limits of duality.* Bloomington, IN: Indiana University Press.

Diamond, L., & Butterworth, M. (2008). Questioning gender and sexual identity: Dynamic links over time. *Sex Roles, 59,* 365–376.

Dozier, R. (2005). Beards, breasts, and bodies: Doing sex in a gendered world. *Gender & Society, 19,* 297-316.

Factor, R., & Rothblum, E. (2008). Exploring gender identity and community among three groups of transgender individuals in the United States: MTFs, FTMs, and genderqueers. *Health Sociology Review, 17,* 235-253.

Johnson, K. (2012). *Transgender, transsexualism, and the queering of gender identities: debates for feminist research.* In Hesse-Biber, S. N. (Ed.), *Handbook of feminist research theory and praxis* (p. 606-626). Los Angeles: Sage Publications.

Kuper, L. E., Nussbaum, R., & Mustanski, B. (2012). Exploring the diversity *Journal of Sex Research, 49,* 244-254.

Nagoshi, J., & Brzuzy, S. (2010). Transgender theory: Embodying research and practice. *Affilia, 25,* 431-443.

Nagoshi, J., Brzuzy, S., & Terrell, H. (2012). Perceptions of gender roles, gender identity, and sexual orientation among transgender individuals. *Feminism & Psychology, 22,* 405-422.

Nagoshi, J., Nagoshi, C., & Brzuzy, S. (2014). *Gender and sexual identity: Transcending feminist and queer theories.* New York: Springer.

Nuttbrock, L. A., Bockting, W. O., Hwahng, S., Rosenblum, A., Mason, M., Macri, M., & Becker, J. (2009). Gender identity *Sexual & Relationship Therapy, 24,* 108-125.

Rankin, S., & Beemyn, G. (2012). Beyond a binary: The lives of gender-nonconforming youth. *About Campus, 17,* 2-10.

Rubin, H. (2003). *Self-made men: Identity and embodiment among transsexual men.* Nashville, TN: Vanderbilt University Press.

Shields, S. (2008). Gender: an intersectionality perspective. *Sex Roles, 59,* 301-11.

Williams, C., Weinberg, M., & Rosenberger, G. (2013). Trans men: Embodiments, identities, and sexualities. *Sociological Forum, 28,* 719-741.

In: Gender Identity
Editor: Beverly L. Miller

ISBN: 978-1-63321-488-0
© 2014 Nova Science Publishers, Inc.

Chapter 4

GENDER DYSPHORIA IN ADULTS AND ADOLESCENTS AS A MENTAL DISORDER ... BUT, WHAT IS A MENTAL DISORDER? A PHENOMENOLOGICAL/EXISTENTIAL ANALYSIS OF A PUZZLING CONDITION

Roberto Vitelli[*]

Assistant Professor of Clinical Psychology,
Dipartimento di Neuroscienze e Scienze della Riproduzione ed Odontostomatologiche
Università degli Studi di Napoli Federico II, Italy

ABSTRACT

Since the origins of humanity the possibility of an area existing beyond the binary subdivision of sexual genders has been incorporated into myth and symbolic representations as expressed through rite, from Plato's Androgyne to Hermaphrodite, from the myth of Attis and Cybele to the figure of Venus Castina. At the same time different cultures have envisaged, and in some cases continue to envisage, outside any "pathologized" category, the possibility of there being a non-correspondence between an individual's biological sex and their subjective experience of belonging to a given sexual gender: for example, the Neapolitan *Femminiello*, the *"two-spirits"* among American natives, and the *Hijras*, who still exist on the Indian sub-continent. Nevertheless, in the West today this existential condition is to some extent shaped, and somehow even produced, by a series of *discourses*, which are first and foremost medical/psychiatric and define and mold its very nature. *Gender Dysphoria*, the clinical taxonomic category which the American Psychiatric Association has recently adopted to replace the existing *Gender Identity Disorder*, refers to an individual's affective/cognitive discontent with the assigned gender and the distress that may accompany the incongruence between one's experienced or expressed gender and one's assigned gender, which in many, but not all, cases also involves a somatic transition by cross-sex hormone treatment and genital surgery (*Sex Reassignment Surgery*) (APA 2013). As Michel Foucault would have it,

---

[*] Corresponding author's email: rvitelli@unina.it.

psychiatric knowledge molds bodies. In any case, the work of preparation and drafting of the recent edition of the DSM, the Diagnostic and Statistical Manual of Mental Disorders (APA 2013), has been accompanied by a lively debate on whether or not it is legal to include the condition within the ranks of Mental Disorders. The result of this debate was to keep the condition in the manual, therefore interpreting it as a manifestation of a Mental Disorder. In the present paper, we will analyze the main historical stages of the process of inclusion of this condition within psychiatric knowledge. We will, therefore, discuss the main problems that this inclusion produces, questioning the very foundations of psychiatric knowledge. Moreover, we will consider the exact nature of this condition within the framework of a phenomenological/existential approach, beyond the simplistic diagnostic criteria proposed by the American manual.

INTRODUCTION

In a very broad and general sense, the term "Gender Identity Variance" (GIV) (Meyer-Bahlburg 2010) commonly refers to existential possibilities that are placed beyond the rigid binarism of gender, i.e. to expressive/behavioural possibilities and inner experiences which are inconsistent with the characteristics of the biological sex at birth and/or go beyond the gender identity categories established at a cultural level.

Since the very origins of humanity the possibility of an area existing beyond the binary subdivision of sexual genders has been incorporated into myth and symbolic representations as expressed through rite, from Plato's Androgyne to Hermaphrodite, from the myth of Attis and Cybele to the figure of Venus Castina (Herdt 1996). At the same time, different cultures have, outside any "pathologized" category, envisaged – and in some cases continue to envisage – the possibility of there being a non-correspondence between an individual's biological sex and their subjective experience of belonging to a given sexual gender: for example, the Neapolitan *Femminiello* (Zito & Valerio 2013), the Thai *Kathoey*, the *"Two-Spirits"* among American natives, the Brazilian *Travesti* or *Pasivo* and the *Hijras*, who continue to exist on the Indian sub-continent (Herdt 1996; Nanda 2008). Nevertheless, in the West, today, this existential condition is traversed and produced by a series of discourses, first and foremost medical/psychiatric, which define and mold its very nature (Billings and Urban 1996).

As an "aporetic" issue par excellence, these conditions have attracted growing attention from the scientific community, as well as significant interest on the media circuit in recent years. Gender variance, also called "gender-non-conformity" or "atypical-gender-identity", tends today to be articulated/substantiated through various discursive practices, which are often strongly opposed to one another: socio-political and anthropological, artistic and medical-psychiatric, psychological and forensic medicine (Vitelli & Valerio 2012).

In particular, the preparation and subsequent publication of the new fifth edition of the DSM, the Diagnostic and Statistical Manual of Mental Disorders which has been recently drafted by the American Psychiatric Association (APA 2013), has raised a lively debate about the legitimacy of inclusion of these conditions within the ranks of mental disorders. Indeed, it is precisely here that we see how difficult it is apparently to produce plain answers; in other words it is here that "the transsexual aporetic quality of the problem" seems to manifest itself. Because psychiatry, in the course of its history, has defined the "pathological nature" of such a condition and set up a complex set of practices around it, we have also to take into account how these psychiatric discursive regimes turn out to be a way to frame subjects' experiences, making them meaningful to themselves and others, and finally to interpret their own identities. (Mason-Schrock 1996; Schrock & Reid 2006) In fact, as Pier Aldo Rovatti, an Italian philosopher, stated a few years ago, psychiatry often produces an effect of alienation/subjugation of the subject to its "discourse", where the individual finds a way to craft self-narratives as an essential form of his/her expressing identity. (Rovatti 2006) Nevertheless, when the American Psychiatric Association was in the process or revising its Diagnostic and Statistical Manual, many activists in the transgender community opposed the hypothesis of maintaining GIVs as "mental disorders" in the DSM and demanded their complete removal. (Vance, Cohen-Kettenis, Drescher, Meyer-Bahlburg, Pfäfflin, & Zucker 2009) In fact, they stated that perpetuating DSM IV-TR's Gender Identity Disorders (APA 2000) in DSM 5 would further stigmatize and harm transgender individuals. (Drescher 2010) However, other stakeholders expressed concern that deleting GID would mean that transgender adults might be denied medical and surgical care.

In the end, the result of this debate was to keep the condition in the manual, therefore interpreting it as a manifestation of a Mental Disorder. However, just as in the 1970s when the American Psychiatric Association queried what a mental disorder was, because it was obliged to decide whether homosexuality, which had been included in the second edition of the Manual (DSM-II, APA 1968), really was such, the question of the exact nature and definition of mental disorders has been raised again. In the present paper, we will analyze the main historical stages of the process of inclusion of gender identity variance within psychiatric knowledge[1]. We will, therefore, discuss the main problems that this inclusion produces, questioning the very foundations of psychiatry. Moreover, we will consider the exact nature of this condition within the framework of a phenomenological/existential approach, beyond the simplistic diagnostic criteria commonly proposed.

GENDER IDENTITY VARIANCE AND MEDICAL DISCOURSE: THE ROOTS

Apart from some relatively unimportant references to the phenomenon present in several authors, e.g., among others, Rudolf Arndt (1835 – 1900), Wilhelm Griesinger (1817-1868) and Jean-Étienne Dominique Esquirol (1772-1840), it is first in the study on the *Contrary Sexual Feeling (köntrâre Sexualempfindung)* carried out by Carl Friedrich Otto Westphal (1833-1930), a pupil of the famous neurologist and psychiatrist Wilhelm Griesinger and a famous professor of psychiatry at Berlin, that we can find the main root of the historical matrix from which Gender Identity Variance has been incorporated into medical discourse. His was a time when sex and sexuality were gaining more and more space in the scientific field. As Michel Foucault put it, it was a time of "'multiplication of discourses concerning sex in the field of exercise of power itself: an institutional incitement to speak about it, and to do

---

[1] Throughout this chapter we will refer mainly to the condition manifesting in adolescence or adulthood. Vice versa, we will not consider gender variance in childhood, although, in some ways, the psychiatrization of the condition in childhood appears even more problematic [World Professionals Association for Transgender Health - WPATH, 2013]. Our choice merely reflects the chapter's limited scope. Interested readers may refer to Zucker [2010] or to the results of the WPATH ICD-11 Consensus Meeting [WPATH, 2013], for a discussion of the condition in childhood.

so more and more" (Foucault 1976, 18). Medical knowledge of sexuality was beginning to structure itself around its various forms, whether they were judged "abnormal" or "normal" according to the criteria of the time.

In 1870 Westphal published in the *Archiv für Psychiatrie* the detailed history of a young woman who, from her earliest years, showed specific personality traits: she liked to dress as a boy, only cared for boys' games and, as she grew up, was sexually attracted only to women, with whom she formed a series of loving relationships, in which the friends obtained sexual gratification through mutual caresses. Westphal perceived that these personality characteristics were congenital, not acquired, so could not be termed "vices"[2]; and, while he insisted on the presence of neurotic elements, his observations showed the absence of anything that could legitimately be termed "insanity". To refer to conditions of this kind, he specifically proposed the expression *könträre Sexualempfindung*[3].

After Westphal's article, the first book which deals with this subject extensively and systematically remains undoubtedly *Psychopathia Sexualis* by Krafft-Ebing, the first edition of which dates back to 1886. Richard Von Krafft-Ebing (1840-1902), for many years Professor of Psychiatry at Vienna University and one of the most distinguished alienists of his time, was one of the first scientific investigators to take a special professional interest in the sexual impulses of individuals. He considered homosexuality as *a perversion*, as a *reversal of the sexual instinct*, in other words as a form of mental disorder, by reason of its departure from procreative heterosexual intercourse[4]. He described two different possibilities: an "acquired" condition and a "congenital" one. With regard to the former, the author describes different degrees for its manifestation, the second of which he called "*Eviration and Defemination*", comparing it with conditions such as those of effeminate persons (*anandreis*, literally, un-masculine) described by Herodotus, and subsequently by Hippocrates, which were said to be frequent among Scythians, or that manifested by the *mujerados* among the Pueblo Indians of New Mexico and by the *berdaches* among the American native Apaches and Navajos. This is how Krafft-Ebing describes this second degree:

---

[2] It is noteworthy that the growing influence of science and technical-scientific knowledge has not been without consequences: if on the one hand it has definitely helped to clear the field from ethical-religious bias, on the other it has attracted the stigma and prejudice associated with mental illness to gender variants.

[3] With reference to the coinage of this term, Foucault noted a major conceptual shift regarding the "psychological, psychiatric, medical category of homosexuality" [Foucault 1976, 42-43], whereas, in fact, Westphal's 1870 article really "can stand as its date of birth": "less by a type of sexual relations than by a certain quality of sexual sensibility, a certain way of inverting in oneself the masculine and the feminine. Homosexuality appeared as one of the faces of sexuality when it was discounted from the practice of sodomy into a kind of interior androgyny, a hermaphrodism of the soul. The sodomite was a regression; the homosexual now is a species." [Foucault 1976, 42-43] Beyond the controversial nature of this passage [Freccero 1999], what appears clear is that at that time a certain confusion or overlapping between homosexuality and gender identity variance was present. It will be a long time before a clearer dividing line between the two categories is defined. At the same time Foucault's notes can be referred also to the condition we are considering here, where the introduction of a noun, of a new category, opened up new horizons, where what was defined was not merely a quality of the subject, but an entirely new existential possibility, somehow molded by psychiatric discursive regimes.

[4] It is clear that Krafft-Ebing viewed unconventional sexual behaviors through the lens of 19th century Darwinian theory: all non-procreative sexual behaviors, now subject to medical scrutiny, were regarded as forms of psychopathology. Although it may seem distant and anachronistic, as we shall see later, neo-Darwinian positions have again been adopted in more recent years for the most appropriate definition of the category of "mental disorders", creating many problems, not only in the interpretation of gender variance, but also, albeit to a lesser extent, of the homosexual condition.

"If, in cases of contrary sexual instinct thus developed, no restoration occurs, then deep and lasting transformations of the psychical personality may occur. The process completing itself in this way may be briefly designated *eviration*. The patient undergoes a deep change of character, particularly in his feelings and inclinations, which become those of a female. After this, he also feels himself to be a woman during the sexual act, has desire only for passive sexual indulgence, and, under certain circumstances, sinks to the level of a prostitute. In this condition of deep and more lasting psycho-sexual transformation, the individual is like the (congenital) *urning*[5] of high grade. In such a case, the possibility of a restoration of the previous mental and sexual personality seems to be excluded."

(Krafft-Ebing 1886-1906, 197)

After the presentation of several autobiographical cases involving such a condition, Krafft-Ebing discusses further degrees of acquired homosexuality: "stages of Transition to *Metamorphosis Sexualis Paranoica*" (in which "bodily sensation is also transformed in the sense of a *transmutatio sexus*" – *ibidem* 202) and "*Metamorphosis Sexualis Paranoica*". This latter term is mostly understood to mean what is today defined as a transsexual condition (Stryker & Whittle 2006), but it should be said that actually the cases discussed by Krafft-Ebing mostly revealed a more complex symptomatology, often with somatic, auditory or olfactory hallucinations, hypochondriac symptoms, ideas of references, various kinds of delusions such as suspicion, persecution, being poisoned or controlled, genealogy. Certainly, however, in the text of Krafft-Ebing some ambiguity regarding the inclusion of the gender variance in the psychotic field can be found, whereas the statements made by the people he encountered, either directly or, more often indirectly in the letters they sent to him, referred to *bodily experiences* they associated with their feeling of belonging to the opposite gender. These were the statements that somehow seem to have induced the author to consider as an expression of a delusion what they said about belonging to a gender different from their "visible" biological sex[6].

However, it is in the discussion of the "*Homo-Sexual Feeling as an Abnormal Congenital Manifestation*" that we can find some interesting remarks regarding the pathologization process of Gender Identity Variance:

"The essential feature of this strange manifestation of the sexual life is the want of sexual sensibility for the opposite sex, even to the extent of horror, while sexual inclination and impulse toward the same sex are present (...) Feeling, thought, will, and the whole character, in cases of the complete development of the anomaly, correspond

---

[5] The term *Urning* (English "Uranian"), was coined by Karl Heinrich Ulrichs, a German writer and official legal adviser for the district court of Hildesheim in the Kingdom of Hanover, who is seen today as a pioneer of the modern gay rights. He employed this term to describe different sexual orientation/gender identities. In his published writings on homosexuality, Ulrichs posited the existence of a "third sex" whose nature is inborn. The essential point in his theory of homosexuality is the doctrine that the male homosexual has a female psyche, which he summed up in the Latin phrase: *anima muliebris virili corpore inclusa* (a female psyche confined in a male body), exactly as many transsexuals actually would put it in subsequent years. Again, what is at stake here is the overlapping between homosexuality and gender identity that was present at that time.

[6] Regarding this issue, we must consider, on the one hand the complex question of the pre-verbal, pre-predicative component of these conditions and the possibility of decoding it beyond the limits of the field of language, and, on the other hand, the difficulties in the very definition of delusion, a question, the latter, which is still far from being finally resolved [Sass & Pienkos 2013].

with the peculiar sexual instinct, but not with the sex which the individual represents anatomically and physiologically. This abnormal mode of feeling may not infrequently be recognized in the manner, dress, and calling of the individuals, who may go so far as to yield to an impulse to don the distinctive clothing corresponding with the sexual role in which they feel themselves to be". (*ibidem*, 222)[7].

As in the case of acquired condition, Krafft-Ebing considers several degrees of "congenital homosexuality", the third of which he calls "*Effemination and Viraginity*". Although it may at first seem a stretch, precisely because of its relevance we shall take a close look at his description of the condition. In fact, it seems to be the first, clear and extensive inclusion of Gender Identity Variance in medical discourse:

"In this group, fully-developed cases in men are female in feelings; in women, males. This abnormality of feeling and of development of character is often apparent in childhood. The boy likes to spend his time with girls, play with dolls, and help his mother about the house; he likes to cook, sew, knit, and develops taste in female toilettes, so that he may even become the adviser of his sister. As he grows older he eschews smoking, drinking, and manly sports, and, on the contrary, finds pleasure in adornment of person, art, *belles-lettres*, etc., even to the extent of giving himself entirely to the cultivation of the beautiful.

If he can assume the *rôle* of a female at a masquerade, it is his greatest delight. He seeks to please his lover, so to speak, by studiously trying to represent what pleases the female-loving man in the opposite sex, - sweetness, sympathy, taste for æsthetics, poetry, etc. Efforts to approach the female appearance in gait, attitude, and style of dress are frequently seen.

The female *urning*, even when a little girl, presents the reverse. Her favorite place is the play-ground of boys. She seeks to rival them in their games. The girl will have nothing to do with dolls; her passion is for playing horse, soldier, and robber. For female employments there is manifested not merely a lack of taste, but often unskillfulness in them. The toilette is neglected, and pleasure found in a course, boyish life. Instead of an inclination for the arts, there is manifested an inclination and taste for the sciences. Occasionally there may be attempts to smoke and drink. Perfumes and cosmetics are abhorred. The consciousness of being born a woman, and, therefore, of being compelled to renounce the University, with its gay life, and the Army, induces painful reflections.

In the inclinations of the amazon for manly sports, the masculine soul in the female bosom manifests itself; and not less in the show of courage and manly feeling. The female *urning* loves to wear her hair and have her clothing in the fashion of men; and it is her greatest pleasure, when opportunity offers, to appear in male attire. Her ideals are historical and contemporary feminine personalities distinguished for mind and energy.

---

[7] The psychopathological area in which Krafft-Ebing places this condition is noteworthy: "Neuroses (hysteria, neurasthenia, epileptoid states, etc.) co-exist. […] In many *urnings*, either temporarily or permanently, insanity of a degenerative character (pathological emotional states, periodical insanity, paranoia, etc.) makes its appearance" [Kraft-Ebing 1886-1906, 225-226]. There are here two points of interest: first, Krafft-Ebing admits the possibility that a psychotic disorder may not be present in all cases. Secondly, at the same time, he appears completely unaware of the secondary effects on the psychological well-being determined by the contextual adverse social responses to such a psychological condition (regarding this last issue, among others, see Prunas et al. 2014). Nevertheless, Krafft-Ebing adds: "The majority of *urnings* are happy in their perverse sexual feeling and impulse, and unhappy only in so far as social and legal barriers stand in the way of the satisfaction of their instinct toward their own sex". [Kraft-Ebing 1886-1906, 226]

With reference to the sexual feeling and instinct of these *urnings*, so thoroughly permeated in all their mental being, the men, without exception, feel themselves to be females; the women feel themselves to be males. (...) In homo-sexual intercourse the man always feels himself, in the act, as a woman; the woman, as a man."

(ibidem, 279-281)

Krafft-Ebing was followed not only by Iwan Bloch (1872-1922), whose work was rich in clinical material and medical/forensic considerations (1907), but also by Magnus Hirschfeld, another author who contributed to the inclusion of Gender Identity Variance in medical discourse and is today clearly recognized as one of the pioneers of the Science of Sexology (Bullough 2003). In 1908 Hirschfeld was among the founders of the Berlin Psychoanalytical Association, along with Iwan Bloch, Otto Juliusburger, Heinrich Koerber and Karl Abraham, although later his relationship with psychoanalysis became somewhat controversial. (Vitelli & Giusti 2013) A homosexual himself, he was a prominent figure in the process of conceptual reinterpretation of homosexuality in the late nineteenth and early twentieth centuries. Moreover, he fought strongly to defend the rights of homosexuals. In 1897 he founded the *Wissenschaftlich-humanitäres Komitee* (Scientific-Humanitarian Committee) with the publisher Max Spohr, the lawyer Eduard Oberg, the writer Max von Bülow and Adolf Brand, who, just a year before, had set up "*Der Eigene* ", an anarchical magazine which gradually dealt more and more with homosexual themes. The main purpose of the Committee was to stimulate scientific research in order to promote the defense of the rights of homosexuals and to mobilize public support for the repeal of Paragraph 175, a law in the German Criminal Code passed in 1871 that criminalized male homosexual behavior. In 1899 Hirschfeld began publishing the *Jahrbuch für sexuelle Zwischenstufen*, the Yearbook for *Intermediate Sexual Types*. This term "*Intermediate Sexual Types*", which appears in the journal's title, refers to the doctrine of *sexual intermediaries*, one of the most important theories produced by the author (Hirschfeld 1913) concerning the existence of a kind of gradient on which you could put the various subjects, a sort of continuous line with two opposite poles, in fact purely virtual, consisting of fully heterosexual women at one extreme and of fully heterosexual men at the other. In other words he postulated the idea of a complex and variable mix within the individual of male and female components, which was to influence the subsequent theories formulated by the Austrian philosopher Otto Weininger (1880-1903) and by Wilhelm Fliess (1858-1928) − the friend of Sigmund Freud who played an important part in the early development of psychoanalysis. Indeed, all these scholars discussed innate psychic bisexuality. However, on closer inspection, Hirschfeld's theory seems to travel on a double track: in fact, while affirming a dimensional approach to the understanding of human sexual gender, thus confirming the "unreal" nature of the binary division of the sexes and the possibility of numerous combinations of the different variables involved (Hirschfeld 1923), he finally seemed to opt for a range of categories: Indeed, along that gradient, he identified several, different conditions, each connected to one of the different variables involved: the sexual organs (cases of hermaphroditism and pseudohermaphroditism), more general physical characteristics (gynecomastia or andromastia, feminae barbatae, androtrichia, etc.), the object of the sexual instinct (heterosexual men and women with behavioral traits related to the opposite sex, as well as homosexuals or bisexuals); and, finally, the individuals' emotional characteristics. With regard to this last condition, Hirschfeld said:

"In Group Four, in which we understand the emotional particularities in direct relation with love life, the ones to be counted as sexual intermediaries are men whose feminine emotions and feelings are reflected in their manner of love, their direction of taste, their gestures and manners, their sensitivity, and many times in their particular way of writing, also men who more or less dress as women or live totally as such; on the other side women of manly character, manly ways of thinking and writing, a strong tendency toward manly passions, manly dress, and naturally women who more or less lead the life of a man. Therefore, transvestites are also to be included in this case" (Hirschfeld 1910, 37[8])

The introduction of the word *transvestism*, and, above all, its conceptual definition, are a focal point in the process of inclusion of gender variance within medical discourse. In fact, this was how Hirschfeld first made a clearer demarcation between this condition, homosexuality (Hirschfeld 1910, 28-29) and the psychotic field (*ibidem*, 33), which Krafft-Ebing had lumped together. This condition was so named by the author for the preference shown by these subjects for the typical clothes of the opposite sex, because of their inner feelings of belonging to the sexual gender opposite to that indicated by their anatomy. In fact, clothes seem to act basically as a *performative sign* as usual (Leone 2010), but in this case in a particularly evident manner, not so much to define the truth/falsehood of what is signaled, but rather, tout court to "construct" subjects' identities: it is through their mode of dress that the subjects described by Hirschfeld *imagined*, in fact, that they *embodied* the opposite sex, after attributing to themselves the specific psychological characteristics socially ascribed to the opposite sexual gender. In this regard, it is interesting to note what Hirschfeld says when he attempts to make a differential diagnosis in reference to the category proposed by Krafft-Ebing, clearly intending to exclude the presence of psychotic traits in such cases:

"No matter how much transvestite men feel women when dressed in women's clothing and women feel like men when dressed in men's clothing, they still remain aware that in reality it is not so. *To be sure, some do imagine – and if so, then the wish is the originator of the thought* – that their skin is softer, their forms rounder, and their movements more gracious than are usual for men, but they know full well, and often are depressed by the fact that they do not physically belong to the desired sex they love." (*my italics*) (*ibidem* 33)

A very subtle intuition of Gender Identity Variants is at stake here, where it would appear clear that when we talk about a female soul trapped in a male body, and vice versa, we are acting, here, from a phenomenological point of view, on the register of the *Imaginary*. Again:

"especially to be considered is that which Krafft-Ebing convincingly made clear in his splendid "Essay on the Explanation of Masochism" ("Versuch einer Erklareung des Masochismus"), that masochism in and of itself depicts a degeneration of a specifically feminine characteristic, while "sadism is to be looked upon as a pathological intensification of the masculine sexual characteristic in its psychical accessories".

---

[8] All Hirschfeld's quotations are taken from the partial English translation by Michael A. Lombardi-Nash, in Stryker and Whittle 2006.

In the case of our transvestites, *almost all characteristics, which impress us at first as being masochistic, easily lead back to the wish for effemination". (my italics)* (*ibidem* 32)

So, according to Hirschfeld, the same "masochistic" instance may more properly be understood as an effect of the *Other* of the Language, of the symbolic abstract oppositions filled with specific values. But we shall discuss this later.

However, to go back to the historical reconstruction, Havelock Ellis's response to Hirschfeld's notations is noteworthy: he judged inadequate the designation of "cross-dressing", because it could be misleading and give people to believe that the main characteristic of their condition was only the tendency to use the clothes of the opposite sex. In fact, he suggested replacing the term "cross-dressing" with that of *sexo-aesthetic inversion* (Ellis 1913), and then, later, with that of *eonism* named after the famous Knight of Eon (Ellis 1920; 1927). Particularly interesting are the reasons for the first option, that is the idea, somehow supported by Hirschfeld himself (1910, 38), of an identification in such cases of the subject with the object loved. By using the word "aesthetic" Ellis intended to refer to what some philosophers had said about empathy as constituting aesthetic experience: for example, in his work *Einleitung in die Ästethic* (Groos 1892), Karl Groos had argued that the basis of aesthetic enjoyment was to be traced back to the phenomena of interior imitation, to the intimate participation in the "life of the object".

Similarly, in his main work *Ästhethic: Psychologie des Schönen und der Kunst* (1903, vol. I and 1906, vol. II), Theodore Lipps had proposed distinguishing three types of enjoyment: in the first, subjects can enjoy a tangible object distinct from themselves, the second is an enjoyment that refers to the subjects themselves (for example where one can enjoy one's physical strength, or skills in various activities), and finally a third, where: "I can enjoy myself in a tangible object separate from me. This is the only kind of aesthetic enjoyment. Aesthetic enjoyment is aimed at objective self-enjoyment" (Lipps, 1906, reported in Vattimo 1977, 179). It is with reference to this last mechanism that Ellis proposed to use the term " *sexo-aesthetic inversion.*" Somehow, Hirschfeld's and Havelock Ellis's intuitions shed light on the psychological functioning, that may sometimes be found in transvestite (transsexual) subjects, but, again, we will discuss this later.

GENDER IDENTITY VARIANCE AND MEDICAL DISCOURSE: THE "TRANSSEXUAL" SIGNIFIER AND THE HANDOVER FROM PSYCHIATRY TO SURGERY

The role played by Hirschfeld in the taxonomic differentiation of the conditions in question, i.e. in their "constitution", certainly cannot be limited to the definition of a specific condition, named "transvestism.", as has been pointed out elsewhere (Bottone et al. 2001; Ekins & King 2001). Indeed, although the authorship of the term *transsexualism* is most often attributed to David Cauldwell, in 1922 Hirschfeld identified specific transvestite "subtypes" (Hirschfeld 1922); and one year later, for one of them he saw fit to use a new expression, *seelischer Transsexualismus*, *Psychic Transsexualism*, or more correctly, *Transsexualism of the Soul* (Hirschfeld 1923, 15). On the other hand his importance in the process we are studying does not end here. Indeed he supervised a team of surgeons who for the first time carried out sex reassignment surgery. The patient was Einar Wegener (Andreas Spanner), a Danish painter, who underwent five operations over a period of two years (1930-1931) to make his/her body look and be as female as possible. The operation was performed following the techniques of Eugen Steinach (1861-1944), the famous Viennese physiologist, who was known not only for performing surgical vasectomies which he believed to produce miraculously rejuvenating effects, but also for carrying out experimental surgery involving the castration of rats and New Guinea pigs and the replanting of fragments of testicular or ovarian tissue (Hoyer 1933). In the historical development we are considering, the importance of Eugen Steinach is much greater than researchers today normally recognize. The 16th-17th Edition of Krafft-Ebing's *Psychopathia Sexualis* was extensively revised by his student Albert Moll, who reports the following fragment of a letter sent by a person presenting a condition of transvestism to Krafft-Ebing:

> "Go to a doctor, throw yourself at his feet, if necessary, and beg him to use you as a subject of experiment. With this in mind I was awakened again to the selfishness of life: Maybe the doctor and the scientist can help you to find a new form of existence. Transplantation, Steinach! He has managed, with a legendary success, to transform the sex of animals. Could not an experiment like this be attempted scientifically on a human being who volunteers to undergo such an operation? On a man who assumes all its consequences himself, and that has only this chance to be saved from folly and inevitable death? (…) I'll ask God to help me to be born again and to give me a little time to live, to give me the opportunity to build myself a new life, without the torments of my present existence, without the continuous struggle, without the conflict, always present to my spirit, between my form which is male and my soul, being and feeling, which are feminine even in the smallest nuances". (Krafft-Ebing 1886-1931, 666).

It appears evident, therefore, that we should not think of a simple unidirectional process of definition of conceptual categories that have defined and organized the psychiatrization of gender variants since the early twentieth century. In other words, it was not just an imposition on the subjects of the psychiatric categories. (Hill 2005) In fact, people who perceived a discrepancy between their internal gender and their biological sex, began to send letters to the most famous exponents of the nascent sexological/psychiatric science asking for help, already in the late nineteenth and early twentieth centuries. What changed in this historical period (Rubin 2006), of course, was the very possibility, on a conceptual level, of defining differently the relationship between sex and gender, the body, and the very idea of the subject (Davidson 2001).

Although the term "transsexualism" appeared in the work of Hirschfeld, it was not greatly developed. It was used again, in December of 1949, when David O. Cauldwell (in Sexology Magazine) described the case of a girl who "obsessively" wanted to be a man: Cauldwell defined this person as a *psychopathic transsexual* and the condition from which this young girl was suffering was classified by Cauldwell as *Psychopathia Trans-Sexualis* (Cauldwell 1949), an expression which explicitly refers to the title of Krafft-Ebing's *Psychopathia Sexualis*.

In any case, the transsexual signifier definitively earns its place in the history of "science" only a few years later. In 1953 a paper entitled "Transvestitism and Transsexualism" was published in the International Journal of Sexology. The author was Harry Benjamin[9], a gerontologist and sexologist, who had been a student of Eugen Steinach. Benjamin wrote this article after "the case of Christine Jorgensen focused attention on the problem as never before" (Benjamin 1966, 25). In fact, two years earlier, in 1951, in Denmark an operation of "*sex reassignment surgery*" was carried out by Christian Hamburger, Georg K. Sturup and E. Dahl - Iversen, who, in 1953, described the operation in the *Journal of the American Medical Association* (Hamburger, Stürup, & Dahl-Iversen 1953). This surgery was not only legal, but also attracted much attention from the media:

> "And so, an unknown George Jorgensen became the world-famous Christine Jorgensen, not the first to undergo such surgery, but the first whose transformation was publicized so widely that the news of this therapeutic possibility spread to the farthest corners of the earth.
>
> The facts of her case, which she herself related with good insight and restraint - unfortunately only in a magazine article - caused emotions to run high among those similarly affected. Suddenly they understood and "found" themselves and saw hope for a release from an unhappy existence[10]. Among the public, there was praise for Christine for the courage of her convictions; also there was disbelief with criticism of her physicians, as well as outright condemnation on moral grounds. Such emotional reactions in lay circles reached the height of absurdity and bigotry when Christine was once barred from a New York restaurant and night club as a guest" (Benjamin 1966, 12)

The name chosen by Jorgensen is extremely indicative of the relationship that she, and more generally the transsexual, will establish with the surgeon from then on. In fact, this name is nothing more than the feminization of her surgeon's name : "*Dr Hamburger was the man to whom I owed so much, above all others. I transposed his first name, Christian, into the feminine Christine*" (Jorgensen 1967, 110). It is evident in her words that the primary object of the "transference" becomes the surgeon. The handover from psychiatry to surgery is thus definitively accomplished. On the other hand, Benjamin's words seem very interesting for another reason, if one considers that, in the wake of the media success of the Jorgensen case, there was a significant increase in applications for sex change in the late fifties. (Frignet 2000, 41) Indeed, in the same year as the publication of Harry Benjamin's famous book "The Transsexual Phenomenon", Johns Hopkins opened the first University-affiliated, multidisciplinary Gender Clinic offering sex reassignment to transsexuals seeking treatment (Green & Money 1969), and more than 40 academic centers in the U.S. would later open gender clinics as well (Denny 1998; 2002)[11].

---

[9] Rejecting psychotherapy as a valid form of treatment, Benjamin helped to pioneer hormonal and surgical methods that are still used today [Russel 2013]. In acknowledgment of his early advocacy of the medical treatment of transsexualism, in 1979 the newly formed Harry Benjamin International Gender Dysphoria Association (HBIGDA), which would go on to develop standards of care (SOC) for treating trans individuals, was named in his honor. This Association's name has been more recently replaced by the new World Professionals Association for Transgender Health (WPATH).

[10] This is exactly what we meant before when we said that "psychiatric discursive regimes turn out to be a way to frame subjects' experiences, making them meaningful to themselves and others, and finally for them to interpret their own identities". We will say something more about this later, discussing the nature of the condition from a phenomenological/existential point of view.

[11] On the basis of a follow-up study published in 1979 by Meyer and Reter [1979], claiming that SRS confers no objective advantage in terms of social rehabilitation, the Johns Hopkins Gender Identity Clinic was finally

THE AMERICAN PSYCHIATRIC ASSOCIATION'S (APA) *DIAGNOSTIC AND STATISTICAL MANUAL OF MENTAL DISORDERS (DSM)*

In reality, however, despite the publication of Benjamin's book and the increasingly evident and dominant inclusion of the gender variant condition within medical discourse, for several years this condition still remained on the sidelines of the official classification systems produced by the APA, the U.S. psychiatric association. Since much psychiatric theorizing of that time continued to conflate sexual orientation and gender identity, many physicians and psychiatrists did not recognize a specific diagnostic category, criticized the use of surgery and hormones to —in their view incorrectly—treat people suffering from what they perceived to be either a severe neurotic, or psychotic, delusional condition in need of psychotherapy and "reality testing" (Drescher 2014). Only in 1980 did it become part of the third edition of the DSM, the famous Diagnostic and Statistical Manual of Mental Disorders, exactly when homosexuality, at least in its "syntonic" variant, was removed. The decision to include transsexualism in the DSM was based on the research and clinical contributions of John Money[12], Harry Benjamin, Robert J. Stoller[13], and Richard Green[14]. The official inclusion was accomplished through a process of "multiplication" of the condition. More precisely, three different categories were considered: a variant manifesting in childhood, the so-called *Gender Identity Disorder of Childhood*, another manifesting in adulthood, named *"Transsexualism"* (which was characterized by a persistent discomfort and sense of inappropriateness about the assigned sex in a person who has reached puberty, and by a persistent preoccupation, for at least two years, with getting rid of one's primary and

---

closed in the same year. After this closure, the activities of several other university centers ceased [Dallas 1998]. This, despite the evident methodological weakness that was soon identified in the above mentioned follow-up study.

[12] John Money (1921-2006), a psychologist and sexologist, had a very important role in the historical process we are considering here. He first began publishing his scientific papers regarding gender identity development in the 1950s [e.g., Money 1955; Money et al. 1957]. He coined the term "gender role". Based on studies of children born with intersex conditions, he theorized that one's inner feeling of being male or female was primarily determined by external, environmental factors.

[13] Robert J. Stoller (1925-1991) was Professor of Psychiatry at the University of California, Los Angeles, Researcher at the Gender Identity Clinic at the same University, and psychoanalyst of the Los Angeles Psychoanalytic Society. He was in the past, and to some extent still is today [Green, 2010], one of the main points of reference for researchers studying "Gender Identity" issues. He was deeply influenced by the theoretical formulations that were produced at that time within the psychoanalytical movement, particularly that of the so-called "middle group" (DW Winnicott, MMR Khan, R. Spitz) and the North American group (M. Mahler, P. Greenacre, RR Greenson, H. Lichtenstein), as well as the Ego Psychology of Hartmann, Kris and Loewenstein. Stoller was among the first to take up the challenge of transsexualism, providing , first, a psychoanalytical interpretation of its development. [Stoller 1968] Actually, beyond the psychoanalytical scenario, he also took into account the scientific input from other disciplines, organizing his observations within a broader theoretical framework: biology, genetics, physiology and pathophysiology, as well as ethology and cognitive science were constant points of reference for him. Stoller traced the origins of male transsexualism back to a non-emergence from primary symbiosis between infant and mother; a phase, he postulated, normally present in the earliest stages of development (*Primary Femininity Stage*, always present in both sexes). He said that this failed *dis-identification* from the mother, favored by an absent father, would result very early in life, possibly by age one or two, in an a-conflictual identification of the child with the mother, and so in the production of a *feminine core gender identity*. [Vitelli 2001]

[14] Richard Green (born 6 June 1936) is an important American sexologist, psychiatrist, lawyer and author specializing in homosexuality and transsexualism, specifically gender identity. Green is the founding editor of the Archives of Sexual Behavior [1971], and served as Editor until 2001. He is also the founding president of the International Academy of Sex Research [1975], which made the Archives its official publication. He served on the American Psychiatric Association DSM-IV Subcommittee on Gender Identity Disorders.

secondary sex characteristics and acquiring the sex characteristics of the other sex), and, finally, a third category called "*Atypical Gender Identity Disorder*". All the identified conditions were placed within the broader category of "*Psychosexual Disorders.*"

In the revised edition, published in 1987, the transsexual category was classified as an Axis II disorder[15], that is within the category of "*disorders typically beginning in infancy, childhood or adolescence*". The authors explained that this move was justified because the first signs of the condition usually appeared at an early age. Among the most important new features introduced in this revised edition, surely, was the addition of a further diagnostic category for cross-gender identified individuals who did not pursue sex reassignment. This new category was named *Gender Identity Disorder of Adolescence or Adulthood, Non-Transsexual Type (GIDAANT)*. Finally, in place of the previous *Atypical Gender Identity Disorder*, a diagnosis of *Gender Identity Disorder Not Otherwise Specified (GIDNOS)* was used for those who did not fulfill criteria for the specific gender identity disorder.

For the fourth edition, published in 1994, the APA Subcommittee which had been specifically delegated to the revision of the diagnostic criteria of the disorder, came up with two main recommendations: the first was to completely eliminate the *GIDAANT* category, because it was not considered sufficiently reliable; the second was to put together the disorder diagnosed in childhood and adolescence with that of adulthood. Starting, then, from the fourth edition of the manual the term *transsexualism* and its differentiation with *GIDAANT* disappeared and a single category, named "*Gender Identity Disorder*" (GID), was considered. The new category was moved from the section "Disorders which usually first appear in infancy, childhood and adolescence" and placed within the superordinate category "*Sexual and Gender Identity Disorders*" on Axis I. This move was justified by the frequent late onset of the disorder, in early or mid-adulthood. Probably, however, one of the most significant changes in the manual was the introduction of a specific new criterion, which referred to "clinically significant distress or impairment in social, occupational, or other important areas of functioning", in some way caused by the mismatch between biological sex and the subjective experience of belonging to a particular gender. In reality, this new criterion was added to almost half of the Manual diagnostic criteria sets, in response to concerns previously expressed (Klein 1978; Spitzer & Williams 1982; Wakefield 1992a) that the DSM criteria were overly inclusive: i.e. it was added with the aim of minimizing false positive diagnoses in situations in which the symptom criteria did not necessarily indicate pathology (Spitzer & Wakefield 1999)[16]. The addition of this criterion, which is still today present within the current criteria set for the new *Gender Dysphoria* category in DSM-5, is interesting because it suggests that people who are not characterized by such distress or impairment could not be

---

[15] Previous DSM editions were organized on a five axes structure: the first referred to Clinical Syndromes (Schizophrenia, Mood Disorders, etc.) ; the second axis contemplated Developmental Disorders and Personality Disorders; the third indicated the Physical Conditions which play a role in the development, continuance, or exacerbation of Axis I and II Disorders; the fourth concerned the Severity of Psychosocial Stressors; lastly, on the final axis, the clinician had to rate the person's level of functioning both at the present time and the highest level within the previous year. The new Edition, DSM-5, recently published [APA 2013], has eliminated this multiaxial structure.

[16] In reality, the clinical significance criterion was a version of a criterion that was used to deal with potential false positives in three DSM-IIIR categories: social phobia, simple phobia, and obsessive-compulsive disorder. Because mild forms of the symptoms of these three disorders were thought to be common in the community, even in cases where there was no disorder, a criterion requiring marked distress or impairment in social functioning was added, although the term "clinically significant" was not used.

regarded as suffering from a mental disorder[17]. We shall come back to this issue later. Again with reference to the changes made in the fourth edition, different subtypes were considered on the basis of specific sexual orientation because this was supposed to provide prognostic value for treatment-related outcomes: in fact, both biological males who maintain that they belong to the female gender (in trans studies these subjects are still commonly referred to as MtF) and biologically female subjects who feel they belong to the male gender (commonly referred to as FtM), were differentiated with regard to sexual orientation as having a sexual attraction for subjects of different/same sex, for subjects of both sexes or for a total absence of sexual "interest"[18].

The next updated edition of the manual - DSM IV-TR (APA 2000) – did not add any specific variation to the diagnostic criteria set of the condition and its place within the manual, apart from some characteristics belonging to certain sexuality-related subtypes. In fact, Ray Blanchard's studies (1989a, 1989b, 1991, 1993a, 1993b), too, postulated the frequent occurrence in the history of biologically male adults sexually attracted to female subjects, or to both males and females, or to neither, of an erotic arousal associated with the thought or image of themselves as members of the female sex (autogynephilia), often with a picture, at least referring to the past history of the subject, of transvestite fetishism[19].

Lastly, as we said before, a new edition of the DSM – DSM-5 - has been recently published (APA 2013). Again as we said before, its preparation and drafting were accompanied by a lively debate on whether or not it is legal to include the condition within the ranks of Mental Disorders. Many LGBTs, and others, maintained that perpetuating DSM-IV-TR's GID diagnoses in DSM-5 would further stigmatize and damage transgender individuals. On the other hand, other members of the movement and advocates of the trans community, as well as several members of the scientific community expressed concern that deleting GID from the DSM would lead third party payers to deny access to care for those transgender adults already struggling with inadequate private and public sources of healthcare

---

[17] The new DSM-5 states: "*Gender dysphoria* refers to the distress that may accompany the incongruence between one's experienced or expressed gender and one's assigned gender. Although not all individuals will experience distress as a result of such incongruence, many are distressed if the desired physical interventions by means of hormones and/or surgery are not available. The current term [Gender Dysphoria] is more descriptive than the previous term *gender identity disorder* and focuses on dysphoria as the clinical problem, not identity per se" [APA 2013, 451]. Anyway the "distress or impairment" criterion continues to appear controversial, because if the manual seems to define gender dysphoria as distressful in itself, i.e. to consider the distress as "inherent" in the condition, then this criterion is redundant. Moreover, as Peggy T. Cohen-Kettenis and Friedemann Pfäfflin stated in a paper of theirs: "Unfortunately, if one does not consider their condition as inherently distressful, a DSM-IV-TR GID diagnosis cannot presently be given to applicants for sex reassignment. This implies that well-functioning applicants who report being free of distress would, for this reason, not be eligible for sex reassignment" [2010, 504]. Evidently a sort of pragmatic approach may have suggested keeping this criterion. As the authors themselves said: "a diagnosis without a distress criterion [...] may not be considered suitable for the reimbursement of treatment". After all, as I said before, such practical purposes led the DSM-5 Work Group on Sexual and Gender Identity Disorder to maintain the condition within the manual.

[18] The usefulness of sexuality related GID specifiers and their prognostic value for treatment related outcomes remain highly controversial. For a review of this issue, see Kohen-Kettenis and Pfäfflin, 2010, esp. pp. 507-508.

[19] The affinity of this "clinical" feature to Havelock Ellis' previously described *sexo-aesthetic inversion* is clear. Despite the criticism of the World Professional Association for Transgender Health [WPATH] on the grounds of lack of empirical evidence for the theory [Gijs & Carroll 2011; Knudson, De Cuypere & Bockting 2011], and the highly controversial nature of this feature [Moser 2010; Serano 2010], the *paraphilia working group for DSM* has included autogynephilia and autoandrophilia (the analogous term which refers to a person assigned female at birth) as subtypes of transvestite disorder. Similarly any reference to autogynephilia has been removed from the Gender Dysphoria category.

funding for medical and surgical treatment. The result of this debate was to keep the condition in the manual. Its new name is *Gender Dysphoria* and its diagnostic criteria are:

> A marked incongruence between one's experienced/expressed gender and assigned gender of at least 6 months' duration as manifested by at least two of the following: 1. A marked incongruence between one's experienced/expressed gender and primary and/or secondary sex characteristics (or in young adolescents, the anticipated secondary sex characteristics). 2. A strong desire to be rid of one's primary and/or secondary sex characteristics because of a marked incongruence with one's experienced/expressed gender (or in young adolescents, a desire to prevent the development of the anticipated secondary characteristics). 3. A strong desire for the primary and/or secondary sex characteristics of the other gender. 4. A strong desire to be of the other gender (or some alternative gender different from one's assigned gender). 5. A strong desire to be treated as the other gender (or some alternative gender different from one's assigned gender). 6. A strong conviction that one has the typical feelings and reactions of the other gender (or some alternative gender different from one's assigned gender).
>
> The condition is associated with clinically significant distress or impairment in social, occupational, or other important areas of functioning.
>
> (APA 2013, 452)

Apart from the specific criteria listed above, the changes that have been made are pretty significant, as they are a compromise solution between different possibilities that had been advanced until then. Among the most important are the following: removal from the sexual disorder chapter and placement in a separate category, no longer bundled with Paraphilias and Sexual Dysfunction (to reduce stigma); a new name where the deletion of the word "disorder" aimed at reducing and "softening" the "psychopathological nature" of the condition as well as minimizing stigmatization of transgender individuals[20]; the acknowledgment of the possibility of non-binary gender identities and expression; the recognition of the possibility of a concomitant disorder of sex development (e.g., congenital adrenogenital disorder, congenital adrenal hyperplasia or androgen insensitivity syndrome), which was not previously contemplated in DSM-IV TR; the removal of subtyping on the basis of sexual orientation; finally, the addition of a *posttransition specifier* to identify individuals who have undergone at least one medical procedure or treatment to support the new gender assignment, and are therefore no longer gender dysphoric but still require access to care for ongoing hormone treatment or other forms of therapy, such as plastic surgery, psychological counselling, and so on.

On the whole, it is evident that the work of mediation between various stakeholders was remarkable. Nevertheless, Gender Identity Variants, according to the APA, continue to be interpreted as a manifestation of a Mental Disorder.

---

[20] *Gender Dysphoria* (from a Greek root for distress), an old diagnostic label originally proposed by Norman Fisk [1973], emphasizes the distress derived from gender assignment and associated sex characteristics, and removes any reference to problems of personal identity (i.e., to cross-gender identification in itself) as was the case in DSM IV-TR *Gender Identity Disorder*.

THE TIMES THEY ARE A-CHANGIN': THE WORLD HEALTH ORGANIZATION'S (WHO) PROCESS OF REVISION OF THE INTERNATIONAL STATISTICAL CLASSIFICATION OF DISEASE AND RELATED HEALTH PROBLEMS (ICD)

The current World Health Organization (WHO) process of revising the *International Statistical Classification of Disease and Related Health Problems (ICD)*, which has already started and will continue until 2017, seems to be going in a very different direction from that expressed by the APA. The current ICD-10 (WHO 1992) considers gender identity variants within the mental disorder section under the broader category of "disorders of adult behavior and personality" and includes five diagnoses: transsexualism, dual-role transvestism, gender identity disorder of childhood, other gender identity disorders, and gender identity disorder unspecified[21]. The ICD-10 diagnosis of transsexualism is an issue about which the WHO has received much interest and many communications from various stakeholders. Many activists, several countries, the Council of Europe Commissioner for Human Rights (2009) and the European Parliament (2011) have insisted that issues related to transgender identity should not be classified as mental disorders in ICD-11. For example, the European Parliament resolution "roundly condemns the fact that homosexuality, bisexuality and transsexuality are still regarded as mental illnesses by several countries, including some within the EU, and calls on states to combat this; calls in particular for the depsychiatrization of the transsexual transgender journey, for free choice of care providers, for changing identity to be simplified, and for costs to be met by social security schemes". The document goes on to "call on the Commission and the World Health Organization to withdraw gender identity disorders from the list of mental and behavioral disorders, and to ensure a non-pathologizing reclassification in the negotiations on the 11th version of the International Classification of Diseases ((ICD-11)". Moreover, The ICD Working Group on Sexual Disorders and Sexual Health also received proposals calling for depathologization and removal of transgender diagnoses from the mental disorders section of the classification from a number of associations and professional organizations. These included the *Agnodice Foundation* (Switzerland), *Aktion Transsexualität und Menschenrecht* (Germany), *Global Action for Trans Equality* (GATE), *LGBT Denmark, Société Française d'Etudes et de prise en Charge du Transsexualisme* (SoFECT, France), and the *World Professional Association for Transgender Health* (WPATH). Also as a result of these requests, in addition to recommending a name change to *Gender Incongruence*, the Working Group on Sexual Disorders and Sexual Health has strongly recommended that the diagnoses be removed from the ICD-11's section on mental and behavioral disorders and possibly be put in an entirely separate chapter, or perhaps in a new chapter entitled "Sexual Health and Sexual Disorders".

---

[21] In ICD-6 (1948), there was no reference to the diagnosis of transsexualism, nor did it appear in ICD-7 (1955); somehow, sexual orientation and gender identity seemed to be conflated in the *homosexuality* category as an inclusive term [that is, as an example] for the diagnostic category *sexual deviation*, which was further classified as a pathological personality under the supra category of *disorders of character, behavior, and intelligence*. A diagnostic label of *transvestitism* (a label that was clearly derived from Hirschfeld's terminology) was introduced for the first time in ICD 8 (1965), although its exact meaning was not specified. ICD-8 (1965), reflecting changing clinical and theoretical views, separated *sexual deviations* (including homosexuality) from *personality disorders*. Further change occurred in ICD-9 (1975), where *transvestitism* was replaced by *transvestism*, and a new separate and exclusionary diagnosis of *transsexualism* was added.

This is the way Jack Drescher, Peggy Cohen-Kettenis and Sam Winter (2012) explain the rationale for such changes:

"The combined stigmatization of being transgender and of having a mental disorder diagnosis creates a doubly burdensome situation for this population that contributes adversely to their health status as well as to their enjoyment and attainment of human rights. For example, transgender people are much more likely to be denied care in general medical or community-based settings given the perception that they must be treated by psychiatric specialists, even for conditions that have nothing to do with being transgender. Difficulty in obtaining transition-related services has also led some transgender people, out of desperation, to expose themselves to significant harm, including HIV infection, through the use of black or grey market hormones, sometimes injected, and thus creating a larger public health problem. In addition, there are unique circumstances in the case of this particular diagnosis that relate to the ability of a person to be viewed as competent to make certain legal decisions. Government agencies in many countries have demonstrated prejudice in extending recognition of change in legal gender status on identity documents such as passports and drivers' licenses. Courts may often rule against transgender people in child custody decisions when their mental disorder diagnosis is used by an ex-spouse to call their competence as parents into question. These are some of the factors that contribute to persuasive human rights and WHO mission-related arguments for moving the category out of the mental disorders section. Given that the WHO's mission is the attainment by all peoples of the highest possible level of health, the WHO must consider whether a policy that appears to be having adverse health (or human rights) consequences for an identifiable group is inconsistent with its mission". (573)

But what kind of scientific discipline is psychiatry, if it is to define its objects on the basis of considerations like these? What is a real mental disorder? How can it be exactly fixed from an ontological and epistemological point of view?

THE DEFINITION OF MENTAL DISORDER: A SLIPPERY SURFACE

Although the trend has been to depathologize gender nonconformity and remove it from the ranks of mental disorders, as we have seen, it is still currently included in a handbook called "Diagnostic and Statistical Manual of Mental Disorders"; therefore, it is considered a form of mental disorder, at least by the American Psychiatric Association. But, the question arises, what actually is a "mental disorder"? The debate on the legality of the inclusion of "gender identity variance" within the ranks of mental disorders is reminiscent of the events that preceded and accompanied the exclusion of homosexuality from the DSM at first, and from the ICD later, in the last century (Meyer-Bahlburg 2010). Today, as then, such a matter leads us inevitably to challenge the status, on a conceptual level, of what is commonly meant by "mental disorder"[22]. Clearly it is necessary to define this, and also what criteria are necessary to label a given psychological condition as a mental disorder.

Strange as it may seem, it was the debate on the issue of homosexuality which led us to question the very nature of mental disorder for the first time, extensively and thoroughly, both on ontological and epistemological levels (Meyer-Bahlburg 2010; Bolton 2008; 2013).

Historically, the depathologization of homosexuality was determined by the convergence of several factors (Drescher 2010): Firstly, a growing number of scientific studies, which had actually been initiated several years before, demonstrated the spread of a homosexual orientation in non-clinical populations of subjects (Kinsey, Pomeroy, & Martin 1948; Kinsey, Pomeroy, Martin, & Gebhard 1953), and the absence of psychopathological symptoms in homosexual samples (Hooker 1957); secondly, the emergence of the anti-psychiatry movement, which affirmed the nature of psychiatry as a social institution, merely masquerading as a medical discipline, but really charged with the social control of minorities (Szasz 1960); finally, the actions of homosexual activists (Drescher 2010) which played a very important role, somehow forcing the APA to remove homosexuality from the DSM in 1973. In fact, after the 1969 Stonewall riots in New York City, gay and lesbian activists, believing psychiatric theories to be a major contributor to homosexual social stigma, disrupted the 1970 and 1971 annual meetings of the APA. Moreover, during the 1971 and 1972 annual APA meetings some gay activists and John Fryer, a medical doctor who appeared as Dr. H Anonymous, a "homosexual psychiatrist", explained to psychiatrists, many of whom were hearing this for the first time, the effects, and in particular the stigma caused by the diagnosis of "homosexuality" (Gittings 2008; Kameny 2009; Silverstein 2009). After these events, the APA embarked upon an internal deliberative process of considering the question of whether homosexuality should remain a psychiatric diagnosis. When Robert Spitzer, the DSM III task force chairman and head of a subcommittee looking into the issue, reviewed the real characteristics of mental disorders, he "concluded that, with the exception of homosexuality and perhaps some of the other 'sexual deviations,' they (the mental disorders) all regularly caused subjective distress or were associated with generalized impairment in social effectiveness of functioning" (Spitzer 1981, 211). Having arrived at this definition of mental disorder, the Nomenclature Committee agreed that homosexuality was not one (Bayer 1981; Drescher 2003; Drescher & Merlino 2007; Hire 2002; Rosario 2003; Sbordone 2003; Spitzer 1981; Stoller et al. 1973). Several other APA committees and deliberative bodies then reviewed their work and approved that decision. Finally, in December 1973, the APA's Board of Trustees (BOT) voted to remove homosexuality from the DSM. Nevertheless, a number of psychiatrists from the psychoanalytical community (Bieber 1987; Socarides 1995) challenged this decision and demanded to hold a referendum within the Association to endorse or invalidate the Board's deliberation. The referendum was actually held and 58% of voters validated the decision taken by the Board: so homosexuality was finally removed from the list of mental disorders, although initially only in the egosyntonic variant, i.e. in a manner limited to those circumstances in which the homosexual

---

[22] Some years ago, Allen Frances pointed out: "Alas, I have read dozens of definitions of mental disorder (and helped to write one) and I can't say that any have the slightest value whatever. Historically, conditions have become mental disorders by accretion and practical necessity, not because they met some independent set of operationalized definitional criteria. Indeed, the concept of mental disorder is so amorphous, protean, and heterogeneous that it inherently defies definition. This is a hole at the center of psychiatric classification." [Frances 2010, 5]

orientation did not lead to any form of discomfort. (Bayer 1981; Drescher 2010)[23] Somehow, this event represents a real watershed in the history of psychiatry: in fact, as well as determining the removal of a condition that up until that moment had been unfairly considered an expression of a mental disorder, it brought with it the start of a serious reflection on the more precise definition of the concept of mental disorder, which, in reality years later still continues to be highly problematic. In any case, the consequences of those far-off events continue to be felt even today, as a true "thorn in the side" of psychiatric knowledge, if it is true that, even many years later, in 2008, Kenneth S. Kendler and Peter Zachar (2008) had this to say:

> "Psychiatrists have had to endure intense criticism for declassifying homosexuality as a mental disorder by taking a vote of the membership. Is psychiatric nosology a scientific endeavor or the expression of shifting political winds? Psychiatry's troubles in this regard are not limited to sexual orientation. Is cross-dressing a disorder? Are oppositional-defiant adolescents mentally ill? Should subthreshold conditions be medicated? It helps psychiatry's case that astronomers held a vote in 2006 to decide whether Pluto is really a planet, but the astronomers' decision to rewrite the definition of a planet has not removed lingering doubts about the scientific legitimacy of psychiatric nosology"
>
> (Kendler & Zachar 2008, 368)[24]

This is extremely important: indeed, it would seem that those distant events have threatened the very foundations of psychiatry as a scientific discipline. Simply highlighting the effects of the inclusion of specific psychological conditions within the ranks of mental disorders, and recognizing that value judgments could play a part in defining certain psychological or behavioral traits as pathological, have determined the search for objective criteria, a rigorous descriptive, neo-kraepelinian approach and a constant monitoring of the possible interference of these value judgments. As Robert Kendell stated:

> "The most fundamental issue, and also the most contentious one, is whether disease and illness are normative concepts based on value judgment, or whether they are value-free scientific terms; In other words, whether they are biomedical terms or socio-political ones" (Kendell 1986, 25)

Specifically in order to define psychiatry as a scientific discipline[25] and not just a "myth", as Thomas Szasz defined it (Szasz 1960), but also to prevent its misuse, Spitzer's

---

[23] Homosexuality was finally removed from the Manual edited by the American Psychiatric Association in 1987, in the third revised edition [APA 1987]. It was deleted from the Handbook prepared by the World Health Organization in 1992, starting from the X Edition of the 'International Classification of Diseases' [ICD].

[24] The authors have recently come back to this issue, comparing the events related to the elimination of homosexuality from the DSM and what happened a few years ago in the astronomical field with the removal of Pluto from the list of planets [Zachar & Kendler 2012]

[25] Regarding this issue, some time ago Somogy Varga stated: "The concept of mental disorder is at the foundation of psychiatry. While adequately defining mental disorder is a notoriously thorny issue with far reaching implications for psychiatric research, diagnosis, socio-political interventions, at least since the publication of the DSM-III there has been a consensus of the fact that a convincing definition of mental disorder is required. In addition, for many, the credibility of psychiatry as a medical discipline to a certain extent depends on a convincing definition." [Varga 2011, 1]

"distress" and impairment", as we have seen before, have been, since the third edition of the American manual (APA 1980), the main criteria by which to establish the legality of the inclusion of specific psychological conditions within the ranks of mental disorders. With minor revisions, the reference to these criteria was also maintained in DSM-III-R (APA 1987), DSM-IV (APA 1994) and DSM-IV-TR (APA 2000).

The introduction to *DSM-5* includes the following definition of mental disorder, which presents some interesting new elements:

> "Although *no definition can capture all aspects of all disorders in the range contained in DSM-5*, the following elements are required:
> A mental disorder is a syndrome characterized by clinically significant disturbance in an individual's cognition, emotion regulation, or behavior that reflects a dysfunction in the psychological, biological, or developmental processes underlying mental functioning. *Mental disorders are usually associated with significant distress or disability* in social, occupational, or other important activities. An expectable or culturally approved response to a common stressor or loss, such as the death of a loved one, is not a mental disorder. Socially deviant behavior (e.g. political, religious, or sexual) and conflicts that are primarily between the individual and society are not mental disorders unless the deviance or conflict results from a dysfunction in the individual, as described above". (*my italics*) (APA 2013, 20)

Firstly, as had already happened in the case of DSM-IV and DSM-IV-TR, the authors stated that "*no definition can capture all aspects of all disorders in the range contained in DSM-5*", in other words that, as the previous two editions of the manual probably pointed out more clearly, "*no definition adequately specifies precise boundaries for the concept "mental disorder*" (APA 1994; 2000). A statement that in itself could turn out to be quite problematic[26], although, indeed, it corresponds to reality. Moreover, unlike in the previous

---

[26] Although the topic may seem futile, resembling the medieval disputes about the nature of "universals", it is clear that this topic is really worthwhile. Phillips, et al. [2012], within their "pluralogue" paper, have identified several possibilities: 1) A "*realistic*" stance, for which mental disorders are something "real", existing "out there" independent of me, within the cerebral structure; they can be intersubjectively appreciated and elucidated as they truly are. This perspective, at least from our point of view, is hardly sustainable. In fact, it tends to deny the presence of value-judgments in the definition of a mental disorder; but the issue is that if on the one hand it seems obvious that any psychic manifestation has its own neuroanatomical correlates, on the other its qualification as pathological rests on value judgments which are irreducible to the physical level: We could also identify a biological substrate underlying a specific psychological condition, but its evaluation as pathological or not is clearly an independent matter. 2) A "*nominalist*" position which denies the existence of "mental disorders" as *universals* (something that can be instantiated by different entities). Authors who espouse a nominalist stance admit that there is "real psychopathology out there but we have no guarantee that their diagnostic constructs sort it out correctly" [5]. For example, we could say that there is no one prototype of "gender dysphoria", but rather a group of existential (clinical) conditions related to "gender non conformity". On the other hand, the very elusiveness of mental disorder categories leads some authors who espouse the nominalist position to recognize the arbitrariness of the inclusion of certain conditions within the ranks of mental disorders [e.g., Zachar and Lobello, in Philips, et al. 2012, 5].3) A "*constructionist*" stance which considers mental disorders not as actual diseases but as mere social constructs, i.e. subjective and culturally driven. This stance, at least from our point of view, is the most reasonable, although it produces considerable problems with regard to the definition of the boundary between normality and pathology. As Allen Frances stated some years ago: "We must accept that our diagnostic classification is the result of historical accretion and accident without any real underlying system or scientific necessity. The rules for entry have varied over time and have rarely been very rigorous. Our mental disorders are no more than fallible social constructs (but nonetheless useful ones if understood and applied properly)". [Frances 2010, 6] 4) A "*pragmatic*" perspective which considers the needs of the multiple user groups (researchers, patients,

editions, the two fundamental criteria identified by Spitzer, i.e. "*significant distress or disability in social, occupational, or other important activities*", are evaluated as not necessarily to be *always* present: In fact, the current edition of the Manual states: "Mental disorders are *usually* associated with significant distress or disability in social, occupational, or other important activities". Evidently, these two criteria do not define a mental disorder by themselves, but rather constitute a quality, a characteristic that may or may not be present. If in medicine, disease is defined by the knowledge of the underlying specific pathophysiological processes, i.e. diseased organs and pathological anatomy, if not the etiology of the symptomatic picture, in psychiatry this knowledge is absent: here you are moving exclusively on the level of syndrome; what defines the disorder is the frequent simultaneous occurrence of specific symptoms, the possible similarity of developments over time (prognosis) and responses to different treatments. A mental disorder is a "syndrome", that is to say "a collection of clinical manifestations coupled with deviance from the "norm"" (Broome 2006, 305). Yes, but what kind of norm is it? In the psychiatric field, far from being able to refer, directly or indirectly, to biological or anatomical data, what defines the disorders are still elements such as thoughts, feelings, behaviors, beliefs, desires, motivations: in other words, all elusive elements that refer to subjective experiences, in respect of which obviously establishing a line of demarcation between the "norm" and the "disease" is a complex and problematic issue. The question is how to identify criteria that can strongly withstand the charge of arbitrariness, of violent action aimed at marginalizing minorities who are characterized by different mental functioning and behavior. The attempt to establish a boundary between the "norm" and mental illness has been made in recent years, inspired by the evolutionary theories which, as we saw before, were already present in Krafft-Ebing's ideas. Although, as we have seen, the American manual tries to limit the influence of moral or cultural references, the problem of drawing the line between normal and abnormal is particularly evident in those conditions which are implicitly or explicitly subject to moral or cultural judgment: e.g. gender identity variants, but also pedophilia, antisocial personality disorder, alcoholism, suicide, persistent minor depressive disorders. In a series of papers starting in the 1970s Boorse has developed a detailed naturalistic (value-free) account of the concept of disease. His aim has been to show that, while medical practice may be value-laden, medical theory is at heart value free, and, hence, scientific. More exactly, he has proposed a theory based on evolutionary and statistical conceptions of health which he dubbed the *Bio-Statistical Model* (*BST*). According to his theory: "1. The reference class is a natural class of organisms of uniform functional design; specifically, an age group of a sex of a species. 2. A normal function of a part or process within members of the reference class is a statistically typical contribution by it to their individual survival and reproduction. 3. Health in a member of the reference class is normal functional ability: the readiness of each internal part to perform all its normal functions on typical occasions with at least typical efficiency. 4. A disease is a type of internal state which impairs health, i.e. reduces one or more functional

---

insurance companies, etc.) and the various consequences not only in the field of care but also in administrative, insurance and legal practices. Sometimes this approach appears to be a sort of "utilitarianism": for example, as we have seen, exactly this kind of approach prompted the Workgroup on Sexual and Gender Identity Disorders to retain Gender Variance within the DSM, trying to balance the necessity of reducing stigma and the necessity of maintaining access to care. 5) A "*nihilist*" stance, mainly expressed by proponents of anti-psychiatry who, as said before, state that mental disorders are only a medical "myth", and that psychiatry is a social institution, merely masquerading as a medical discipline, but really charged with the social control of minorities. [Szasz 1960]

abilities below typical efficiency". (1977, 555). Although, following his thought, such a definition would be value-free, i.e. it puts aside any reference to cultural factors or value judgment (1997), the identification of specific classes of reference for the definition of a diseased state produces several paradoxes: not least, once again, as Rachel Cooper pointed out (2005, 17), that related to the pathologization of homosexuality. Boorse himself recognizes the validity of this point, stating, however, that defining a condition as pathological does not necessarily mean that it must receive medical treatment. (Boorse 1997, 11-12) A really paradoxical statement, as Somogy Varga rightly pointed out, if it is true "that the account of disease is deflated, and quite far from our normal use of the concept of disease, which includes that a disease is actually a bad thing to have" (2011, 4), in other words, by definition, something that implies and requires health restoration, that is to say a cure!

On the same wavelength, another naturalistic, but more detailed, medical model of disease has been proposed by Jerome C. Wakefield with his "hybrid naturalism". According to the New York University Professor, a mental disorder can be defined as a "harmful dysfunction", "where "harmful" is a value term, referring to conditions judged negative by sociocultural standards, and "dysfunction" is a scientific factual term". (2007, 149):

> "A condition is a disorder if and only if (a) the condition causes some harm or deprivation of benefit to the person as judged by the standards of the person's culture (the value criterion), and (b) the condition results from the inability of some internal mechanism to perform its natural function, wherein a natural function is an effect that is part of the evolutionary explanation of the existence and structure of the mechanism (the explanatory criterion)" (Wakefield 1992, 384).

In this way, the author considers a comprehensive model which takes into account both aspects: the sociocultural standards and a more elusive "factual term based on evolutionistic biology that refers to the failure of an internal mechanism in the execution of one of its natural functions"[27], i.e., the physical cerebral structures (the hardware) as well as the mental functions and dispositions, such as, for example, the motivational, cognitive, affective and perceptual mechanisms (the software). (Wakefield 2004) On the basis of these assumptions, Wakefield himself, in a paper written with Michael B. First (Wakefield and First 2003, reported in Meyer Bahlburg 2010), stated that "Gender Identity Disorder" cannot be considered as a mental disorder, since it lacks one of the two necessary conditions: the impairment of functioning and/or the subjective distress (i.e., the "harmful" component). Therefore, it should be considered rather as a "simple dysfunction" (sic!) but, as stated by Meyer-Bahlburg (2010), the definition of "dysfunction" is the same as, and no less problematic than, that of "pathology". In any case, this way of thinking seems to have persuaded the DSM 5 Gender Identity Subworkgroup to retain the Gender Variant category within the Manual, but at the same time to outline the necessity of a *clinically significant distress or impairment in social, occupational, or other important areas of functioning*. The problematic nature of Wakefield's proposal is evident when one considers that, on the one hand, the reference to contextual elements and therefore to the historical and cultural process

---

[27] Regarding the elusive nature of the "dysfunction" component, Derek Bolton had this to say: "The point is rather that for the vast majority of syndromes in the [psychiatric] manuals we *just do not know* whether they involve failure of a natural designed function or whether they are designed or acquired strategic responses to environmental conditions, or indeed whether they are designed adaptive responses". [Bolton 2008, 131]

seems important, on the other hand their borders appear difficult to draw. What kind of sociocultural standards must be considered? Western standards? Are we sure that they are the same everywhere?

Moreover, as Derek Bolton stated some years ago:

> "Concerning the judgment of abnormality in terms of comparison with an average reference group, it is unclear exactly what normal reference group is being invoked, and why deviance from it should be considered a dysfunction rather than just difference". (Bolton 2008, 9)

In other words, it seems an extremely ideological vision that may be expressed as an equation like conformism = normal = health. Following this point of view, the sense of subjective well-being, corresponding to identity with current values and lifestyles, or the recognition of belonging to a specific prevalent sector of society, are assumed acritically as a parameter for clinical judgment. (Grasso & Stampa 2006) So, although Wakefield's intention is to refute the anti-psychiatric arguments, and in particular those of Thomas Szasz (Wakefield 2004), these seem to come back in through the back door. Once again, not only homosexuality but today mainly gender non-conformity appear to be Psychiatry's Achilles' heel, where psychiatry seems to be a tool of social control that serves to pathologize the natural variations within humanity. Some years ago, in the above-mentioned paper, Meyer-Bahlburg stated: "Of course, there is always the question how much of social stigma is associated with the observable gender atypicality rather than the psychiatric label by itself." (2010, 11). It is a very interesting point because it takes us back to the similarities with the removal of homosexuality from the DSM in the seventies. As we have said before, several factors triggered this event: the results of scientific research demonstrating the spread of a homosexual orientation among non-clinical populations, the absence of psychopathology among homosexuals, homosexual activism and finally the action of the social and political movements, generically referred to as "anti-psychiatric". (Drescher 2010) Now this last phenomenon, in particular, did not come from nowhere: what characterized those years was an ethical-cultural spirit profoundly different from what we find today, a particular context where, as Renzo Carli and Rosa Maria Paniccia (2011) pointed out, it was necessary and also of great value to recognize and welcome diversity. Those times were indeed very different from today, which is characterized, on the contrary, by a backlash of negative individualism and the rejection, more or less violent, of "the other than self".

A PHENOMENOLOGICAL/EXISTENTIAL INTERPRETATION

We have elsewhere proposed a different reading of male transsexualism in adulthood from a phenomenological/existential point of view (Vitelli 2012). Here we shall try to summarize the main ideas. Phenomenology has been utilized in various ways by authors doing trans work (Ahmed 2006; Murphy 2009; Rubin 1998; 2003; Campbell & I'Anson 2007; Salamon 2010; Richards 2011; Owen 2012). As we have seen, today the temperature surrounding the trans issue is absolutely incandescent. There are several ideological standpoints competing for precedence, but, as the main phenomenological rule states, bracketing together all past knowledge/presuppositions (*phenomenological reduction*) generally allows phenomena to speak for themselves, and this may lead to a clearer and fuller analysis of the transsexual experience beyond the simplistic diagnostic criteria through which it is currently defined. In this way it might be possible to discover the *existential a-priori* that marks out the condition we are examining, the very 'categories' that make the anchoring and orientation in the *Lifeworld* possible [28]. In effect, what is at stake here is not solely and simply a transcendence of the *contingent* nature of what is a *given* in bodily anatomy referable to the difference between the sexes, the rising up of an individual above their own *facticity* through technical advancement, but rather a specific and more complex existential way of being: a specific *world-design*, a specific form of *being-in-the-world*, of *being-with-the-other*.

As we have seen before, the new DSM 5 would emphasize the issue of dysphoria rather than that of identity, but as may be readily acknowledged, *Gender Identity* is a key part of personal identity. What is at stake here is a more or less vivid sense of one's own personality trait or inner feeling, a diachronic and/or synchronic sum of such content, but, the question arises, what exactly do male/female transsexuals mean when they refer to themselves as being *inhabited by a female/male soul*? If it is true that judgments that I make about myself are always constrained by social expectations and cultural values, in this case, referring to Jean Paul Sartre, consciousness may direct its own *Ego* (*Moi*) as a *noematic correlative*, as a *self-representation* (Sartre 1937), defining its quality solely and exclusively on the basis of what the social *says* about the *feminine* or the *masculine*[29]. In this sense, it is clear that pre-verbal inner experiences regarding gender identity are always signified right within a horizon of meanings opened up by the *signifier of sexual difference*, which is a culturally and therefore historically determined perspective or background of intelligibility. It is within this field that we may unequivocally place this "speaking out" about this: what, indeed, is sexual gender if not a specific self-ascription, a reflective appropriation, and a thematic self-identification, in other words the *effect* of specific linguistic practices, a social construct, a set of socially-constructive attributive rules and restrictions transcendent of pure biological fact? What has been recently done within the DSM-5 regarding the possibility of belonging to some other gender than male or female, appears, in this sense, extremely important. It allows us to imagine a truly dramatic change. Indeed, as Jean Paul Sartre himself states in his *Search for a Method*, "the most individual possible is only the internalization and enrichment of a social possible" (Sartre 1957, 95), and, as we said before, psychiatric discursive mechanisms present themselves as a prominent locus of production for such "social possibles". (Rovatti 2006) So, the DSM change will probably have a great influence on the way subjects will frame their own experience, making it meaningful to themselves and others. In any case, beyond this important conceptual turn, probably as a result of the weight of past history, it is true that the *transsexual signifier* has gained prominence since its introduction and has given rise to a widespread diffusion of the *transsexual phenomenon*, as observed in recent years. (Chiland 1997) According to the new edition of the DSM (APA 2013), "Transsexual denotes an individual who seeks, or has undergone, a social transition from male to female (MtF) or female to male (FtM), which in many, but not all, cases also involves a somatic transition by

---

[28] For the issue of the *existential a-priori*, see Needleman 1963; Kraus 2010.

[29] As Sartre states in *The Transcendence of the Ego*, if "the *me* appears only with the reflective act, as the noematic correlative of a reflective intention" [Sartre 1937, 12], then "the influence of preconceived ideas and social factors is preponderant here" [ibidem, 16] in determining its "qualities".

cross-sex hormone treatment and genital surgery" (451). That is to say that the male transsexual, in his opposition to *his bodily appearance*, claims his own *true soul* as *female*, and the female transsexual her own *soul* as *male*; in other words, the register by which such individuals define themselves is clearly binary. One of the people whom Giulia Macoratti, an Italian researcher, interviewed a few years ago for an essay of hers had the following to say on the subject: "*The "top", for a (male) transsexual, is to be Woman, not just a woman... It is what a man sees in a woman... Because (transsexuals) think with a man's brain.*" (Macoratti 2005, 154). A very odd statement, wherein, on the one hand the subject seems to affirm the possibility of *being two in one*, greatly complicating the most common idea about the nature of inner experiences that are present at least in some cases with respect to the sexual gender; on the other, the MtF transsexual clearly refers to an *imaginary* ideal of femininity. This last aspect is very important because what we are dealing with here, at least in many MtF transsexuals, is the importance, if not the rigidity of *a specific feminine body-image*[30]. In the case of subjects requesting a "somatic transition", *Femininity* is the signifier that models their own body. This is used as a plastic material which is continually redesigned, in pursuit of a logic guided exactly by subjection to such an *imaginary* ideal of femininity: an ideal that sits above any actual reality, but to which, nonetheless, individuals seem to wish to devote themselves in an asymptotic and irrealizing movement. In fact, beyond long-lasting hormonal therapy, transsexuals often undergo a series of different operations to feminize or masculinize the body: eg, breast/chest, external genitalia and/or internal facial structures, body contouring. The reasons for such *bodily adjustments* are easily understood. As Edmund Husserl pointed out, I am not simply a pure and formal subject of experience, but rather I become aware of myself specifically as a human person only within a public sphere (Husserl 1973, 175; 1952, 204–05). At the same time, as a long phenomenological tradition demonstrates, the body plays a crucial role in the interpersonal context (Gallagher & Zahavi 2010). Indeed, all of us see ourselves through the eyes of other people just because we are *embodied subjects*. Talking about the three-way division he makes into the *body as-being-for-itself*, the *body-for-others* and the *alienated-body*, Sartre states:

> "I exist my body: this is its first dimension of being. My body is utilized and known by the Other: this is its second dimension. But in so far as *I am for others*, the Other is revealed to me as the subject for whom I am an object. Even there the question, as we have seen, is of my fundamental relation with the Other. I exist therefore for myself as known by the Other – in particular, in my very facticity. I exist for myself as a body

---

[30] In her book, explicitly dedicated to the issue of *Body Images*, Gail Weiss writes: "The turbulence that characterizes our lived bodily experience, a turbulence which, for Lacan, is psychically rejected in favor of a projected (imaginary) identification with the specular image, can, as he well recognized, never be denied altogether. Indeed, I would maintain that this turbulence is expressed and even accentuated in the transitions we continually make between one body image and another. For the nonpathological subject, I am suggesting, it is the very multiplicity of these body images which guarantees that we cannot invest too heavily in any one of them, and these multiple body images themselves offer points of resistance to the development of too strong an identification with a singularly alienating specular (or even cultural) image. That is, these multiple body images serve to destabilize the hegemony of any particular body image ideal, and are precisely what allows us to maintain a sense of corporeal fluidity." [Weiss 1999, 100] Although from an existentialist point of view the question of the pathological nature, or not, of a given condition is of little or no interest, surely the observation of the importance that in some subjects *a single body image* can assume, definitely seems relevant if we consider what happens in many, but not all, MtF transsexuals.

known by the Other. This is the third ontological dimension of my body." (Sartre 1943, 351).

Sartre's third ontological dimension is absolutely important for self-awareness. As Shaun Gallagher and Dan Zahavi said, "embodiment brings intersubjectivity and sociality into the picture, and draws attention to the question of how certain forms of self-consciousness are intersubjectively mediated, and may depend on one's social relations to others" (Gallagher & Zahavi 2010). So, the effective meaning of the feminized/masculinized body obtained by cross-sex hormone treatment and genital surgery may only really be understood in the intersubjective arena (Owen 2012). The question of femininity/masculinity is something that happens "*among the subjects*".

A few years ago, the French philosopher and psychologist Patricia Mercader wrote:

> "From a general standpoint, one may wonder whether a morphological transformation can be considered to be a 'sex change': what is transformed is the appearance of the body, in other words, the way the individual is perceived and perceives him/herself, the way in which he or she is acknowledged in social life." (Mercader 1994, 18)

Indeed the desire to modify sexual characteristics may be easily understood, if we consider that, in some cases, it is mainly on the surface of the body that transsexuals place the matrix of their own being: in what, in Sartre's terminology, is the *alienated body*. Subject is both reduced to her visible surfaces and judged by them by others, even by herself[31].

It is true that for all of us the desire-fuelled gaze of the other is always an important element in defining our own gender identity.

As Sartre writes,

> "My *first* apprehension of the Other as having a sex does not come when I conclude from the distribution of his hair, from the coarseness of his hands, the sound of his voice, his strength that he is of the masculine sex. We are dealing there with derived conclusions which refer to an original state. The first apprehension of the Other's sexuality in so far as it is lived and suffered can be only desire; it is by desiring the Other (or by discovering myself as incapable of desiring him) or by apprehending his desire for me that I discover his being-sexed. Desire reveals to me simultaneously *my* being-sexed and *his* being sexed, *my* body as sex and *his* body." (Sartre 1943, 384)

The French philosopher's words are equally relevant if they are compared with what Loredana, a Neapolitan transsexual, had to say:

---

[31] It is noteworthy that Sandra Bartky has referred this dynamic more generally to women's experiences, invoking the "fashion-beauty complex" [Bartky 1990]. A woman, she states, is today reduced to her visible surfaces and judged by them by others, even by herself, according to specific standards of beauty, slenderness, etc. In such a way, a woman usually tends to tacitly accept, co-posit and reinforce such social shaping forces, becoming "a self-policing subject, a self committed to a restless self-surveillance" [80]. This issue has been discussed also by Ellyn Kaschack [1992], Iris Young [1990] and Gail Weiss [1999]. In any case, what we imagine to be at stake in the transsexuals' experience is the special and profound importance that such dynamics often play in the stabilizing process of personal identity.

"I will not deny, however, that working as a prostitute is something we like. It is the desire that we read in the eyes of those men, who, by day, do not look at us and laugh at us, but, at night, belong to us, pay money to have us!" (Cipolla, Rossi & Cardone 2010, 77)

It is, indeed, the gaze of the Other/other that mainly the female transsexual (MtF) in many (but not all) cases looks for as a prosthetic support, as a constant and necessary source of confirmation of her own self-declaration/self-display, and therefore of her own "assumed identity". The *irrealizing* action of the imaginary register (Sartre 1940) is, in this case, effectively targets the modification of one's own bodily appearance, motivated precisely by the body's nature as a body offered to the gaze. The problem is that the *other-than-Self*'s non-'inert' nature and the individual's dependency on his/her gaze, the enigmatic and "disorienting" nature of the *alter-ego* as Szilasi defines it (quoted by Binswanger 1965/1972, 71), often makes it a potential source of threat in the transsexual's mind. The other holds the secret of what she is. It follows that the other may choose to bestow or withhold her recognition of what she is. Another transsexual, quoted in a study by Alessandro Salvini, an Italian Professor of Clinical Psychology, says this: "*Those who are outside that door waiting to judge me can make me feel like a fully successful woman, or as if I have some original manufacturing defect.*" (Salvini 1999, 260). The sexual encounter itself may be at risk or become a troubling experience, just as Katy, another transsexual who was interviewed some years ago by Porpora Marcasciano, a sociologist and a leading exponent of the Italian transsexual movement, says:

"Sometimes I thought that my partner was staying with me just looking for my male genitalia. This really upset me because I felt like a woman, but if the other was looking for my masculine side, it automatically demolished, cancelled my perception of myself. This thought was a kind of worm that has gnawed at me for years. It is a problem that I often find myself facing, that the homosexuality of my partner could neutralize my being a woman." (Marcasciano 2008, 81-82)

A tragic antinomy is therefore set up in such cases on an existential level: if, on the one hand, the other is established as a constant potential source of threat, on the other, as previously said, the other's gaze is important for the identity stabilizing process[32].

The price paid for such an intersubjective dynamic may seem extremely high, with the ever-present risk of annulling any *real and deep* co-existentive encounter, the possibility of precluding an authentic dialogical dimension.

---

[32] The difference between MtF and FtM subjects is well expressed by Anne A. Lawrence: "Being regarded and treated as a member of one's preferred gender during the real-life experience [cross-living as a member of the preferred gender before SRS] is usually easier for FtM transsexuals than for MtF transsexuals. (...) While it is difficult for both MtF and FtM transsexuals to eradicate all evidence of their birth sex, residual signs of maleness in MtF transsexuals can often interfere with their being considered female, while residual signs of femaleness in FtM transsexuals may interfere little if at all with their being considered male". [Lawrence 2008, 447]

CONCLUSION

This paper has focused on some controversial issues surrounding gender identity variance. We have shown how, in the West today, this existential condition is to some extent shaped, and somehow even produced, by a series of discourses, which are first and foremost medical/psychiatric and define and mold its very nature. We have analyzed the main historical stages of the process of inclusion of this condition within psychiatric knowledge, and discussed the main problems that this inclusion produces in that it questions the very foundations of psychiatric knowledge. Finally, we have considered the exact nature of this condition within the framework of a phenomenological/existential approach.

Since the *handover* from psychiatry to surgery, psychiatrists and clinical psychologists today have plied their trade as official technical consultants or experts, essentially carrying out a merely diagnostic function. Gender Identity psychiatrists are renowned for acting as "gatekeepers" to hormones and surgery. (Speer & Parsons 2006) As a result, many individuals who could profit from a therapeutic relationship avoid establishing one. But how would it be possible for us to rethink the clinical encounter beyond its mere diagnostic value? Well, probably psychological work should aim to improve the subject's psychological sense of security, reducing, when necessary, his/her dependence on the other. On the other hand it should be recognized that today violence and discrimination against transgender people are still extremely common and pervasive. The gaze of the other is actually quite threatening and really unwilling to accept or appreciate diversity, so life can be very difficult for gender non-conforming people. Psychiatrists, as well as Clinical Psychologists, become nothing more than representatives of a broader social context, perceived, rightly, as hostile. The same psychiatrization of the condition probably contributes to a such state of affairs.

So, beyond any psychiatric or psychological discourse, the battle for a more peaceful world, for a full acceptance of all the existential possibilities – and gender non conformity is one of these - seems to be an important way to give a fully existential life-meaning to gender non conforming people. Their existential experience, as we have tried to describe here, is certainly a very complex one, although the problems they live with do not derive from psychiatric discourse alone, but from a much broader societal-cultural context. Clearly, what needs to be changed is the very basis of Western contemporary culture. What is needed today is acceptance, far more than medical categories.

REFERENCES

Ahmed, S. (2006). *Queer Phenomenology: Orientation, Objects, Others*. Durham and London: Duke University Press.

American Psychiatric Association (APA). (1968). *Diagnostic and statistical manual of mental disorders (2nd ed.)*. Washington, DC: Author.

American Psychiatric Association (APA). (1980). *Diagnostic and statistical manual of mental disorders (3rd ed.)*. Washington, DC: Author.

American Psychiatric Association (APA) (1987). *Diagnostic and statistical manual of mental disorders (3rd ed., rev.)*. Washington, DC: Author.

American Psychiatric Association. (APA) (1994). *Diagnostic and statistical manual of mental disorders (4th ed.)*. Washington, DC: Author.

American Psychiatric Association. (APA) (2000). *Diagnostic and statistical manual of mental disorders (4th ed., text rev.)*. Washington, DC: Author.

American Psychiatric Association (APA) (2013). *Diagnostic and Statistical Manual of Mental Disorders, Fifth Edition, DSM-5*. Arlington, VA: Author.

Bartky, S. L. (1990). *Femininity and Domination: Studies in the Phenomenology of Oppression*. New York: Routledge, Chapman & Hall.

Bayer, R. (1981). *Homosexuality and American psychiatry: The politics of diagnosis*. New York: Basic Books.

Benjamin, H. (1953). *Transvestism and transsexualism*. International Journal of Sexology, 7: 12-14.

Benjamin, H. (1966). *The Transsexual Phenomenon*. New York: The Julian Press, Inc. Publishers. Retrieved March 14, 2014, from http://www.mut23.de/ texte/Harry% 20Benjamin%20-%20The%20Transsexual%20Phenomenon.pdf. Copyright of the electronic edition by Symposium Publishing, Düsseldorf, 1999.

Bieber, I. (1987). On arriving at the American Psychiatric Association decision on homosexuality. In H. T. Engelhardt & A. L. Caplan (Eds.), *Scientific controversies: Case studies in the resolution and closure of disputes in science and technology* (pp. 417–436). New York: Cambridge University Press.

Billings, D.B. & Urban, T. (1996). The socio-medical construction of transsexualism: an interpretation and critique. Originally published in: *Social Problems*, 1982, 29, 266-282. Republished in R. Ekins, & D. King (Eds.) (1996), *Blending genders: social aspects of cross-dressing and sex-changing* (pp. 99-117). London: Routledge.

Binswanger, L. (1965/1972). *Delirio: Antropoanalisi e Fenomenologia* (It. Tr. by E. Borgna). Venice: Marsilio Editore.

Blanchard, R. (1989a). The classification and labeling of non homosexual gender dysphorias. *Archives of Sexual Behavior*, 18, 315-334.

Blanchard, R. (1989b). The concept of autogynephilia and the typology of male gender dysphoria. *Journal of Nervous and Mental Disease*, 177, 616-623.

Blanchard, R. (1991). Clinical observations and systematic studies of autogynephilia. *Journal of Sex and Marital Therapy*, 17, 235-251.

Blanchard, R. (1993a). The she-male phenomenon and the concept of partial autogynephilia. *Journal of Sex and Marital Therapy*, 19, 69-76.

Blanchard, R. (1993b). Varieties of autogynephilia and their relationship to gender dysphoria. *Archives of Sexual Behavior*, 22, 241-251.

Bloch, I. (1907). *Das sexualleben unserer Zeit in seinen Beziehungen zur modernen Kultur. Marcus Verlagsbuchhandlung*. Berlin. English Tr. By M. E. Paul (1909) *The Sexual Life of Our Time in Its Relations to Modern Civilization*. London: Rebman.

Bolton, D. (2008, 2009). *What is mental disorder? An essay in philosophy, science, and value*. Oxford, UK: Oxford University Press.

Bolton, D. (2013). What is Mental Illness? In K. W. M. Fulford, M. Davies, R. G. T. Gipps, G. Graham, J. Z. Sadler, G. Stanghellini, & T. Thornton (Eds.). *The Oxford Handbook of Philosophy and Psychiatry* (pp. 434-450). Oxford (UK): Oxford University Press.

Boorse, C. (1977). Health as a theoretical concept. *Philosophy of Science*, 44(4), 542-573.

Boorse, C. (1997). A Rebuttal on health. In J. F. Humber, & R. F. Almeder (Eds.). *What is Disease?* (pp. 1- 134). Totowa: New Jersey: Humana Press.

Broome, M. R. (2006), Taxonomy and Ontology in Psychiatry: A Survey of Recent Literature. *Philosophy, Psychiatry, & Psychology*, 13(4), 303-319.

Bottone, M., Galiani, R., & Valerio, P. (2001). Introduzione. In P. Valerio, M. Bottone, R. Galiani, & R. Vitelli (Eds.). *Il Transessualismo: saggi psicoanalitici*. Milan: Franco Angeli Editore.

Bullough V. L. (2003), Magnus Hirschfeld, an often overlooked pioneer. *Sexuality and Culture*, 7(1), 62-72.

Campbell, J.S.J.O., & I'Anson, C. (2007). Beyond Gender Essentialism and the Social Construction of Gender: Redefining the Conception of Gender Through a Reinvestigation of Transgender Theory. *International Studies in Philosophy*, 39 (1), 19-30.

Carli, R., & Paniccia, R.M. (2001). *La cultura dei servizi di salute mentale in Italia: dai malati psichiatrici alla nuova utenza - l'evoluzione della domanda di aiuto e delle dinamiche di rapporto*. Milan: Franco Angeli Editore.

Chiland, C. (1997, 2003). *Transsexualism: illusion and reality* (English Trans. by P. Slotkin,). Middletown – CT: Wesleyan University Press.

Cipolla, A., Rossi, L. & Cardone A. (2010). La prostituzione transessuale. In A. Morniroli (Ed.), *Vite clandestine: frammenti, racconti e altro sulla prostituzione e la tratta di esseri umani in provincia di Napoli*, (pp. 77-94). Naples: Gesco Edizioni.

Cohen-Kettenis, P. T., & Pfäfflin, F. (2010). The DSM Diagnostic Criteria for Gender Identity Disorder in Adolescents and Adults. *Archives of Sexual Behavior*, 39(2), 499– 513.

Cooper, R. (2005). *Classifying madness: a philosophical examination of the diagnostic and statistical manual of mental disorders*. Dordrecht, Netherlands: Springer.

Council of Europe. Commissioner for Human Rights. *Issue Paper: Human Rights and Gender Identity*. 2009. Retrieved April 29, 2014, from https://wcd.coe.int/ ViewDoc.jsp?id=1476365.

Dallas, D. (1998). A selective bibliography of transsexualism. *Journal of Gay and Lesbians Psychotherapy*, 6 (2), 35-66.

Davidson, A. I. (2001). *The Emergence of Sexuality: Historical Epistemology and the Formation of Concepts*. Cambridge, Mass.: Harvard University Press.

Denny, D. (1998), *Current Concepts in Transgender Identity: Towards a New Synthesis*. New York: Garland Publishers.

Denny, D. (2002). A selective bibliography of transsexualism. *Journal of Gay & Lesbian Psychotherapy*, 6 (2), 35-66.

Drescher, J. (2003). An interview with Robert L. Spitzer, MD. *Journal of Gay & Lesbian Psychotherapy*, 7(3), 97–111.

Drescher, J. (2010). Queer diagnoses: parallels and contrast in the history of homosexuality, gender variance, and the diagnostic and statistical manual. *Archives of Sexual Behaviour*, 39, 427-460.

Drescher, J. (2014). Gender Identity Diagnoses: History and Controversies. In B. P. C. Kreukels, T. D. Steensma & A. L.C. de Vrie (Eds.). *Gender Dysphoria and Disorders of Sex Development*, (pp. 137-150). New York Heidelberg Dordrecht London: Spinger Ed.

Drescher, J., Cohen-Kettenis, P. & Winter, S. (2012). Minding the body: Situating gender identity diagnoses in the ICD-11. *International Review of Psychiatry*, 24(6), 568–577.

Drescher, J., & Merlino, J. P. (Eds.). (2007). *American psychiatry and homosexuality: An oral history*. New York: Harrington Park Press.

Ekins, R., King, D. (2001). Pioneers of Transgendering: The Popular Sexology of David O. Cauldwell. *International Journal of Transgenderism*, 5, 2. Retrieved March 14, 2014, from http://www.symposion.com/ijt/cauldwell/cauldwell_01.htm.

Ellis, H. (1913). Sexo-aesthetic inversion. *Alienist and Neurologist*, 34, 249-279.

Ellis, H. (1920). *Eonism. Medical Review of Reviews*, New York, 3-12.

Ellis H. (1927), *Studies in the Psychology of Sex, Vol. II: Sexual Inversion*. Retrieved March 14, 2014, from http://www.gutenberg.org/files/13611/13611-h/13611-h.htm.

European Parliament: *28 September 2011 on human rights, sexual orientation and gender identity at the United Nations. 2011*. Retrieved April 29, 2014, from www.europarl.europa.eu/sides/getDoc.do?pubRef=-//EP//TEXT+TA+P7-TA-2011-0427+0+DOC+XML+V0//EN

Fisk, N. (1973). Gender Dysphoria Sindrome (The How, What, and Why of a Disease). In D. Laub, & P. Gandy (Eds.). *Proceedings of the second interdisciplinary symposium on gender dysphoria syndrome*. Stanford, CA, Stanford University Medical Center: University of California Press.

Foucault, M. (1976). *The History of Sexuality: Volume 1: An Introduction*. English Tr. Robert Hurley. NY: Random House - Pantheon Books, 1978.

Frances, A. (2010). DSM in Philosophyland: Curiouser and Curiouser. *Bulletin of the Association for the Advancement of Philosophy and Psychiatry*, 17(2), 3-7. Retrieved March 14, 2014, from http://alien.dowling.edu/~cperring/aapp/bulletin_v_ 17_2/Vol17N2.pdf

Freccero, C. (1999). Acts, Identities, and Sexuality's (Pre)Modern Regimes. *Journal of Women's History*, 11(2), 186-192.

Frignet, H. (2000) *Le transsexualisme*. Paris: Desclée de Brower.

Gallagher, S., & Zahavi, D. (2010), Phenomenological Approaches to Self-Consciousness. In E. N. Zalta (Ed.). *The Stanford Encyclopedia of Philosophy* (Winter 2010 Edition), Retrieved March 14, 2014, from http://plato.stanford.edu/archives/win2010/entries/self-consciousness-phenomenological/>.

Gijs, L., & Carroll, R. A. (2011). Should Transvestic Fetishism Be Classified in DSM 5? Recommendations from the WPATH Consensus Process for Revision of the Diagnosis of Transvestic Fetishism. *International Journal of Transgenderism*, 12(4), 189.

Gittings, B. (2008). Show and tell. *Journal of Gay and Lesbian Mental Health*, 12(3), 289–294.

Grasso, M., & Stampa, P. (2006). Chi ha slegato Roger Rabbit? Diagnosi psichiatrica e modelli di salute mentale: Osservazioni su alcune criticità metodologiche per la ricerca in psicoterapia. *Rivista di Psicologia Clinica. Teoria e metodi dell'intervento*, 1, 102-117.

Groos, K. (1892), *Einleitung in die Ästethic*. Giessen: Ricker.

Green, R. (2010). Robert Stoller's Sex and Gender: 40 years on. *Archives of Sexual Behavior*, 39(6), 1457-65.

Green, R., & Money, J. (Eds) (1969). *Transsexualism and Sex Reassignment*. Baltimore, MD: The Johns Hopkins Press.

Hamburger, C., Stürup, G. K., & Dahl-Iversen, E. (1953). Transvestism: Hormonal Psychiatric and Surgical Treatment. *Journal of American Medical Association,* 152, 30, 391 - 396.

Herdt, G. (Ed.). (1996). *Third sex, third gender: beyond sexual dimorphism in culture and history*. New York: Zone Books.

Hill, D. B. (2005). Sexuality and Gender in Hirschfeld's Die Transvestiten: A case of the 'Elusive Evidence of the Ordinary'. *Journal of the History of Sexuality*, 14 (3), 316-332.

Hire, R. O. (2002). An interview with Robert Jean Campbell III, MD. *Journal of Gay & Lesbian Psychotherapy*, 6(3), 81–96.

Hirschfeld, M. (1910). Die Transvestiten, eine Untersuchung über den erotischen Verkleidungstrieb mit umfangreichem casuistischem und historischem Material. In: Medizinischer Verlag, Berlin; Ferdinand Spohr, Leipzig, 1925. Partial English Translation by Michael A. Lombardi-Nash, in: S. Stryker e S. Whittle (eds), *The Transgender Studies Reader* (pp. 28-39). New York: Routledge, 2006.

Hirschfeld, M. (1913). *Geschlechtsübergänge: Mischungen männlicher und weiblicher Geschlechtscharaktere. (Sexuelle Zwischenstufen.) Erweiterte Ausgabe eines auf der 76. Naturforscherversammlung zu Breslau gehaltenen Vortrages. 2*. Leipzig: Auflage Verlag von Max Spohr (Inh. Ferd. Spohr).

Hirschfeld, M. (1922). *Sexualpathologie. Ein Lehrbuch für Ärtze und Studierende*. Bonn: A. Marcus & Webers Verlag.

Hirschfeld, M. (1923). Die intersexuelle Konstitution. *Jahrbuch für sexuelle Zwischenstufen*, 23, 3-27.

Hooker, E. A. (1957). The adjustment of the male overt homosexual. *Journal of Projective Techniques*, 21, 18–31.

Hoyer, N. (Ed.) (1933). *Man into Woman. An Authentic Story of a Change of Sex. The True Story of the Miraculous Transformation of the Danish Painter, Einar Wegener (Andreas Spanner)*. New York: Dutton.

Husserl, E. (1952). *Ideen zu einer reinen Phänomenologie und phänomenologischen Philosophie. Zweites Buch: Phänomenologische Untersuchungen zur Konstitution*, Edited by M. Biemel. The Hague, Netherlands: Martinus Nijhoff; English translation: *Ideas Pertaining to a Pure Phenomenology and to a Phenomenological Philosophy, Second Book. Studies in the Phenomenology of Constitution*, Translated by R. Rojcewicz and A. Schuwer. Dordrecht: Kluwer, 1989.

Husserl, E. (1973). Zur Phänomenologie der Intersubjektivität II. *Husserliana XIV*. Den Haag: Martinus Nijhoff.

Jorgensen, C. (1967, 2000). *A personal biography*. San Francisco: Cleis Press.

Kameny, F. (2009). How it all started. *Journal of Gay & Lesbian Mental Health*, 13(2), 76–81.

Kaschack, E. (1992). *Engendered Lives: A New Psychology of Women's Experience*. New York: Basic Books.

Cauldwell, D. O. (1949) Psychopathia Trans-sexualis. *Sexology Magazine*, December. Republished in: S. Stryker e S. Whittle (eds), *The Transgender Studies Reader* (pp. 40-44). New York: Routledge, 2006.

Kendell, R.E. (1986). What are mental disorders?. In A.M. Freedman, R. Brotman, I. Silverman, & D. Hutson (Eds.). *Issues in psychiatric classification: science, practice and social policy* (pp 23-45). New York: Human Sciences Press.

Kendler, K.S., & Zachar, P. (2008). The incredible insecurity of psychiatric nosology. In K. Kendler, & J. Parnas (Eds.). *Philosophical issues in psychiatry: explanation, phenomenology, and nosology* (pp. 368-383). Baltimore: John Hopkins University Press.

Kinsey, A. C., Pomeroy, W. B., & Martin, C. E. (1948). *Sexual behavior in the human male*. Philadelphia: W. B. Saunders.

Kinsey, A. C., Pomeroy, W. B., Martin, C. E., & Gebhard, P. H. (1953). *Sexual behavior in the human female*. Philadelphia: W. B. Saunders.

Klein, D.F. (1978). A proposed definition of mental disorder. In D.F. Klein, & R.L. Spitzer (Eds). *Critical Issues in Psychiatric Diagnosis* (pp 41–72). New York: Raven Press.

Knudson, G., De Cuypere, G., & Bockting, W. (2011). Second Response of the World Professional Association for Transgender Health to the Proposed Revision of the Diagnosis of Transvestic Disorder for DSM 5. *International Journal of Transgenderism*, 13, 9-12.

Krafft-Ebing, von R. (1886-1906). *Psychopathia Sexualis 7th edition*. (English translation by Charles Gilbert Chaddock). Philadelphia: The F. A. Davis Company Publishers- London: F. G. Rebman, 1894.

Krafft-Ebing, von R. (1886-1931). *Psychopathia sexualis XVI-XVII edition*. It. Trans. by Piero Giolla. Milan: Carlo Manfredi Editore, 1966.

Kraus, A. (2010). Existential a prioris and the phenomenology of schizophrenia. *Dialogues in Philosophy, Mental and Neuro Sciences*, 3(1), 1-7.

Lawrence, A. A. (2008). Gender identity disorders in adults: Diagnosis and treatment. In D. L. Rowland & L. Incrocci (Eds.), *Handbook of sexual and gender identity disorders* (pp. 423-456). Hoboken, NJ: John Wiley & Sons.

Leone, M. (2010). Pudibondi e spudorati: Riflessioni semiotiche sul linguaggio del corpo (s)vestito. *Rivista Italiana di Filosofia del Linguaggio*, 2, 74-94.

Lipps, T. (1903-1906). *Ästhetik. Psychologie des Schönen und der Kunst*. Hamburg/Leipzig: Voss.

Macoratti, G. (2005). Transessuali e transgender: la costruzione di un'identità negata. In C. Fasola (Ed.), *L'identità: l'altro come coscienza di sé* (pp.143-58). Turin: Utet Libreria.

Marcasciano, P. (2008). *Favolose narranti: Storie di transessuali*. Rome: Manifestolibri.

Mason-Schrock, D. (1996). Transsexuals' Narrative Contruction of the "True Self". *Social Psychology Quarterly*, 59(3), 176-192.

Mercader, P. (1994). *L'illusion transsexuelle*. Paris: Edition L'Hartmattan.

Meyer-Bahlburg, H.F.L. (2010). From mental disorder to iatrogenic hypogonadism: dilemmas in conceptualizing gender identity variants as psychiatric conditions. *Archives of Sexual Behavior*, 39, 461-476.

Meyer, J. K., & Reter, D. (1979). Sex reassigment: follow up. *Archives of General Psychiatry*, 36, 1010-1015.

Money, J. (1955). Hermaphroditism, gender and precocity in hyperadrenocorticism: Psychologic findings. *Bulletin of the Johns Hopkins Hospital*, 96, 253–264.

Money, J., Hampson. J.G., & Hampson, J.L. (1957). Imprinting and the establishment of Gender Role. *AMA Archives of Neurology and Psychiatry*, 77(3):333–336.

Moser, C. (2010). Blanchard's Autogynephilia Theory: A Critique. *Journal of Homosexuality*, 57(6), 790–809.

Murphy, A. V. (2009). Sexuality. In H. L. Dreyfus & M. A. Wrathall (Eds.). *A Companion to Phenomenology and Existentialism* (pp.489-501). Oxford, UK: Blackwell Publishing Ltd.

Nanda, S. (2008). Cross-Cultural Issues. In D. L. Rowland & L. Incrocci (Eds). *Handbook of Sexual and Gender Identity Disorders* (pp.457-485). Hoboken, New Jersey: John Wiley & Sons,.

Needleman, J. (1963). Introduction to Being-In-The-World. In L. Binswanger (1963). *Being-in-the-world: Selected papers of Ludwig Binswanger* (J. Needleman, Trans.). New York: Basic Books.

Owen, I. R. (2012). The phenomenological psychology of gender: How trans-sexuality and intersexuality express the general case of self as a cultural object. In D. Lohmar & J. Brudzinska (Eds.). *Founding psychoanalysis phenomenologically: Phenomenological theory of subjectivity and the psychoanalytical experience* (pp. 199-212). Phaenomenologica, 199. Dordrecht: Springer Science & Business Media.

Phillips, J., et al. (2012). The six most essential questions in psychiatric diagnosis: a pluralogue part 1: conceptual and definitional issues in psychiatric diagnosis. *Philosophy, Ethics, and Humanities in Medicine*, 7:3. Retrieved April 29, 2014 from http://www.ncbi.nlm.nih.gov/pmc/articles/PMC3305603/

Prunas A., Vitelli R., Agnello F., Curti E., Fazzari P., Giannini F., Hartmann D., & Bini M. (2014). Defensive functioning in MtF and FtM transsexuals. *Comprehensive Psychiatry*, 55(4): 966-71.

Richards, C. (2011). Transsexualism and Existentialism. *Existential Analysis*, 22 (2), 272-279.

Rosario, V. A. (2003). An interview with Judd Marmor, MD. *Journal of Gay & Lesbian Psychotherapy*, 7(4), 23–34.

Rovatti, P.A. (2006). *La filosofia può curare? La consulenza filosofica in questione*. Milan: Raffaello Cortina Editore.

Rubin, H. (1998). Phenomenology as Method in Trans Studies. *GLQ: A Journal of Lesbian and Gay Studies*, 4(2), 263-281.

Rubin, H. (2003). *Self-Made Men: Identity and Embodiment among Transsexual Men*. Nashville: Vanderbilt University Press.

Rubin, H. (2006). The logic of treatment. In S. Stryker & S. Whittle (Eds.). *The transgender Studies Reader* (pp.482-498). New York – London: Routledge.

Russell, S. (2013). Deconstructing a DSM Diagnosis: Gender Identity Disorder (GID) in Adolescents and Adults. *Western Undergraduate Psychology Journal*, 1: Iss. 1, Article 1. Retrieved March 14, 2014, from http://ir.lib.uwo.ca/wupj/vol1/iss1/1

Salamon, G. (2010). *Assuming a Body: Transgender and Rhetorics of Materiality*. New York Chichester, West Sussex: Columbia University Press.

Salvini, A. (1999). Transessualismo e riorganizzazione della rappresentazione narrativa di sé: un punto di vista clinico. *Rivista di Sessuologia*, 23 (3), 257-268.

Sartre, J. P. (1937). *The Transcendence of the Ego: A sketch for a phenomenological description* (English trans. by Andrew Brown). London and New York: Routledge, 2004. Retrieved March 14, 2014, from http://cliffordglee.com/Site/EXSupplementalReadings_files/36578062-0415320682-Jean-Pau-Sartre-The-Transcendence-of-the-Ego-a-Sketch-for-a-Phenomenological-Description- Routledge.pdf

Sartre, J. P. (1940). *The Imaginary: A phenomenological Psychology of the Imagination* (English Trans. by J. Webber). London and New York: Routledge, 2004.

Sartre, J. P. (1943). *Being and Nothingness*. (English trans. by Hazel E. Barnes). New York: Philosophical Library, 1956.

Sartre, J. P. (1957), *Search for a Method*, (English tr. by H. Barnes). New York: Random House, 1958.

Sass, L. A., & Pienkos, E. (2013). Delusion: The Phenomenological Approach. In K. W. M. Fulford, M. Davies, R. G. T. Gipps, G. Graham, J. Z. Sadlre, G. Stanghellini, & T. Thornton (Eds.). *The Oxford Handbook of Philosophy and Psychiatry* (pp. 632-657). Oxford (UK): Oxford University Press.

Sbordone, A. J. (2003). An interview with Charles Silverstein, PhD. *Journal of Gay & Lesbian Psychotherapy*, 7(4), 49–61.

Schrock, D. P. & Reid, L. L. (2006). Transsexuals' Sexual Stories. *Archives of Sexual Behavior*, Vol. 35 (1), 75-86.

Serano, J. M. (2010). The Case Against Autogynephilia. *International Journal of Transgenderism*, 12(3), 176–187.

Silverstein, C. (2009). The implications of removing homosexuality from the DSM as a mental disorder (Letter to the editor). *Archives of Sexual Behavior*, 38, 161–163.

Socarides, C. W. (1995). *Homosexuality: A freedom too far*. Phoenix, AZ: Adam Margrave Books.

Speer, S.A., & Parsons, C. (2006). Gatekeeping Gender: Some Features of the Use of Hypothetical Questions in the Psychiatric Assessment of Transsexual Patients. *Discourse and Society*, 17(6), 785-812.

Spitzer, R. L. (1981). The diagnostic status of homosexuality in DSM III: Are formulation of the issues. *American Journal of Psychiatry*, 138, 210–215.

Spitzer, R. L., & Wakefield J. C. (1999). DSM-IV Diagnostic Criterion for Clinical Significance: Does It Help Solve the False Positives Problem?. *American Journal of Psychiatry*, 156:1856–1864.

Spitzer, R.L., & Williams, J.B.W. (1982). The definition and diagnosis of mental disorder, in W.R. Gove (Ed), *Deviance and Mental Illness: Sage Annual Reviews of Studies in Deviance, vol 6* (pp 15–31). Beverly Hills, California: Sage Publications.

Stoller, R. J. (1968). *Sex and Gender: The Development of Masculinity and Femininity*. London - New York: Karnak Books.

Stoller, R. J., Marmor, J., Bieber, I., Gold, R., Socarides, C. W., Green, R., et al. (1973). A symposium: Should homosexuality be in the APA nomenclature? *American Journal of Psychiatry*, 130, 1207– 1216.

Stryker, S., & Whittle, S. (Eds) (2006). *The Transgender Studies Reader*. New York: Routledge.

Szasz, T. S. (1960). The myth of mental illness. *American Psychologist*, 15, 113–118.

Vance, S. R., Cohen-Kettenis, P. T., Drescher, J., Meyer-Bahlburg, H. F. L., Pfäffl in, F., & Zucker, K. J. (2010). Opinions about the *DSM* Gender Identity Disorder diagnosis: Results from an international survey administered to organizations concerned with the welfare of transgender people. *International Journal of Transgenderism, 12* (1), 1–24.

Varga, S. (2011). Defining mental disorder. Exploring the "natural function" approach. *Philosophy, Ethics and Humanities in Medicine*, 21(6), 1. Retrieved March 14, 2014, from http://www.peh-med.com/content/6/1/1.

Vattimo, G. (Ed.) (1977), *Estetica Moderna*. Il Mulino, Bologna.

Vitelli, R. (2001). Transessualismo e identità di genere. L'opera di Robert J. Stoller – Presentazione. In P. Valerio, M. Bottone, R. Galiani, & R. Vitelli (Eds.). *Il Transessualismo – Saggi Psicoanalitici* (pp. 29-45). Milan: Franco Angeli.

Vitelli, R. (2012). Il Transessualismo Maschile e la Maschera: Una Lettura Daseinsanalitica. In R. Vitelli, & P. Valerio (Eds.). *Sesso e Genere: uno sguardo tra storia e nuove prospettive* (pp.113-152). Naples: Liguori Editore.

Vitelli, R., & Giusti, Z. (2012). Per un'archeologia del soggetto transessuale: un'introduzione a *Die Transvestiten* di Magnus Hirschfeld e a *Psychopathia transexualis* di David Cauldwell. In: R. Vitelli & P. Valerio (Eds), *Sesso e Genere: uno sguardo tra storia e nuove prospettive* (pp 7-26). Naples: Liguori Editore.

Vitelli, R., & Valerio, P. (Eds) (2012). *Sesso e Genere: uno sguardo tra storia e nuove prospettive*. Naples: Liguori Editore.

Wakefield, J. (1992). The concept of mental disorder – on the boundary between biological facts and social value. *American Psychologist*, 47, 373–88.

Wakefield, J.C. (2004). Realtà e valori nel concetto di salute mentale: il disturbo come disfunzione dannosa. *Psicoterapia e Scienze Umane*, 38(4), 439-464.

Wakefield, J.C. (2007). The concept of mental disorder: diagnostic implications of the harmful dysfunction analysis. *World Psychiatry*, 6(3), 149-156.

Wakefield, J.C., & First, M.B. (2003). Classifying the distinction between disorder and nondisorder: Confronting the overdiagnosis (false positive) problem in DSM-V. In K. A. Philips, M. B. First, & H. A. Pincus, (Eds.). *Advancing DSM: Dilemmas in psychiatric diagnosis* (pp. 23-56). Arlington, WA: American Psychiatric Association.

Weiss, G. (1999). *Body Images: Embodiment as Intercorporeality*. New York: Routledge.

Westphal, C. (1870). Die konträre Sexualempfindung. *Archiv für Psychiatrie*, 2, 73-108.

World Health Organization (WHO), (1992). *The ICD-10 classification of mental and behavioural disorders: clinical descriptions and diagnostic guidelines*. Geneva: World Health Organization.

World Professionals Association for Transgender Health – WPATH (2013). *WPATH Consensus Process Regarding Transgender and Transsexual-Related Diagnoses in ICD-11 – 31 May 2013*. Retrieved March 14, 2014, from http://www.wpath.org/uploaded_files/140/files/ICD%20Meeting%20Packet-Report-Final-sm.pdf.

Young, I. (1990). *Throwing Like a Girl and Other Essays in Feminist Philosophy and Social Theory*. Bloomington: Indiana University Press.

Zito, E., & Valerio, P. (Eds) (2013). *Genere: Femminielli - esplorazioni antropologiche e psicologiche*. Naples: Dante & Descartes.

Zachar, P., & Kendler, K. S. (2012). The removal of pluto from the class of planets and homosexuality from the class of psychiatric disorders: a comparison. *Philosophy, Ethics, and Humanities in Medicine*, 7, 4.

Zachar, P., & Lobello, S. G. (2012). Commentary: A Game for Every Kind of Umpire (Almost). In J.Phillips, et al. (Eds). The six most essential questions in psychiatric diagnosis: a pluralogue part 1: conceptual and definitional issues in psychiatric diagnosis. *Philosophy, Ethics, and Humanities in Medicine*, 7:3. Retrieved April 29, 2014 from http://www.ncbi.nlm.nih.gov/pmc/articles/PMC3305603/

Zucker, K. J. (2010). The DSM diagnostic criteria for gender identity disorder in children. *Archives of Sexual Behavior*, 39(2), 477- 498.

In: Gender Identity
Editor: Beverly L. Miller

ISBN: 978-1-63321-488-0
© 2014 Nova Science Publishers, Inc.

Chapter 5

GENDER DYSPHORIA IN CHILDREN AND ADOLESCENTS

Davide Dèttore[1,3], Jiska Ristori[2,3] and Paolo Antonelli[3]

[1]Department of Health Sciences, University of Florence, Florence, Italy
[2]Department of Clinical Physiopathology, University of Florence, Florence, Italy
[3]Unity for Atypical Gender Identities in Developmental Age
Miller Institute, Florence, Italy

ABSTRACT

Gender Dysphoria (GD) is a complex and most probably multifactorially caused condition and it is increasingly a matter of interest in the media and scientific literature. In particular, it is expressed by a significant discomfort that is usually associated with the incongruence between natal sex and gender identity and it represents a dimensional phenomenon that can occur with different degrees of intensity. The most extreme form of GD is usually accompanied by a desire for gender reassignment (GR). GD can have an early onset, since preschool age, with extremely variable and hard to predict clinical outcomes. Etiopathogenic theories are still uncertain and no specific etiological factor determining atypical gender development has been found to date, but there seems to be an increasing evidence of a biologic and/or genetic component involved. Professionals that deal with this kind of issues need to be able to recognize gender variant youth in order to perform an early assessment, to support awareness and structuring of sexual identity dimensions, to prevent associated psychopathology (if present), and consequently to improve the quality of life. Despite international guidelines being available, treatment of gender dysphoric children and adolescents is still controversial and there is currently poor consensus on psychological and medical intervention. Specialized GD services appear to be important in order to prevent suffering and distress and ensure psychosocial wellbeing of gender variant children/adolescents and their families. Aim of this chapter is to deal with psychological, medical and ethic aspects related to GD in children and adolescents, and to provide an overview of current debates and clinical options available internationally.

INTRODUCTION

Gender atypical development in youth is increasingly a matter of interest in the media and scientific literature (Sills, 2014). In general, there seems to be a much greater public awareness of the complexities that gender-variant children encounter in their day-to-day lives (Zucker & Wood, 2011). Issues regarding the psychotherapeutic and medical needs of gender variant and gender dysphoric youth are in fact perhaps the area of transgender healthcare that elicits more controversy (Dèttore et al., in press; Lev, 2004).

Considering the great variability of terminology in the transgender field, definitions used in this chapter follow below. *Gender Identity* consists in the continuous and persistent sense of the Self as a male, a female (Money, 1975), or other gender, different from the binary of two genders (Dèttore et al., in press). The concept of *Gender Identity* differs from the ones of *Gender Role* and *Sexual Orientation*. In particular, *Gender Role* indicates behaviors, attitudes, and personality traits which, within a given society and historical period, are typically attributed to, expected from, or preferred by persons of one gender (Steensma, Kreukels, de Vries, & Cohen-Kettenis, 2013). *Sexual Orientation* can be defined by a person's responsiveness to sexual stimuli. The most salient dimension of sexual orientation is the sex of the person to whom one is attracted (Fisher et al., in press). Furthermore, the terms *Gender Variance* and *Transgederism* describe a various group of individuals who cross or transcend culturally defined categories of gender (Fisher et al., in press) and are generally used with reference to individuals who present features of atypical gender identity development (Di Ceglie, 2013).

Moreover, *Gender Dysphoria* (GD) is characterized by a marked incongruence between one's gender identity and assigned gender, associated with clinically significant distress or impairment in social, occupational or other important areas of functioning (DSM-5; APA, 2013). GD is not a homogeneous condition, but represents a dimensional phenomenon that can occur with different degrees of intensity of which only the most extreme form is usually accompanied by a desire for gender reassignment (GR; Dèttore et al., in press). According to these definitions, a transsexual person is an individual who identifies as a member of the opposite gender and, consequently to his/her GD, wishes to adapt the body to his/her gender identity through both medical and surgical reassignment, as much as technically possible (Fisher et al., in press). On the other hand, some individuals who experience gender variance do not necessarily wish a complete cross-gender identification, do not always need clinical attention (Diamond & Butterworth, 2008; Lee, 2001), may or may not experience distress and they may or may not want to live as "the other gender" (Cohen-Kettenis & Pfäfflin, 2010).

GD can have an early onset, since preschool age, with extremely variable and hard to predict outcomes. Younger children may report GD, yet most of them will ultimately not meet criteria for GD once they become pubertal (Bradley & Zucker, 1997). Prospective follow-up studies show that childhood GD does not invariably persists into adolescence and adulthood. If the results from all outcome studies are combined, about 15% (range 2%-27%) of the GD children appear to remain gender dysphoric in adolescence (Steensma, Biemond, de Boer, & Cohen-Kettenis, 2011). While in prepubertal children there seems to be a greater fluidity, malleability and variability in outcomes (Byne et al., 2012), the persistence of GD into adolescence and adulthood appears to be much higher (Coleman et al., 2011) and seems to be more likely if the GD has been more severe in childhood (Spack et al., 2012; Steensma, van der Ende, Verhulst, & Cohen-Kettenis, 2013; Wallien & Cohen-Kettenis, 2008). For example, in the follow-up study conducted by de Vries, Noens, Cohen-Kettenis, van Berckelaer-Onnes and Doreleijers (2010), 70 adolescents, diagnosed with GD and given gonadotropin-releasing hormone analogues (GnRHa), all continued with GR.

Steensma et al. (2011) underline the importance of adolescence and in particular the period between 10 and 13 years to be crucial in the process of persisting or desisting of GD. Three possible contributing factors were identified as involved in the increase or decrease of gender discomfort: puberty, changes in the environment associated with being more explicitly treated as one's natal sex (first years in high school), and sexuality (Steensma et al. 2011).

GD youths often present with psychological symptoms, including anxiety, depression, suicidal ideation and attempts, self-harm behaviors (Spack et al., 2012), low self-esteem, lack of self-worth and are often socially isolated or bullied by peers and adults (Fisher et al., in press). Although there are cases of comorbid psychiatric disorders, these psychological symptoms are often the result of the discomfort GD individuals feel in their own bodies and of the social rejection they experience (Fisher et al., in press; Spack et al., 2012). In particular, these psychological symptoms seem to worsen with the onset of puberty, when adolescents have to experience the effects of a body that changes in an unwanted direction (Hembree et al., 2009). Also retrospective accounts from adult transsexuals indicate that psychological problems, such as depression and anxiety, often arise during puberty as a consequence of the distress that accompanies their bodily changes (Fisher et al., in press; Kreukels & Cohen-Kettenis, 2011).

GD is a complex and most probably multifactorially caused phenomenon. Adolescents with GD have no proven genetic, anatomic, or hormonal abnormalities (Hembree et al., 2009). Etiopathogenic theories are still uncertain and no specific etiological factor determining atypical gender development has been found to date (Dèttore et al., in press). With the current state of knowledge it remains plausible that a complex interaction between a biological predisposition in combination with intra- and inter- personal factors contribute to a development of GD (de Vries & Cohen-Kettenis, 2012).

Treatment of GD youth is controversial and there is currently no consensus on psychological and medical intervention. This is likely related to the fact that there are no properly designed outcome studies evaluating psychological interventions and only a few studies evaluating medical interventions (Dèttore et al., in press; de Vries & Cohen-Kettenis, 2012).

Considering differences in outcomes, prepubertal children and adolescents with GD do not undergo the same diagnostic procedures and goals.

Regarding children, Zucker, Wood, Singh and Bradley (2012) advocate a developmental and biopsychosocial model of treatment. Goals for treatment are formulated on a case-by-case basis and may include reduction in GD and acceptance of the biologic sex (Zucker et al., 2012). According to the Dutch Approach, the clinical management of children with GD contains elements of a therapeutic approach but is not directed at the GD itself; it focuses instead on treating emotional, behavioural and family problems that may or may not have an impact on the child's GD (de Vries & Cohen-Kettenis, 2012).

Regarding adolescents, after a careful psycho-diagnostic evaluation medical intervention can be considered under strict conditions (de Vries & Cohen-Kettenis, 2012). International published guidelines for the treatment of adolescents with GD (Hembree et al., 2009), as well as the latest *Standards of Care* (SOC, 7th edition; Coleman et al., 2011) by the *World*

Professional Association for Transgender Health (WPATH), have recommended suppression of puberty by using reversible GnRHa at Tanner stage 2/3 for adolescents who fulfill strict eligibility criteria (Hembree et al., 2009). Furthermore, GD adolescents, whose GD persists and that fulfill specific criteria, may be eligible for early cross-sex hormone treatment (CHT; between 16 and 18 years), followed by GR surgery at 18 years. Both general and psychological functioning seems to benefit in selected adolescents with GD (de Vries & Cohen-Kettenis, 2012; de Vries, Steensma, Doreleijers, & Cohen-Kettenis, 2011) that meet specific criteria (Coleman et al., 2011; Fisher et al., in press).

GD clinics in Europe, as well as in Northern America, have been characterized by increase in the number of referrals and by a decline in age at which medical interventions, aiming at GR, are requested (de Vries & Cohen-Kettenis, 2012; Steensma, Kreukels et al., 2013; Zucker et al., 2012). Early GR may be a solution for some selected GD adolescents, but of course it is important to offer different types of help according to a range of diverse needs (Di Ceglie, 2013). Many academic centers treat adults with GD, but few pediatric centers provide specific care for adolescents with GD. Specialized GD services appear to be important in order to prevent suffering and distress and ensure psychosocial wellbeing of gender variant children/adolescents and their families. Furthermore, professionals that deal with this kind of issues need to be able to recognize gender variant youth in order to perform an early assessment, to support awareness and structuring of sexual identity dimensions, to prevent associated psychopathology (if present), and consequently to improve the quality of life (Spack, 2013).

Aim of this chapter is to deal with psychological, medical and ethic aspects related to GD in children and adolescents, and to provide an overview of current debates and clinical options available internationally.

GENDER DYSPHORIA IN CHILDREN

In most cases, gender identity and gender role are congruent with each other and in line with natal sex. Furthermore, for the vast majority of people gender identity is established in toddlerhood, is consistent with biological sex and remains fixed (Adelson, 2012). This counts also for children with gender non-conformity in toy, play, and playmate preferences. Gender non-conformity is in fact not the same as GD (Coleman et al., 2011). In particular, gender non-conformity refers to the extent to which a person's gender identity, role, or expression differs from the cultural norms prescribed for people of a particular gender (Adelson, 2012). Conversely, as outlined before, GD refers to the discomfort or distress that is caused by a discrepancy between a person's gender identity and assigned gender at birth (Knudson, DeCuypere, & Bockting, 2010). Only some gender non-conforming people experience GD at some point in their lives.

The diagnosis of GD in childhood, once called Gender Identity Disorder, appeared in the psychiatric nomenclature for the first time in the DSM-III (APA, 1980) and is currently listed in the *Diagnostic and Statistical Manual of Mental Disorders, 5 Edition* (DSM-5; APA, 2013). In particular, the diagnostic criteria to be fulfilled for GD in childhood are outlined as follows:

A A marked incongruence between one's experienced/expressed gender and assigned gender, of at least 6 months' duration, as manifested by at least six of the following (one of which must be Criterion A1):

1 A strong desire to be of the other gender or an insistence that one is the other gender (or some alternative gender different from one's assigned gender);

2 In boys (assigned gender), a strong preference for cross-dressing or simulating female attire; or in girls (assigned gender), a strong preference for wearing only typical masculine clothing and a strong resistance to the wearing of typical feminine clothing;

3 A strong preference for cross-gender roles in make-believe play or fantasy play;

4 A strong preference for the toys, games, or activities stereotypically used or engaged in by the other gender;

5 A strong preference for playmates of the other gender;

6 In boys (assigned gender), a strong rejection of typically masculine toys, games, and activities and a strong avoidance of rough-and-tumble play; or in girls (assigned gender), a strong rejection of typically feminine toys, games, and activities;

7 A strong dislike of one's sexual anatomy;

8 A strong desire for the primary and/or secondary sex characteristics that match one's experienced gender.

B The condition is associated with clinically significant distress or impairment in social, school, or other important areas of functioning.

Furthermore, the diagnosis requires to specify if GD comes or not with a Disorder of Sex Development (DSD; e.g., a congenital adrenogenital disorder such as congenital adrenal hyperplasia or androgen insensitivity syndrome). DSD are a wide range of congenital conditions characterized by different levels of prenatal androgens resulting in variability of any component of sexual differentiation, included gender psychosexual development (Fisher et al., in press). DSD are not considered anymore as a criterion for differential diagnosis for GD as it happened in previous editions of the DSM, but the two conditions can now coexist since there is good clinical evidence that individuals with a DSD can experience GD (Richter-Appelt & Sandberg, 2010).

In the diagnosis and treatment of GD children, the perspective of development must be taken into account (de Vries & Cohen-Kettenis, 2012). Gender variant behavior and even the wish to be of the other gender can in fact be either a phase or a normal developmental variant without any adverse consequences for a child's current functioning (de Vries & Cohen-Kettenis, 2012; Bartlett, Vasey, & Bukowsky, 2000). In some cases, GD with an acute onset can be understood as a stress response to a specific event, as for example a newborn sibling of the opposite sex (Zucker & Bradley, 1995). In other cases, cross-gender behaviors may be associated with self-soothing or reduction of anxiety. However, for GD children, cross-gender behaviors do not represent a transient phase or an expression of gender non-conformity, but reflect a deep and persistent cross-gender identification that causes significant discomfort with their assigned gender and impairment in main areas of functioning. As mentioned before, GD is a dimensional phenomenon and, as it happens in adults, also in children there appears to be heterogeneity in GD features: some children demonstrate extremely gender non-conforming behaviors and wishes, accompanied by persistent and severe discomfort with their primary sex characteristics. In other children, these characteristics are less intense or only partially present (Cohen-Kettenis, Steensma, & de Vries, 2011; Knudson et al., 2010).

Preschool children, as young as age two, may show features that could indicate GD (de Vries & Cohen-Kettenis, 2012). From a developmental perspective, the onset seems to occur during the same period that more typical sex-dimorphic behaviors can be observed in young children (Zucker & Bradley, 1995). For example, sex-typed toy preferences exist as early as age 12-24 months (Jadva, Hines, & Golombok, 2010), with boys showing more interest in a car compared to a doll and vice versa. Furthermore, pre-pubertals with GD may express the wish or assert to be or that they will grow to be the other gender. In addition, they may prefer clothing, toys and games that are commonly associated with the other gender and may show marked cross-gender identification in role-playing, dreams, and fantasies. Also, they usually prefer playing with other-sex peers. In some cases, they may be perceived by strangers as the other gender and may ask to be called by a name of the other gender. Usually, they display intense negative reactions to parental attempts to contrast cross-gender behavior and some may refuse to attend school or social events where such behaviors are not allowed. Anatomic disphoria may be present; for example natal males may refuse to urinate in a sitting position or some natal girls may express a desire to have a penis or claim to have a penis or that they will grow one when older (APA, 2013; Zucker & Bradley, 1995). They may also state that they do not want to develop breasts. It has been observed that young children are less likely than older children, adolescents and adults to express extreme and persistent anatomic dysphoria. Expressions of anatomic dysphoria seem, in fact, more common with the onset of puberty (APA, 2013).

At the moment, the majority of the demographic information about transgender youth comes from research performed in the main clinics specialized in GD: Canada, the United Kingdom, and the Netherlands (Steensma et al., 2014; Zucker, 2010). There have not been formal epidemiologic studies to assess the prevalence of gender variance and GD in childhood (Shumer & Spack, 2013). The *Child Behavior Checklist* (CBCL; Achenbach & Edelbrock, 1983) has been used as a tool to estimate the prevalence of gender variance in childhood. In reviews of American and Dutch CBCL, results from non-referred patients (aged 4-11), 5-12% of children had affirmative answers to items focusing on gender variance (Verhulst, Van der Ende, & Koot, 1996; Zucker, Bradley, & Sanikhani, 1997), percentage that seems to decrease from ages 4-5 to ages 6-13 years (Bradley & Zucker, 1997). Regarding the Italian situation, a study was conducted by Dèttore, Ristori and Casale (2011) on 350 children aged between 3 and 5 years and the prevalence of gender variant responses was found to be 5.23% in males, 3.93% in females and 4.57% in the total sample.

GD during childhood does not inevitably continue into adulthood (Coleman et al., 2011). This is an important difference between GD in childhood and adolescence. Follow-up studies of prepubertal children, who were referred to clinics for assessment of GD, show how GD persisted into adulthood in about 6-23% of cases (Cohen-Kettenis, 2001; Zucker & Bradley, 1995). Boys in these studies were more likely to identify as gay in adulthood than as transgender (Green, 1985; Zucker & Bradley, 1995). Many gender-variant children will in fact ultimately develop a non-heterosexual orientation in adolescence (Wallien & Cohen-Kettenis, 2008). Other studies, also including girls, showed a 12-27% persistence rate of GD into adulthood (Drummond, Bradley, Peterson-Badali, & Zucker, 2008; Wallien & Cohen-Kettenis, 2008). Conversely, GD in children that intensifies with onset of puberty rarely subsides (Spack et al., 2012; Steensma & Cohen-Kettenis, 2011; Steensma et al., 2011).

Additional research is needed to refine estimates of the prevalence and persistence of GD in different populations worldwide (Coleman et al., 2011).

Also sex ratio is different between GD children and adolescents (Coleman et al., 2011). In clinically referred prepubertal (under 12 years) GD children, the male/female ratio ranges from 6:1 to 3:1 (Zucker, 2004), while in clinically referred GD adolescents (older than 12 years), the male/female ratio is close to 1:1 (Cohen-Kettenis & Pfäfflin, 2010). The disparity in childhood referrals for concerns regarding gender identity may reflect a true higher prevalence of gender issues in boys because of a greater biological vulnerability or it could be due to social factors. For example, cross gender behaviors could be less accepted in boys than in girls and therefore come more easily to the adult's attention.

Preoccupation with cross-gender wishes may develop at all ages after the first 2-3 years of childhood and often interfers with daily activities (APA, 2013). Children with GD seem to failure to develop age-typical same-sex peer relationships and skills; this may lead to isolation from peer groups and to distress. Furthermore, empirical studies have reported the presence of general behavior problems in both boys and girls with GD (Cohen-Kettenis, Owen, Kaijser, Bradley, & Zucker, 2003; Zucker & Bradley, 1995). These studies have shown that children with GD, on average, display levels of general psychopathology similar to those of demographically matched clinical controls and greater than those of non-referred controls (Zucker & Wood, 2011). In particular, boys with GD seem to show more internalizing than externalizing problems, whereas girls with GD seem to be characterized by more evenly distributed internalizing and externalizing problems (Zucker & Wood, 2011).

The association between GD and other psychological and behavioral problems can be considered in several ways. It may be that the distress associated with the desire to be of the other gender leads to socioemotional problems, including depression and anxiety. Also, psychological and behavioral problems could be related with poor peer relations due to social ostracism and rejection by same-sex peers. Furthermore, in prepubertal children, increasing age is associated with having more behavioral or emotional problems, this seems to be related to the increasing non-acceptance of gender variant behaviors by others (APA, 2013). Some children may be teased, bullied, or ostracized either in the family and/or in school because of their unusual presentation due to the incongruence between their self-perception and the body. GD, along with atypical gender expression, is in fact associated with high levels of stigmatization and discrimination (APA, 2013); this can be since an early age and can contribute to negative self-concept, increased rates of mental disorder comorbidity and early school drop-out (APA, 2013). Therefore, gender variant children can be vulnerable to develop a negative sense of Self (Yunger, Carver, & Perry, 2004). However, also in some non-Western cultures, anxiety has been found to be relatively common in individuals with GD, even in societies with accepting attitudes toward gender-variant behavior (APA, 2013). Furthermore, it is relatively common for gender dysphoric children to have co-existing internalizing disorders, such as anxiety and depression (Cohen-Kettenis et al., 2003; Wallien, Swaab, & Cohen-Kettenis, 2007; Zucker, Owen, Bradley, & Ameeriar, 2002).

In recent years, there has been an emerging interest in the possible co-occurrence of GD with Autistic Spectrum Disorders (ASD), as reviewed in de Vries et al. (2010). The prevalence of ASD seems to be higher in clinically referred gender dysphoric children than in the general population (de Vries et al., 2010). In particular, a number of clinicians have reported an apparent increase in the number of GD children and adolescents who appear to meet the criteria for a high-functioning ASD, such as Asperger's Pervasive Developmental

Disorder Not Otherwise Specified (Zucker, Wood, & VanderLaan, 2013). One explanation for a possible linkage between GD and ASD is the intense focus/obsessional interest in specific activities (Baron-Cohen & Wheelwright, 1999; Klin, Danovitch, Merz, & Volkmar, 2007). These children and adolescents appear to develop a fixation on gender, in much the same way that they develop other types of intense/obsessional/restricted interests (e.g., in street routes, in makes of dishwashers).

No unequivocal etiological factor or set of factors determining atypical gender development has been found to date, but with the current state of knowledge it is plausible that a complex interaction between a biological predisposition in combination with intra- and inter- personal factors contribute to a development of GD (Dèttore et al., in press). The phenomenon of GD remains unclear and it is probably multifactorial (Di Ceglie, 2013). Heritability studies have demonstrated the role of a genetic factor for the development of GD. Conversely, at the moment, a convincing candidate gene has yet not been identified (Klink & Den Heijer, 2013).

Since the appearance of the diagnosis of Gender Identity Disorder in the DSM, as well as through the action of the media, awareness about gender identity issues has increased and families have started to seek professional help (Di Ceglie, 2013). In recent years some specialized professional services have been set, especially in Western countries. In general, these have been characterized by an increase of the rate of referrals over the years and by a decrease of age referrals (de Vries & Cohen Ketenis, 2012). There is a general agreement that children with strong and persistent cross-sex identification causing emotional distress should be evaluated by a mental health professional (MHP) with a specific training in gender identity and GD issues. As recently reviewed by Zucker and Wood (2011), MHPs use a variety of gender identity specific tools and general assessments to aid in the diagnosis of GD and identification of coexisting comorbidities.

At the moment there is no consensus among professionals in the transgender health care regarding appropriate intervention or even appropriate goals of intervention for children diagnosed with GD. Considering that children with atypical gender identity development all present differently within the GD phenomenon, several types of help, according to a range of diverse needs, should be offered (Di Ceglie, 2013). Furthermore, the optimal approach in treating GD minors is controversial, as children have limited capacities to participate in decision-making regarding their own treatment and no legal ability to provide informed consent. Therefore they must rely on caregivers to make treatment decisions on their behalf, including those that will influence the course of their lives in the long term (Byne et al., 2012). Also, there is a lack of randomized controlled treatment outcomes studies (Drescher & Byne, 2013). General agreement does exist that avoidance of adult homosexuality is not an ethic goal in the treatment of GD, as homosexuality is not defined as a psychiatric disorder (Shumer & Spack, 2013). Furthermore, one overarching goal of psychotherapeutic treatment for childhood GD is to optimize the psychological adjustment and wellbeing of the child (Byne et al., 2012). In addition, professional interventions can help to alleviate distress in the child, assist the development of a child and observe the persistence or desistence of the GD at the beginning of puberty (Di Ceglie, 2013). In general, the reasons for offering professional help include the following: to explore whether or not there is a connection between GD and the associated difficulties, and devise the appropriate form of help.

In 1998 the Royal College of Psychiatrists published guidelines for the management of GD in children and adolescents. The guidelines emphasize the importance of adopting a developmental approach and that care should be provided within a well integrated, specialist multidisciplinary team which ensures that all aspects of a child's development are taken into consideration, including the family and social contexts in which the child lives. These guidelines were largely adopted by the *Harry Benjamin International Gender Dysphoria Association* (HBIGDA), now known as *World Professional Association for Transgendered Health* (WPATH) and recently revised in the *Standards of Care - 7 version* (Coleman et al., 2011).

In the past, several approaches to working with children with GD have been identified in the professional literature (Byne et al., 2012). In particular, behavioural and psychodynamic therapies have been largely used for this population with overall dissatisfactory results (Möller, Schreier, Li, & Romer, 2009). These have been focused on trying to intervene on GD by working with the child and the caregivers in order to decrease both cross-gender behaviors and identification. The underlying assumption was that these approaches could decrease the likelihood that GD would persist into adolescence and culminate in later adult transsexualism (Zucker, 2008). For various reasons (e.g., social stigma, likelihood of hormonal and surgical procedures with their associated risks and costs), persistence was considered to be an undesirable outcome by some (Green, 1985; Rekers & Morey, 1989; Zucker, 2008). At present, these interventions are referred as unethical by the WPATH SOC (Coleman et al., 2011). In line, some clinical associations, like the *American Academy of Child & Adolescent Psychiatry*, have explicitly formulated their position against psychological interventions that aim to treat non-conforming behaviors (Adelson, 2012).

In the report by the *American Psychiatric Association* (Byne et al., 2012), approaches to working with children with GD were classified in three groups. None of these supports the possibility of a medical intervention in children with GD. The first focuses on working with the child and caregivers to lessen GD and to decrease cross-gender behaviors, even if now it is considered as unethical by the WPATH SOC (Coleman et al., 2011). A second supports the goal to allow the developmental trajectory of gender identity to unfold naturally, without pursuing or encouraging a specific outcome. A third approach may entail affirmation of the child's cross gender identification by MHPs and family members.

In particular, Zucker et al. (2012) advocate a developmental and biopsychosocial model of treatment. Goals for treatment are formulated on a case by case basis, but may include elimination of peer ostracism, treatment of other psychopathology, reduction in GD and acceptance of the biologic sex (Zucker et al., 2012).

The Dutch Approach to GD in children and adolescents has become worldwide famous and pioneer in the field. In particular, intervention of GD in childhood it is not focused on reducing GD, but rather on treating emotional, behavioral and family problems that may have an impact on the child's GD (de Vries & Cohen-Kettenis, 2012). Considering that GD can exist in different degrees and can manifest itself in different ways (de Vries & Cohen-Kettenis, 2012), different procedures are performed. In particular, after evaluating GD and all aspects of the child's functioning (cognitive level, psychosocial functioning and school performance), an individual recommendation is given. If no concomitant problems have been observed and the child has sensitive parents, it can be sufficient to give advice on how to handle GD and support the child and the family in dealing with uncertainties of outcomes by adopting an attitude of *watchful waiting* (Di Ceglie, 2013). In particular, parents are encouraged in finding a balance between an accepting and supportive attitude toward GD, while at the same time protecting the child against any negative reactions and remaining realistic about the actual situation (de Vries & Cohen-Kettenis, 2012). Conversely, if from the psychological evaluation other concomitant psychological problems may occur, the child should be referred. As outlined before, in some cases gender variant behaviors can be a reaction to certain events and situations and can therefore reduce with psychotherapy. In general, it seems that many children with GD can benefit from psychotherapy aimed at securing a positive self-image or dealing with negative reactions from others (de Vries & Cohen-Kettenis, 2012). Without this support, these children may develop problems in social relationships, emotional and behavioral problems, low self-esteem or problems in school (de Vries & Cohen-Kettenis, 2012). The Dutch Approach does not provide any medical intervention before puberty (de Vries & Cohen-Kettenis, 2012). Once GD children reach puberty and in a selected number of cases, the distress brought about by pubertal changes can be alleviated by early pubertal suppression through the use of GnRHa, as described more in detail in the next paragraph.

Di Ceglie, since 1989, has set up the *Gender Identity Development Service* in the United Kingdom and has developed a model of management of GD youth. Emphasis is placed on fostering recognition and non judgmental acceptance of gender identity problems, ameliorating associated behavioral, emotional, and relationship difficulties, breaking the cycle of secrecy and encouraging exploration of the mind-body relationship by promoting close collaboration among professionals in different specialties, including pediatric endocrinology (Di Ceglie, 1998). In addition, Di Ceglie (2013) underlines the need to work on stigma, which is often related to the experience of atypical gender identity and is at times internalized by the individual with GD. It is also valuable to alleviate the feeling of shame that some children/adolescents and their families experience and enable people to develop skills in handling social interactions and dealing with possible hostility (Di Ceglie, 2013).

Spack et al. (2012) in the USA support the use of an early individual psychotherapy and family therapy that encourage acceptance of the child's budding gender development while simultaneously emphasizing the importance of remaining open to the fluidity of his or her gender identity and sexual orientation.

Hill, Menvielle, Sica and Johnson (2010) advocate an affirmative intervention, helping parents to support their child's declared gender rather than attempting to have the child conforming to the natal sex. There is an increasing parental support for young children living as their desired gender; however, desires may struggle with returning to live as their assigned gender at birth when their original desire to live as the opposite gender had been so strongly supported and encouraged by parents and providers, and even accepted by peers (Steensma & Cohen-Kettenis, 2011).

Finally, some words should be spent about social gender transition in childhood. This is in fact a controversial issue and divergent views are held by health professionals (Coleman et al., 2011). Several factors should be considered when and if a child should socially have a transition to his or her affirmed gender (Edwards-Leeper & Spack, 2012). Some children may prefer to live in their affirmed gender only at home or others may become depressed if not permitted to present in the desired gender in all life areas (Edwards-Leeper & Spack, 2012). The Endocrine Society's clinical practice guidelines oppose complete social role change in prepubertal children with GD (Hembree et al., 2009). Considering the low persistence of childhood GD, also the Dutch Team recommends not to make a complete social transition before the very early stages of puberty. It should be considered that a change back to the original gender role can be highly distressing and even result in postponement of this second social transition on the child's part (Steensma & Cohen-Kettenis, 2011). Furthermore, some children may not feel free to switch back to the gender assigned to his or her biological sex if he or she so desires in the future (Edwards-Leeper & Spack, 2012). In a qualitative follow-up study, several youth reported difficulties in realizing they no longer wanted to live in the role of the other gender and in making this clear to other people (Steensma et al., 2011). Another reason against early social transition is preventing children to develop a sense of reality too far and different from their physical reality, which could make extremely difficult the protracted treatments they will later need. MHPs can help families to make decisions regarding the timing and process of any gender role changes for their young children. They should provide information and help parents to weigh the potential benefits and challenges of particular choices (Coleman et al., 2011). MHPs can assist parents in identifying potential in between solutions or compromises (e.g., only when on vacation). It is also important that parents and professionals explicitly let the child know that there is a way back by keeping all options open. Parents are invited to create a safe environment where their child can feel free to experiment and develop optimally. In this regard, they are also advised to set boundaries in cross-gender behavior. For example, cross-dressing in a homo-transphobic neighborhood could expose a GD child to violence and aggression and therefore the child needs to be protected in order to be safe. In general, there seems to be agreement that the child's wishes and desires have to be supported by allowing the child to live in his or her affirmed gender to the extent that is deemed safe to do so for the child and the family (Coleman et al., 2011).

GENDER DYSPHORIA IN ADOLESCENCE

As previously described, GD can have an early onset with variable and hard to predict clinical outcomes (Korte et al., 2008). The diagnostic criteria of GD in adolescents may be indicators of a slight form of gender variance, or an early expression of a homosexual, bisexual, transgender or gender queer development, which may or not be accompanied by GD (de Vries & Cohen-Kettenis, 2012). As outlined before, from current studies it seems that a percentage between 12% and 27% of children diagnosed with GD in childhood will maintain GD also in adolescence and adulthood (Steensma et al., 2011). While childhood GD includes a wide range of outcomes, when it persists in the beginning of puberty, it will rarely desist into later adolescence and adulthood (de Vries & Cohen-Kettenis, 2012). To date, clinicians and researchers do not know when and how GD persists or desists. Clinical experience has shown that this often happens just before or just after the onset of puberty (de Vries & Cohen-Kettenis, 2012). Pubertal development can sometimes, even in well-established cases of GD in childhood, change the course of gender identity development, in line with the recent research on desisting and persisting GD after childhood by Steensma et al. (2011). The Authors suggest that young people, who changed their perceived gender identity, considered the period between 10 and 13 years of age to be crucial, associated with being more explicitly treated as one's natal sex; both persisters and desisters stated that the changes in their social environment (e.g., first years in high school), the anticipated and actual feminization or masculinization of their bodies, and their first experiences of falling in love and sexual attraction had influenced their gender related interest and behavior, feelings of gender discomfort and gender identification (Steensma et al., 2011).

Also regarding demographic information about transgender adolescents, most information come from the main clinics specialized in GD worldwide. There is no record of the characteristics of teenagers who are gender variant, but do not have GD or who seek other help than in specialized clinics (Khatchadourian, Amed, & Metzger, 2014; Steensma, van der Ende et al., 2013; Steensma et al., 2014; Zucker, 2010). Moreover, some observational studies that have reported the clinical characteristics of the Italian GD adult population referring to different clinics (Bandini et al., 2011; Bandini et al., 2013; Caldarera & Pfäfflin, 2011; Fisher et al., 2010; Fisher et al., 2013; Imbimbo et al., 2009; Madeddu, Prunas, & Hartmann, 2009; Meriggiola, Jannini, Lenzi, Maggi, & Manieri, 2010) can be useful to have some retrospective information about the sample during their adolescence. In particular, both female to male (FtM) and male to female (MtF) groups reported an early GD onset (before the age of 7). These Italian results about GD onset are in line with worldwide data (Cohen-Kettenis & Pfäfflin, 2010; Zucker et al., 2006).

At the moment, the patho-biological basis of GD is not yet known and the diagnosis is based primarily on psychological methods (Cohen-Kettenis et al., 2008; Sills, 2014). In May 2013 the DSM-5 (APA, 2013) was published with changes in name and criteria for GD in adolescence, as follows:

A   A marked incongruence between one's experienced/expressed gender and assigned gender, of at least 6 months duration, as manifested by 2 or more of the following indicators:
  a   A marked incongruence between one's experienced/expressed gender and primary and/or secondary sex characteristics (or, in young adolescents, the anticipated secondary sex characteristics);
  b   A strong desire to be rid of one's primary and/or secondary sex characteristics because of a marked incongruence with one's experienced/expressed gender (or, in young adolescents, a desire to prevent the development of the anticipated secondary sex characteristics);
  c   A strong desire for the primary and/or secondary sex characteristics of the other gender;
  d   A strong desire to be of the other gender (or some alternative gender different from one's assigned gender);
  e   A strong desire to be treated as the other gender (or some alternative gender different from one's assigned gender);
  f   A strong conviction that one has the typical feelings and reactions of the other gender (or some alternative gender different from one's assigned gender).
B   The condition is associated with clinically significant distress or impairment in social, occupational, or other important areas of functioning, or with a significantly increased risk of suffering, such as distress or disability.

Also for adolescents, the diagnosis specifies two subtypes, with or without DSD. In the DSM-5 diagnosis, the DSM-IV-TR criterion C (*The disturbance is not concurrent with a physical intersex condition*) has been abandoned.

The main differential diagnoses in adolescence from GD are an ego-dystonic homosexual orientation, transvestic fetishism, disorders in the psychotic spectrum (Korte et al., 2008) and body dysmorphic disorder (à Campo, Nijman, Merckelbach, & Evers, 2003). In particular, not all adolescents with GD manifest a clear and explicit desire for hormonal/surgical GR: these adolescents can be concerned about some aspects of their gender identity or other dimensions of their sexual identity (Dèttore et al., in press). Adolescents with a homosexual orientation have often a history of cross-gender behaviors and interests in childhood and may have trouble distinguishing the dimension of sexual orientation from gender identity or may find it difficult to accept their homosexuality due to more or less severe forms of internalized homonegativity (Lippa, 2008; Rottnek, 1999). In other cases, cross-dressing behaviors may be transient, occasional, compulsive or associated with a state of sexual arousal (as in transvestic fetishism) and they may be mistaken with a desire for hormonal/surgical GR: this can occur in individuals with or without psychiatric disorders (Dèttore et al., in press). In the specific case of psychotic spectrum conditions, delusions of belonging to the other gender may be present; in cases of major psychopathologies, the opportunity for a medical transition must be carefully evaluated and postponed in order to allow first the treatment of the psychiatric disorder and assess the levels of the psychosocial functioning over time (de Vries et al., 2006). Another point of evaluation is the adolescent's body image. For example, it can occur that adolescents may be frustrated as they perceive that their bodies will not feminize or masculinize at the same rhythm as in their peers. Additionally, more intense internal conflicts and stronger negative emotions can be present if secondary sex characteristics are already developed before the beginning of treatment: this case frequently leads to breast binding or to other attempts of concealing breasts, penis and/or testicles; and emotions and feelings of shame, guilt, frustration and regret may be present as the treatment has not begun earlier (Dèttore et al., in press).

Considering the developmental processes of adolescence, which often includes testing of different identities and expressions of the Self, special attention is required in the case of adolescents who arrive with a specific request for partial body changes: more frequently oriented towards a hormone therapy or some surgery only, to minimize the male or female phenotypic characteristics, but not to a complete GR (Dèttore et al., in press). In these cases forms of psychotherapy are probably more appropriate in order to clarify their situation and observe its evolution to make sure that any decision will be taken in a conscious way. Even in cases of adolescents who have a clear diagnosis of GD, but who do not show any psychological skills of resilience and who do not have adequate social support, it is sometimes advisable to postpone the CHT and/or surgery and try to create the basis for a positive outcome in the event of a possible GR (Cohen-Kettenis et al., 2008).

As for the differences between children and adolescents with GD, even if formal epidemiologic studies on GD are lacking, as described in the previous paragraph, an important difference is in the proportion for which dysphoria persists into adulthood and another one is in the sex ratios for each age group (Coleman et al., 2011). In most children GD will disappear before, or early in, puberty; however, in some children these feelings will intensify and body aversion will develop or increase as they become adolescents and their secondary sex characteristics develop (Cohen-Kettenis, 2001; Cohen-Kettenis & Pfäfflin, 2003; Drummond et al., 2008; Wallien & Cohen-Kettenis, 2008; Zucker & Bradley, 1995). Findings from one study suggest that more extreme gender nonconformity in childhood is associated with persistence of GD into late adolescence and early adulthood (Wallien & Cohen-Kettenis, 2008); but many adolescents and adults presenting with GD do not report a history of childhood gender-nonconforming behaviors (Docter, 1988; Landén, Wålinder, & Lundström, 1998). Thus, it can be a surprise to others (family of origin, friends and community members) when a youth's GD first becomes evident in adolescence. Adolescents who experience their primary and/or secondary sex characteristics and their sex assigned at birth as inconsistent with their gender identity may be intensely distressed about it, and many GD adolescents have a strong wish for hormones and surgery. Moreover, increasing numbers of adolescents have already begun living in their desired gender role upon entering high school (Cohen-Kettenis & Pfäfflin, 2003). Already for all these reasons, it is understandable the importance of having specialized services for GD adolescents.

Furthermore, adolescents with GD are often characterized by emotional and behavioral problems, self-harm, use and abuse of drugs, higher suicide risk and psychiatric comorbidity (Dèttore, 2005; Grossman & D'Augelli, 2007; Fisher et al., in press). In particular, adolescents seen in gender identity clinics tend to report higher rates of internalizing psychopathologies, compared with peers in the general population (D'Augelli, Grossman, & Starks, 2006; Wallien et al., 2007). Conversely, a Dutch study reports that adolescents seen in a GD clinic show less psychiatric comorbidity than a clinically referred psychiatric population (de Vries & Cohen-Kettenis, 2012). It is important to underline that a recent study reported that adolescents' behavioral and emotional problems, as well as depressive symptoms, decreased and general functioning significantly improved with access to a specialized GD service (de Vries et al., 2011).

Adolescents with GD often report being victims of discrimination and social stigma (de Vries et al., 2006; Nuttbrock et al., 2009) and, as it happens in childhood, this may have an impact on their psychological health.

Furthermore, suffering from GD and not being able to present socially in the desired gender role can lead to different problems. For example, adolescents with GD often have difficulties in connecting socially and romantically with peers while still in the undesired gender role, with the high risk for bullying and violence (Fisher et al., in press); the physical changes that come with puberty can further increase social marginalization, isolation from family, dropping out of school, and may lead them to the street and sometimes to criminal activity (Delemarre & Cohen-Kettenis, 2006; Spack, 2013).

Thus, when supporting and treating adolescents with GD (but also working with children), health professionals should broadly conform to the following WPATH SOC guidelines (Coleman et al., 2011, pp. 15-16):

1   MHPs should help families to have an accepting and nurturing response to the concerns of their gender dysphoric adolescent; families play in fact an important role in the psychological health and well-being of youth, and this also applies to peers and mentors from the community, who can be another source of social support (Brill & Pepper, 2008; Lev, 2004);

2   Psychotherapy should focus on reducing an adolescent's distress related to the GD and on ameliorating any other psychosocial difficulties; for youth pursuing sex reassignment, psychotherapy may focus on supporting them before, during and after reassignment (de Vries et al., 2006; Zucker, 2006);

3   Families should be supported in managing uncertainty and anxiety about their adolescent's psychosexual outcomes and in helping youth to develop a positive self-concept;

4   MHPs should not impose a binary view of gender: they should give ample room for people to explore different options for gender expression; correspondingly, hormonal or surgical interventions are appropriate for some adolescents but not for others;

5   Adolescents and their families should be supported in making difficult decisions regarding the extent to which adolescents are allowed to express a gender role that is consistent with their gender identity, as well as the timing of changes in gender role and possible social transition: for example, an adolescent might attend school while undergoing social transition only partly (e.g., by wearing clothing and having a hairstyle that reflects gender identity) or completely (e.g., by also using a name and pronouns congruent with gender identity); difficult issues include whether and when to inform other people of the adolescent's situation, and how others in their lives might respond;

6   Health professionals should support adolescents and their families as educators and advocates in their interactions with community members and authorities such as teachers, school boards and courts;

7   MHPs should strive to maintain a therapeutic relationship with gender-nonconforming adolescents and their families throughout any subsequent social changes or physical interventions: this ensures that decisions about gender expression and the treatment of GD are thoughtfully and recurrently considered; the same reasoning applies if an adolescent has already socially changed gender role prior to being seen by a MHP.

Considering the complexity of GD in adolescence, an early assessment of gender variant adolescents seems therefore important to support awareness and structuring of sexual identity dimensions, to prevent associated psychopathologies (if present), and consequently to improve quality of life and psychosocial wellbeing (de Vries & Cohen-Kettenis, 2012). Furthermore, there is a general agreement that an early evaluation of GD adolescents seems necessary to ward off an eventual delay or arrest in emotional, social or intellectual development (Fisher et al., in press).

Also regarding GD treatment in adolescence, behavioral and psychodynamic approaches were used with the major goal of persuading the adolescent that the real gender was the gender of assignment (Giordano, 2012). As outlined before, it is clear that any similar assumptions and goals are misplaced as research and clinical experience suggest that gender identity development is a complex phenomenon and that gender identity is not always congruent with physical appearance (Giordano, 2012). Therefore, effective therapy should be the one that helps the adolescent to flourish as a unique individual, whatever the innate gender is (Giordano, 2012). In this regard, it is important that in the therapeutic relationship, the clinician holds a neutral attitude regarding any possible outcome, in order to help the adolescent to explore openly the GD.

In continuity with what described in the previous paragraph regarding intervention for GD in childhood, models of care of gender dysphoric adolescents are controversial and there is currently no unanimous consensus on psychological and medical interventions.

Among adolescents referred to gender identity clinics, the number considered eligible for early medical treatment differs among countries and centers; for example, not all gender clinics offer puberty suppression: if such treatment is offered, the pubertal stage at which adolescents are allowed to begin varies from Tanner stage 2 to stage 4 (Delemarre-van de

Waal & Cohen-Kettenis, 2006; Zucker et al., 2012). The percentages of treated adolescents are likely influenced by the organization of health care, insurance aspects, cultural differences, opinions of health professionals and diagnostic procedures offered in different settings (Coleman et al., 2011).

Yet in selected cases and if specific criteria are satisfied, the main reference model is now considered the Dutch Approach, that is increasingly becoming a worldwide benchmark for assessment and treatment of adolescents with GD (de Vries & Cohen-Kettenis, 2012; Cohen-Kettenis et al., 2011; de Vries et al., 2006; de Vries & Cohen-Kettenis, 2012). In particular, the Dutch Team was pioneering in the field of GD beacuse they were the first to offer early medical interventions to adolescents.

As promoted within the Dutch Approach, the few studies evaluating medical interventions in GD adolescents seem to indicate that the administration of GnRHa (around age 12) to suppress puberty and early CHT (between 16 and 18 years), followed by GR surgery at 18 years, can be effective and positive for both general and mental functioning of selected adolescents with GD (de Vries et al., 2011; de Vries & Cohen-Kettenis, 2012).

In particular, the Dutch Approach is characterized by a multidimensional and multiphasic protocol including: medical and psychological assessment, possible psychotherapy, real life experience, puberty suppression, and hormonal and surgical reassignment (Dèttore et al., in press). This protocol requires a multidisciplinary team, consisting of child psychologists and psychiatrists, psychometrists, pediatric endocrinologists for the first phases, and, in the later surgical phases from the age of 18 years, it requires plastic surgeons, gynecologists and urologists (de Vries & Cohen-Kettenis, 2012). Furthermore, the psycho-diagnostic phase includes interviews with the adolescent and the parents, and the administration of psychometric tests, which are clinically useful and enable cross-clinic research, as evaluative comparisons or descriptions of populations. Moreover, it focuses on an evaluation of the adolescent's general psychological functioning as well as on GD. In particular, onset of the atypical gender attitudes and behaviors, their characteristics and pervasiveness of expression in the different life contexts are evaluated. Furthermore, if GD is present and a medical intervention is considered to be useful, the assessment process evaluates any psychological and/or social risk factors that could possibly interfere with the good outcome of the intervention and, if present, have usually to be treated before the GD. During the diagnostic process the adolescent has also to be accurately informed about the short and long term intervention consequences, as well as the limits of the hormone and surgical treatment in order to prevent unrealistic and frustrating expectations (de Vries & Cohen-Kettenis, 2012).

After this first diagnostic phase, with no medical intervention, an extended diagnostic phase, involving the administration of GnRHa, follows. GnRHa temporarily suppress the endogenous production of sex steroids, and thus leave the adolescents in a 'limbo' in which they can explore their real gender without the distress of developing in a body that they may perceive as alien (Cohen-Kettenis et al., 2011; de Vries et al., 2006; de Vries & Cohen-Kettenis, 2012; Fisher et al., in press).

International clinical guidelines (Hembree et al., 2009) and evidence gathered so far show that for adolescents with serious and persistent GD the best outcome is provided by beginning treatment with puberty suppressant medications as soon as pubertal changes happen, approximately at Tanner Stage 2 (Coleman et al., 2011; de Vries et al., 2006; Hembree et al., 2009; Wylie, Fung, Boshier, & Rotchell, 2009). GD typically becomes increasingly more significant at the onset of Tanner 2 puberty, when physical changes become unbearable

(Hembree et al., 2009; Spack, 2013). At this moment gender dysphoric adolescents may become aware that they cannot avoid the natural expression and shaping of their natal sex (Fisher et al., in press), which is incongruent with their gender identity (Spack, 2013). As outlined before, these undesired changes may seriously interfere with healthy psychological functioning and well-being (Hembree et al., 2009; Spack, 2013), and therefore an early medical intervention through the suppression of pubertal development is recommended in adolescents with GD before the irreversible development of secondary sex characteristics. Before starting the medical intervention with GnRHa, applicants need to meet the eligibility criteria in line with the WPATH SOC (Coleman et al., 2011): it is fundamental to begin at a time when the person is considered by the clinicians able to make an informed conscious and mature decision on that medical intervention (Spack, 2013).

These WPATH criteria for puberty-suppressing hormones for adolescents (Coleman et al., 2011) are:

1   The adolescent has demonstrated a long-lasting and intense pattern of gender nonconformity or GD (whether suppressed or expressed);
2   GD emerged or worsened with the onset of puberty;
3   Any coexisting psychological, medical, or social problems that could interfere with treatment (e.g., that may compromise treatment adherence) have been addressed, such that the adolescent's situation and functioning are stable enough to start treatment;
4   The adolescent has given informed consent and, particularly when the adolescent has not reached the age of medical consent, the parents or other caretakers or guardians have consented to the treatment and are involved in supporting the adolescent throughout the treatment process.

The last phase starts the GR, first using CHT: adolescents who have continued to strongly and consistently identify herself/himself with the other gender during the course of GnRHa treatment and still meet the initial criteria for starting a medical treatment are candidates for this next step in intervention (Edwards-Leeper & Spack, 2012). This step inducing the desired puberty by CHT is recommended at the age of 16 years, if eligibility criteria are met (Cohen-Kettenis et al., 2011; de Vries et al., 2006; de Vries & Cohen-Kettenis, 2012).

These criteria for hormone therapy, in line with the WPATH SOC (Coleman et al., 2011), are as follows:

1   Persistent, well-documented GD;
2   Capacity to make a fully informed decision and to consent for treatment;
3   Age of majority in a given country (if younger, follow the SOC outlined below);
4   If significant medical or mental health concerns are present, they must be reasonably well-controlled.

The WPATH SOC (Coleman et al., 2011) in fact underline that adolescents may be eligible to begin feminizing/masculinizing hormone therapy, preferably with parental consent: in many countries 16-year-olds are legal adults for medical decision-making and do not require parental consent, but ideally treatment decisions should be made among the adolescent, the family and the treatment team. Moreover, regimens for hormone therapy in gender dysphoric adolescents differ substantially from those used in adults (Hembree et al., 2009). The hormone regimens for youth are adapted to account for the somatic, emotional and mental development that occurs throughout adolescence (Hembree et al., 2009).

This intervention is partially reversible, meaning that the achieved modifications in external secondary sex characteristics will not disappear completely in case of discontinuation of CHT (Delamarre-van de Waal & Cohen-Kettenis, 2006).

The protocol of the induction of puberty in GD adolescents consists of a slow and progressive increase of sex steroids to adult dose. The sex steroid treatment should attempt to replicate the normal timing of puberty optimizing the pubertal growth spurt, the body composition for the assigned sex and the bone mineral accrual (Bertelloni, Dati, & Baroncelli, 2008; Hembree et al., 2009). Specifically, physical masculinization in FtM individuals is obtained through testosterone esters in an increasing dose, which results in suppressing menses, growing libido and gradually clitoral enlargement, although the final size never reaches the size of a normal penis (Delamarre-van de Waal & Cohen-Kettenis, 2006; Palmert & Dunkel, 2012; Spack, 2013). If still present, mild breast mass will become more atrophic and can even disappear (Delamarre-van de Waal & Cohen-Kettenis, 2006). In the case of MtF individuals, a female pubertal induction is obtained by using oestrogens at gradually increasing doses: too high oestrogen doses lead in fact to premature closure of the epiphyses and impaired adult height (Hembree et al., 2009; Palmert & Dunkel, 2012).

Finally, if desired, the last step of GR can be taken through surgical gender assignment when individuals are 18 years old or older, and if WPATH SOC eligibility criteria are fulfilled (Coleman et al., 2011).

First, in agreement with the WPATH SOC (Coleman et al., 2011), for the MtF individual surgical procedures may include the following:

1 Breast/chest surgery: augmentation mammoplasty (implants/lipofilling);
2 Genital surgery: penectomy, orchiectomy, vaginoplasty, clitoroplasty, vulvoplasty;
3 Nongenital, nonbreast surgical interventions: facial feminization surgery, liposuction, lipofilling, voice surgery, thyroid cartilage reduction, gluteal augmentation (implants/lipofilling), hair reconstruction, and various aesthetic procedures.

And for the FtM individual surgical procedures may include the following:

1 Breast/chest surgery: subcutaneous mastectomy, creation of a male chest;
2 Genital surgery: hysterectomy/salpingo-oophorectomy, reconstruction of the fixed part of the urethra, which can be combined with a metoidioplasty or with a phalloplasty (employing a pedicled or free vascularized flap), vaginectomy, scrotoplasty, and implantation of erection and/or testicular prostheses;
3 Nongenital, nonbreast surgical interventions: voice surgery (rare), liposuction, lipofilling, pectoral implants, and various aesthetic procedures.

These WPATH SOC eligibility criteria (Coleman et al., 2011) are based on the available evidence and expert clinical consensus, different recommendations are made for different surgeries, as well as the number and sequence of surgical procedures may vary from individual to individual according to their clinical needs. In summary, a criterion for all breast/chest and genital surgeries is documentation of persistent GD by a qualified MHP. For some surgeries, additional criteria include preparation and treatment consisting of feminizing/masculinizing hormone therapy and one year of continuous living in a gender role that is congruent with one's gender identity.

The sex reassignment surgery in GD individuals is a completely irreversible medical treatment (de Vries & Cohen-Kettenis, 2012).

Several studies have shown that only CHT or GR surgery were likely to have a positive impact in decreasing the levels of GD (Murad et al., 2010). These important findings seem to be confirmed by a recent study in adolescents showing that the GR surgery preceded by the GnRHa treatment is effective in overcoming GD (de Vries, in press). The concerns that early medical treatment has unfavorable physical effects have therefore to this date not been confirmed (Delamarre-van de Waal & Cohen-Kettenis, 2006; Kreukels & Cohen-Kettenis, 2011).

Last but not least, ethical concerns should be considered. The GnRHa have been provided since the late 1990s and the published body of literature shows that they have various important benefits (Giordano, 2012), as for example the following: the GnRHa reduce the adolescent's suffering (Cohen-Kettenis et al., 2008); the GnRHa aid in prolonging the diagnostic phase, as the body remains in a neutral early pubertal state, and therefore this phase, similarly to the real-life experience of living in the desired gender, provides time for the adolescent to continue meeting the clinicians and to self-explore without the severe distress caused by the pubertal changes (Hembree et al., 2009; Spack, 2013); the GnRHa improve the precision of the diagnosis (Cohen-Kettenis & Pfäfflin, 2003), and they can help to identify adolescents who are false positives (Delamarre-van de Waal & Cohen-Kettenis, 2006); the physical effects of pubertal suppression with the GnRHa are fully reversible, in fact if, after extensive exploring of his/her gender reassignment wish, the adolescent decides not to follow through with the transition to the opposite gender, the pubertal suppression can be discontinued and the spontaneous pubertal development will resume immediately and the individual will achieve his/her full maturation in the biological direction (Hembree et al., 2009; Manasco et al., 1988); the physical treatment outcome following medical interventions in adolescence is far more satisfactory than when treatment is started at an age at which secondary sex characteristics have already been developed (Delamarre-van de Waal & Cohen-Kettenis, 2006; Hembree et al., 2009; Smith, van Goozen, & Cohen-Kettenis, 2001); the GnRHa reduce the invasiveness of future medical and surgical interventions (Cohen-Kettenis & Pfäfflin, 2003); this reversible intervention with the GnRHa prevents emotional and psychological suffering which can be risky for self-harming behaviors and suicide attempts (Cohen-Kettenis et al., 2008; Edwards-Leeper & Spack, 2012; Grossman & D'Augelli, 2007).

However, the provision of the GnRHa has raised acute ethical dilemmas: intervening in the spontaneous development of puberty may seem morally unacceptable – as "playing god", or as interfering with "nature" (Giordano, 2012). In particular, this concern regards whether it is ethical or not to interfere with the future of the adolescent. For example, Stein (2013) argues that the "wait and see" approach by using GnRHa with GD adolescents might not be neutral position, but, on the other hand, it could encourage GD persistence through both biological and psychological mechanisms. However, it should be considered that the choice of not intervening is not a neutral option and that not taking any action may also interfere with the person's future. Insofar as interference with what is thought of as a "spontaneous" or "natural" development is likely to alleviate suffering and promote psychosocial wellbeing, therefore there is a strong reason in favor of interfering (Giordano, 2012). It should also be remembered that pubertal suppression with the GnRHa is reversible: if an adolescent decides to interrupt the treatment and let his/her body develop in the gender of assignment, s/he can stop the treatment and no irreversible modifications on his/her body will have taken place (Giordano, 2012).

So far the published clinical evidence shows that the outcome for gender dysphoric adolescents medically treated early on is vastly superior to the outcome of gender dysphoric adolescents who are left untreated until complete pubertal development (de Vries et al., 2011; Giordano, 2012).

This latter group is exposed to a series of health perils, psychological and social problems, which are to a significant extent resolved or prevented with the administration of the GnRHa, and the high suicide attempt rates afflicting gender dysphoric adolescents go down to zero in the population of gender dysphoric adolescents who receive medical treatment early in the first phases of intervention (Spack, 2013). Also regarding the hypothetical interference of GnRHa on the physiologic accretion of bone mass during puberty, studies show that, although a significant decrease of bone mass is seen during GnRHa treatment, during the long-term treatment of adolescents with GD, a continued increase of bone mass is observed. During cross-sex hormones, in fact, a catch-up of bone accretion produces results that are comparable with the normal physiologic increase (Delamarre, 2013).

CONCLUSION

Gender Dysphoria (GD) in children and adolescents is a complex and most probably multifactorially caused phenomenon that requires further studies. Although both children and adolescents are involved into a rapid and dramatic developmental process (physical, psychological, and sexual), there are a number of differences in the phenomenology, developmental course, and treatment approaches for GD in children and adolescents (Coleman et al., 2011).

Considering the great fluidity and variability in outcomes between gender dysphoric children and adolescents (particularly in prepubertal children), children and adolescents with GD do not undergo the same diagnostic procedures and models of care.

In the report by the *American Psychiatric Association* (Byne et al., 2012), the approaches to working with GD children were classified into three groups, but none of them supports the possibility of a medical intervention in GD children. The first one focuses on working with the child and caregivers to lessen GD and decrease cross-gender behaviors (although now it is considered as an unethical approach). The second approach supports instead the goal to allow the developmental trajectory of gender identity to unfold naturally without pursuing or encouraging a specific outcome; while the third one can entail affirmation of the child's cross-gender identification by MHPs and family members.

For example, Zucker et al. (2012), within the Toronto gender identity clinic, advocate a developmental and biopsychosocial model of intervention for GD children: treatment goals are formulated on a case-by-case basis and they can include reduction in GD and acceptance of the natal sex. On the other side, according to the Dutch Approach within the Amsterdam gender clinic, the clinical management of gender dysphoric children contains elements of a therapeutic approach, not directed at the GD itself, but it focuses on treating emotional, behavioral and family problems that may have an impact on the child's GD (de Vries & Cohen-Kettenis, 2012).

As for GD adolescents, in line with the Dutch Approach, which is now considered the main reference model of care, after a careful psycho-diagnostic assessment, medical interventions can be considered under strict conditions (de Vries & Cohen-Kettenis, 2012). International published guidelines for the treatment of GD adolescents (Hembree et al., 2009), as well as the latest WPATH SOC (7th edition; Coleman et al., 2011), have recommended the suppression of puberty by using reversible GnRHa at Tanner stage 2/3 for adolescents fulfilling strict eligibility criteria. Moreover, GD adolescents, whose GD persists and that fullfill specific criteria, may be eligible for early CHT (between 16 and 18 years old), followed by GR surgery at 18 years old (de Vries & Cohen-Kettenis, 2012). The benefits of this combined approach have been illustrated in the literature and they vastly outweigh any potential side-effects of the medications involved (de Vries & Cohen-Kettenis, 2012; de Vries et al., 2011; Spack, 2013). Furthermore, providing this combined approach, it is essential that all professionals, parts of the gender team, are aware of and understand the contributions of each discipline, and that they communicate throughout the process (Hembree et al., 2009).

Correspondingly, professionals working with gender dysphoric children and adolescents are in a delicate and difficult situation as for the clinical decisions. They may intervene in the case of false positives, thus causing damage, or choose not to intervene, and as a consequence not alleviate the suffering of gender dysphoric young people who actually need these interventions. Lately, the demand for specialized services for GD in childhood and adolescence has grown, as well as the age of children and adolescents who come to the attention of specialists and require a GR has decreased considerably. It is not unusual that children of 12 years old have an explicit request for a medical/surgical GR: this raises ethical and clinical issues with no easy solution (Cohen-Kettenis et al., 2011; de Vries & Cohen-Kettenis, 2012).

The individual, after the treatment has commenced, has to be made aware of the possibility of interrupting the therapy if that seems preferable to him or her. The certain and real side effects of not receiving the treatment might, for many, outweigh the potential risks of this intervention. Minors can make an informed and rational choice to take the potential risks of treatment, including those who have not been fully established, when the alternative is, in terms of probabilities, much worse for them (Giordano, 2012).

In summary, structured guidelines for the assessment and treatment of gender dysphoric children and adolescents will assist clinicians to help solving the acute sense of unhappiness and developing the resources to live peacefully with their families and peer groups (Byne et al., 2012).

Concluding, in response to the criticism that has been formulated against the early treatment of adolescents starting with puberty suppression using the GnRHa (Korte et al., 2008), the Dutch Gender Team underlines the importance of considering also the consequences of non-treatment: it does not represent a neutral option and, in some cases, can lead to negative consequences in the long-term for those individuals who have to wait until after their puberty to begin the CHT. These people could be pushed to behave in an irresponsible and dangerous way to have access to the CHT, the confidence in professional help could be undermined, and finally the developmental processes and psychological functioning could be impaired. Some gender dysphoric adolescents may develop psychiatric problems, such as depression, suicidal tendencies, anxiety, oppositional defiant disorders, or they may become school drop-outs, or even react with complete social withdrawal (Cohen-Kettenis et al., 2011; Fisher et al., in press). The puberty suppression seems to be beneficial for gender dysphoric adolescents by giving a relief of their prolonged severe suffering and distress, and by improving their quality of life (Steensma, Kreukels et al., 2013). The philosophy *in dubio abstine* could therefore be harmful (de Vries & Cohen-Kettenis, 2012; Fisher et al., in press).

REFERENCES

à Campo, J., Nijman, H., Merckelbach, H., & Evers, C. (2003). Psychiatric Comorbidity of Gender Identity Disorders: A Survey Among Dutch Psychiatrists. *American Journal of Psychiatry, 160*, 1332-1336.

Achenbach, T. M., & Edelbrock, C. (1983). *Manual for the child behavior checklist and revised child behavior profile.* Burlington: University of Vermont Department of Psychiatry.

Achenbach, T. M., & Rescorla, L. A. (2001). *Manual for the ASEBA school-age forms and profiles.* Burlington (VT): University of Vermont - Research Centre for Children, Youth and Families.

Adelson, S. L. (2012). Practice parameter on gay, lesbian, or bisexual sexual orientation, gender nonconformity, and gender discordance in children and adolescents. *Journal of the American Academy of Child and Adolescent Psychiatry, 51*, 957-974.

American Psychiatric Association (1980). *Diagnostic and Statistical Manual of Mental Disorders (Third Edition).* Washington, DC: American Psychiatric Association.

American Psychiatric Association (2000). *Diagnostic and Statistical Manual of Mental Disorders (Fourth Edition, Text Revision).* Washington, DC: American Psychiatric Association.

American Psychiatric Association (2013). *Diagnostic and Statistical Manual of Mental Disorders (Edition Five).* Washington, DC: American Psychiatric Association.

Bandini, E., Fisher, A. D., Castellini, G., Lo Sauro, C., Lelli, L., Meriggiola, M. C., Casale, H., Benni, L., Ferruccio, N., Faravelli, C., Dèttore, D., Maggi, M., & Ricca, V. (2013). Gender identity disorder and eating disorders: similarities and differences in terms of body uneasiness. *Journal of Sexual Medicine, 10*, 1012-1023.

Bandini, E., Fisher, A. D., Ricca, V., Ristori, J., Meriggiola, M. C., Jannini, E. A., Manieri, C., Corona, G., Monami, M., Fanni, E., Galleni, A., Forti, G., Mannucci, E., & Maggi, M. (2011). Childhood maltreatment in subjects with male-to-female gender identity disorder. *International Journal of Impotence Research, 23*, 276-285.

Baron-Cohen, S., & Wheelwright, S. (1999). 'Obsessions' in children with autism or Asperger syndrome: Content analysis in terms of core domains of cognition. *British Journal of Psychiatry, 175*, 484-490.

Bartlett, N. H., Vasey, P. L., & Bukowsky, W. M. (2000). Is gender identity disorder in children a mental disorder? *Sex Roles, 43*, 753-785.

Bertelloni, S., Dati, E., & Baroncelli, G. I. (2008). Disorders of sex development: Hormonal management in adolescence. *Gynecological Endocrinology, 24*, 339-346.

Bradley, S. J., & Zucker, K. J. (1997). Gender identity disorder: a review of the past 10 years. *Journal of the American Academy of Child and Adolescent Psychiatry, 36*(7), 872-880.

Brill, S. A., & Pepper, R. (2008). *The transgender child: A handbook for families and professionals.* Berkeley, CA: Cleis Press.

Byne, W., Bradley, S. J., Coleman, E., Eyler, A. E., Green, R., Menvielle, E. J., Meyer-Bahlburg, H. F. L., Pleak, R. R., & Tompkins, D. A. (2012). Report of the American Psychiatric Association Task Force on Treatment of Gender Identity Disorder. *Archives of Sexual Behavior, 41*(4), 759-796.

Caldarera, A., & Pfäfflin, F. (2011). Transsexualism and sex reassignment surgery in Italy. *International Journal of Transgenderism, 13*, 26-36.

Cohen-Kettenis, P. T. (2001). Gender identity disorder in DSM? *Journal of the American Academy of Child & Adolescent Psychiatry, 40*(4), 391-391.

Cohen-Kettenis, P. T., Delemarre-van de Waal, H. A., & Gooren, L. J. G. (2008). The Treatment of Adolescent Transsexuals: Changing Insights. *Journal of Sexual Medicine, 5*, 1892-1897.

Cohen-Kettenis, P. T., Owen, A., Kaijser, V. G., Bradley, S. J., & Zucker, K. J. (2003). Demographic characteristics, social competence, and behavior problems in children with gender identity disorder: A cross-national, cross-clinic comparative analysis. *Journal of Abnormal Child Psychology, 31*, 41-53.

Cohen-Kettenis, P. T., & Pfäfflin, F. (2003). *Transgenderism and Intersexuality in Childhood and Adolescence. Making Choices.* London: Sage Publications.

Cohen-Kettenis, P. T., & Pfäfflin, F. (2010). The DSM diagnostic criteria for gender identity disorder in adolescents and adults. *Archives of Sexual Behavior, 39*, 499-513.

Cohen-Kettenis, P. T., Schagen, S. E., Steensma, T. D., de Vries, A. L., & Delemarre-van de Waal, H. A. (2011). Puberty suppression in a gender-dysphoric adolescent: A 22-year follow-up. *Archives of Sexual Behavior, 40*(4), 843-847.

Cohen-Kettenis, P. T., Steensma, T. D., & de Vries, A. L. C. (2011). Treatment of adolescents with gender dysphoria in the Netherlands. *Child and Adolescent Psychiatric Clinics of North America, 20*, 689-700.

Coleman, E., Bockting, W., Botzer, M., Cohen-Kettenis, P. T., De Cuypere, G., Feldman, J., Fraser, L., Green, J., Knudson, G., Meyer, W. J., Monstrey, S., Adler, R. K, Brown, G. R., Devor, A. H., Ehrbar, R., Ettner, R., Eyler, E., Garofalo, R., Karasic, D. H., Lev, A. I., Mayer, G., Meyer-Bahlburg, H., Hall, B. P., Pfäfflin, F., Rachlin, K., Robinson, B., Schechter, L. S., Tangpricha, V., van Trotsenburg, M., Vitale, A., Winter, S., Whittle, S., Wylie, K. R., & Zucker, K. (2011). Standards of Care for the Health of Transsexual, Transgender, and Gender-Nonconforming People, Version 7. *International Journal of Transgenderism, 13*, 165-232.

D'Augelli, A. D., Grossman, A. H., & Starks, M. T. (2006). Childhood gender, atypicality, victimization, and PTSD among lesbian, gay, and bisexual youth. *Journal of Interpersonal Violence, 21*, 1462-1476.

Delamarre-van de Waal, H. A. (2013). Early Medical Intervention in Adolescents with Gender Dysphoria. In B. P. C. Kreukels, T. D. Steensma, & de Vries, A. L. C. (Eds.), *Gender Dysphoria and Disorders of Sex Development, Progress in Care and Knowledge* (Chapter 8). New York: Springer.

Delamarre-van de Waal, H. A., & Cohen-Kettenis, P. T. (2006). Clinical management of gender identity disorder in adolescents: A protocol on psychological and pediatric endocrinology aspects. *European Journal of Endocrinology*, *155*, 131-137.

Deogracias, J. J., Johnson, L. L., Meyer-Bahlburg, H. F. L., Kessler, S. J., Schober, J. M., & Zucker, K. J. (2007). *The Gender Identity/Gender Dysphoria Questionnaire for Adolescents and Adults. Journal of Sex Research*, *44*, 370-379.

Dèttore, D. (2005). *Il Disturbo dell'Identità di Genere.* Milano: McGraw-Hill.

Dèttore, D., Ristori, J., Antonelli, P., Bandini, E., Fisher, A. D., Villani, S., de Vries, A. L. C., Steensma, T. D., & Cohen-Kettenis, P. T. (in press). Gender dysphoria in adolescents: the need for a shared assessment protocol and the proposal of the AGIR protocol. *Journal of Psychopathology*.

Dèttore, D., Ristori, J., & Casale, S. (2011). GID and Gender Variant Children in Italy: a study in preschool children. *Journal of Gay and Lesbian Mental Health*, *15*, 12-29.

de Vries, A. L., & Cohen-Kettenis, P. T. (2012). Clinical Managment of Gender Dysphoria in Children and Adolescents: The Dutch Approach. *Journal of Homosexuality*, *59*, 301-320.

de Vries, A., Cohen-Kettenis, P. T., & Delemarre-Van de Waal, H. (2006). Clinical Management of Gender Dysphoria in Adolescents. *International Journal of Transgenderism*, *9*, 83-94.

de Vries, A. L., Noens, I., Cohen-Kettenis, P. T., van Berckelaer-Onnes, I., & Doreleijers, T. (2010). Autism spectrum disorders in gender dysphoric children and adolescents. *Journal of Autism and Developmental Disorders*, *40*, 930-936.

de Vries, A., Steensma, T. D., Doreleijers, T. A., & Cohen-Kettenis, P. T. (2011). Puberty suppression in adolescents with gender identity disorder: a prospective follow-up study. *Journal of Sexual Medicine*, *8*(8), 2276-2283.

Diamond, L. M., & Butterworth, M. (2008). Questioning gender and sexual identity: dynamic links over time. *Sex Roles*, *59*, 365-376.

Di Ceglie, D. (1998). Management and therapeutic aims with children and adolescents with gender identity disorders and their families. In D. Di Ceglie & D. Freedman (Eds.), *A stranger in my own body: Atypical gender identity development and mental health* (pp. 185-197). London: Karnac Books.

Di Ceglie, D. (2013). Care for Gender-Dysphoric Children. In B. P. C. Kreukels, T. D. Steensma, & de Vries, A. L. C. (Eds.), *Gender Dysphoria and Disorders of Sex Development, Progress in Care and Knowledge* (Chapter 8). New York: Springer.

Docter, R. F. (1988). *Transvestites and transsexuals: Toward a theory of cross-gender behavior.* New York, NY: Plenum Press.

Drescher, J., & Byne, W. (2012). GD/GV Children and Adolescents: Summarizing What We Know and What we Yet Have to Learn. *Journal of Homosexuality*, *59*, 501-510.

Drescher, J., & Byne, W. (2013). *Treating transgender children and adolescents: An interdisciplinary discussion.* New York, NY: Routledge.

Drummond, K. D., Bradley, S. J., Badali-Peterson, M., & Zucker, K. J. (2008). A followup study of girls with gender identity disorder. *Developmental Psychology*, *44*, 34-45.

Edwards-Leeper, L., & Spack, N. P. (2012). Psychological Evaluation and Medical Treatment of Transgender Youth in an Interdisciplinary "Gender Management Service" (GeMS) in a Major Pediatric Center. *Journal of Homosexuality*, *59*, 321-336.

Fisher, A. D., Bandini, E., Casale, H., Ferruccio, N., Meriggiola, M. C., Gualerzi, A., Manieri, C., Jannini, E., Mannucci, E., Monami, M., Stomaci, N., Delle Rose, A., Susini,

T., Ricca, V., & Maggi, M. (2013). Sociodemographic and Clinical Features of Gender Identity Disorder: An Italian Multicentric Evaluation. *Journal of Sexual Medicine*, *10*, 408-419.

Fisher, A. D., Bandini, E., Ricca, V., Ferruccio, N., Corona, G., Meriggiola, M. C., Jannini, E. A., Manieri, C., Ristori, J., Forti, G., Mannucci, E., & Maggi, M. (2010). Dimensional profiles of male to female gender identity disorder: An exploratory research. *Journal of Sexual Medicine*, *7*, 2487-2498.

Fisher, A. D., Ristori, J., Bandini, E., Giordano, S., Mosconi, M., Jannini, E. A., Godano, A., Greggio, N. A., Ricca, V., Dèttore, D., & Maggi, M. (in press). SIAMS-SIE-SIEDP-ONIG position statement on medical treatment in gender-dysphoric adolescents. *Journal of Endocrinological Investigation*.

Giordano, S. (2012). *Children with Gender Identity Disorder, a clinical, ethical and legal analysis*. London and New York: Routledge.

Green, R. (1985). Gender identity in childhood and later sexual orientation: Follow-up of 78 males. *The American Journal of Psychiatry*, *142*, 339-341.

Grossman, A. H., & D'Augelli, A. (2007). Transgender youth and life-threatening behaviors. *Suicide and Life-Threatening Behavior*, *37*(5), 527-537.

Hembree, W. C., Cohen-Kettenis, P. T., Delemarre-van de Waal, H. A., Gooren, L. J., Meyer, W. J.[3rd], Spack, N. P., Tangpricha, V., & Montori, V. M. (2009). Endocrine treatment of transsexuals persons: an Endocrine Society clinical practice guideline. *Journal of Clinical Endocrinology & Metabolism*, *94*, 3132-3154.

Hill, D. B., Menvielle, E., Sica, K. M., & Johnson, A. (2010). An affirmative intervention for families with gender variant children: Parental ratings of child mental health and gender. *Journal of Sex and Marital Therapy*, *36*, 6-23.

Imbimbo, C., Verze, P., Palmieri, A., Longo, N., Fusco, F., Arcaniolo, D., & Mirone, V. (2009). A report from a single institute's 14-year experience in treatment of male-to-female transsexuals. *Journal of Sexual Medicine*, *6*, 2736-2745.

Institute of Medicin (2011). *The health of lesbian, gay, bisexual, and transgender people: Building a foundation for better understanding*. Washington, DC: The National Academies Press.

Jadva, V., Hines, M., & Golombok, S. (2010). Infants' preferences for toys, colors, and shapes: Sex differences and similarities. *Archives of Sexual Behavior*, *39*, 1261-1273.

Khatchadourian, K., Amed, S., & Metzger, D. L. (2014). Clinical Management of Youth with Gender Dysphoria in Vancouver. *The Journal of Pediatrics*, *164*(4), 906-911.

Klin, A., Danovitch, J. H., Merz, A. B., & Volkmar, F. R. (2007). Circumscribed interests in higher functioning individuals with autism spectrum disorders: An exploratory study. *Research and Practice for Persons with Severe Disabilities*, *32*, 89-100.

Klink, D., & Den Heijer, M. (2013). Genetic Aspects of Gender Identity Development and Gender Dysphoria. In B. P. C. Kreukels, T. D. Steensma, & de Vries, A. L. C. (Eds.), *Gender Dysphoria and Disorders of Sex Development, Progress in Care and Knowledge* (Chapter 2). New York: Springer.

Knudson, G. A., DeCuypere, G., & Bockting, W. (2010). Recommendations for revision of the DSM diagnoses of gender identity disorders: Consensus statement of the World Professional Association for Transgender Health. *International Journal of Transgenderism*, *12*(2), 115-118.

Korte, A., Goecker, D., Krude, H., Lehmkuhl, U., Grüters-Kieslich, A., & Beier, K. M. (2008). Gender Identity Disorders in Childhood and Adolescence. *Deutschees Ärtzenblatt, 105*(48), 834-841.

Kreukels, B. P., & Cohen-Kettenis, P. T. (2011). Puberty suppression in gender identity disorder: the Amsterdam experience. *Nature Reviews Endocrinology, 7*(8), 466-472.

Kuyper, L. (2012). Transgenders in Nederland: prevalentie en attitudes. *Tijdschrift voor Seksuologie, 36,* 129-135.

Landén, M., Wålinder, J., & Lundström, B. (1998). Clinical characteristics of a total cohort of female and male applicants for sex reassignment: A descriptive study. *Acta Psychiatrica Scandinavica, 97*(3), 189-194.

Lee, T. (2001). Trans(re)lations: lesbian and female to male transsexual accounts of identity. *Women's Studies International Forum, 24,* 347-357.

Lev, A. I. (2004). *Transgender Emergence.* NewYork-London-Oxford: The Haworth Clinical Practice Press.

Lindgren, T. W., & Pauly, I. B. (1975). A body image scale for evaluating transsexuals. *Archives of Sexual Behavior, 4*(6), 639-656.

Lippa, R. A. (2008). The Relation Between Childhood Gender Nonconformity and Adult Masculinity–Femininity and Anxiety in Heterosexual and Homosexual Men and Women. *Sex Roles, 59*(9/10), 684-693.

Madeddu, F., Prunas, A., & Hartmann, D. (2009). Prevalence of axis II disorders in a sample of clients undertaking psychiatric evaluation for sex reassignment surgery. *Psychiatric Quarterly, 80,* 261-267.

Manasco, P. K., Pescovitz, O. H., Feuillan, P. P., Hench, K. D., Barnes, K. M., Jones, J., Hill, S. C., Loriaux, D. L., & Cutler Jr, G. B. (1988). Resumption of puberty after long term lutenizing hormone-releasing hormone treatment of central precocious puberty. *Journal of Clinical Endocrinology & Metabolism, 67,* 368-372.

Meriggiola, M. C., Jannini, E. A., Lenzi, A., Maggi, M., & Manieri, C. (2010). Endocrine treatment of transsexual persons: An Endocrine Society clinical practice guideline. Commentary from an European perspective. *European Journal of Endocrinology, 162,* 831-833.

Money, J. (1975). Ablatio penis: Normal male infant sex-reassigned as girl. *Archives of Sexual Behavior, 4,* 65-71.

Möller, B., Schreier, H., Li, A., & Romer, G. (2009). Gender Identity Disorder in Children and Adolescents. *Current problems in pediatric and adolescent health care, 39*(5), 117-143.

Murad, M. H., Elamin, M. B., Garcia, M. Z., Mullan, R. J., Murad, A., Erwin, P. J., & Montori, V. M. (2010). Hormonal therapy and sex reassignment: A systematic review and meta-analysis of quality of life and psychosocial outcomes. *Clinical Endocrinology, 72,* 214-231.

Nuttbrock, L., Hwahng, S., Bockting, W., Rosenblum, A., Mason, M., Macri, M., & Becker, J. (2009). Psychiatric impact of gender-related abuse across the life course of male-to-female transgender persons. *Journal of Sex Research, 47*(1), 12-23.

Palmert, M. R., & Dunkel, L. (2012). Delayed puberty. *New England Journal of Medicine, 366,* 443-453.

Rekers, G. A., & Morey, S. M. (1989). Personality problems associated with childhood gender disturbance. *Italian Journal of Clinical and Cultural Psychology, 1,* 85-90.

Richter-Appelt, H., & Sandberg, D. E. (2010). Should disorders of sex development be an exclusion criterion for gender identity disorder in DSM 5? *International Journal of Transgenderism, 12,* 94-99.

Rottnek, M. (1999). *Sissies & tomboys: Gender nonconformity & homosexual childhood.* New York: New York University Press.

Royal College of Psychiatrists (1998). *Gender identity disorders in children and adolescents - Guidance for management. Council Report CR63.* London: Royal College of Psychiatrists.

Shaffer, D., Gould, M. S., Brasic, J., Ambrosini, P., Fisher, P., Bird, H., & Aluwahlia, S. (1983). A Children's Global Assessment Scale (CGAS). *Archives of General Psychiatry, 40,* 1228-1231.

Shumer, D. E., & Spack, N. P. (2013). Current management of gender identity disorder in childhood and adolescence: guidelines, barriers and areas of controversy. *www.co-endocrinology.com.*

Sills, I. N. (2014). Increasing Expertise in Caring for the Gender Dysphoric Child and Transgender Adolescent. *The Journal of pediatrics, 164*(4), 689-690.

Smith, Y. L., van Goozen, S. H. M., & Cohen-Kettenis, P. T. (2001). Adolescents with gender identity disorder who were accepted or rejected for sex reassignment surgery: a prospective follow-up study. *Journal of the American Academy of Child and Adolescent Psychiatry, 40,* 472-481.

Spack, N. P. (2013). Management of Transgenderism. *JAMA, 309*(5), 478-484.

Spack, N. P., Edwards-Leeper, L., Feldman, H. A., Leibowitz, S., Mandel, F., Diamond, D. A., & Vance, S. R. (2012). Children and adolescents with gender identity disorder referred to a pediatric medical center. *Pediatrics, 129,* 418-425.

Steensma, T. D., Biemond, R., de Boer, F., & Cohen-Kettenis, P. T. (2011). Desisting and persisting gender dysphoria after childhood: a qualitative follow-up study. *Clinical Child Psychology and Psychiatry, 16*(4), 499-516.

Steensma, T. D., & Cohen-Kettenis, P. T. (2011). Gender transitioning before puberty? *Archives of Sexual Behavior, 40,* 649-650.

Steensma, T. D., Kreukels, P. C., de Vries, A. L. C., & Cohen-Kettenis, P. T. (2013). Gender identity development in adolescence. *Hormones and Behavior, 64,* 288-297.

Steensma, T. D., Kreukels, B., Jürgensen, M., Thyen, U., de Vries, A., & Cohen-Kettenis, P. T. (in press). The Utrecht Gender Dysphoria Scale: A validation study. *Archives of Sexual Behavior.*

Steensma, T. D., van der Ende, J., Verhulst, F. C., & Cohen-Kettenis, P. T. (2013). Gender Variance in Childhood and Sexual Orientation in Adulthood: A Prospective Study. *The Journal of Sexual Medicine, 10*(11), 2723-2733.

Steensma, T. D., Zucker, K. J., Kreukels, B. P. C., VanderLaan, D. P., Wood, H., Fuentes, A., & Cohen-Kettenis, P. T. (2014). Behavioral and Emotional Problems on the Teacher's Report Form: A Cross-National, Cross-Clinic Comparative Analysis of Gender Dysphoric Children and Adolescents. *Journal of Abnormal Child Psychology, 42*(4), 635-647.

Stein, E. (2013). Commentary on the treatment of gender variant and gender dysphoric children and adolescents: common themes and ethical reflections. In J. Descher & W. Byne (Eds.), *Treating transgender children and adolescente. An interdisciplinary discussion* (pp. 186-206). New York, NY: Routledge.

Verhulst, F. C., Van der Ende, J., & Koot, H. M. (1996). *Handleiding voor de CBCL 4–18 (Manual for the Child Behavior Checklist and Revised Child Behavior Profile)*. Rotterdam, the Netherlands: Sophia Kinderziekenhuis/Academisch Ziekenhuis Rotterdam/Erasmus Universiteit.

Wallien, M. S. C., & Cohen-Kettenis, P. T. (2008). Psychosexual outcome of gender-dysphoric children. *Journal of the American Academy of Child and Adolescent Psychiatry, 47*, 1413-1423.

Wallien, M. S. C., Swaab, H., & Cohen-Kettenis, P. T. (2007). Psychiatric comorbidity among children with gender identity disorder. *Journal of the American Academy of Child and Adolescent Psychiatry, 46*, 1307-1314.

Wylie, K. R., Fung, R., Boshier, C., & Rotchell, M. (2009). Recommendations of Endocrine Treatment for Patients with Gender Dysphoria. *Sexual and Relationship Therapy, 24*(2), 175-187.

Yunger, J. L., Carver P. R., & Perry, D. G. (2004). Does gender identity influence children's psychological well-being? *Developmental Psychology, 40*, 572-582.

Zucker, K. J. (2004). Gender identity development and issues. *Child and Adolescent Psychiatric Clinics of North America, 13*(3), 551-568.

Zucker, K. J. (2006). "I'm half-boy, half-girl": Play psychotherapy and parent counseling for gender identity disorder. In R. L. Spitzer, M. B. First, J. B. W. Williams & M. Gibbons (Eds.), *DSM-IV-TR casebook, volume 2* (pp. 321-334). Arlington, VA: American Psychiatric Publishing, Inc.

Zucker, K. J. (2008). Associated psychopathology in children and adolescents with gender identity disorder. In H. F. L. Meyer-Bahlburg (Chair), *From mental disorder to iatrogenic hypogonadism: Dilemmas in conceptualizing gender identity disorder (GID) as a psychiatric condition*. Symposium presented at the meeting of the American Academy of Child and Adolescent Psychiatry, Chicago.

Zucker, K. J. (2010). The DSM Diagnostic Criteria for Gender Identity Disorder in Children. *Archives of Sexual Behavior, 39*, 477-498.

Zucker, K., & Bradley, S. (1995). *Gender identity disorders and psychosexual problems in children and adolescents*. New York: Guilford Press.

Zucker, K. J., Bradley, S. J., Lowry Sullivan, C. B., Kuksis, M., Birkenfeld-Adams, A., & Mitchell, J. N. (1993). A gender identity interview for children. *Journal of Personality Assessment, 61*, 443-456.

Zucker, K. J., Bradley, S. J., & Sanikhani, M. (1997). Sex differences in referral rates of children with gender identity disorder: Some hypotheses. *Journal of Abnormal Child Psychology, 25*, 217-227.

Zucker, K. J., Mitchell, J., Bradley, S., Tkachuk, J., Cantor, J. M., & Allin, S. M. (2006). The recalled Childhood Gender Identity/Gender Role Questionnaire: Psychometric Properties. *Sex Roles, 54*(7/8), 469-483.

Zucker, K. J., Owen, A., Bradley, S. J., & Ameeriar, L. (2002). Gender-dysphoric children and adolescents: A comparative analysis of demographic characteristics and behavioral problems. *Clinical Child Psychology and Psychiatry, 7*, 398-411.

Zucker, K. J., & Wood, H. (2011). Assessment of gender variance in children. *Child and Adolescent Psychiatric Clinics of North America, 20*, 665-680.

Zucker, K. J., Wood, H., Singh, D., & Bradley, S. J. (2012). A developmental, biopsychosocial model for the treatment of children with gender identity disorder. *Journal of Homosexuality, 59*, 369-397.

Zucker, K. J., Wood, H., & VanderLaan, D. P. (2013). Models of Psychopathology in Children and Adolescents with Gender Dysphoria. In B. P. C. Kreukels, T. D. Steensma, & de Vries, A. L. C. (Eds.), *Gender Dysphoria and Disorders of Sex Development, Progress in Care and Knowledge* (Chapter 9). New York: Springer.

In: Gender Identity
Editor: Beverly L. Miller

ISBN: 978-1-63321-488-0
© 2014 Nova Science Publishers, Inc.

Chapter 6

THE GENETICS OF TRANSSEXUALISM

Rosa Fernández, Ph.D.[1], Isabel Esteva, M.D.[2], Esther Gómez-Gil, M.D.[3], Teresa Rumbo, Ph.D.[1], Mari Cruz Almaraz, Ph.D.[2], Ester Roda, Ph.D.[3], Juan-Jesús Haro-Mora, Ph.D.[2], Antonio Guillamón, M.D.[4] and Eduardo Pásaro, Ph.D.[1,*]

[1]Departamento de Psicología. Área Psicobiología,
Universidad de A Coruña, A Coruña, Spain
[2]Unidad de Transexualidad e Identidad de Género,
Hospital Carlos Haya, Málaga, Spain
[3]Unidad de Identidad de Género, Hospital Clinic, Barcelona, Spain
[4]Departamento de Psicobiología, UNED, Madrid, Spain

ABSTRACT

Transsexualism is a gender identity disorder with a multifactorial etiology. Neurodevelopmental processes and genetic factors seem to be implicated.

The aim of this study was to investigate the association between the genotype and female-to-male (FtM) and male-to-female (MtF) transsexualism by performing a karyotype and molecular analysis of three variable regions of the genes $ER\beta$ (estrogen receptor β), AR (androgen receptor) and $CYP19A1$ (aromatase).

Methods: We carried out a cytogenetic and molecular analysis in 273 FtMs, 442 MtFs, 371 control females and 473 control males. The control groups were healthy, age- and geographical origin-matched. The karyotype was investigated by G-banding and by high-density (HD) array in the transsexual group. The molecular analysis involved three tandem variable regions of genes $ER\beta$ (CA repeats in intron 5), AR (CAG repeats in exon 1) and $CYP19A1$ (TTTA repeats in intron 4). The allele and genotype frequencies, after division into short (S) and long (L) alleles, were obtained.

---

* Corresponding author: Eduardo Pásaro Méndez, Departamento de Psicología (Área Psicobiología), Universidad de A Coruña, Campus Elviña, 15071. A Coruña. Spain, E-mail address: eduardo.pasaro@udc.es, Teleph: +34 981 16 70 00, Fax: +34 981 16 71 15.

Results: No karyotype aberration has been linked to transsexualism (FtM or MtF), and prevalence of aneuploidy (3%) appears to be slightly higher than in the general population (0.53%). Concerning the molecular study, FtMs differed significantly from control females with respect to the median repeat length polymorphism $ER\beta$ ($P = 0.002$) but not to the length of the other two studied polymorphisms. The repeat numbers in $ER\beta$ were significantly higher in FtMs than in the female control group, and the likelihood of developing transsexualism was higher (odds ratio: 2.001 [1.15–3.46]) in the subjects with the genotype homozygous for long alleles.

No significant difference in allelic or genotypic distribution of any gene examined was found between MtFs and control males. Moreover, molecular findings presented no evidence of an association between the sex hormone-related genes ($ER\beta$, AR, and $CYP19A1$) and MtF transsexualism.

INTRODUCTION

As sexual differentiation of the genitals takes places in the first two months of pregnancy, and sexual differentiation of the brain starts during the second half of pregnancy (Bao and Swaab, 2011), these two processes may be influenced independently of each other, resulting in gender disphoria or transsexualism. If this is the case, one might expect to find, in transsexuals, male sexual organs and female brain structures, or vice versa. This also means that in the case of an ambiguous gender at birth, the degree of masculinization of the genitals may not reflect the same degree of masculinization of the brain (Swaab, 2007).

Transsexuality is characterized by a conviction of having been born in the wrong body. Male-to-female (MtF) and female-to-male (FtM) transsexuals are characterized by persistent other-sex identification and uneasiness with their assigned gender (American Psychiatric Association, 2000). The prevalence of transsexuality is 1:10,000 for MtF and 1:30,000 for FtM (Swaab, 2007).

It is not possible to identify a single cause for transsexualism, rather its origin seems to be multifactorial (Kockett and Fahrner, 1987; Bakker et al., 1993; Landen et al., 1996; Gooren, 2006). Important works have shown that it is associated with neurodevelopmental processes of the brain (Zhou et al., 1995; Kruijver et al., 2000; Bocklandt and Vilain, 2007; Luders et al., 2009; Luders et al., 2012; Zubiaurre-Elorza et al., 2013; Zubiaurre-Elorza et al., 2014) while others imply the involvement of genetic factors (Henningsson et al., 2005; Ujike et al., 2009; Hare et al., 2009; Fernández et al., 2013; Fernández et al., 2014).

One of the lines of research on biological determinants of transsexualism is based on sexual dimorphic brain nuclei. In humans several hypothalamic nuclei have been reported to be sexually dimorphic with respect to size and/or shape: Postmortem brain studies have shown that the volume and the number of neurons of the central part of the bed nucleus of the *stria terminalis* (BSTc) and the third interstitial nucleus of the anterior hypothalamus (INAH3) are feminized in MtF transsexuals (Zhou et al., 1995; Kruijver et al., 2000). A similar pattern was reported in the INAH3 of FtMs (García-Falgueras and Swaab, 2008).

Recently, the gray and white matter regions of the brain of FtMs were studied before and after cross-sex hormonal treatment. The white matter microstructure pattern in untreated FtMs was closer to males than to females; before testosterone treatment they presented a female phenotype with a masculine and/or defeminized profile in brain bundles that are related to complex cognitive function (Rametti et al., 2011). Only these bundles respond to androgenization and they do so in the way that males respond (Rametti et al., 2012). In relation to the gray matter, untreated FtMs showed evidence of subcortical gray matter masculinization; they presented a masculinization of their right putamen. However, their cortical thickness (CTh) did not differ from control females but it was greater than in males in the parietal and frontal cortices (Zubiaurre-Elorza et al., 2014).

Luders et al., (2009) analyzed magnetic resonance imaging (MRI) data of 24 MtFs not yet treated with cross-sex hormones to determine whether gray matter volumes in MtFs more closely resemble people who share their biological sex, or people who share their gender identity. The results revealed that regional gray matter variation in MtFs is more similar to the pattern found in men than in women. However, MtFs show a significantly larger volume of regional gray matter in the right putamen compared to men. These findings provide new evidence that transsexualism is associated with a distinct cerebral pattern, which supports the assumption that brain anatomy plays a role in gender identity (Luders et al., 2009).

Rametti et al., (2011) conducted a microstructure analysis of white matter by DTI (diffusion tensor imaging) in 18 MtF, finding that MtF transsexuals differed from both male and female controls bilaterally in the superior longitudinal fasciculus, the right anterior cingulum, the right forceps minor, and the right corticospinal tract. These findings reveal that the white matter microstructure pattern in untreated MtF transsexuals falls halfway between the pattern of male and female controls. Some fasciculi do not complete the masculinization process in MtF transsexuals during brain development.

The idea of genetic factor involvement in transsexualism has come mainly from familial studies (Green and Keverne, 2000; Green, 2000), familial cases of twins being concordant for transsexualism (Gómez-Gil et al., 2010; Heylens et al., 2012), and from molecular genetic studies of certain polymorphisms of androgen and estrogen system genes (Sosa et al., 2004; Henningsson et al., 2005; Bentz et al., 2008; Hare et al., 2009; Ujike et al., 2009; Fernández et al., 2013; Fernández et al., 2014).

But sexual differentiation of the brain in mammals is significantly influenced by sex hormones and other circulating hormones (Baba et al., 2007). The androgen receptor gene (AR) is implicated in the differentiation of the cortical cortex. The possession of an allele with a smaller number of CAG repeats confers more efficient functioning of the receptor and is associated with "masculinization" of the cortex in adolescence (Raznahan et al., 2010).

For the estrogen receptor gene (ER), two subtypes, the alpha ERα and beta ERβ, have been identified (Enmark and Gustafsson, 1999). Expression of the beta subtype is clearly higher in several brain regions (Osterlund and Hurd, 2001) and male mice lacking functional ERβ have an incompletely defeminized brain and behavior (Kudwa et al., 2005). Estrogen receptor α is primarily involved in masculinization, while estrogen receptor β has a major role in defeminization of sexual behaviors (Kudwa et al., 2005).

Moreover, animal studies have clearly demonstrated that prenatal exposure to testosterone plays a primary role in neural and behavioral sexual differentiation (Hines, 2006). Testosterone binds to and activates androgen receptors (ARs) and is converted to estrogen by aromatase cytochrome P450 (CYP19A1) in the brain and consequently activates the central estrogen receptors ERα and ERβ. It may cause masculinization directly by activation of AR or indirectly by activation of ERs (Sato et al., 2004; Kudwa et al., 2006).

Aromatase cytochrome P450, which is necessary for the conversion of androgens to estrogens, plays an important role in the sexual differentiation of the brain. In humans, the gene CYP19A1 is expressed in multiple areas of the brain, notably the temporal and frontal neocortex, the hippocampus, and the hypothalamus (Stoffel-Wagner et al., 1999; Hayes et al., 2000). It is believed that sex differences in estrogen levels as a result of aromatization of androgen may explain the sexual dimorphisms found in the hypothalamus (Gorski, 1991).

Hence, the genes coding for the *ERβ*, *AR* and *CYP19A1* are reasonable candidates in the quest for genes that may influence the likelihood of developing transsexualism.

Previous studies analyzing these genes have presented discordant results. Henningsson et al. (2005) in a genetic study of transsexualism in a population consisting of 29 MtFs from Sweden found significant differences when they examined the *ERβ* gene but not with respect to the other two studied polymorphisms (*AR* and *CYP19A1*). Hare et al. (2009) in a population consisting of 112 MtFs from Australia and Los Angeles (California) and 258 control non-transsexual males from Australia found a significant association between longer *AR* gene polymorphisms and MtF. Finally, Ujike et al., (2009) in a Japanese population of 168 FtMs and 74 MtFs found no significant differences in allelic or genotypic distribution of any gene examined (*AR*, *ERα*, *ERβ*, *CYP19A1*, and six polymorphisms: rs2008112, rs508653, V660L, H770H, rs572698 and PROGINS) between MtFs and control males or between FtMs and control females.

The aim of our study was to investigate the possible association of the karyotype and the sex hormone-related genes *ERβ*, *AR*, and *CYP19A1* with FtM and MtF transsexualism by performing a molecular analysis of the variable regions of these genes in 273 FtMs, 442 MtFs, 371 control females and 473 control males.

METHOD

Subjects

The subjects comprised 273 FtMs, 442 MtFs, 371 control females and 473 control males. The control groups were age- and geographical origin-matched females and males. The selection of FtMs and MtFs was conducted through both the Andalusian Gender Identity Unit (Carlos Haya Hospital of Málaga, Spain) and the Gender Identity Units of Catalonia (Clínic Hospital of Barcelona, Spain).

The diagnoses were made using the *Diagnostic and Statistical Manual of Mental Disorders* (DSM-IV) (American Psychiatric Association, 2000) and the International Classification of Diseases, tenth edition (ICD-10) (*World Health Organization (WHO)*, 1993). All patients received medical examinations by an endocrinologist to rule out the anomaly of the external genitalia and internal sex organs. Participants had no endocrine, neurological or major psychiatric comorbidity.

Sociodemographic, clinical, and psychiatric data that included any family background of transsexuality were completed for all patients as part of similar standard clinical assessments at both clinics (Esteva de Antonio et al., 2001; Bergero et al., 2001; Gómez-Gil et al., 2009).

The control groups (XX and XY) consisted of a random group of individuals from a Spanish population, previously used in metabolic and genetic studies (Soriguer et al., 2013; Fernandez-Real et al., 2013), age and sex adjusted with the FtM and MtF groups. They were free of any neurological, systemic, or psychiatric illness, as verified by a detailed interview. The study only included heterosexual controls without karyotype alterations.

The study was initiated after obtaining approval from the Ethics Committees of the University of A Coruña, Clínic Hospital (Barcelona), and Carlos Haya Hospital (Málaga). We drafted a protocol and obtained written, informed consent from each of the participants in the study.

Genetic Analysis

Cytogenetic Analyses

Peripheral blood samples were extracted for cytological and molecular analyses. Chromosomes were prepared according to standard techniques from peripheral blood (Moorhead et al., 1960) and the preparations were treated with trypsin to obtain G-banding (Seabright, 1971). Patients with chromosomal aberrations like translocations, inversions or chromosome number aberration were discarded.

Genotype Assessment by High-Density (HD) Array

Genomic DNA was extracted using the DNeasy Blood & Tissue Kit from Qiagen (Madrid, Spain). The genome-wide DNA copy number analyses were performed with CytoScan™ HD Array (Affymetrix, Madrid, Spain) in accordance with the manufacturer's instructions.

Molecular Analyses

The polymorphic regions were amplified by polymerase chain reaction (PCR) following the protocol outlined in Table 1. All genotyping was performed in a blinded fashion, and in triplicate in case of failure reactions. Finally, the fragments were analyzed by automated capillary electrophoresis 3130 XL Genetic Analyzer from Applied Biosystems (Madrid, Spain).

Statistical Analysis

Independent samples were analyzed by taking the medians of Mann-Whitney U and chi-square tests, using the median length of the alleles. To calculate the cutoff point to differentiate between S and L alleles, we took into account the median of the polymorphisms of individual genes from control groups.

Analyses were performed using SPSS 17.0 software (SPSS, Chicago, IL, USA). A P value ≤ 0.05 was considered significant. Interactions between the three polymorphisms were evaluated using a binary logistic regression model.

RESULTS

FtM Group

The analysis by HD array allowed us to examine the karyotype at the molecular level. Eleven patients from the FtM group were excluded for small autosomic pericentromeric inversions or translocations. We were unable to find any karyotypic alteration specific to transsexualism since genetic variants found in the FtM group have not clinical significance.

With respect to the analysis of polymorphisms, the FtM group (Table 2) showed 16 alleles for *ER*β, in a range of repeats between 19-35 (>85% alleles have 24 to 30 CA repeats); nineteen different alleles for the *AR* gene, the number of repeats extending between 7 and 28 (>90% alleles have 16-24 CAG repeats); and 11 alleles for the *CYP19A1* gene with a characteristic "U" distribution.

In the control female group the molecular analysis showed 14 alleles for the *ER*β gene extending between 18 and 31 repeats; the *AR* gene showed 16 alleles between 12 and 28 repeats and the gene *CYP19A1* showed 10 alleles between 4 and 14 repeats with the same characteristic "U" distribution.

Significant differences were found only in the *ER*β gene when we compared the number of repeats in both populations, with a higher value in the FtM group. The *P* value obtained in the Mann-Whitney *U*-test was 0.002 (Table 3).

To calculate the allele frequencies, we differentiated between short and long alleles, taking into account the median of the polymorphisms for individual genes from control group. So, for the *ER*β gene the difference between short and long alleles remained at 26 repeats, for the *AR* gene at 19 repeats and for *CYP19A1* at 8 repeats (Table 4). After this separation no significant differences were found in the distribution of long and short alleles for *AR* or *CYP19A1* but they were significant for the *ER*ß gene (*P* = 0.001 for the chi-square test) (Table 4). The odds ratio (OR) data for the allele frequency show significant values for the L allele vs. the S: OR = 1.508 with confidence intervals at 95% (1.777–1.911).

In a second step, the lengths of the three polymorphisms were subclassified to obtain genotype frequencies. The genotypes were determined as SS, LL and heterozygous SL (Table 5). The data show a significant association between phenotype and the *ER*β gene, *P* = 0.001 for the chi-square test. For all other variables no significant association was established (Table 5).

The OR data indicate a significant association only for the genotype LL versus SS: OR = 2.001 with confidence intervals at 95% (1.154 – 3.464) establishing that the probability of FtM transsexualism is greater for the genotype LL compared to SS.

Finally, we applied a binary logistic regression model. The three variables and all the possible interactions between them were included. We used the Wald statistic to evaluate the significance of coefficients (Table 6). The model fits the data based on the values of -2LL (701.761) and Cox-Snell R^2 (0.095) and Nagelkerke (0.129). None of these interactions were statistically significant.

MtF Group

The analysis by HD array allowed us to examine the karyotype at molecular level in the MtF population. Nine patients (2.04%) were excluded for diverse karyotype alterations described in Table 7. The aneuploidies found included two Klinefelter syndrome (47,XXY), two deletions of the terminal Yq arm (46,XY,Yqh-), three inversions (46,XY inv(12)(p11:q21); 46,XY inv(9)(p11:q12); 46,XY inv(2)(p11:q13)); two Robertsonian translocations (45,XY,t(13q:14q); 45,XY,t(9;22)/46XY). We were unable to find any karyotypic alteration specific to transsexualism.

With respect to the analysis of polymorphisms, the MtF group showed 16 alleles for *ER*β (Table 8), in a range of repetitions between 19-35 (>85% alleles have 24 to 29 CA repeats);

21 different alleles for the *AR* gene, in a range between 6 and 29 repetitions (almost 80% alleles have 16-22 CAG repeats); and 8 alleles for the *CYP19A1* gene in a range between 4-23 repetitions with a characteristic "U" distribution (>87% alleles have 7-8 or 12 TTTA repeats).

In the male control group, the molecular analysis showed 13 alleles for the *ERβ* gene extending between 19 and 31 repetitions (Table 8) (>88% alleles have 24 to 29 CA repeats); the *AR* gene showed 12 alleles between 12 and 25 repetitions (>86% alleles have 16-21 CAG repeats) and the gene *CYP19A1* showed 7 alleles between 7 and 14 repetitions with the same characteristic "U" distribution (86% alleles have 7-8 or 12 TTTA repeats).

Significant differences were found only in the *CYP19A1* gene when we compared the number of repeats in both populations (Table 9), but this significance disappears when calculating allele and genotype frequencies (Tables 10 and 11).

To calculate the allele frequencies we differentiate between S and L alleles, taking into account the median of the polymorphisms from control group. So, for the *ERβ* gene the difference between S and L alleles remained at 27 repeats, for the *AR* gene at 19 repeats and for *CYP19A1* at 8 repeats (Table 10). After this separation no significant differences were found in the distribution of S and L alleles for the genes.

In a second step, the lengths of the three polymorphisms were subclassified to obtain genotype frequencies (Table 11). The genotypes were determined as SS, LL, and heterozygous SL for the genes *ERβ* and *CYP19A1*, and S or L for the gene *AR*. For all variables no significant association was established. The odds ratio data indicate no significant differences (Table 12).

Finally, we applied a binary logistic regression model. The three variables and all the possible interactions among them were included in the model. We used the Wald statistic to evaluate the significance of the model coefficients (Table 13). None of these interactions were statistically significant.

DISCUSSION

We investigated the possible influence of the sex hormone-related genes *ERβ*, *AR*, and *CYP19A1* on the etiology of FtM and MtF transsexualism by performing a molecular analysis of the variable regions (the CA repeats in intron 5 of *ERβ*, the CAG repeats in exon 1 of *AR*, and the TTTA repeats in intron 4 of *CYP19A1*) in 273 FtMs, 442 MtFs, 371 control females and 473 control males. To the best of our knowledge, this is the largest group of transsexuals analyzed so far.

In accordance with previous data of aneuploidy in transsexual populations (Hengstschlager et al., 2003; Bearman G, 2007; Wylie and Steward, 2008; Inoubli et al., 2011; Auer et al., 2013), our data show a low incidence of chromosomal abnormalities in the transsexual population (3%) but slightly higher than in the general population (0.53%) (Maeda et al., 1991). Maeda et al. (1991) found 93 karyotype aberrations (52 in males, 41 in females) corresponding to a prevalence of 0.63% in a series of 14,835 liveborn infants.

The analysis by HD array showed no karyotypic alteration specific to transsexualism, which is in accordance with earlier reports based in the analysis of the karyotype from G bands. But, interestingly, the prevalence that was found in the current study was very similar to the previously reported ones (Hengstschlager et al., 2003; Bearman G. 2007; Wylie and

Steward, 2008; Inoubli et al., 2011; Auer et al., 2013). Inoubli et al. (2011) in a retrospective study of 368 transsexual individuals found a normal karyotype in 97.55%. Prevalence of abnormal karyotypes was 3.19% among MtFs, and 0.85% among FtMs. Auer et al., (2013) in a retrospective study of the Barr body and the karyotype in 270 transsexual individuals (165 MtF/105 FtM) reported that the prevalence of chromosomal abnormality in both groups was 1.5% (2.9% in the FtM and 0.6% in the MtF group). Wylie and Steward, (2008) found only one abnormal karyotype 47,XYY/46,XY in a population of 52 transsexual individuals. Hengstschlager et al., (2003) in an extensive cytogenetic and molecular analysis in a transsexual population of 30 MtFs and 31 FtMs could not detect any chromosomal aberrations with the exception of one balanced translocation 46,XY,t(6;17)(p21.3;q23). Bearman (2007) reported 2.5% variant karyotypes in about 400 transsexuals.

Our case series is the largest number of analyses of karyotypes from FtM and MtF reported in the literature, and it confirms that genetic aberrations detectable at the chromosome level are not significantly associated with transsexualism.

To the best of our knowledge, this is the first time that a technique of genotype assessment by HD array has been applied to research transsexualism. This allowed us to perform an exhaustive analysis of any type of small chromosomal alteration. So using this new advanced technique of molecular karyotyping and looking for the homogeneity of the sample analyzed, we excluded any chromosome alteration that may be disturbing the results.

With regard to the molecular study, to investigate the possible influence of the sex hormone-related genes on the etiology of transsexualism, we grouped the data into S and L alleles according to the median repeat length polymorphism obtained from control groups, obtaining the individual's genotype (SS, SL or LL) for the genes $ER\beta$, $CYP19A1$ and AR only in females, and (S or L) for the gene AR in males.

FtMs differed from the female control group with respect to the median length of the $ER\beta$ polymorphism but not with respect to the length of the other two studied genes. Considering the data for categorical variables of S and L alleles, and the genotypes SS, SL, and LL, we found significant P values for $ER\beta$ gene and genotype frequencies but not for AR and $CYP19A1$ genes. A greater number of CA repeats corresponds to greater probabilities of FtM transsexualism.

In the case of the AR and $CYP19A1$ genes, we did not find any relationship between the genes and FtM transsexualism. However, in the case of exon 5 of the $ER\beta$ gene, and contrary to that described by Ujike et al. (2009), we found a direct relationship between the length of the variable region and FtM transsexualism, so the greater the number of repeats, the greater the susceptibility to transsexualism.

Although there are numerous studies showing the inverse relationship between the length of the AR gene and the activity of the hormone-receptor complex (Chamberlain et al., 1994; Kazemi-Esfarjani et al., 1995; Tut et al., 1997), there are no data indicating that this same inverse relationship exists in the case of $ER\beta$. Some works bear on this possibility; Kudwa et al., (2006) found that male mice lacking functional $Er\beta$, when treated with the appropriate hormonal priming, display significantly more female-like sexual receptivity than littermates. Yet, lack of functional ERβ receptors does not impair normal expression of adult masculine sexual behavior.

They found no evidence showing that masculinization is deficient in ERβKO males (rats genetically modified without the $Er\beta$ gene); however, they propose that the defeminization process is incomplete in ERβKO males. Our data, like previous studies (Westberg et al.,

2001; Kudwa et al., 2005), support the finding that a functioning ERβ receptor is directly proportional to the size of the analyzed polymorphism, so a greater number of repeats implies greater transcription activation, therefore, an increase in ERβ receptor function, and finally, an increase in defeminization in females. Thus, one could propose that the greater efficiency of the estrogen-receptor complex by a high number of repeats would lead to a reduction in feminization, favoring a defeminization process (Even et al., 1994). Defeminization of the corticospinal tract has been described in FtMs (Rametti et al., 2011).

Westberg et al., (2001) found that women with relatively few CA repeats of the *ERβ* gene displayed higher testosterone levels and lower sex steroid hormone-binding globulin levels than those with many CA repeats. The apparent association between a short CA repeat region of the *ERβ* gene and high levels of testosterone suggests that this variant of the gene leads to a less active receptor (Hsiao et al., 1999). Needless to say, a detailed discussion of the possible mechanisms underlying the apparent association between the *ERβ* gene polymorphism studied and the hormonal activity must await further clarification of the influence of this polymorphism on receptor function.

With regard to the molecular study, MtFs did not differ from the male control group with respect to the median length of none of the polymorphisms. Considering the data for categorical variables of S and L alleles, and the genotypes, we did not find any significant values for *ERβ*, *AR* or *CYP19A1* genes.

Our data complement a previous study on transsexualism from Ujike et al. (2009), who examined the same three polymorphisms in a transsexual Japanese population (MtF and FtM). These authors analyzed so far the largest MtF population (74 MtF and 168 FtM), although the sample analyzed by us in this paper surpasses that analyzed by Ujike et al. In accordance with our study, these authors did not find any association either between the three polymorphisms and MtF transsexualism nor any interactions between the genetic variables.

Moreover, there are another two works addressing the molecular analysis of transsexualism: Henningsson et al., (2005) in a population of 29 Swedish MtFs, found significant differences when they examined the *ERβ* gene. They found that CA repeats in *ERβ* were significantly higher in MtFs than in controls. Furthermore, a logistic regression analysis also indicated significant associations of the three genes with MtF. However, because the P values were marginal and the patient number was quite small, the possibility of a type I error cannot be fully excluded.

In 2009, Hare et al., tried to replicate the findings in a larger sample consisting of 112 MtFs from Australia and Los Angeles (California) and 258 non-transsexual control males from Australia, and found significantly longer repeats of *AR* in patients than in controls, but not of *ERβ* or *CYP19A1*. However, the P value was again marginal ($P = 0.04$), and they compared different populations (Australian and Los Angeles (USA)). There might be differences between the two populations in this polymorphism that could be altering the statistics data (Sasaki et al., 2003). To the best of our knowledge, little is known about the distribution of these repeats among different human populations.

The number in our Spanish MtF sample was 442 MtFs, the largest MtF population analyzed so far, and it showed no significant association of MtF with *AR*, *ERβ* or *CYP19A1*. Significant differences ($P = 0.022$) were found only in the *CYP19A1* gene when we compared the number of repeats in both populations, but this significance disappears ($P = 0.079$ and $P = 0.205$) when calculating allele and genotype frequencies (Tables 11-13).

Aromatase cytochrome P450 (*CYP19A1*) is necessary for the conversion of androgens to estrogens, and it plays an important role in the sexual differentiation of the brain, but it has been previously demonstrated that variation in the gene for this subunit of the aromatase enzyme complex is not likely to be a major factor in male sexual orientation (DuPree et al., 2004).

The present study has several strengths. To the best of our knowledge, this is the first time that a technique of HD Array is applied to research transsexualism. This technique allows us to exclude any chromosome alterations that may be disturbing the results. Furthermore, this study has one of the largest sample sizes of MtFs analyzed.

However, there were some limitations in the present study. First, there are other variable regions and other genes that could be analyzed and that could complement our study. A second limitation, common to all human genetic studies, is that we were limited by the DNA sequence variability present in the particular population we studied.

Thus, our results do not suggest that *AR, ERβ* and aromatase per se play a role in the development of MtF transsexualism, and that naturally occurring variations in genes *AR, ERβ* and *CYP19A1* may not play a major role in MtF transsexualism.

CONCLUSION

1. Our data reveals that genetic aberrations detectable at the chromosome level are not significantly associated with transsexualism. The analysis of the karyotype only provides very limited information in the transsexual population.
2. Our data confirm a low incidence of chromosomal abnormalities in the transsexual population (3%) but higher than in the general population (0.53%).
3. Our data support the association between the *ERβ* gene and FtM transsexualism. The higher number of CA repeats implies greater transcription activation, and therefore, also lower feminization or a greater defeminization. Thus, the susceptibility to transsexualism was higher in the subjects with genotype homozygous LL (long/long alleles).
4. MtF transsexualism is not influenced by the regions analyzed.

ACKNOWLEDGMENTS

This work was supported by grants PSI2010-15115 (EP) and PSI2011-24496 (AG). We are grateful to the patients and control subjects who voluntarily participated in the study.

All authors contributed to and have approved the final manuscript. The authors declare no conflict of interest.

Table 1. Description of the polymorphic regions analyzed

Gene	Description	Position	Tandem repeat	Primers	Cycles and temperatures
ERβ	(Tsukamoto et al., 1998)	14q22–24	(CA)n intron 5	5'-AACAAAATGTTGAATGAGTGGG-3' 5'-GGTAAACCATGTCTGTACC-3' FAM	35 cycles: 92 °C 40 sec 57 °C 40 sec 72 °C 40 sec 72 °C 10 min
AR	(Sleddens et al., 1992)	Xq11-12	(CAG)n exon 1	5'-GTTCCTCATCCAGGACCAGGTA-3' 5'-GTGCGCGAAGTGATCCAGA-3' HEX	35 cycles: 92 °C 1 min 56 °C 1 min 72 °C 1 min 72 °C 10min
CYP19A1	(Polymeropoulos et al., 1991)	15q21.1	(TTTA)n intron 4	5'-TTACAGTGAGCCAAGGTCGT-3' 5'-GCAGGTACTTAGTTAGCTAC-3' NED	35 cycles: 92 °C 1 min 58 °C 1 min 72 °C 1 min 72 °C 10 min

Table 2. The alleles identified in this study. The table lists the frequencies of the alleles in XX controls and FtM for the *ERβ*, *AR* and *CYP19A1* genes

ERβ repeat length	Frequency control group	Frequency FtM	AR repeat length	Frequency control group	Frequency FtM	CYP19A1 repeat length	Frequency control group	Frequency FtM
18	1.01%	0.00%	7	0.00%	0.21%	4	0.81%	0.20%
19	4.66%	0.42%	8	0.00%	0.00%	5	0.00%	0.00%
20	5.26%	3.15%	9	0.00%	0.00%	6	0.40%	0.41%
21	8.30%	2.31%	10	0.00%	0.00%	7	30.73%	34.90%
22	6.28%	2.31%	11	0.00%	1.07%	8	24.12%	18.78%
23	1.21%	2.31%	12	1.62%	0.43%	9	4.99%	5.71%
24	8.70%	9.66%	13	0.00%	0.21%	10	1.62%	0.41%
25	3.44%	3.99%	14	0.40%	1.07%	11	7.95%	2.45%

Table 2. (Continued)

ERβ repeat length	Frequency control group	Frequency FtM	AR repeat length	Frequency control group	Frequency FtM	CYP19A1 repeat length	Frequency control group	Frequency FtM
26	9.31%	7.98%	15	0.81%	1.50%	12	28.57%	33.47%
27	22.06%	24.16%	16	10.93%	9.40%	13	0.67%	2.65%
28	21.05%	26.26%	17	17.81%	13.68%	14	0.13%	0.20%
29	6.68%	10.50%	18	14.98%	14.53%	15	0.00%	0.41%
30	1.21%	4.62%	19	13.77%	13.68%			
31	0.81%	1.05%	20	8.91%	12.18%			
32	0.00%	0.21%	21	11.74%	12.18%			
33	0.00%	0.21%	22	7.29%	8.12%			
34	0.00%	0.00%	23	4.86%	5.98%			
35	0.00%	0.84%	24	4.45%	3.21%			
			25	0.40%	1.50%			
			26	1.62%	0.43%			
			27	0.00%	0.43%			
			28	0.40%	0.21%			

Table 3. Median data of tandem repeats of *ERβ*, *AR*, and *CYP19A1* in FtM and XX control group

Gene	Group	N	Mean of tandem repeats	SD	Mann-Whitney U-test	P value
ERβ	Control group	371	25.56	1.90	31918	0.002[a]
	FtM group	238	26.83	1.86		
AR	Control group	365	19.27	1.88	40992	0.402[b]
	FtM group	236	19.45	2.19		
CYP19A1	Control group	371	9.33	1.56	42524	0.160[b]
	FtM group	245	9.51	2.24		

[a] Significant differences with respect to control group; $P \leq 0.05$.
[b] Nonsignificant differences with respect to control group; $P > 0.05$.
FtM = female-to-male; SD = standard deviation.

Table 4. Data of the allele frequencies for *ERβ*, *AR*, and *CYP19A1* after division into short and long alleles

Gene	Allele	Frequencies FtM group	Frequencies Control group	Chi-square test	P value
ERβ	Short (<26)	150 (31.51%)	303 (40.84%)	9.759	0.001[a]
	Long (≥26)	326 (68.49%)	439 (59.16%)		
		476 (100%)	742 (100%)		
AR	Short (<19)	253 (53.6%)	374 (44.38%)	1.618	0.203[b]
	Long (≥19)	219 (46.4%)	376 (55.62%)		
		472 (100%)	730 (100%)		
CYP19A1	Short (<8)	285 (52.2%)	416 (56.06%)	0.53	0.466[b]
	Long (≥8)	205 (41.8%)	326 (43.94%)		
		490 (100%)	742 (100%)		

[a] Significant differences with respect to control group; $P \leq 0.05$.

[b] Nonsignificant differences with respect to control group; $P > 0.05$.

FtM = female-to-male.

Table 5. Frequencies of the genotypes for *ERβ*, *AR*, and *CYP19A1* after division into SS, SL, and LL genotypes

Gene	Genotype	Frequencies FtM group	Frequencies Control group	Chi-square test	P value
ERβ	SS	24 (10.08%)	51 (13.75%)	13.086	0.001[a]
	SL	102 (42.86%)	201 (54.18%)		
	LL	112 (47.11%)	119 (32.08%)		
Total		238 (100%)	371 (100%)		
AR	SS	73 (30.9%)	101 (26.93%)	1.497	0.473[b]
	SL	107 (45.3%)	172 (45.87%)		
	LL	56 (23.7%)	102 (27.20%)		
Total		236 (100%)	365 (100%)		
CYP19A1	SS	79 (32.2%)	113 (30.46%)	0.656	0.720[b]
	SL	127 (51.8%)	190 (51.21%)		
	LL	39 (15.09%)	68 (18.33%)		

Table 5. (Continued)

Gene	Genotype	Frequencies FtM group	Frequencies Control group	Chi-square test	P value
Total		245 (100%)	371 (100%)		

[a] Significant differences with respect to control group; $P \leq 0.05$.
[b] Nonsignificant differences with respect to control group; $P > 0.05$.

FtM = female-to-male; L = long allele; S = short allele.

Table 6. Binary logistic regression analyses of gene–gene interactions for susceptibility to FtM Transsexualism

Gene	df	Wald	P value
ERβ	1	11.626	0.001[a]
AR	1	3.223	0.073[b]
CYP19A1	1	1.337	0.248[b]
AR by ERβ	2	0.716	0.397[b]
AR by CYP19A1	2	0.296	0.586[b]
CYP19A1 by ERβ	2	0.076	0.783[b]
AR by CYP19A1 by ERβ	3	0.523	0.470[b]

[a] Significant differences with respect to control group; $P \leq 0.05$.
[b] Nonsignificant differences with respect to control group; $P > 0.05$.

FtM = female-to-male.
df = degrees of freedom.

Table 7. Altered karyotypes found in MtF group that were excluded from the study

Karyotype	N	%
Karyotype available	442	100%
Unremarkable karyotype	433	97.96%
47,XXY	2	0.45%

Karyotype	N	%
46.XY,Yqh-	2	0.45%
46.XY inv(12)(p11:q21)	1	0.23%
46.XY inv(9)(p11:q12)	1	0.23%
46.XY inv(2)(p11:q13)	1	0.23%
45.XY,t(13q:14q)	1	0.23%
45XY,t(9;22)/46XY	1	0.23%

Table 8. The alleles identified in this study. The table lists the frequencies of the alleles in male control group and MtF for the _ERβ_, _AR_ and _CYP19A1_ genes

ERβ repeat length	Frequency control group	Frequency MtF	AR repeat length	Frequency control group	Frequency MtF	CYP19A1 repeat length	Frequency control group	Frequency MtF
18	0.00%	0.00%	6	0.00%	0.23%	4	0.00%	1.16%
19	0.36%	0.36%	7	0.00%	0.00%	5	0.00%	0.00%
20	4.63%	3.45%	8	0.00%	0.00%	6	0.00%	0.00%
21	1.42%	2.86%	9	0.00%	0.00%	7	26.92%	33.87%
22	1.07%	2.14%	10	0.00%	0.23%	8	27.27%	23.35%
23	1.07%	2.14%	11	0.00%	1.17%	9	8.04%	6.24%
24	8.54%	13.45%	12	2.14%	1.87%	10	0.00%	0.00%
25	6.05%	3.81%	13	0.00%	0.70%	11	2.45%	1.50%
26	14.59%	9.52%	14	0.71%	1.64%	12	31.82%	30.40%
27	22.42%	23.93%	15	0.00%	2.11%	13	3.15%	3.24%
28	25.98%	23.57%	16	9.29%	10.07%	14	0.35%	0.23%
29	11.39%	10.24%	17	17.14%	14.05%	15	0.00%	0.00%
30	2.14%	2.50%	18	21.43%	14.05%			
31	0.36%	1.07%	19	12.14%	11.01%			
32	0.00%	0.60%	20	15.00%	10.07%			
33	0.00%	0.00%	21	12.86%	10.07%			
34	0.00%	0.12%	22	4.29%	11.24%			
35	0.00%	0.24%	23	2.14%	4.92%			
			24	1.43%	2.11%			

Table 8. (Continued)

ERβ repeat length	Frequency control group	Frequency MtF	AR repeat length	Frequency control group	Frequency MtF	CYP19A1 repeat length	Frequency control group	Frequency MtF
			25	1.43%	1.17%			
			26	0.00%	1.41%			
			27	0.00%	1.17%			
			28	0.00%	0.47%			
			29	0.00%	0.23%			

Table 9. Dates of the median data of tandem repeats of *ERβ*, *AR* and *CYP19A1* in MtF and male control group

Gene	Group	N	Mean of tandem repeats	SD	Mann-Whitney U- test	P value
ERβ	Control group	471	26.49	2.40	379964.5	0.342[b]
	MtF group	414	26.41	2.51		
AR	Control group	467	18.90	2.77	93499.0	0.226[b]
	MtF group	420	19.05	3.21		
CYP19A1	Control group	472	9.29	2.19	379771.5	0.022[a]
	MtF group	428	9.11	2.34		

[a] Significant differences with respect to control group; $P \leq 0.05$.
[b] Nonsignificant differences with respect to control group; $P > 0.05$.
MtF = male-to-female; SD = standard deviation.

Table 10. Data of the allele frequencies for *ERβ*, *AR* and *CYP19A1* after division into short and long alleles

Gene	Allele	Frequencies MtF group	Frequencies Control group	Chi-square test	P value
ERβ	Short (<27)	311 (37.56%)	359 (38.12%)	0.057	0.8443[b]
	Long (≥27)	517 (62.44%)	583 (61.88%)		
Total		828 (100%)	942 (100%)		

Gene	Allele	Frequencies MtF group	Frequencies Control group	Chi-square test	P value
AR	Short (<19)	194 (46.19%)	230 (49.25%)	0.832	0.381 [b]
	Long (≥19)	226 (53.81%)	237 (50.75%)		
Total		420 (100%)	467 (100%)		
CYP19A1	Short (≤8)	504 (58.88%)	517 (54.77%)	3.091	0.079 [b]
	Long (>8)	352 (41.12%)	427 (45.23%)		
Total		856 (100%)	944 (100%)		

[a] Significant differences with respect to control group; $P \leq 0.05$.
[b] Nonsignificant differences with respect to control group; $P > 0.05$.

MtF = male-to-female.

Table 11. Frequencies of the genotypes for ERβ, *AR* and *CYP19A1* after division into SS, SL and LL genotypes

Gene	Genotype	Frequencies MtF group	Frequencies Control group	Chi-square test	P value
ERβ	SS	48 (11.59%)	55 (11.68%)	0.101	0.9479 [b]
	SL	215 (51.93%)	249 (52.87%)		
	LL	151 (36.47%)	167 (35.46%)		
Total		414 (100%)	471 (100%)		
AR	S	194 (46.19%)	230 (49.25%)	0.836	0.3818 [b]
	L	226 (53.81%)	237 (50.75%)		
Total		420 (100%)	467 (100%)		
CYP19A1	SS	149 (34.81%)	145 (30.72%)	3.143	0.205 [b]
	SL	206 (48.13%)	227 (48.09%)		
	LL	73 (17.06%)	100 (21.19%)		
Total		428 (100%)	472 (100%)		

[a] Significant differences with respect to control group; $P \leq 0.05$.
[b] Nonsignificant differences with respect to control group; $P > 0.05$.

MtF = male-to-female; L = long allele; S = short allele.

Table 12. The Odds Ratio values

Gene	Odds Ratio	P value
ERβ OR Long /Short (L/S)	1.0237 (0.8444 to 1.2410)	0.8118[b]
AR OR Long /Short (L/S)	1.1305 (0.8682 to 1.4722)	0.3624[b]
CYP19A1 OR Long /Short (L/S)	0.8456 (0.7014 to 1.0195)	0.0788[b]
ERβ OR Long-Long /Short-Short (LL/SS)	1.0361 (0.6637 to 1.6173)	0.8761[b]
AR OR Long-Long /Short-Short (LL/SS)	1.1305 (0.8682 to 1.4722)	0.3624[b]
CYP19A1 OR Long-Long /Short-Short (LL/SS)	0.7104 (0.4865 to 1.0373)	0.0767[b]

[a] Significant differences with respect to control group; $P \leq 0.05$.
[b] Nonsignificant differences with respect to control group; $P > 0.05$.

Table 13. Binary logistic regression analyses of gene–gene interactions for susceptibility to MtF transsexualism

Gene	df	Wald	P value
ERβ	1	-0.538	0.591[b]
AR	1	0.638	0.523[b]
CYP19A1	1	-1.432	0.152[b]
AR by ERβ	2	-0.047	0.962[b]
AR by CYP19A1	2	0.172	0.864[b]
CYP19A1 by ERβ	2	1.244	0.214[b]
AR by CYP19A1 by ERβ	3	-0.685	0.493[b]

[a] Significant differences with respect to control group; $P \leq 0.05$.
[b] Nonsignificant differences with respect to control group; $P > 0.05$.

MtF = male-to-female.

df = degrees of freedom.

REFERENCES

American Psychiatric Association (2000) Diagnostic and Statistical Manual of Mental Disorders, 4th ed. DSM-IV-TR, Washington, DC.

Auer, M.K., Fuss, J., Stalla, G.K., and Athanasoulia, A.P. (2013) Twenty years of endocrinologic treatment in transsexualism: analyzing the role of chromosomal analysis and hormonal profiling in the diagnostic work-up. *Fertil. Steril.* 100(4):1103-10.

Baba, T., Endo, T., Honnma, H., Kitajima, Y., Hayashi, T., Ikeda, H., Masumori, N., Kamiya, H., Moriwaka, O., and Saito, T. (2007) Association between polycystic ovary syndrome and female-to-male transsexuality. *Hum. Reprod.* 22(4):1011-6.

Bakker, A., van Kesteren, P.J., Gooren, L.J., and Bezemer, P.D. (1993) The prevalence of transsexualism in The Netherlands. *Acta Psychiatr. Scand.* 87(4):237-238.

Bao, A.M. and Swaab, D.F. (2011) Sexual differentiation of the human brain: relation to gender identity, sexual orientation and neuropsychiatric disorders. *Front Neuroendocrinol.* 32(2):214-26.

Bearman G. (2007) Karyotyping and genetics in the transgendered population. In: Ettner R, Monstrey S, Eyler AE, eds. *Principles of transgender medicine and surgery.* New York: Haworth Press.

Bentz, E.K., Hefler, L.A., Kaufmann, U., Huber, J.C., Kolbus, A., and Tempfer, C.B. (2008) A polymorphism of the CYP17 gene related to sex steroid metabolism is associated with female-to-male but not male-to-female transsexualism. *Fertil. Steril.* 90(1):56-59.

Bergero, M.T. , Cano, O.G., Esteva de Antonio, I., Giraldo, F., Gornemann, S.I., and Álvarez, O.P. (2001) Evaluación diagnóstica y seguimiento psicológico en la Unidad de Trastornos de Identidad de Género de Andalucía (Málaga). *Cir. Plast. Iberlatinamer.* 27:263-272.

Bocklandt, S. and Vilain, E. (2007) Sex differences in brain and behavior: hormones versus genes. *Adv. Genet.* 59:245-66.

Chamberlain, N.L., Driver, E.D., and Miesfeld, R.L. (1994) The length and location of CAG trinucleotide repeats in the androgen receptor N-terminal domain affect transactivation function. *Nucleic Acids Res.* 22(15):3181-3186.

DuPree, M.G. , Mustanski, B.S., Bocklandt, S., Nievergelt, C., and Hamer, D.H. (2004) A candidate gene study of CYP19 (aromatase) and male sexual orientation. *Behav. Genet.* 34(3):243-50.

Enmark, E. and Gustafsson, J.A. (1999) Oestrogen receptors - an overview. *J. Intern. Med.* 246(2):133-138.

Esteva de Antonio, I., Bergero Miguel, T., Giraldo Ansio, F., Cano Oncala, G., Ruyz de Adana, S. , Crespillo Gómez, C., and Soriguer Escofet, F. (2001) Unidad de trastornos de identidad de género en Andalucía. Experiencia del primer año de funcionamiento [Gender identity disorder unit in Andalusia. The experience of the first year]. Endocrinolologia y Nutricion 49:71–74.

Even, M.D., Laughlin, M.H., Krause, G.F., and vom Saal, F.S. (1994) Differences in blood flow to uterine segments and placentae in relation to sex, intrauterine location and side in pregnant rats. *J. Reprod. Fertil.* 102(1):245-252.

Fernandez-Real, J.M., Corella, D., Goumidi, L., Mercader, J.M., Valdes, S., Rojo Martinez, G., Ortega, F., Martinez-Larrad, M.T., Gomez-Zumaquero, J.M., Salas-Salvado, J.,

Martinez Gonzalez, M.A., Covas, M.I., Botas, P., Delgado, E., Cottel, D., Ferrieres, J., Amouyel, P., Ricart, W., Ros, E., Meirhaeghe, A., Serrano-Rios, M., Soriguer, F., and Estruch, R. (2013) Thyroid hormone receptor alpha gene variants increase the risk of developing obesity and show gene-diet interactions. *Int. J. Obes.* (Lond) 37:1499-1505.

Fernández, R., Esteva, I., Gómez-Gil, E., Rumbo, T., Almaraz, M.C., Roda, E., Haro-Mora, J.J., Guillamón, A., and Pásaro, E. (2013) The (CA)n Polymorphism of ERbeta Gene is Associated with FtM Transsexualism. *J. Sex Med.* 11:720-28.

Fernández, R., Esteva, I., Gómez-Gil, E., Rumbo, T., Almaraz, M.C., Roda, E., Haro-Mora, J.J., Guillamón, A., and Pásaro, E. (2014): The genes ERβ, AR and CYP19A1 are not associated with MtF transsexual individuals. *J. Sex Med.* In press.

García-Falgueras, A. and Swaab, D.F. (2008) A sex difference in the hypothalamic uncinate nucleus: relationship to gender identity. *Brain* 131(Pt 12):3132-3146.

Gooren, L. (2006) The biology of human psychosexual differentiation. Horm Behav 50(4):589-601.

Gorski RA (1991) Sexual differentiation of the endocrine brain and its control. In M. Motta (ed.), *Brain Endocrinology*. New York: Raven.

Green, R. (2000) Birth order and ratio of brothers to sisters in transsexuals. Psychol Med. 30(4):789-95.

Green, R. and Keverne, E.B. (2000) The disparate maternal aunt-uncle ratio in male transsexuals: an explanation invoking genomic imprinting. *J. Theor. Biol.* 202(1):55-63.

Gómez-Gil, E., Esteva, I., Almaraz, M.C., Pasaro, E., Segovia, S., and Guillamon, A. (2010) Familiality of gender identity disorder in non-twin siblings. *Arch. Sex Behav.* 39(2):546-52.

Gómez-Gil, E., Trilla, A., Salamero, M., Godas, T., and Valdés, M. (2009) Sociodemographic, clinical, and psychiatric characteristics of transsexuals from Spain. *Arch. Sex Behav.* 38(3):378-392.

Hare, L., Bernard, P., Sánchez, F.J., Baird, P.N., Vilain, E., Kennedy, T., and Harley, V.R. (2009) Androgen receptor repeat length polymorphism associated with male-to-female transsexualism. *Biol. Psychiatry* 65(1):93-96.

Hayes, F.J., Seminara, S.B., Decruz, S., Boepple, P.A., and Crowley, W.F. Jr (2000) Aromatase inhibition in the human male reveals a hypothalamic site of estrogen feedback. *J. Clin. Endocrinol. Metab.* 85(9):3027-35.

Hengstschlager, M., van Trotsenburg, M., Repa, C., Marton, E., Huber, J.C., and Bernaschek, G. (2003) Sex chromosome aberrations and transsexualism. *Fertil. Steril.* 79(3):639-40.

Henningsson, S., Westberg, L., Nilsson, S., Lundstrom, B., Ekselius, L., Bodlund, O., Lindstrom, E., Hellstrand, M., Rosmond, R., Eriksson, E., and Landen, M. (2005) Sex steroid-related genes and male-to-female transsexualism. *Psychoneuroendocrinology* 30(7):657-664.

Heylens, G., De Cuypere, G., Zucker, K.J., Schelfaut, C., Elaut, E., Vanden Bossche, H., De Baere, E., and T'Sjoen, G. (2012) Gender identity disorder in twins: a review of the case report literature. *J. Sex Med.* 9(3):751-7.

Hines, M. (2006) Prenatal testosterone and gender-related behaviour. *Eur. J. Endocrinol.* 155 (Suppl 1):115-121.

Hsiao, P.W., Lin, D.L., Nakao, R., and Chang, C. (1999) The linkage of Kennedy's neuron disease to ARA24, the first identified androgen receptor polyglutamine region-associated coactivator. *J. Biol. Chem.* 274(29):20229-20234.

Inoubli, A., De Cuypere, G., Rubens, R., Heylens, G., Elaut, E., Van Caenegem, E., Menten, B., and T'Sjoen, G. (2011) Karyotyping, is it worthwhile in transsexualism? J *Sex Med.* 8(2):475-8.

Kazemi-Esfarjani, P., Trifiro, M.A., and Pinsky, L. (1995) Evidence for a repressive function of the long polyglutamine tract in the human androgen receptor: possible pathogenetic relevance for the (CAG)n-expanded neuronopathies. *Hum. Mol. Genet.* 4(4):523-527.

Kockett, G. and Fahrner, E.M. (1987) Transsexuals who have not undergone surgery: A follow up study. *Arch. Sex Behav.* 16:511-22.

Kruijver, F.P., Zhou, J.N., Pool, C.W., Hofman, M.A., Gooren, L.J., and Swaab, D.F. (2000) Male-to-female transsexuals have female neuron numbers in a limbic nucleus. *J. Clin. Endocrinol. Metab.* 85(5):2034-2041.

Kudwa, A.E., Bodo, C., Gustafsson, J.A., and Rissman, E.F. (2005) A previously uncharacterized role for estrogen receptor beta: defeminization of male brain and behavior. *Proc. Natl. Acad. Sci. U S A* 102(12):4608-4612.

Kudwa, A.E., Michopoulos, V., Gatewood, J.D., and Rissman, E.F. (2006) Roles of estrogen receptors alpha and beta in differentiation of mouse sexual behavior. *Neuroscience* 138(3):921-928.

Landen, M., Walinder, J., and Lundstrom, B. (1996) Incidence and sex ratio of transsexualism in Sweden. *Acta Psychiatr. Scand.* 93(4):261-263.

Luders, E., Sanchez, F.J., Gaser, C., Toga, A.W., Narr, K.L., Hamilton, L.S., and Vilain, E. (2009) Regional gray matter variation in male-to-female transsexualism. *Neuroimage* 46(4):904-7.

Luders, E., Sanchez, F.J., Tosun, D., Shattuck, D.W., Gaser, C., Vilain, E., and Toga, A.W. (2012) Increased Cortical Thickness in Male-to-Female Transsexualism. *J. Behav. Brain. Sci.* 2(3):357-362.

Maeda, T., Ohno, M., Matsunobu, A., Yoshihara, K., and Yabe, N. (1991) A cytogenetic survey of 14,835 consecutive liveborns. *Jinrui Idengaku Zasshi* 36(1):117-29.

Moorhead, P.S., Nowell, P.C., Mellman, W.J., Battips, D.M., and Hungerford, D.A. (1960) Chromosome preparations of leukocytes cultured from human peripheral blood. *Exp. Cell Res.* 20:613-616.

Osterlund, M.K. and Hurd, Y.L. (2001) Estrogen receptors in the human forebrain and the relation to neuropsychiatric disorders. *Prog. Neurobiol.* 64(3):251-267.

Polymeropoulos, M.H., Xiao, H., Rath, D.S., and Merril, C.R. (1991) Tetranucleotide repeat polymorphism at the human aromatase cytochrome P-450 gene (CYP19). *Nucleic Acids Res.* 19(1):195.

Rametti, G., Carrillo, B., Gomez-Gil, E., Junque, C., Zubiarre-Elorza, L., Segovia, S., Gomez, A., and Guillamon, A. (2011) The microstructure of white matter in male to female transsexuals before cross-sex hormonal treatment. A DTI study. *J. Psychiatr. Res.* 45(7):949-54.

Rametti, G., Carrillo, B., Gomez-Gil, E., Junque, C., Zubiaurre-Elorza, L., Segovia, S., Gomez, A., Karadi, K., and Guillamon, A. (2012) Effects of androgenization on the white matter microstructure of female-to-male transsexuals. A diffusion tensor imaging study. *Psychoneuroendocrinology* 37(8):1261-9.

Rametti, G., Carrillo, B., Gómez-Gil, E., Junqué, C. , Segovia, S., Gómez, A., and Guillamón, A. (2011) White matter microstructure in female to male transsexuals before cross-sex hormonal treatment. A diffusion tensor imaging study. *J. Psychiatr. Res.* 45(2):199-204.

Raznahan, A., Lee, Y., Stidd, R., Long, R., Greenstein, D., Clasen, L., Addington, A., Gogtay, N., Rapoport, J.L., and Giedd, J.N. (2010) Longitudinally mapping the influence of sex and androgen signaling on the dynamics of human cortical maturation in adolescence. *Proc. Natl. Acad. Sci. U S A* 107(39):16988-93.

Sasaki, M., Kaneuchi, M., Sakuragi, N., Fujimoto, S., Carroll, P.R., and Dahiya, R. (2003) The polyglycine and polyglutamine repeats in the androgen receptor gene in Japanese and Caucasian populations. *Biochem. Biophys. Res. Commun.* 312(4):1244-7.

Sato, T., Matsumoto, T., Kawano, H., Watanabe, T., Uematsu, Y., Sekine, K., Fukuda, T., Aihara, K., Krust, A., Yamada, T., Nakamichi, Y., Yamamoto, Y., Nakamura, T., Yoshimura, K., Yoshizawa, T., Metzger, D., Chambon, P., and Kato, S. (2004) Brain masculinization requires androgen receptor function. *Proc. Natl. Acad. Sci. U S A* 101(6):1673-1678.

Seabright, M. (1971) A rapid banding technique for human chromosomes. *Lancet* 2(7731):971-972.

Sleddens, H.F., Oostra, B.A., Brinkmann, A.O., and Trapman, J. (1992) Trinucleotide repeat polymorphism in the androgen receptor gene (AR). *Nucleic Acids Res.* 20(6):1427.

Soriguer, F., Gutierrez-Repiso, C., Rubio-Martin, E., Garcia-Fuentes, E., Almaraz, M.C., Colomo, N., Esteva de Antonio, I., de Adana, M.S., Chaves, F.J., Morcillo, S., Valdes, S., and Rojo-Martinez, G. (2013) Metabolically healthy but obese, a matter of time? Findings from the prospective pizarra study. *J. Clin. Endocrinol. Metab.* 98(6):2318-25.

Sosa, M., Jodar, E., Arbelo, E., Dominguez, C., Saavedra, P., Torres, A., Salido, E., Liminana, J.M., Gomez De Tejada, M.J., and Hernandez, D. (2004) Serum lipids and estrogen receptor gene polymorphisms in male-to-female transsexuals: effects of estrogen treatment. *Eur. J. Intern. Med.* 15(4):231-237.

Stoffel-Wagner, B., Watzka, M., Schramm, J., Bidlingmaier, F., and Klingmuller, D. (1999) Expression of CYP19 (aromatase) mRNA in different areas of the human brain. *J. Steroid Biochem. Mol. Biol.* 70(4-6):237-41.

Swaab, D.F. (2007) Sexual differentiation of the brain and behavior. *Best Pract. Res. Clin. Endocrinol. Metab.* 21(3):431-44.

Tsukamoto, K., Inoue, S., Hosoi, T., Orimo, H., and Emi, M. (1998) Isolation and radiation hybrid mapping of dinucleotide repeat polymorphism at the human estrogen receptor beta locus. *J. Hum. Genet.* 43(1):73-74.

Tut, T.G., Ghadessy, F.J., Trifiro, M.A., Pinsky, L., and Yong, E.L. (1997) Long polyglutamine tracts in the androgen receptor are associated with reduced trans-activation, impaired sperm production, and male infertility. *J. Clin. Endocrinol. Metab.* 82(11):3777-3782.

Ujike, H., Otani, K., Nakatsuka, M., Ishii, K., Sasaki, A., Oishi, T., Sato, T., Okahisa, Y., Matsumoto, Y., Namba, Y., Kimata, Y., and Kuroda, S. (2009) Association study of gender identity disorder and sex hormone-related genes. *Prog. Neuropsychopharmacol. Biol. Psychiatry* 33(7):1241-1244.

Westberg, L. , Baghaei, F., Rosmond, R., Hellstrand, M., Landen, M., Jansson, M., Holm, G., Bjorntorp, P., and Eriksson, E. (2001) Polymorphisms of the androgen receptor gene and the estrogen receptor beta gene are associated with androgen levels in women. *J. Clin. Endocrinol. Metab.* 86(6):2562-2568.

World Health Organization (WHO) (1993) The ICD-10. Classification of Mental and Behavioural Disorders. Diagnostic Criteria for Research, Geneva.

Wylie KR, Steward D (2008) A Consecutive Series of 52 Transsexual People Presenting for Assessment and Chromosomal Analysis at a Gender Identity Clinic. *International Journal of Transgenderism* 10:147-148.

Zhou, J.N., Hofman, M.A., Gooren, L.J., and Swaab, D.F. (1995) A sex difference in the human brain and its relation to transsexuality. *Nature* 378(6552):68-70.

Zubiaurre-Elorza, L., Junque, C., Gomez-Gil, E., and Guillamon, A. (2014) Effects of Cross-Sex Hormone Treatment on Cortical Thickness in Transsexual Individuals. *J. Sex Med.* 11(5):1248-61.

Zubiaurre-Elorza, L., Junque, C., Gomez-Gil, E., Segovia, S., Carrillo, B., Rametti, G., and Guillamon, A. (2013) Cortical thickness in untreated transsexuals. *Cereb. Cortex* 23(12):2855-62.

In: Gender Identity
Editor: Beverly L. Miller

ISBN: 978-1-63321-488-0
© 2014 Nova Science Publishers, Inc.

Chapter 7

GENDER IDENTITY, CULTURE OF HONOR AND GENDER VIOLENCE: SOCIAL AND PERSONAL IMPLICATIONS

Esther Lopez-Zafra[1]*, Ph.D.
and Noelia Rodríguez-Espartal[2], Ph.D.
[2]Full Profesor of Social Psychology
[2]Assistant profesor of Social Psychology;
Department of Social Psychology, University of Jaén, Spain

ABSTRACT

Gender violence is a social problem that has a great impact in Spain (Ferrer and Bosch, 2013). This complex process has also personal implications in women's health (physical and mental health) and social implications (laws or cultural constrains, among others) that affect interpersonal relationships. To analyze this phenomenon a wide range of variables should be taken into account. Two of these important variables are cultural level (culture of honor) and individual level (gender identity). Our studies show that there is a relationship between gender identity and culture of honor. Specifically, individuals high in masculine gender identity give more importance to culture of honor whereas high feminine gender identity relates with a lower concern to honor affairs. In this book chapter for *Gender Identity: Disorders, Developmental Perspectives and Social Implications*, we analyze the role that this relation has on gender violence and their consequences and social implications. Specifically, we summarize a series of studies that examine gender identity, culture of honor and gender violence both in prisoners and in non prisoners' men and in general population. Our results would help to better understand gender violence and the role that gender identity has in this complex, personal and social, phenomenon.

Keywords: Culture of honor, gender identity, gender violence

---

* Corresponding author email: elopez@ujaen.es.

INTRODUCTION

Gender violence is a social problem that has a great impact in Spain (Ferrer and Bosch, 2013). This complex process has also personal implications in women's health (physical and mental health) and social implications (law, cultural constrains, among others) that affect interpersonal relationships. The explanation of this phenomenon is multicausal, taking into account individual (victims, aggressors) and social aspects (social group, economic affairs) whereby culture has a great impact both in psychological and social aspects. Thus, we can assert that gender violence is a psychosocial phenomenon that should be also addressed from a cultural perspective. Examples of the importance of the cultural issue are differences among countries in the number of cases, justifications given or even legal aspects. These cultural patterns influence individuals perceptions about their legitimacy to use violence, the social dominance that one group can exert over other group (i.e. men over women) and the importance gender identity has in their own personal identity.

A main macrosocial aspect to explain gender violence has to do with gender inequality. Gender equality is an unresolved issue all over the world. The Gender Gap Report (GGR; 2013) shows that equality indices rank from countries as Iceland that occupies the first position (index= 0.87[1]) followed by Finland (I= .842), (Norway I= .841) or Sweden (I= .81) to Syria in the 133 position of the rank (I=.566) followed by Chad (rank= 134; I= .558), Pakistan (rank= 135; I= .545) and Yemen (rank= 136; I= .512). Even in the top level of the rank, we see that gender gap index is 0.8 when a real equality index between men and women should be equal to 1. Thus, gender equality is not real in any country in the world. However, a greater gap means a greater inequality and lowest opportunities for women all over the world, and the lowest the gap, the best.

If we pay attention to the countries both at the top and at the bottom, and look at the statistics about gender violence, we can infer that violence is related to a highest inequality among the sexes, and culture of honor is an important variable to consider in those countries at the bottom.

Embedded with this aspect are the differing cultural dimensions among those countries and cultures. Culture refers to a system of shared beliefs, values, and expectations developed to meet basic subsistence needs, social values, and the exercise of one's skills in a particular geographical niche (Bond, 2005). Culture is compound by symbols, norms, values and beliefs. All these components give sense to social life, and have prescriptive and proscriptive implications, that is, what should or not be done. Hofstede (1980) concluded that there are several cultural dimensions that make the countries differ on the value given to different aspects. Two of these dimensions are distance power and masculinity, although individualism is the most known dimension.

Masculinity has to do with gender identity. In Hofstede´s classification masculinity refers to the value given to traditional gender roles. Masculine values include competition, assertiveness, ambition, power and wealth. In a masculine culture, most people believe that men should be the bread winners and should study and work; whereas women should be house holders and shouldn´t have to work or study if they don´t want. As an example, we can compare four of the countries in the GGR (two at the top and two at the bottom) with Hofstede´s study: Iceland and Finland vs. Syria and Pakistan. As shown in Figure 1. Pakistan

---

[1] The equality index Ranks from 0= total inequality to 1= total equality

and Syria score higher both in power distance and masculinity than Iceland or Finland. Specifically, with a very low score of 30 or 33 respectively, it is clear that in Iceland and Finland hierarchy is established for convenience, superiors are always accessible and managers rely on individual employees and teams for their expertise. At the same time, communication is informal, direct and participative. On the other hand, with an extremely low score of 10, Iceland is considered a definitively feminine society and Finland with a 26 is thus considered a feminine society. In feminine countries the focus is on "working in order to live", managers strive for consensus, people value equality, solidarity and quality in their working lives. Conflicts are resolved by compromise and negotiation. Incentives such as free time and flexibility are favored. Focus is on well-being and status is not shown or emphasized.

However, Syria with a high score of 80 is a hierarchical society, but Pakistan with an intermediate score of 55 it is not possible to determine a preference in this dimension. This means that people accept a hierarchical order in which everybody has a place and which needs no further justification. Hierarchy in an organization is seen as reflecting inherent inequalities, centralization is popular, subordinates expect to be told what to do and the ideal boss is a benevolent autocrat. But in the case of masculinity, both countries score 50 and 52 which is an exactly intermediate score and it cannot be said if Pakistan or Syria has a preference to masculinity of femininity. However, inequalities in the social system reflect in gender relations and gender roles are clearly defined in countries as Syria or Pakistan (FNUAP, 2005). In those countries, violations and violence against women are very frequent and culture of honor is an important concept to take into account.

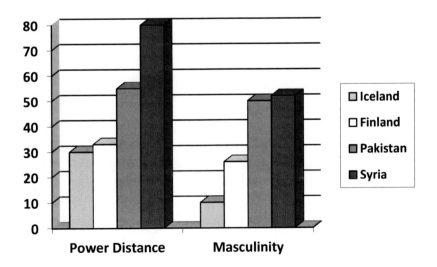

Figure 1. Power distance and Masculinity in top and bottom countries at GGR.

Culture of honor refers to a psychological mechanism that underlies cultural norms that perpetuate and justify violence as a result of group learning about how to defend property or the environment. In such cultures, women are the property of men and gender violence could be exerted to control women. In fact, in countries such as Spain, in 2009, the rate of foreign women killed by their partners or former partners is almost five times the rate of the Spanish (Amnesty International, 2014), being immigrants of culture of honor countries the most affected.

HONOR CULTURE AND GENDER IDENTITY

In India multiple sexual abuses is related to a punishment against women. Men feel they are the law and can make women lose honor as a consequence of their "wrong" behavior. However, these violence and abuses committed by men take no consequences. In Jordanian, honor codes are stipulated by law and women can be punished by this law. In other countries as Morocco pregnant women out of marriage suffer from social exclusion. These examples are very evident, but other subtle forms of sexism and gender violence due to honor culture are present all over the world.

In the frame of cultural differences, culture of honor emerges to explain why men in certain cultures perceive themselves as the guardians of women´s honor, even with the use of violence. It is a wide concept beyond individual honor or own behavior. It is assumed that honor also depends on others´ actions and violence is the correct form to restore it. Honor refers to self-worth in own eyes and in the eyes of others (Pitt-Rivers, 1965, 1968, 1977). Honor is related to reputation, honesty, moral integrity and trustworthiness (Peristiany, 1965). We can distinguish four honor codes based on their central themes: morality-based honor (focused on honesty and trust), family-based honor (focused on the family's collective reputation, depending on each individual family member), feminine honor (based on modesty and sexual restraint of women) and masculine honor (emphasizing the physical protection of the family and its property and masculine gender stereotypes) (see Rodriguez Mosquera, Liskow & DiBona, 2011 for a review of the types of honor). Studies have analyzed individuals' reactions to offenses to honor. Individuals who value honor are expected to protect their own reputations and the reputations of their families. These expectations are thought to be important for both women and men (Rodriguez Mosquera, 2011), although men defend their reputations in a more physical manner than women do.

The proposal or theory about the culture of honor was primarily designed to explain why certain cultures perpetuate or justify violence as a result of group learning about how to defend property or environment (Cohen, Nisbett, Bowdle, and Schwarz, 1996), and this can be reflected in the judicial level by applying different yardsticks to the law and issuing statements, and even justifying some attacks and defense the consequences of violence (Cohen, 1996). This occurs mainly when it comes to relating with honor situations (Nisbett and Cohen, 1997). Finally, when these rules are even legitimated at a legal level, collective representations or mental ideas of what it is right or not to do and about the consequences become a cultural product. When it reaches this level, and is rooted in the culture, its importance is unquestionable and generates cultural differences in their expression (Lopez-Zafra, 2007a). In summary, the concept of honor culture refers to the set of cultural norms generated by history, law and social policy that allow capital punishment and mistreatment of women and children (Cohen, 1996), perpetuated by the interpretations and media laws made on honor-related acts (Cohen and Nisbett, 1997, Lopez-Zafra, 2007b).

The psychosocial perspective is relatively recent in origin and has, as main objective, the study of emotional reactions in the defense of male honor in the culture of honor in the southern United States (Nisbett and Cohen, 1994, Cohen, Nisbett, Bowdle & Schwarz, 1996; Nisbett and Cohen, 1996). Early studies that address this concept as such relate to emotional reactions that can be justified by the defense of their own. An increasing number of research take the concept of honor as central to explain comparative reactions to offenses across cultures and within the culture in terms of the importance given to honor (Pérez, Páez and Navarro, 2001).

There is a higher incidence of the culture of honor in less industrialized countries or in developing countries, where the concept of ownership extends not only to land but also to people than in developed countries. But the worst is that the idea of property over people is much stronger in the case of women who are profoundly limited in their freedom.

Gender and gender identity are crucial concepts to understand this process. Men are abusing women under cultural constrains and, although it is higher in countries with a lower development and lower gender equality, men could perceive all over the world that they are superior to women.

In fact, research has shown that there are sex differences and gender identity differences in culture of honor. The study by Lopez-Zafra, (2008) shows that, since the idea of defending the honor falls on men, they score higher than women in the variable culture of honor. Specifically, significant differences between men and women in all factors of the Culture of Honor scale emerge (Lopez-Zafra, 2007). Men give more importance to individual honor and believe that society and the law should defend the honor of the people, but they also consider as more legitimate the use of violence to an offense than women. As for the overall assessment of honor, men again score significantly higher than women (see Figure 2). It is on factors 1 (Individual honor) and 3 (using violence is legitime) in which there is a greater distance between them, that is, men more than women emphasize the defense of honor even with the use of violence. Thus, it is confirmed that it is men who perceive up to them to ensure the honor and demand it in their environment, social group and society in general.

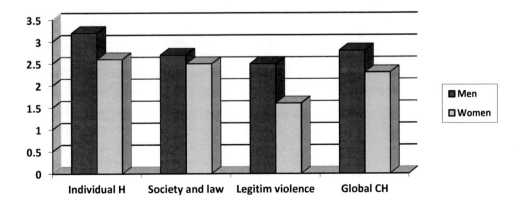

Figure 2. Sex differences in Culture of Honor dimensions and global CH.

Men may perceive that they should restore honor and that their peers reinforce these standards of aggression (Vandello, Cohen and Ransom, 2008). This proposal has been extended to research that take the concept of honor as central to their explanations to compare reactions to offenses with their gender identity or masculinity in different cultures. In this case, we find that the cultural values that emphasize female loyalty and sacrifice and male honor can indirectly reinforce violence in the relationship and reward women who remain in abusive relationships (e.g. Brazil vs. U.S. Vandello and Cohen, 2003; Chile vs Canada or Latino vs. Anglo American Vandello, Cohen, Grandon and Franiuk, 2009).

An egalitarian society based on equality in couple relationships and not on dominance, is a society where the culture of honor has a limited role. However, a society with a patriarchal model, with beliefs that reflects historical patterns of parental authority of "pater familiae" considers that men has some violence canon allowing them to act aggressively, provided that no exceeded. Persistent unequal power relations allow this aggression and social tolerance of violence against women (López-Sáez, 2006). Thus, violence against women is justified by a breach of their gender role (Ferrer and Bosch, 2000).

Gender role refers to a series of believes in which there is consensus about the characteristics of men and women who become policy on what should and should not be done for each sex (Eagly, 1987; Eagly, Wood and Diekman, 2000). This gender role plays an important role especially in cultures based on honor that involves a set of identity characteristics known as machismo. An example is the study of Rodríguez, Manstead and Fischer (1999) who observed differences between Spain and Holland. The culture of honor is characterized by the salience of honor codes related to gender. The female honor focuses on sexual shame (virginity, modesty and sexual restrictions) wheras male honor focuses on virility in protection of the family, and a reputation as a hard man. This culture of honor is stronger in Spain than in the Netherlands and affects attitudes toward sex roles. Indeed, emotional responses to insults that threaten the family honor are different depending on the nationality and gender, the Spaniards in general react more intensely than Netherlanders and even more Spanish men (Rodriguez, Manstead and Fischer, 2002).

A much broader and comprehensive study is the one conducted by Vandello and Cohen (2003). They carried out two studies comparing a culture of honor with a culture of no honor considering the one hand, perceptions about a man who has been deceived by his wife and his violent reaction to this and the other, the reactions of people to a real situation of violence. In the first study, with participants in Brazil and Illinois (USA), the results show a clear difference between the cultures of honor and not honor. Americans perceived that a man who responded with violence was less reliable and less man before an episode of infidelity, whereas Brazilians felt it was slightly more man and that he was restoring honor through violence. Although in both cases the violence was condemned, Brazilians showed some justification for its use. In the second study, cultural differences also occur in reaction to a woman who has experienced violence. Participants from honor cultures (Hispanics and Southerners USA) showed a more favorable impression on a woman expressing loyalty and respentance, they also thought that she was stronger if she decided to continue the relationship, while the North were more favorable to a woman who manifest independence and the intention of leaving the abuser whereas they thought she was weak if considering to continue the relationship. In summary, a variation between-and intra-cultures in honor syndrome may explain violence against women (Lopez-Zafra, 2007b).

Thus, not only sex but gender identity could explain differences on being prone to give high importance to culture of honor. Gender identity has the prescriptive aspect of the characteristics associated to women and men, that is, women should be weak and dependent and men should be aggressive and independent.

In the study by Lopez-Zafra, (2008), correlational analyzes between the different dimensions of gender identity and culture of honor clearly showed that the culture of honor correlated significantly with agency - instrumental dimension. This dimension corresponds to the items and factors associated with masculinity, i.e., people who score high on masculinity do well in culture of honor, while not the case with femininity since the correlation between the Communal Dimension and Culture of honor is not significant and is even reversed. Furthermore, in this study the K-Means cluster analysis showed that two groups emerged: people giving high importance to honor (high culture of honor group) and people giving low importance to honor (low culture of honor group). These two groups differed in the agentic/instrumental dimension, which is related to masculinity, showing higher scores in the high culture of honor group.

When considering couples, Lopez-Zafra, (2008) showed that the importance given to culture of honor was important for their satisfaction with the partner. The important thing was to have similar scores, that is, both members score high or low. In these cases, people felt more satisfied than when one of the partner scored high and the other scored low in culture of honor. This was also related to gender identity. In congruent couples (both scoring similar in culture of honor) people scored lower higher in feminine gender identity.

GENDER IDENTITY AND GENDER VIOLENCE

Social cognitive theory considers that gender identity is constructed by cognitive processing of experiences; it allows learning about social gender roles and rules about which the proper sex behaviors are (Ruiz, 2004). In this sense, learning stands as the means of transmitting values, attitudes and rules, and the development of stereotypes in childhood play an essential role in how the relations between men and women are established. Gender stereotypes refer to the characteristics linked to women and men as members of the sex category and can be understood as behavioral scripts that serve to limit the daily behavior of both men and women, strengthening appropriate behavior and eliminating inadequate ones (Gaudí-Rodríguez, 2009). Thus, gender stereotypes maintain inequalities and can be considered a responsible factor in violent behavior toward women.

Gender roles derive from the segregation of activities considered congruent for women and for men and are presented as anchored in today's society. It is more or less rooted, depending on the culture, but leading to inequalities in which women are subordinated to man (Lopez-Zafra and García-Retamero, 2012). These differences identified between men and women allow us to say that the gender stereotyped attributes are socially constructed, and therefore can and should change. The concept of socialization refers to the way the male culture and female culture, understood as ways of experiencing the world. In these cultures roles influence life, i.e., how to act socially expected that men and women. And what is usually expected in patriarchal cultures, which are more likely to exert violence against women, is that men assume a role of domination based on power relations, whereas women assume a submissive role focused on the world of emotions and family relationships. As men perceive their gender stereotype as important, women are perceived as weak and hostile (Ruiz, 2004).

In this sense, there are very representative data obtained by Cantera and Blanch (2010) who conducted a study to assess the extent to which gender stereotypes are rooted in today's society. They found that the social perception of relationships is based on traditional gender stereotypes, ie man – breadwinner and woman - caregiver, and that the paradigm of violence, that is, man-violent, woman-pacific is involved in the perception of partner violence. It is also interesting to note that both men and women agree to when adopting a gender perspective, being women who stress the differences with regard to gender role behaviors. These stereotypes about gender and violence contribute to the social visibility of this problem, and also make invisible other types of intimate partner violence, as for example, the one exercised by the woman to the man, or the one in gay couples (Cantera and Blanch, 2010; Cantera and Gamero, 2007).

Thus, beliefs are anchored in patriarchal culture and imply a way of understanding the relationships between men and women based on the difference, asymmetry and abuse of power. From this point of view, a relationship which builds its structure in this patriarchal culture involves structural violence by definition (Dobash and Dobash, 1979).

These sexist beliefs and attitudes yield a gender effect on both adult and adolescent population (Ferrer, Bosch, Ramis and Navarro, 2006). In this sense, boys are more sexist and show more benevolent sexist attitudes (Lameiras and Rodíguez, 2002), whereas women and girls favor equality between men and women in the distribution of household tasks and family decision-making, as well as the participation of women in public life and in decision-making (Díaz-Aguado, 2003; Díaz-Aguado and Martínez, 2001; Expósito, Moya and Glick, 1998; Ferreret al., 2006; Gómez and Esteban, 1995; Moya and Expósito, 2001).

Thus, gender and gender role attitudes are among the most important predictors of sexism (Berkel, Vandiser and Bahner, 2004; Mullender, 2000). Regarding sexism, men show more tolerant attitudes toward abusers and intimate partner violence (Ferrer et al.,; 2006; Locke and Richman, 1999; Harris and Cook, 1994; Markowitz, 2002; Nayak, Birne, Martin and Abraham, 2003; Pierce and Harris, 1993; Yosihoka, Di Noia and Ullah, 2001). Furthermore, these beliefs are related to the tendency to blame the victim, to legitimize the attitudes and behaviors of offenders and sustain myths about gender violence beliefs about traditional gender roles, the subordination of women to men, the restriction of the rights of women and male dominance (Berkelet al., 2004; Mullender, 2000; Nayak et al., 2003; Yanes and González, 2000).The relationship established by male abusers between inequality and control is so strong that one cannot be explained without the other. Similarly, it is also clear their tendency to accept the positive relationship between masculinity and violence, which leads them to justify and legitimize violence as if it were their "right" (Fernández-Llebrez, 2005).

Also, the stories of men who have committed violence against women can help us to conclude about how they see social roles of women and men (Rodríguez-Espartal, 2012; Boira, 2010). In their conception of the relationship and ideal partner, they consider that their partner should be a housewife, servant and supplier of men's desires. Their speech is childish, they have an idyllic setting in which the man, lord and master, defines both what should be as family and social roles that partners should play. They justify it by arguing that this is something imposed by *tradition* and they alert about the dangers of transgressions. In their speech, these men tend to highlight the consequences when things are not as they should be, showing an aggressive and challenging position for the victim whose effects can be dramatic (Cantera and Gamero, 2007; Boira, 2010).

In this sense, when talking about violence against women, the instrumental element is crucial. That is, murdering a woman it is often called a crime for self-justification or moral crime in which the perpetrator acts for consistency and conviction. This action is a result of their idea of how relations are, how the family structure is. They impose a model of family structure on the basis of intimidation, coercion, threats, etc.. (Lorente, 2005). However, there are different types of machismo, and the predominance of patriarchal ideology is not always manifested directly, clearly and violent, but sometimes it is associated with more everyday aspects of the relationship justifying that the victim is the guilty person in the couple. That is, the roles in the relationship, the dailymaking of decisions, (e.g. for organizing the house, the education of children, money and shopping...) are assumed by these men as the main natural actor and manager of the relationship (Bordieu, 2000). It is from this point on that these men start implementing the strategies needed to maintain the status quo; actions based on the pressure and the fear of a possible backlash of man, aimed at controlling and mastering the situation.

Studies conducted with men convicted by intimate partner violence against women (IPVAW) show these gender stereotypes. For example, different studies show that they describe themselves as tender, loving, affectionate, friendly, spiritual, unable to plan, conformist, timid, passive, resigned, unsure of themselves, and not undecided like risk. These characteristics are in fact, culturally attributed to the female gender stereotype (Aguilera, 2004; Rodríguez-Espartal, 2012). The explanation is twofold: first, and related to what in the 70s and 80s was called *men combat without victory*, they feel ambivalence and conflict regarding their gender identity (Aguilera 2004; Ferrer, 2000; Rodríguez-Espartal, 2013; Viveros, 2001), and in the construction of their masculinity they assume their inability to get rid of their feminine aspects. Thus, they feel an identity crisis, not knowing what to do and how to act to be truly men. They do not understand that the rigidity of the male and female stereotypes has been fading today (Aguilera, 2004). Second, social desirability can explain this result (Rodríguez-Espartal, 2012). These prisoners are aware of the social impact of intimate partner violence and, in particular, the negative view the society has of the perpetrator. Thus, due to social desirability they will put up with socially attributed to the feminine characteristics to be also seen as victims in this process. It is very important to take into account this aspect when interventions are performed with male abusers.

The meaning and significance that these men give to their violent behavior is given by (Aguilera, 2004): a) making external attributions about the causes of aggression to their partners; b) considering aggression as a way to confirm their authority at home and to justify aggression, because of personality as a trait; c) considering that women are responsible for their aggressiveness, asserting that: their women do not understand them, their women are flirtatious or rude or their women are unable to meet their obligations as wives.

These rigid gender roles are also related to other variables as control and jealousy. The violent men towards women do not tolerate women´s independence; they want to keep their relationship under control. They also express an excessive emotional dependence on her partner, considering that they are abandoned when a woman makes any other activity, resulting in the appearance of jealousy (Aguilera, 2004). Also, Cabrera (2010) found in a group of prisoners convicted by intimate partner violence (IPVAW), a strong role of the family in the rigid gender roles they endorse. Using qualitative analyses of stories of life, this author finds that these men were part of masculinized families in which the expressions of femininity were heavily punished, both physically and emotionally. The role differentiation is very clear in these families: the father is serious, aloof and breadwinner, bringing money to their homes and asking for explanations about how the money was expended, imposing order and control. The mother is remembered as the expressive part of the couple and the family, more affectionate but less valued, responsible for managing the house and money but always under strict supervision of the parent.

Also related with gender roles, other studies show that they provoke deterioration of the relationship with continuous disrespect and the use of power and control to maintain the situation (Castellanos, 2010); sociocognitive machismo schemas steaming from a sexist socialization that justifies male superiority over women causes rigidity of thought (Castillo et al., 2005). Furthermore, Dobash, Dobash, Wilson and Daly (1992) demonstrated how the historical domination of husbands over their wives, including the use of violence, has been reinforced by cultural beliefs. In many cultures, violence is considered normal and a prerogative of men / husbands. The socialization of children tends to reflect the standards and related cultural values. Thus, boys are encouraged to be sexually active and aggressive while girls are taught to resist sexual activity and be sweet (García-Moreno, 2000). In this sense, unequal power relations allowing this aggression and social tolerance of violence against women persist (López-Sáez, 2006). Moreover, violence against women is justified by a breach of their gender role or gender stereotype (Ferrer and Bosch, 2000) and this could be a reflection of sexism and of the inability of many men to adapt to new forms of egalitarian coexistence between men and women (García, 2004; Lorente, 2008). In fact, gender differences have been observed around the culture of honor (Sackelford, 2005), the idea of honor may be influencing gender violence as an idea of masculinity and femininity which implies control by the man stands and submission by the woman (Puente and Cohen, 2003), that is, when a division of social roles between men and women occurs. In fact, as shown above male gender identity or agency was significantly associated with a greater emphasis given to honor (Lopez-Zafra, 2008; 2010). Furthermore, a study about distorted thoughts and their relationship to variables involved in violence, showed an association with culture of honor. Torres and Lopez-Zafra (2010) found that individual honor of violent men influence distorted thoughts towards women. This data has is supported by subsequent studies (Lopez-Zafra, Rodríguez-Espartal, López-Turrillo and Berrios-Martos, 2011; Rodríguez-Espartal, López-Turrillo and Lopez-Zafra, 2011).

Bearing these comments in mind, it seems that education on egalitarian values would be an important point to work with children, future men and women in the fight against gender violence. However, this education must have close supervision and be made and implemented by professionals in gender issues. In this sense, new masculinities are developing and could be seen as positive. But it also happens that some men generate a resistance to this change making them even more radical in their traditional approaches to the roles of men and women in society. These new masculinities incorporate the desire for certain identification with feminine values as feminization of interpersonal values is considered positively; but on the other hand, some men fear a risk for their identity and social power.

In sum, there are two approaches in masculinities: males that identify with the feminization of values, softness or approach to the feminine world (Keen, 1999; Moore, 1994; Seidler, 2000), and a more traditional and even reactionary claiming of men under a different paradigm (benevolent sexism) with persistence of hard, powerful and traditional man (Bly, 1990).

In agreement with Fernández (2010), we consider that only when new masculine and feminine identifications that uncheck traditional stereotypical traits emerge, will be possible the strengthening of the new identities and a substantive progress in the redistribution of power and social roles. Gender identifications with general and interpersonal values are essential to consider in the future of equality and gender equity.

CONCLUSION

IPVAW is a very complex phenomenon. Society is aware of the consequences and the social problem it causes (Ferrer, and Bosch, 2013). However, women suffer from violence in different forms and intimate partner violence implies the closest relation a woman can have: the aggressor is the person you think you are in love with. The factors that help to explain why this process take place are both individual and social. Regarding the social aspect, it is important to take into account how the social structure allows and maintains, and even legitimize, the use of violence inside couple relations. Power, social dominance and inequality are part of cultures of honor that consider that a woman is a property of her couple and even is inferior than the man.

As for the individual aspect, it also has a social influence. We refer to gender identity that is related to gender stereotypes, and gender stereotypes derive from gender social roles. Thus, the division of the work and chores that men and women perform (gender roles) are related to the characteristics they are attributed as women and men (gender stereotypes) and they identify with these characteristics to a different extent (gender identity).

As far as a man identifies extremely with the social description of masculine stereotypes and considers that he is in a higher position than a woman, he would endorse masculine traditional roles and would exercise power as the basis of this relation. This is unjustifiable but benevolent sexism emerges as a more social desirability way to impose traditional standards. Thus, if we want to fight against IPVAW, it is important to consider the cultural, social and individual levels of analysis and intervene in all of them, beginning with the importance of gender identity to avoid disorders in identity and interpersonal relations.

REFERENCES

Aguilera, A. (2004). Características psicológicas del hombre golpeador de su compañera permanente, residente en la ciudad de Bucaramanga. *MedUnab, 7, 20,*73-83.

Amnistía Internacional (2014). Violencia contra las mujeres retrieved from http://www. es.amnesty.org/temas/mujeres/violencia-contra-las-mujeres/magnitud-cifras-y-datos/

Amitay, O. & Mongrain, M. (2007). From Emotional Intelligence to Intelligence Choice of Partner. *The Journal of Social Psychology*, 147 (4), 325-343.

Berkel, L.A., Vandiser, B. J. & Bahner, A.D. (2004). Gender role attitudes, religion and spirituality as predictors of domestic violence attitudes in white college students. *Journal of College Student Development, 45*(2), 119-133.

Bly, R. (1990). *Iron John: a Book About Men.* Shaftesbury, Dorset: Element Books.

Boira, S. (2010). *Hombres maltratadores. Historias de violencia masculine.* Zaragoza: Sagardiana. Estudios Feministas.

Bourdieu, Pierre (2000): Propos sur le champ politique. Lyon: Presses Universitaires.

Buss, D. M. (2000). *The dangerous passion.* New York: Free Press.

Cabrera, M. (2010). Acercándonos al hombre que ejerce la violencia de género: clasificación y descripción de un grupo de maltratadores. *Nómadas. Revista Crítica de Ciencias Sociales y Jurídicas, 25,* 1-24.

Cantera, L.M., & Blanch, J.M. (2010). Percepción Social de la Violencia en la Pareja desde los Estereotipos de Género. *IntervenciónPsicosocial, 19* (2), 121-127.

Cantera, L. &Gamero, V. (2007). La violencia en la pareja a la luz de los esterotipos de género. *Psico, 38*(3), 233-237.

Castellanos, F. (2010). Variables psicológicas de los penados por delitos de violencia de género en medidas penales alternativas. *Seminario de violencia de género.* UAM+CSIC.ICFS. Universidad Autónoma de Madrid. Disponible en http://www.uam.es/otros/forenses/vdg/b7.pdf

Castillo, T., Estepa, Z., Guerrero, J., Rivera, G., Ruiz, A. & Sánchez, C. (2005), *Programa de tratamiento en prisión para agresores en el ámbito familiar. Grupo de trabajo sobre violencia de género,* Documentos Penitenciarios 2: Madrid.

Cohen, D. (1996). Law, social policy and violence: the impact of the regional cultures. *Journal of Personality and Social Psychology,* 70 (5), 961-978

Cohen, D. (1998). Culture, social organization and social psychology. *Journal of Personality and Social Psychology.*75, 408-419.

Cohen, D. &Nisbett, R.E. (1997). Field experiments examining the culture of honor: the role of institutions in perpetuating norms about violence. *Personality and Social Psychology Bulletin.* 23(11) 1188-1199.

Cohen, D., Vandello, J. &Rantilla, A. (1998). The sacred and the social: cultures of honor and violence. En P. Gilbert & B. Andrews (Eds.) *Shame: Interpersonal behavior, psychopatology and culture* (pp. 261-282). Nueva York. Oxford University Press.

Cohen, D.; Nisbett, R.E.; Bowdle, B.F. & Schwarz, N. (1996). Insult, aggression, and the southern culture of honor: an experimental ethnography. *Journal of personality and social psychology, 70 (5),* 945-960.

Cramer, D. (2004) Satisfaction with a Romantic Relationship, Depression, Support and Conflict.*Psychology and Psychotherapy-Theory Research and Practice* 77(4):449-461.

Díaz-Aguado, M.J. (2003). Adolescencia, sexismo y violencia de género. *Papeles del Psicólogo., 23*(84), 35-44.

Díaz-Aguado, M.J. & Martínez, A. (2001).*La construcción de la igualdad y la prevención de la violencia contra la mujer desde la educación secundaria.* Madrid: Instituto de la Mujer.

Dobash, R. (1979). *Violence against Wives: A Case against the Patriarchy.* New York: Free Press.

Dobash, R. Dobash P., R.E., Wilson, M., & Daly, M. (1992). The myth of sexual symmetry in marital violence. *Social Problems 39,* 71-79.

Eagly, A. H. (1987). Sex differences in social behavior: A social-roleinterpretation. Hillsdale, NJ: Lawrence Erlbaum.

Eagly, A. H., Wood, W., & Diekman, A. B. (2000). Social role theory of sex differences and similarities: A current appraisal. En T. Eckes & H. M. Trautmer (Eds.), *The developmental social psychology of gender* (pp. 123–174). Mahwah, NJ: Erlbaum.

Expósito, F., Moya, M. & Glick, P. (1998). Sexismo Ambivalente: medición y correlatos. *Revista de Psicología Social, 55,* 893-905.

Fernández, C. (2010). La equidad de género: presente y horizonte próximo. *Quaderns de Psicologia, 12*(2), 93-104.

Fernández-Llebrez, F. (2005). Masculinidades y violencia de género, ¿por qué algunoshombres maltratan a sus parejas (mujeres)? Disponible enhttp://www. berdingune.euskadi.net/u89congizon/es/contenidos/informacion/material/es_gizonduz/adj untos/masculinidadesyviolenciadegenero.pdf

Ferrer, V.A. & Bosch, E. (2000). Violencia de género y misoginia: reflexiones psicosociales sobre un posible factor explicativo. *Papeles del psicólogo* 75,13-19.

Ferrer, M. V., & Bosch, E. (2013). Gender violence as a social problem in Spain: Attitudes and acceptability. *Sex Roles,* on-line. doi:10.1007/s11199-013-0322-z

Ferrer, V.A., Bosch, E., Ramis, M. C. & Navarro, C. (2006).Las creencias y actitudes sobre la violencia contra las mujeres en la pareja: Determinantes sociodemográficos, familiares y formativos. *Anales de Psicología, 22*(2), 251- 259.

Gaudi-Rodríguez, J. (2009): Mitos y violencia de género (I). Obtenido:http://www.correo-gto.com.mx/notas.asp?id=134312 el 213 de abril de 2014.

Ghazal, R. & Cohen, D. (2002). Honor and values in Saudi Arabia. *Unpublished manuscript, University of Waterloo.*

Grandon, R. & Cohen, D. (2002). Violence, jealousy and loyalty in Chile and Canada.Unpublished manuscript, University of Waterloo.

Gómez-Esteban, C. (1995).*Mujeres e igualdad de oportunidades.*Estudio CIS 2194.Octubre 1995. Datos de Opinión, 2. Disponibleen http://www.cis.es/boletin/2/est2.html

Harris, R.J. & Cook, C.A. (1994). Attributions about spouse abuse: it matters who the batterers and victims are. *Sex Roles, 30,* 553-565.

Hofstede, G. (1998). *Masculinity and Femininity: The Taboo Dimension of National Cultures.* Thousand Oaks CA: Sage Publications

Keen, S. (1999). *Ser hombre.* Madrid: Gaia ediciones.

Lameiras, M. & Rodríguez, Y. (2002). Evaluación del sexismo moderno en los adolescentes. *Revista de Psicología Social, 17*(2), 119-127.

Locke, L.M. & Richman, C.L. (1999). Attitudes toward domestic violence: race and gender issues. *Sex Roles, 40*(3/4), 227-247.

López-Sáez, M. (2006). Mujeres maltratadas y asesinadas por sus parejas. Violencia ¿de qué género? En E. López-Zafra & M.P. Berrios (eds). *La violencia en las relaciones familiares y de pareja.* (pp. Xx) Madrid. El Lunar.

Lopez-Zafra, E. (2007a). Elaboración de una escala para medir Cultura del Honor. *Revista de Psicología Social,* 22 (1), 31-42.

Lopez-Zafra, E. (2007b). El componente cultural de la violencia. En J. F. Morales, M. Moya, E. Gaviria e I. Cuadrado (coord.). *Psicología Social.*(441-454). Madrid. McGraw- Hill.

Lopez-Zafra, E. (2008). Relación entre Cultura del Honor e Identidad de género: el papel del sexo, edad y nivel de estudios en la predisposición a la violencia. *Estudios de Psicología*, 29 (2), 209-220.

Lopez-Zafra, E. Berrios, M.P & Augusto, J. M. (2008). *Introducción a la Psicología Social.* Jaén. Del Lunar.

Lopez-Zafra, E. & Garcia-Retamero, R. (2012). Do gender stereotypes change? *Journal of GenderStudies, 21* ,191-205.

Lopez-Zafra, E. & López Sáez, M. (2001). Por qué las mujeres se consideran más o menos femeninas y los hombres más o menos masculinos. Explicaciones sobre su autoconcepto de identidad de género. *Revista de Psicología Social,* 16 (2), 193-207.

Lopez-Zafra, E. & López Sáez, M. (2002). Violencia y género: el papel de la variable género y las nuevas formas de discriminación sexual. En Bel Bravo, M. (dir.) E*tnia y género: la cultura occidental de los últimos tres siglos.* (pp. 75-96). Servicio de Publicaciones de la Universidad de Jaén.

Lopez-Zafra, E. & Rodríguez Espartal, N. (2008). Relación entre cultura del honor, celos y satisfacción de pareja. *Boletín de Psicología,* 94, 7-22.

Lpez-Zafra, E., Rodríguez, N. & Jiménez, I. (2008). Cultura del Honor e Inteligencia Emocional: ¿conceptos relacionados o incompatibles? *Summa Psicológica* UST, 5 (2), 17- 26.

Lopez-Zafra, E., Rodríguez-Espartal, N., López-Turrillo, E., Berrios-Martos, M.P., Augusto-Landa, J.M. & García-León, A. (2011). Emotional intelligence, culture of honor, and distorted thoughts of gender violence prisoners: results of a cognitive-behavioral intervention. *Abstracts del III International Congress on Emotional Intelligence*, Opatija, Coracia.

Lorente, M. (2007). Violencia de género, educación y socialización: acciones y reacciones. *Revista de Educación, 342,* 19-35.

Lorente, M. (2009). *Balance de la aplicación de cuatro años de ley integral en la administración de justicia.* Conferencia inaugural presentada en el III Congreso del observatorio contra la violencia doméstica y de género. Madrid, España.

Lucas, T.; Parkhill, M.R; Wendorf, C.A.; Imameglu, E.O. et al. (2008). Cultural and evolutionary components of marital satisfaction: A multidimensional assessment of measurement. *Journal of Cross-Cultural Psychology, 39,* 1, 109-115.

Markowitz, F.E. (2001). Attitudes and family violence: linking intergenerational and cultural theories. *Journal of Family Violence, 16,* 205-218.

Minkov, M. & Hofstede, G. (2012). Hofstede's fifth dimension: New evidence from the World Values Survey. *Journal of Cross-Cultural Psychology*, 43, 3-14.

Moore, H.S. (1994). *A Passion for difference.*Cambridge: Polity Press.

Moya, M. & Exposito, F. (2001).Antecedentes y consecuencias del neosexismo en varones y mujeres de la misma organización laboral. En D. Caballero, M.T. Méndez y J. Pastor (Eds.), *La mirada psicosociológica*(pp. 619-625). Madrid: Biblioteca Nueva.

Mujeres en la Red (2001). Réplica al informe del consejo general del poder judicialsobre la problemática derivada de la violencia domestica. Obtenido de http://www.nodo50.org/mujeresred/violencia-contra_informe.html

Mullender, A. (2000). *La violencia doméstica. Una nueva visión de un viejo problema.* Barcelona: Paidós.

Nayak, M. B., Byrne, C.A., Martín, M.H. & Abraham, A.G. (2003). Attitudes toward violence against women: a cross-nation study. *Sex Roles, 49*(7), 333-342.

Nisbett, R.E. (1993). Violence and U.S. regional culture.*American Psychologist*, 48,441-449.

Nisbett, R.E. & Cohen, D. (1996). *Culture of honor.* Boulder, Westview Press.

Pérez, J.A.; Páez, D. & Navarro Pertusa, E. (2001). Conflicto de mentalidades: cultura del honor frente a liberación de la mujer. *Revista electrónica de motivación y emoción, 4,* n° 8-9.

Pierce, M. & Harris, R.J. (1993). The effect of provocation, ethnicity, and injury description of men´s and women´s perceptions of a wife-battering incident. *Journal of Applied and Social Psychology, 23,* 767-790.

Puente, S. & Cohen, D. (2003). Jeaolusy and the Meaning (or Nonmeaning of Violence. *Personality and social psychology bulletin, 29* (4), 449-460.

Rodríguez-Espartal, N. (2012). Intervención con presos por violencia de género.Propuesta y resultados de un programa basado en Inteligencia Emocional. TesisDoctoral. Jaén: Universidad de Jaén, Facultad de Humanidades y Ciencias de laEducación.

Rodríguez-Espartal, N. & López-Zafra, E. (2007). Cultura del honor y relaciones interpersonales en parejas jóvenes universitarias. En C. Guillén & R. Guil (eds). *Psicología Social: un encuentro de perspectivas* (531-536). Cádiz. Asociación de profesionales de Psicología Social.

Rodríguez-Espartal, N., López-Turrillo, E. & Lopez-Zafra, E. (2011). Inteligencia emocional, cultural del honor y pensamientos distorsionados en un grupo de presos condenados por violencia de género, tras un tratamiento cognitivo- conductual. *Libro de resúmenes del I Symposium sobr eAbuso Psicológico.* Granada.

Rodríguez, P., Manstead, A. R. S. & Fischer, A. (1999). Male honor, female honor and attitudes towards sex-roles in Spain and the Netherlands. Comunicación presentada al 12th Meeting of Experimental Social Psychology. Oxford.

Rodríguez, P., Manstead, A. R. S. & Fischer, A. (2002). The role of honor concerns in emotional reactions to offences. *Cognition and Emotion.* 16 (1): 143-163.

Ruiz, Y. (2004). La violencia contra la mujer en la sociedadactual: análisis y propuestas de intervención. *Jornadas de Fomento de la Investigació*: Castellón.

Salovey, P. &Grewal, D. (2005).The Science of emotional intelligence. *Currents Directions in Psychological Science, 14,* 281-285.

Salovey, P., Mayer, J, D., Goldman, S., Turvey, C., &Palfai, T. (1995). Emotional attention, clarity, and repair: Exploring emotional intelligence using the Trait Meta-Mood Scale. In J. W. Pennebaker (Ed). Emotion, disclosure and health (pp. 125-154). Washington, D. C.: American Psychological Association.

Seidler, V. (2000).*Unreasonable men. Masculinity and social theory.* México: Paidós.

Segall, M.H. (1988). Cultural roots of aggressive behavior. M.H. Bond (ed.) *The cross-cultural challenge to social psychology.* Londres. SAGE. (pp. 208-217).

Shackelford, T. K. (2005).An Evolutionary Psychological perspective on cultures of honor. *Evolutionary Psychology, 3,* 381-391.

Shackelford, T.K.; Gotees, A.T.; Buss, D.M.; Euler, H.A. & Oiré, S. (2005). When we hurt the ones we love: predicting violence against women from men´s mate retention tactics. *Personal Relationships, 12,* 447-463.

Smith, L., Heaven, P. &Ciarrochi, J. (2008).Trait emotional intelligence, conflict communication patterns, and relatioship satisfaction.*Personality and Individual differences,* 44, 1314-1325.

Spence, J.T., Helmreich, R.L. &Stapp, J., (1974). The Personal Attributes Questionnaire: A measure of sex role stereotypes and masculinity-feminity*. ISAS Catalog of Selected Documents in Psychology,* 4, 43, n° 617.

Stith, S.M.; Green, M.N.; Smith D.B. & Ward, D.B. (2008). Marital satisfaction and marital discord as risk markers for intimate partner violence: A meta-analytic review. *Journal of Family Violence*, 23,3, 149- 161.

Torres-Fúnez, E. & Lopez-Zafra, E., (2010).Diferencias en cultura del honor, inteligenciaemocional y pensamientos distorsionados sobre las mujeres en reclusos y no reclusos. *Boletín de Psicología. 100,* 71-78.

Triandis, H. C. (1996). The psychological measurement of cultural syndromes. *American Psychologist, 51,* 407-415.

UNFPA - United Nations Population Fund State of World Population, (2005).The Human Rights of Girls and Women. Obtenido dehttp://www.unfpa.org/swp/2005/english/ch3/

Vandello, J.A. & Cohen, D. (2003). Male honor and female fidelity: Implicit cultural scripts that perpetuate domestic violence. *Journal of personality and social psychology, 84, (5),* 997-1010.

Vandello, J.A. & Cohen, D. (2004). When believing is seeing: sustaining norms of violence in cultures of honor. En M. Schaller; E. Christian & S. Crandall (eds.) *The psychological foundations of culture,* (281-304). Nueva Yersey: Lawrence Erlbaum Associates.

Vandello, J.A. & Cohen, D. (2008). Culture, Gender, and Men's Intimate Partner Violence.*Social and Personality Psychology Compass* 2 (2), 652–667.

Vandello, J.A.; Cohen, D. & Ransom (2008). U.S. Southern and Northern differences in perceptions of norms about aggression: Mechanisms for the perpetuation of a culture of honor. *Journal of cross-cultural psychology*, 39, 162-177.

Vandello, J.A.; Cohen, D., Grandon, R., Franiuk, R.(2009). Stand by Your Man: Indirect Prescriptions for Honorable Violence and Feminine Loyalty in Canada, Chile, and the United Status. *Journal of Cross Cultural Psychology*.40(1): 81 - 104.

Viveros, M. (2001). Masculinidades. Diversidades regionales y cambios generacionales en Colombia. In M. Viveros; J. Olavarría & Fuller, N. *Hombres e identidades de género. Investigaciones desde América Latina.* Colombia: Universidad Nacional de Colombia.

Winters, J., Clift, R. & Dutton, D. (2004). An Exploratory Study of Emotional Intelligence and Domestic Abuse.*Journal of Family Violence*, 19 (5), 255-267.

Yanes, J.M. & González, R. (2000). Correlatos cognitivos asociados a la experiencia de violencia intraparental. *Psicothema, 12*(1), 41-47.

Yela, C.; Jiménez-Burillo, F. & Sangrador, J.L. (2003). Las dos caras del amor: funciones, mitos, paradojas y renuncias. En S. Worchel, J. Cooper, G. R. Goethals& J.M. Olson (eds) *Psicología Social.* Madrid. Thomson.

Yoshioka, M.R., DiNoia, J. & Ullah, K. (2000). Attitudes toward marital violence. *Violence Against Women, 7*(8), 900-926.

In: Gender Identity   ISBN: 978-1-63321-488-0
Editor: Beverly L. Miller   © 2014 Nova Science Publishers, Inc.

Chapter 8

WHERE SHOULD GENDER IDENTITY DISORDER GO? REFLECTIONS ON THE ICD-11 REFORM

*Simona Giordano**

CSEP, The University of Manchester,
The School of Law, Williamson Building,
Manchester, England

ABSTRACT

Gender Identity Disorder (GID) is included in the ICD-10 among the Mental and Behavioural Disorders (so called F-Codes) (F64). The World Health Organization is currently preparing the eleventh version of the ICD, to be published in 2015 or 2017. Members of the WHO Working Group on the Classification of Sexual Disorders and Sexual Health propose the removal of GID from the Mental and Behavioural Disorders and its inclusion in a non-psychiatric category. One motion is to rename the condition 'Gender Incongruence', and place it within a new category called 'Certain conditions related to sexual health', thereby formalising the idea that whatever the condition is, it is not a disorder.

Retaining GID within the ICD is thought to facilitate access to publicly funded or otherwise subsidised medical treatment. Whereas removing GID from mental illnesses is certainly a step forward in the recognition of the diversity of individual gender and sexual orientations, it may be asked whether it is still too small a step. Why should gender differences be included at all in diagnostic manuals? On what grounds? This chapter explores the reasons for and against retention of the diagnostic category of GID in the ICD, and it discusses where it should eventually be placed.

It will conclude that, as proposed by some LGBT groups, gender variance could be enclosed within the so-called Z coded of the ICD. These are non-pathologising codes, currently listed under the "Factors influencing health status and contact with health services".

---

* E-mail: simona.giordano@manchester.ac.uk.

1. INTRODUCTION

Gender Identity Disorder (GID) is included in the ICD-10 [1] among the Mental and Behavioural Disorders (so called F-Codes) (F64). The World Health Organization is currently preparing the eleventh version of the ICD, to be published in 2015 or 2017.

As per February 2014, the WHO Working Group has not published proposals relating to the category of gender identity [2]. However, members of the WHO Working Group on the Classification of Sexual Disorders and Sexual Health have published two papers [3, 4]. In these papers the authors propose the removal of GID from the Mental and Behavioural Disorders and its inclusion in a non-psychiatric category. One motion is to rename the condition 'Gender Incongruence', and place it within a new category called 'Certain conditions related to sexual health', thereby formalising the idea that whatever the condition is, it is not a disorder. The Working Group wishes to retain the condition within the ICD, as this is thought to facilitate access to publicly funded or otherwise subsidised medical treatment.

These proposals represent an important step towards the recognition of the human rights of every person, regardless of his/her sex and gender orientation. Already in 2010 the Council of Europe stressed that considering transgender/transsexual people[1] as afflicted by mental illness contradicts the statement, contained in the Universal Declaration of Human Rights, that "all human beings are born free and equal in dignity and rights" [5]: gender identity, like sexual orientation, is one of the most important and intimate aspects of who we are. The psychiatric diagnosis in particular, in spite of some potential advantages [6] has psychological and social adverse implications [7, 8]. Considering gender variance as a mental disorder seems to be, to use Marcuse's epithet, a form of "repressive tolerance" [9].

Whereas removing GID from mental illnesses is certainly a step forward in the recognition of the diversity of individual gender and sexual orientations, it may be asked whether it is still too small a step.

Why should gender differences be included at all in diagnostic manuals? On what grounds?

The main concern, as noted above, is not one of principle, but a practical one: the ability of transgender people to access publicly funded care or to obtain reimbursement under insurance schemes. But this is not the only concern, as we shall see.

An alternative solution is proposed by some LGBT groups. Gender variance, it is suggested, could be enclosed within the so-called Z coded of the ICD. These are non-pathologising codes, currently listed under the "Factors influencing health status and contact with health services". It will be argued that the users' proposal to place gender variance within the Z Codes is reasonable, ethically sound, and pragmatic; it represents a viable alternative to either complete exclusion from the ICD or pathologisation of gender variance.

Let us now move to the exploration of the main arguments for and against retention of GID in the ICD-11 (including those of purely pragmatic nature).

---

[1] For the purposes of this paper I will use the terms transgenderism/transsexualism, gender variance as interchangeable. I will privilege the term 'gender minorities' and will use it wherever possible.

2. GID Should Remain in the ICD Because It Is a 'Biological' Disorder

This argument could go somewhat like this: there is no ground to regard gender variance as *mental illness*, and therefore it should be removed from the Mental and Behavioural Disorders (from the F-Codes). However, it should be retained in the ICD because there is evidence that transgenderism has biological origins.

If a biological cause, or set of causes, of transgenderism could be found, this would contribute to the specificity of the diagnosis, and to the tailoring of appropriate medical treatments. The debate on whether GID should be included or not in the diagnostic manuals would be resolved. If, for example, it were found that atypical gender identity development is caused by, say, endocrine factors, this would help to collocate GID within the ICD (for example, with the endocrine disorders). Moreover, there would be no need (or less need) to 'argue for' the entitlement to medical treatment. As sufferers from a clear illness of corroborated biological origins, patients would 'quite clearly', so the argument may go, be entitled to the needed medical care, without having to bear the stigma of mental illness. The stakes are, thus, high.

That GID may be caused by some biological factors seems to reflect the experience of some transgender people and their families. They often refer to their perceived gender as 'innate'; the families of transgender children often insist on the resiliency of the child's 'innate' gender. Nothing can 'persuade' someone with a certain gender identity that that identity is not really the right one.

A large body of research has thus attempted to unravel the genetic, hormonal and neuro-developmental factors that might cause atypical gender identity development [10-17]. The higher prevalence of gender variance amongst people with intersex conditions than in the 'normal' population seems to suggest that chromosomal and hormonal factors may be involved in the aetiology of gender variance. However, not all intersex people have atypical gender; in fact, the majority of them identify themselves unequivocally as either males or females [18, 19], regardless of their chromosomal make up, and this suggests that the relationship between chromosomal make up and gender identity is far more complex than one may think.

Research has also attempted to disentangle the 'real' nature of gender variance; thus the relationship between transgenderism and other conditions [20, 21], such as separation anxiety disorder [22], body integrity identity disorder [23] and psychoses [24] has been the subject of extensive study. In recent years (2011-14) the association sometimes observed between gender variance and disorders on the autism spectrum [25] and eating disorders has been studied [26-28]. Research has also been devoted to analyse and interpret the familiality (occurrence of gender variance within one family, or study of the recurrent features of families in which gender variance appears) [29].

Nevertheless, despite some researchers' arguments for a biological basis for gender variance (see above), it is not clear what that basis is. Findings should be interpreted with caution, as a biological basis is likely to exist for *all gender identity development*, and it is not yet clear what neurological and biological factors produce atypical gender identity development compared to 'typical' gender identity development; indeed it is not even clear what biological factors produce a 'normal' gender identification and how [30].

Gender identity seems to result from an interplay of biological and social factors, and cognitive interpretations that are unique to each individual [31]. All processes of gender identification require a complex negotiation of preferences, inclinations, biological make up, social expectations, personal experiences, and acquisition of social roles. This means that males and females are not, and cannot be, homogeneous groups. As each individual is unique and different to any other, his/her way of being 'a male' or 'a female' will necessarily be unique and different.

There are thus various forms and ways of being, "multiple social identities" [32], and it is not possible, at least at this stage, to differentiate between healthy and pathological gender identities on scientific or clinical grounds (that is, on the basis of 'some observable facts'). That differentiation, if it takes place, takes place on other grounds; for example on the basis of value judgments relating to how humans should function, or of normative models of sex and gender 'normality'.

Considering that there are no clear clinical or scientific grounds to differentiate healthy from pathological gender identities, it could be argued that GID has no place in diagnostic manuals; we have as much reason to regard gender non-conformity as illness as we do to regard gender conformity as illness – which is to say, none.

From this point of view, it may be concluded that GID should be removed entirely from the ICD, in the same way as homosexuality and bisexuality have been. Once it was understood that there are many normal types of sexual orientation, the grounds for keeping homosexuality in the ICD vanished. The same should apply, in principle, to gender variance: once it is understood that the binary 'male/female' is misguiding and scientifically unfounded, GID should be removed from the ICD. But there are other aspects to be considered, and other arguments for and against retention of GID in the ICD.

3. GID SHOULD REMAIN IN THE ICD: SUFFERING IS INDICATION OF PATHOLOGY

It could be argued that even if the causes of gender identity (whether 'typical' or 'atypical') are (as yet) unknown, without a doubt in the vast majority of cases gender identity development does not cause distress. Most people grow in the gender assigned to them at birth, and do so quite comfortably. People whose gender is different from the gender of assignment are often afflicted by great confusion and distress. Moreover, gender variance is nearly always connected with ill social adjustment and functioning [33] and is often associated with poor psychological and social outcome [34], especially when proper medical care is not provided timely. This could all indicate that, even if the aetiology is not known, gender variance must be an illness of some kind, and thus has to be retained in the ICD.

3.1. Why Suffering Is Not an Indication of Pathology

The problem with this argument is that many conditions are associated with suffering and significant impairment in the life of the individual and the family. For some people, events such as divorce, bereavement, infertility, and so on may cause profound distress and have undesirable effects on psychological and social functioning; but they are not for that reason illnesses. This suggests that either many more conditions should be listed in diagnostic manuals, or that 'suffering' may be a shaky ground for inclusion of a condition in diagnostic manuals.

Moreover, distress may be an *adequate* response to adversities. In the case of gender variance, the psycho-social ill-adjustment typically associated with gender variance seems to be, to a significant extent, a function of societal inability to embrace gender differences as normal (and non-pathological), and treat them as such [35]. We shall return shortly on this point (see next Section).

Suffice to note now that suffering needs to be understood, and it is not a sufficient ground to conceptualise certain conditions as illnesses. In fact it is not even a necessary ground. Some forms of cancer at some stages may cause no suffering, and yet we may agree that they are pathological.

So suffering is not necessarily an indication of pathology; and absence of suffering is not necessarily an indication of health. Suffering, instead, as anticipated above, needs to be understood.

3.2. Understanding Suffering

Understanding people's suffering involves attempting to disentangle their predicaments. Gender variance can be associated with inherent suffering: people may feel terrified and revolted by their physical characteristics. But a large part of the distress associated with gender variance is a function of societal inability to embrace gender differences as normal, and in societies where the gender divide is not as marked, gender non-conforming people suffer less [35].

Lesbian, gay, bisexual, and transgender (LGBT) individuals are subjected to high degrees of discrimination, abuse and violence [36, 37]. Homophobic bullying in schools in England is common, and has severe long-term effects [38]. Children who are victims of it are five times more likely than other students to fail to attend school, and twice as likely not to pursue further education [39]. Substance abuse, homelessness, prostitution, HIV infection, self-harm, depression, anxiety [40], and suicide [41] are also included among the results of homophobic bullying [42].

Even in absence of physical or verbal abuse, the marginalisation of gender minorities is apparent: marriage, employment, and many legal rights are often a function of 'gender' [43]. Birth itself is marked by gender predictions and those who do not fit a mainstream gender divide are often left in a legal and social vacuum.

Some transgender people narrate the grief associated with having to continually pretend to be someone they are not, being scared of being caught or uncovered[2]. Suffering is therefore inextricably intertwined with the social response that transgender people receive. This does not mean that gender variance is a 'social construct' - that it is all caused by wrong gender stereotypes. It means instead that there is an important social dimension to gender, and that people's suffering should also be understood in that light.

---

[2] Personal communication with transgender individuals.

To describe gender minorities as ill because they often suffer and lack serene psycho-social adjustment is to condemn them to a double jeopardy: they often do not have the possibility of serene psychological and social adjustment, and then they are regarded as ill because they have not adjusted well.

4. GENDER VARIANCE IS AN ILLNESS BECAUSE IT IS A VARIATION FROM WHAT NORMALLY HAPPENS

It could still be argued that the vast majority of people develop quite 'naturally' in the gender of rearing, and therefore gender variance must be a disorder, here meant as a deviation from the norm [44-49]. The gender we are assigned is generally in line with our biological features, and these reflect a 'normal functioning' for our species: these biological features allow us to integrate in society with certain roles, but more importantly, to reproduce, to pass on our genes, ultimately to preserve our species. A deviation from this functioning, which seems to be 'normal' for our species, is in itself an illustration of pathology.

Indeed, in the attempt to define it, some have proposed that 'illness' should be understood as a deviation from "normal species functioning" [50, 51].

This argument is slightly more sophisticated than the one considered in the previous section. The argument in the previous section suggested that gender minorities are ill *because they suffer*. However we noted that not all people who suffer are ill, and not all those who are ill suffer. This second argument instead suggests that whether or not people suffer, they are ill *if and because* their condition represents a variation from 'normal species functioning'. So, for example, a gender non-conforming child who is perfectly happy to cross-dress is still afflicted with a disorder, whether or not at that point in time s/he experiences any suffering.

This argument has the merit of reducing or eliminating the emphasis on suffering as a criterion for the medicalization of certain human conditions. However, the argument has important pitfalls, which emerge once we try to qualify what 'normal species functioning' may be.

'Normal species functioning' could be what happens to the majority of people. But what happens to the majority of people, even to the vast majority of people, cannot be taken as an indication of what is healthy. The vast majority of people are right-handed, and yet being left handed is not pathological. The majority of adults in Western countries perhaps is short-sighted (or long-sighted), and yet having a full vision is not for that reason an illness.

'Normal species functioning' could also be defined in terms of the ability to reproduce (indeed this argument has been used in the literature) [52]. The desire to change gender may be seen from this perspective as 'against nature' or 'inherently' unhealthy. But many transgender people do actually reproduce; and many people who do not cross genders do not or cannot reproduce. If reproduction or the ability to reproduce was the ground to consider individuals healthy, it would follow that post-menopausal women or infertile people are ill, which surely is at least dubious.

If the arguments elaborated so far are persuasive, then it seems to follow that there are no reasons, clinical or epistemological, to consider gender variance as a disorder or an illness.

Whether or not GID should be removed from the diagnostic manuals also depends on other considerations. In what follows I will consider the 'pragmatic' reasons for and against retention of GID in the ICD.

5. THE PROVISION OF TREATMENT: THE ARGUMENT FOR RETAINING GID IN THE ICD

One important argument in favour of retaining the category of GID within the ICD is that it facilitates access to treatment. Not just access to *publicly funded* or otherwise *subsidised care*, but to *treatment*, whether privately paid for or not. Why should a doctor treat people in absence of illness? Why would they mutilate 'healthy' bodies?

One possible answer may be: because that benefits the patients (and because the patients so request)[3].

But how would a doctor know that the patient (or should we say client, if gender variance is de-pathologised?) is going to benefit from a certain medical intervention without a clear diagnosis? Even in cases in which the amputation of healthy limbs has been regarded as lawful in the UK, this only happened because the person was said to suffer from Body Dysmorphic Disorder [53]. Maybe the limbs were healthy, but the person had a disorder. At least so the argument may go.

Without the boundaries of a diagnosis, wouldn't doctors tumble down a slippery slope at the end of which they may be required to perform tasks that they may see as contrary to the goals of medicine?

Indeed, there are known cases of 'odd' or ethically suspicious medical requests. Some people are known to have demanded to look *less human*, for example. The story of the Cat Woman is well known. The woman underwent massive reconstructive surgery to look like a cat. It is also known that a growing number of people seek surgery to obtain 'Caucasian' traits: examples of these are blepharoplasty for Asian people [54-56], or skin bleaching and nose filing for black people [57-59].

A doctor can of course always refuse to perform such operations if they think that these are contrary to the goals of medicine.

However, there will be (there are) doctors who *do not see* these operations as contrary to the goals of medicine. It would then be up to individual doctors to decide whether or not a woman who wants to look feline *will* look feline or whether a transgender person will obtain the requested treatments.

But this also means that transgender people could *lose* their *entitlement* to medical care: whether or not their requests are satisfied, in this scenario, depends on whether or not they find a doctor who is 'compassionate' enough, or 'knowledgeable' enough, or even 'unscrupulous' enough, to provide treatment. Is this a desirable situation?

---

[3] For reasons of space I will leave aside here this second horn of the problem, namely the issue of respect for autonomy and informed consent. I will assume here that the requesting people have the legal capacity to provide valid consent. It is to be noted that in England people do not have a right to obtain medical treatment, even if they are requesting that treatment with capacity. The doctors can refuse to satisfy a competent request if they believe that the treatment required is not in the person's best interests. Burke v. GMC [2005] EWCA Civ 1003.

There is one further concern: once GID disappeared as a 'disorder', society may further stigmatise gender non-conforming people because, if they are not afflicted by illness, then it must mean that they 'choose' or 'want' bodily mutilations for no reason, just because 'they are odd'.

In truth, how many of us do not think that there must be something 'odd' at least with someone who undergoes surgery after surgery to look like a cat? Where would the difference be between cases like hers and cases of people who want to amend their sexual characteristics? The psychiatric diagnosis, thrown out by the door, would enter back by the window, fed in by the very de-medicalisation of GID.

The concerns presented here will be examined in turn.

5.1. Gender Variance Is Different from the Other Conditions

It needs to be noted that gender variance is not comparable to other types of discomfort with our bodies, some of which have been listed above (but the list could of course be much longer).

Whereas people may be unhappy with their own body in the most disparate ways, there is wide agreement on the 'features' of gender variance. The predicaments of gender non-conforming people are often similar (though the interventions requested or needed may vary). Non-conforming gender behaviours may manifest themselves in many cases very early (at the age of 2 to 4) [60] and are often persistent.

It is thus likely that gender variance has to do with early development of gender identity, rather than with the susceptibility to and acquisition of social stereotypes (as is arguably the case for many other forms of body dissatisfaction). Gender variance is also different in other ways: it is not dissatisfaction with the physical features or with how some body parts look; it is dissatisfaction with the identity that a certain body reveals and reflects. The causes of gender variance are unknown and are probably multiple [61, 62], and I have suggested that seeking the 'causes' of gender variance may even be misleading: however, the severity in which gender variance may manifest itself and its early onset indicate that there is something non-negotiable about gender identification: as noted above, when a gender identity is adopted, typically it is not possible to convince the person that s/he has got it wrong. This applies to adults as well as to children.

Even when gender identity fluctuates, there is not much that can be done to convince the individual that s/he is either a man or a woman.

In this sense we can still talk about gender variance as a phenomenon that has identifiable features and a predictable outcome based on the evidence gathered by the clinical community and on the experience of gender non-conforming people, and still regard it as different in many important ways from other types of body discomfort. We can still provide medical care based on the evidence collected and published so far: we can rely on the body of medical opinion that has realised guidelines on good clinical care, on the appropriate standards of care that sufferers can expect [63, 64].

All of that can be accepted without having to either accept that gender variance is an illness, or to accept that if it is not an illness it is *on a par* with other forms of body dissatisfaction.

5.2. Some Normative Implications in Clinical Care

It is noted that where gender variance is persistent, the psycho-social adjustment of the transgender person is typically very difficult [65]. People who receive timely and appropriate medical care have better lives [66-68]. If not treated, instead, the psychological and social sequelae for many transgender people are grim [69]. It could be argued that two grounds here *at least* legitimise medical treatment (*at least* because these grounds can produce a *moral obligation* to provide medical treatment): the sufferers' ability to benefit from treatment and the harm that is likely to result from withholding medical treatment.

Now, of course one could argue that if an amputation of a healthy limb is likely to prevent a person from attempting suicide, that amputation *should be carried out*. In cases like these presented to the Courts in the UK, treatment has been regarded as lawful because it was considered as life saving [70].

That, however, does not imply that the condition of the person who has discomfort with healthy limb and gender variance are *on a par*. Indeed, it is likely that various forms of body dissatisfaction are markedly different from one another, that the predicaments and the psychological dynamics of the people concerned are significantly different, and that care can and should be differentiated accordingly[4] (think of the dissatisfaction experienced by people with anorexia – the degree of dissatisfaction may be as profound as in gender variance, but that does not make the conditions *on a par*) [71].

It would also be invidious to argue that GID should stay in the ICD *so that people can obtain the needed care*. Why then not create a category of Asian Identity Disorder, so that Asian women can obtain the 'needed' blepharoplasty? Why not create a category of YID (Youngish Identity Disorder) for women over 40s who 'need' some cosmetic treatments? There is no need to proceed this way in order to explain why medical treatment is ethically justified (or even ethically mandatory). The provision of medical treatment can be justified on other grounds, rather than the 'finding' of 'a disorder' (we shall discuss these grounds shortly).

There are further arguments and concerns.

5.3. The Unscrupulous Doctor

If GID were removed from the ICD, wouldn't doctors and patients lose clarity concerning the parameters of good medical care? Wouldn't that expose gender minorities to unscrupulous doctors, willing to perform surgery on request without careful assessment of whether this is in the patient's best interests? What would happen, so the argument may go, to people with psychoses, or other vulnerable groups who *may believe* they want cross-gender treatment but who are unlikely to benefit from it? Both patients and society may need to know what the boundaries of good and ethical clinical practice are: people must have an idea of what doctors may ethically do and what doctors should refrain from doing.

---

[4] I have indeed explored the body dissatisfaction typical of people with anorexia and bulimia nervosa, and the results of my analysis and of the review of the literature suggest that the phenomenology of eating disorders and gender variance are extremely different. The fact that both groups are unhappy with the way their body is, per se, is immaterial. See endnote 71.

This concern is obviously extremely important. But it is not clear that retaining GID in the ICD offers this kind of protection, and it not clear that de-pathologising GID will expose gender minorities and other vulnerable groups to these kinds of hazard.

Deleting GID from the ICD does not and should not imply 'throwing away the baby with the bathwater'. It does not and should not mean getting rid of, for example, the Standards of Care [63], based on decades of data collection and analysis. Doctors still owe a duty of care to the people to whom they offer treatment, and still ought to intervene in their best interests. These interests do not necessarily become 'fluid' or open to whatever interpretation because a certain condition is de-pathologised. For example, fertility treatment can be highly sophisticated, and is tightly regulated in England: yet infertility is not a 'disorder' listed in the ICD. Pregnancy is not a disorder, and yet there are accepted standards of clinical care and at times sophisticated forms of healthcare intervention that are provided to pregnant women. The removal of GID from the ICD does not entail and should not create a 'Wild West of gender treatment'. Indeed, it is unethical to provide medical treatment only on the condition that gender minorities continue to be regarded as 'ill'. That is precisely the type of 'repressive tolerance' Marcuse talked about. If not based on the finding of an illness, on what grounds shall gender treatment be provided? And how can good clinical care be guaranteed?

6. THE JUSTIFICATION OF MEDICAL TREATMENT

Medical care in cases of gender variance can be morally justified if and when three conditions are met: first, the person must be in distress, and his/her suffering cannot be ameliorated with psychological/social intervention (for example, with psychotherapy, family or school involvement in cases of children); second, the sufferer has been assessed by specialists according to published literature and/or to international clinical guidelines, such as the Standards of Care [63, 64], and it must be sufficiently clear that the person's gender identification is such that the person will benefit from medical intervention. Using clinical guidelines to understand the predicaments of a person with gender variance, utilising the evidence collected so far to assess the person's issues and make a likely prediction of the outcomes is a part of good and responsible clinical care, and does not imply accepting that gender variance is an illness. Finally, it should be expected that non-treatment is the most risky option: for example it should be probable that the overall psycho-social sequelae associated with non-treatment are pernicious and worse for the applicant than that associated with treatment. The WPATH Standards of Care, for example, include harm reduction as a legitimate goal of clinical intervention [63]. It can thus be argued that medical intervention can be provided, and also provided according to parameters of good clinical care, even if the condition is de-medicalised [72].

7. RETAINING GID IN THE ICD FACILITATES SUBSIDISED MEDICAL CARE

Another concern is whether removing GID from the ICD will hinder the patients' entitlement to *subsidised* medical care.

The treatments needed by gender minorities are often life long, and in many cases they involve extensive and invasive surgery. Full realignment surgery is not always necessary; for example, some people may wish to be recognised as women at home and as men on the workplace, or *vice versa*; some people only wish to receive hormonal intervention in order to feminise or masculinise their body partially, some may wish to only receive partial surgery (for a variety of reasons), whereas some people need full realignment surgery. But in most cases some form of medical treatment is necessary, and sometimes treatment, as noted, is costly and life-long. For many transgender people, receiving medical treatment is a matter of life or death.

In many countries, even now that GID is formally regarded as an illness, not all treatments will be publicly funded; for example, laser hair removal may not be funded, and yet it is obviously necessary for a transgender woman not to present herself socially with stubborn facial hair. These treatments are expensive, especially considering the discrimination in the job market that many transgender people still suffer. In England provision of medical treatment will be based on the budget of the Local Authorities, so it is not guaranteed that certain treatments will be publicly funded, even if GID is listed in the ICD.

Moreover, the idea that only the conditions listed in the ICD as disorders 'deserve' public expense, or that only people afflicted by those alignments may present legitimate claims to NHS treatment is misguided. Even if whatever has to do with gender were de-medicalised (like homosexuality and heterosexuality), this, in principle, should have no bearing upon access to medical treatment. I have explained why this is so elsewhere [73] but let me summarise a few important points.

First, it should be noted that there are many conditions that are treated medically in spite of not being 'illnesses'. If treatment for these conditions is subsidised, then *prima facie* treatment for gender minorities should not be withdrawn based on the removal of the category from the diagnostic manuals.

We have seen earlier that, for example, medical treatment is routinely offered to women in pregnancy, although pregnancy is not an illness. Fertility treatment, breast reconstructions after accidents or breast cancer, surgery for bat ears and hormonal treatment for excessive or retarded growth[5] are all examples of interventions provided to people, although there is no illness to treat. These medical treatments are typically funded publicly or reimbursed under many insurance schemes [74]. If these treatments are subsidised, it means that we are ready to accept that some conditions may require public or otherwise funded treatment, even in absence of illness.

Second, there is a more fundamental, conceptual problem in the claim that publicly funded or otherwise subsidised care should be offered only in case of ascertained disorders. The problem is that the definition of disability/disorder/illness is not just a matter of empirical or scientific observation, but of value [75].

As Brazier and Glover write, "unless the law can settle upon some coherent and defensible definition of illness, the elasticity of concept of illness may snap" [70, p.375]. This means that the 'presence' of a 'disability' or 'illness' cannot be simply 'established': people have very divergent views on whether a condition is a disorder or disability or not, or even an advantage.

---

[5] I owe this observation to Peter Clayton.

Disability-right activists have for a long time made this point as the pivot of their protests against a 'disabiling' environment; some deaf couples have deliberately attempted to have deaf children because they regarded deafness as an advantage [76]. Therefore the 'finding' of a disorder or illness cannot be the criterion upon which it is decided whether an individual will receive publicly funded care or not.

Finally, there are ways to guarantee appropriate care that do not pass through pathologisation. The Yogyakarta Principles on the Application of Human Rights Law to Sexual Orientation and Gender Identity, at Principle 18, states: "a person's sexual orientation and gender identity are not, in and by themselves, medical conditions and are not to be treated, cured or suppressed" [77]. Following this, in May 2012 the Argentinian senate passed a law which recognises the human right of transgender people to access medical care (including surgery) without any kind of diagnosis [78].

Retaining GID in diagnostic manuals, thus, does not necessarily serve the pragmatic purpose of obtaining proper medical care, or subsidised medical care, and removal of GID from the diagnostic manuals should not necessarily hinder access to subsidised care.

8. A SUBTLE BUT IMPORTANT DIFFERENCE: *DIA-APART* AND FINDING 'THE ILLNESS'

The assumption that only if there is a certified illness people have a legitimate claim to treatment, especially publicly funded treatment, is very much entrenched in the way many people think about gender treatments: transgender people usually obtain medical care only when a specialist, or team of specialists, makes a diagnosis that excludes other possible causes (such as an intersex condition). Making a diagnosis seems to be equated to the finding of a disorder or illness. It may be requested that the patient has a social transition prior to the provision of hormonal and surgical treatment, to evaluate whether s/he is *really transgender* [63] Transgender patients often have to 'demonstrate' that they have a 'disorder'; that 'disorder' has to be certified by a specialist (generally a psychiatrist), and only when it is 'certified' that the person has 'the illness' s/he can then receive the needed treatments.

This way of proceeding may have some important benefits: it is certainly vital that decisions to undertake irreversible mutilating surgery are not rushed, and that the patient and doctor assess carefully together the expectations of the patient and whether the available treatments can indeed fulfill those expectations. The 'informed consent' process in these cases has to encompass a lot more than plain provision of information relating to the benefits and risks of proposed treatments and alternatives. There is thus something seemingly beneficial to the patient in this 'diagnostic' process.

However, there is a subtle but important differentiation to make, one to which I alluded earlier. Establishing whether the patient's predicaments are such that the person is going to benefit from the long, invasive treatments that s/he requests is a matter of good clinical care. Initiating gender treatment is certainly not a decision that either patients or doctors would want to take lightly: both should in principle be satisfied that treatment is in the best interests of the patient and that the patient is going to benefit from it. But stressing the importance of such an assessment does not equate to 'finding the illness'.

To make a diagnosis literally means to 'distinguish' to 'discern'. In this sense making a diagnosis is useful and important: it helps to discern what the patient's predicaments and expectations are, and to assess how likely it is that the treatments available enhance the patient's welfare and/or decrease his/her suffering. This does not equate, and should not equate, to 'finding an illness'. It could be that having a non-conforming gender is a perfectly 'normal', 'natural' event (as there are different gender identities and not only two), and that many people are simply less lucky than others and need medical care in order to develop a body that allows them to express more fully who they are. It is thus crucial to discuss with the person what types of intervention can be most helpful to fulfill the person's needs. That is completely different from evaluating whether the patient 'ticks' the boxes of GID, as contained in one diagnostic manual or another, and a patient should not be put in the invidious position of 'having to prove' to be ill in order to obtain the treatments that are necessary to express him or herself fully within society.

From this point of view, the removal of GID should not preclude a 'diagnostic' process, meant literally as the understanding, the discernment, and the recognition of the patient's needs.

9. GID SHOULD BE RETAINED IN THE ICD AS THIS PROMOTES RESEARCH

One argument to retain a medical diagnosis of gender variance is that it may encourage further research.

Whereas research on gender identity development is crucial to the good management of various gender identities, there is no reason to believe that by de-pathologising gender variance research would be hindered. Psychology studies many phenomena that are not pathological: much of the research on gender identity development was not carried out on subjects thought to be ill. There is no reason to presuppose that atypical gender identity development should receive less attention if it is de-pathologised.

10. GID SHOULD BE RETAINED IN THE ICD BECAUSE THIS MAKES PEOPLE FEEL BETTER

The finding of 'an illness' may provide a sort of (possibly reassuring) 'explanation' for seemingly inexplicable experiences; it can protect both sufferers and the significant others from feelings of guilt and blame, which are often associated with 'abnormal' behaviours and experiences.

Indeed the person may not know or understand what is 'going wrong' with her/him, and being told that what is happening is a recognised disorder, with a name and clinical features that recur in a similar way in other people, may soothe one's anxiety [79].

But it is not clear why a sufferer and her/his family may not be equally reassured at hearing that gender variance is a normal way in which gender may develop, that many people have an 'atypical' gender development, that there is no pathology to worry about, and that there is a wide range of medical, social and lifestyle interventions that can help the person. It is unclear why a statement of normality should be less reassuring than a diagnosis of pathology.

11. A Viable Compromise: The Proposal to Enclose GID in the Z Codes

Global Action for Trans Equality proposes to enclose gender variance among the Z Codes of the ICD.

"Categories Z00-Z99 are provided for occasions when circumstances other than a disease, injury or external cause classifiable to categories A==-Y89 are recorded as 'diagnoses' or 'problems'. This can arise in two main ways:

a. When a person who may or may not be sick encounters the health services for some specific purpose, such as to receive limited care or service for a current condition, to donate an organ or tissue, to receive prophylactic vaccination or to discuss a problem which is in itself not a disease or injury.
b. When some circumstance or problem is present which influences the person's health status but is not in itself a current illness or injury. Such factors may be elicited during population surveys, when the person may or may not be currently sick, or be recorded as an additional factor to be borne in mind when the person is receiving care for some illness or injury" [80].

Problems relating to, for example, persecution or discrimination on the basis of membership of some groups, or on the basis of personal characteristics, such as unusual physical appearance, are covered by the Z Codes. Minority stress and distress are also covered by these Codes.

As we saw at the beginning of this paper, the WHO Working Group on the Classification of Sexual Disorders and Sexual Health is airing the possibility of creating a new category of conditions relating to sexual health, and enclose gender variance in that category (with a name that is currently not decided).

There are two main problems with this proposal (others have been highlighted by LGBT groups) [81].

One is that gender variance is not necessarily a condition related to sexual health. There are aspects of gender realignment treatments that of course relate to sexual health (and reproductive health). For example, phalloplasty ideally needs to be carried out in a way that allows the person to retain sensitivity and the possibility to have orgasms. During vaginoplasty, the vagina ideally should have dimensions that allow penetrative sex (one of the reasons that some surgeons are reluctant to carry out surgery on male-to-female minors is that the tissue available for a creation of a sensitive vagina is not sufficient until the penis has reached certain dimensions)[6]; but gender variance is not necessarily and primarily a problem of sexual health.

---

[6] Personal communication from surgeons.

The other problem is that the inclusion of gender variance among problems relating to sexual health associates again gender variance with conditions that can be regarded as 'medical' (such as some dysfunctions in sexuality for example).

Thus, unless sound reasons are produced to enclose gender variance within this category, if the consensus is to retain gender variance within the ICD, it seems more appropriate overall to enclose it under the Z Codes.

CONCLUSION

Once upon the time, the humankind was composed of three types of being: males, females and the ill. Now we have no reason to regard those who are neither males nor females as ill. In fact, as sex and gender development have been studied more, we have also lost the certainty that we can identify who the males and the females are [6].

Accepting the existence of a variety of ways of being means looking beyond the stereotypical gender divide, and accepting that all people "are born equal in dignity and right" [82] regardless of their sex and gender orientations, and that their difference should not be regarded as deviance.

In the absence of sound reasons, epistemological or otherwise, for retaining the diagnosis of GID, the pathologisation of gender variance, far from serving the interests of the people affected, may illustrate societal inability or unwillingness to recognise the full legitimacy of gender minorities, and to consider atypical gender development as one of the different ways in which identity can be formed.

Retaining the diagnosis of GID risks reinforcing the view that there are only two possible sound ways of being: male or female - a view that has to give way to the recognition of a much more nuanced and varied picture.

Retaining the diagnosis risks reinforcing discrimination against those who are a part of a minority, by perpetuating the view of atypical gender identification as a deviance. This contradicts the moral imperative, that we all share, to have equal concern and respect for all members of the human family [82], regardless of arbitrary features, such as age, race, sexual orientation or gender. Thus if gender variance has to find ay space within the new ICD, the only place that it can ethically occupy is within the Z Codes, those that include conditions of suffering that require medical, psychological and social attention and resources, but which are not *per se* pathologies.

ACKNOWLEDGMENT

I wish to thank Iain Brassington for his extensive comments on this paper.

REFERENCES

[1] World Health Organisation (WHO) (1992). ICD-10, *International Statistical Classification of diseases*. Geneva: WHO.

[2]   http://apps.who.int/classifications/icd11/browse/f/en Last accessed 4 April 2014.

[3]   Drescher, J., Cohen-Kettenis, P., and Winter, S. (2012). Minding the body: situating gender identity diagnoses in the ICD-11. *International Review of Psychiatry,* (December, 24, 6), pp.568-77.

[4]   Drescher, J. (2013). Controversies in gender diagnoses. *LGBT Health,* (1, 1), pp.9-13. Available at http://online.liebertpub.com/doi/pdf/10.1089/lgbt.2013.1500 Last accessed 4 April 2014.

[5]   http://www.un.org/en/documents/udhr/ Last accessed 4 April 2014.

[6]   Giordano, S. (2011). Where Christ did not go: men, women and Frusculicchi. Gender Identity Disorder (GID): epistemological and ethical issues relating to the psychiatric diagnosis. *Monash. Bioethics Review,* (29, 4), pp.12.1-22.

[7]   Stuart, H. (2006). Mental illness and employment . *Current Opinion in Psychiatry,* (19, 5), pp. 522–526.

[8]   Bartel, A. and Taubman, P. (1986). Some Economic and Demographic Consequences of Mental Illness. *Journal of Labor Economy,* (4, 2), pp. 243-256.

[9]   Marcuse, H. (1965). Repressive tolerance. Available online at http://ada.evergreen.edu/~arunc/texts/frankfurt/marcuse/tolerance.pdf Last accessed 4 April 2014.

[10]   Besser, M. Carr, S., Cohen-Kettenis, P. T, Connolly, P. De Sutter, P. Diamond, M., Di Ceglie, D., Higashi, Y., Jones, L., Kruijver, F. P. M., Martin, J., Playdon, Z.-J., Ralph, D., Reed, T., Reid, R., Reiner, W. G., Swaab, D., Terry, T., Wilson, P. Wylie, K. (2006). Atypical Gender Development – A Review. *International Journal of Transgenderism,* (9, 1), pp. 29-44.

[11]   Zucker K. J. (2006). Commentary on "Atypical Gender Development-A Review". *International Journal of Transgenderism,* (9,1), pp. 53-59.

[12]   Soleman, R. S., Shagen, S. E. Veltman, D. J., Kreukels, B. P. C., Cohen-Kettenis, P. T., Lambalk, C. B. Wouters, F., Delemarre-van de Waal, H. A. (2013). Sex differences in verbal fluency during adolescence: a functional magnetic resonance imaging study in gender dysphoric and control boys and girls. *Journal of Sexual Medicine,* (10, 8), pp.1969-1977.

[13]   Santarnecchi, E., Vatti, G., Dettore, D., and Rossi, A. (2012) Intrinsic cerebral connectivity analysis in an untreated female to male transsexual subject. A first attempt using resting state fMRI. *Neuroendocrinology,* (96, 3), pp.188-93.

[14]   Shin-ichi Hisasue, Shoko Sasaki, Taiji Tsukamoto, and Shigeo Horie. (2012). The relationship between second to fourth digit ratio and female gender identity. *Journal of Sexual Medicine,* (9, 11), pp.2903-09.

[15]   Case, L. K. and Ramachandran, V. S. (2012). Alternating gender incongruity: a new neuropsychiatric syndrome providing insight into the dynamic plasticity of brain-sex. *Medical Hypotheses,* (78, 5), pp.626-31.

[16]   Fuss, J., Biedermann, S. W., Stalla, G. K. and Auer, M. K. (2013). On the quest for a biomechanism of transsexualism: is there a role for BDNF? *Journal of Psychiatric Research,* (47, 12), pp.2015-27.

[17]   Fontanari, A. M. V., Andreazza, T., Costa, T. B., Koff, W. J., Aguiar, B., Ferrari, P., Massuda, R., Pedrini, M., Silveira, E., Belmonte-deAbreu, P. S., Gama, C. S., Kauer-Stant'Anna, M., Kapczinski, F. and Lobato, M. I. R. (2013). Serum concentration of

brain derived neurotrophic factor in patients with gender identity disorder. *Journal of Psychiatric Research,* (47, 10), pp.1546-48.

[18] Wallien, M. S. C., Zucker, K. J. , Steensma, T. D. and Cohen-Kettenis P.T. (2008). 2D:4D finger-length ratios in children and adults with gender identity disorder. *Hormonal Behavior,* (54, 3), pp.450-454.

[19] Nawata Hideyuki, Ogomori Koji, Tanaka Mariko, Nishimura Ryoji, Urashima Hajime, Yano Rika, Takano Koichi and Kuwabara Yasuo. (2010). Regional cerebral blood flow changes in female to male gender identity disorder. *Psychiatry And Clinical Neurosciences,* (64, 2), pp.157-161.

[20] Seishi Terada, Yosuke Matsumoto, Toshiki Sato, Nobuyuki Okabe, Yuki Kishimoto and Yosuke Uchitomi (2012). Factors predicting psychiatric comorbidity in gender dysphoric adults. *Psychiatry Research,* (200, 2/3), pp.469-474.

[21] Fisher, A. D., Bandini, E., Casale, H., Ferruccio, N., Meriggiola, M. C., Gualerzi, A., Manieri, C., Jannini, E., Mannucci, E., Monami, M., Stomaci, N., Delle Rose, A:, Susini, T., Ricca, V., Maggi, M. (2013). Sociodemographic and clinical features of gender identity disorder: an Italian multicentric evaluation. *Journal of Sexual Medicine,* (10, 2), pp.408-429.

[22] Wu, L. T., Gersing, K. R., Swartz, M. S., Burchett, B., Li, T. K., Blazer, D. G. (2013). Using electronic health records data to assess comorbidities of substance use and psychiatric diagnoses and treatment settings among adults. *Journal of Psychiatric Research,* (47, 4), pp.555-563.

[23] Moller, J., Oddo, S. and Strin, A. (2013). Body integrity disorder (BIID). *Personlichkeitsstorungen Theorie und Therapie,* (17, 2), pp.100-109.

[24] Fagel, S. A., Swaab, H., De Sonneville, L. M., Van Rijn, S., Pieterse, J. K., Scheepers, F. and Van Engeland, H. (2013). Development of schizothypal symptoms following psychiatric disorders in childhood or adolescence. *European Child and Adolescent Psychiatry,* (22, 1), pp.683-692.

[25] Jones, R. M., Wheelwright, S., Darrell, K., Martin, E., Green, R., Di Ceglie, D. and Baron-Cohen, S. (2012). Brief report, female to male transsexual people and autistic traits. *Journal of Autism and Developmental Disorders,* (42, 2), pp.301-306.

[26] Algars, M., Alanko, K., Santtila, P. and Sandnabba, K. N. (2012). Disordered eating and gender identity disorder: a qualitative study. *Eating Disorders: the Journal of Treatment and Prevention,* (20, 4), pp.300-311.

[27] Bandini, E., Fisher, A. D., Castellini, G., Lo Sauro, C., Lelli, L., Meriggiola, M. C., Casale, H., Benni, L., Ferruccio, N., Faravelli, C., Dettore, D., Maggi, M. and Ricca, V. (2013). Gender identity disorder and eating disorders: similarities and differences in terms of body uneasiness. *Journal of Sexual Medicine,* (10, 4), pp.1012-23.

[28] Ewan, L. A., Middleman, A. B. and Feldmann, J. (2014). Treatment of anorexia nervosa in the context of transsexuality: a case report. *International Journal of Eating Disorders,* (47, 1), pp.112-15.

[29] Heylens, G., De Cuypere, G., Zucker, K. J., Schelfaut, C., Elaut, E., Vanden Bossche, H., De Baere, E. and T'Sjoen, G. (2012). Gender identity disorder in twins: a review of the case report literature. *Journal of Sexual Medicine,* (9, 3), pp.751-757.

[30] Deaux, K. and Stewart, A. J. (2001). Framing Gender Identities. In R. K. Unger (Ed.), *Handbook of the Psychology of Women and Gender* (pp. 84-100). London/New York: Wiley.

[31] Archer J. and Lloyd B. (2002). *Sex and Gender*. Cambridge: Cambridge University Press, pp. 75–76.

[32] Bolin, A. (1996). Transcending and Transgendering: Male-to-Female Transsexuals, Dichotomy and Diversity. In Gilbert Herdt (Ed.), *Third Sex Third Gender, beyond Sexual Dimorphism in Culture and History* (pp. 447-486). New York: Zone Books.

[33] Giordano S. (2008). Ethics of Management of Gender Atypical Organisation in Children and Adolescents. In M. Boylan (Ed.), International Public Health Policy and Ethics (pp.249-272). Dordrecht: Springer.

[34] Cohen-Kettenis, P. T. and. Pfäfflin, F. (2003). Transgenderism and Intersexuality in Childhood and Adolescence. *Making choices*. London: Sage Publications.

[35] Connolly, P. (2003). Transgendered Peoples of Samoa, Tonga and India: Diversity of Psychosocial Challenges, Coping, and Styles of Gender Reassignment, Harry Benjamin International Gender Dysphoria Association Conference, Ghent, Belgium.

[36] GLSEN (2011). The 2011 National School Climate Survey. Available at http://www.glsen.org/sites/default/files/2011%20National%20School%20Climate%20Survey%20Full%20Report.pdf Last accessed 4 April 2014.

[37] Di Ceglie, D. (2000). Gender identity disorder in young people. *Advances in Psychiatric Treatment*, (6), pp. 458–466.

[38] Rivers, I. (2011). *Homophobic bullying: research and theoretical perspectives*. Oxford: Oxford University Press.

[39] Hall Horace, R. (2006). Teach to Reach: addressing lesbian, gay, bisexual and transgender youth issues in the classroom. *The New Educator*, (2), pp. 149-157.

[40] Department of health (2004). Stand up for us: challenging homophobia in schools. Available at http://www.nice.org.uk/niceMedia/documents/stand_up_for_us.pdf Last accessed 4 April 2014.

[41] Di Ceglie D. (1998). A stranger in my own body. London: Karnal Books.

[42] Whittle, S., Turner, L.and Al-Alami, M. (2007). Engendered Penalties: Transgender and Transsexual People's Experiences of Inequality and Discrimination. Equality Reviews. Available online at http://www.pfc.org.uk/pdf/EngenderedPenalties.pdf Last accessed 4 April 2014.

[43] Kitzinger, C. (2001). Sexualities. In Rhoda K. Unger (Ed.), Handbook of the psychology of women and gender (pp.272-288). New Jersey: Wiley.

[44] Cole, P. (2007). The body politic: theorising disability and impairment. *Journal of Applied Philosophy*, (24), pp.169-176.

[45] Edwards, S. D. (2005). Disability: definitions, value and identity. Oxford: Radcliffe.

[46] Kristiansen, K., Behmas, S. and Shakespeare T. (Eds.) (2009). *Arguing about disability: philosophical perspectives*. London: Routledge.

[47] Nordenfelt, L. (1997). The importance of a disability/handicap distinction. *Journal of Medicine and Philosophy*, (22), pp.607-622.

[48] Shakespeare, T. (2006). *Disability rights and wrongs*. London: Routledge.

[49] Smith, S. R. (2009). Social justice and disability: competing interpretation of the medical and social models. In K. Kristiansen, S. Behmas and T. Shakespeare (Eds.), *Arguing about disability: philosophical perspectives* (pp. 15-29). London: Routledge.

[50] Boorse, C. (1987). Concepts of health. In Donald VanDeveer and Tom Regan (Eds.), *Health Care Ethics: an Introduction* (pp. 359-393). Philadelphia: Temple University Press.

[51] An interesting account may also be found in Rudnick, A. (2013). What is a psychiatric disability. *Health Care Analysis,* published online 24 January 2013. Last accessed 6 April 2014.

[52] Herdt, G. (1996). Introduction: Third Sexes and Third Genders. In Gilbert Herdt (Ed.), Third Sex Third Gender, beyond Sexual Dimorphism in Culture and History (pp. 21-81). New York, Zone Books.

[53] http://news.bbc.co.uk/1/hi/scotland/625680.stm Last accessed 6 April 2014.

[54] Kaw, E. (2003). Medicalization of Racial features: Asian American women and Cosmetic Surgery. *Medical Anthropology Quarterly*, (7,1): 74-89.

[55] Haiken, E. (1997). Venus Envy. A History of Cosmetic Surgery. Baltimore: Johns Hopkins University Press.

[56] Baumann, S. (2008). The moral underpinnings of beauty: A meaning-based explanation for light and dark complexions in advertising. *Poetics* (36), pp. 2-23.

[57] Charles, C. A. D. (2003). Skin-bleaching, self-hate, and black identity in Jamaica. *Journal of Black Studies*, (33), pp. 711-728.

[58] Little, M. O. (1996). Suspect Norms of Appearance and the Ethics of Complicity. In I. de Beaufort, M. Hilhorst and S. Holm (Eds.), In the *Eye of the beholder: Ethics and Medical Change of Appearance,* Copenhagen: Scandinavian University press.

[59] Little, M. O. (1998). Cosmetic Surgery, Suspect Norms, and the Ethics of Complicity. In E. Parens (Ed.), Enhancing Human Traits: Conceptual Complexities and Ethical Implications Washington DC: Georgetown University Press.

[60] Manners, P. J. (2009). Gender Identity Disorder in Adolescence: A Review of the Literature. *Child and Adolescent Mental Health*, (14, 2), pp. 62–68.

[61] Moller B., Schreier H., Li A. and Romer G. (2009). Gender Identity Disorder in Children and Adolescents. *Current Problems in Pediatric and Adolescent Health Care*, (39,5), pp. 117-143.

[62] Nawata H., Ogomori K., Tanaka M., Nishimura R., Urashima H., Yano R., Takano K. and Kuwabara Y. (2010). Regional cerebral blood flow changes in female to male gender identity disorder. *Psychiatry and Clinical Neurosciences*, (64,2), pp.157-161.

[63] World Professional Association for Transgender Health (WPATH) (2012). Standards of Care for the Health of Transsexual, Transgender, and Gender Nonconforming People, Seventh Version. Online at http://www.wpath.org/uploaded_files/140/files/ Standards%20of%20Care,%20V7%20Full%20Book.pdf Last accessed 6 April 2014.

[64] Endocrine Society (2009). Hembree, W. C., Cohen-Kettenis, P. T., Delemarre-van de, H., Gooren, L. J. Meyer, W. J., Spack, N., Tangpricha, V. and MontoriReprint, V. M. (2009). Endocrine Treatment of Transsexual Persons: An Endocrine Society Clinical Practice Guideline. First published in the *Journal of Clinical Endocrinology and Metabolism* (94, 9), pp. 3132–3154. At http://www.endo-society Last accessed 6 April 2014.

[65] Imbimbo C., Verze P., Palmieri A., Longo N., Fusco F., Arcaniolo D. and Mirone V. (2009). A report from a single institute's 14-year experience in treatment of male-to-female transsexuals. *Journal of Sexual Medicine*, (6,10), pp. 2736-2745.

[66] Pfafflin, F. (1992). Regrets After Sex Reassignment Surgery. *Journal of Psychology and Human Sexuality,* (5), pp. 69-85.

[67] Coleman, E., Bockting, W., Botzer, M., Cohen-Kettenis, P., DeCuypere, G., Feldman, J., Fraser, L., Green, J., Knudson, G., Meyer, W. J., Monstrey, S., Adler, R. K., Brown,

G. R., Devor, A. H., Ehrbar, R., Ettner, R., Eyler, E., Garofalo, R., Karasic, D. H., Lev, A. I., Mayer, G., Meyer-Bahlburg, H., Hall, B. P., Pfaefflin, F., Rachlin, K., Robinson, B., Schechter, L. S., Tangpricha, V., van Trotsenburg, M., Vitale, A., Winter, S., Whittle, S., Wylie, K. R., and Zucker, K. (2011). World Professional Association for Transgender Health Standards of Care for the Health of Transsexual, Transgender, and Gender-Nonconforming People, Version 7. *International Journal of Transgenderism*, (13), pp.165–232.

[68] Olsson, Stig-Eric, and Moller, A. Regret after Sex Reassignment Surgery in a Male-to-Female Transsexual: A Long-Term Follow-Up. *Archives of Sexual Behavior,* (35, 4), pp. 501–506.

[69] Delemarre-van de Waal A. H. and Cohen-Kettenis T. P. (2006). Clinical management of gender identity disorder in adolescents: a protocol on psychological and paediatric endocrinology aspects. *European Journal of Endocrinology*, (155, suppl 1), pp. 131-137.

[70] Brazier M. and Glover N. (2000). Does Medical Law have a future? In David Hayton (Ed.), Law's Future (pp.371-88). Oxford: Hart Publishing.

[71] Giordano, S. (2005). Understanding Eating Disorders. Oxford and New York: Oxford University Press.

[72] Giordano S. (2008). Lives in a chiaroscuro. Should we suspend the puberty of children with Gender Identity Disorder? *Journal of Medical Ethics*, (34,8), pp. 580-586.

[73] Giordano, S. (2011). Sliding Doors: Should treatment of Gender Identity Disorder and other body modifications be privately funded? Medicine Health Care and Philosophy, (December), pp. 1-10.

[74] Giordano, S. (2011). Where Christ did not go: men, women and Frusculicchi. Gender Identity Disorder (GID): epistemological and ethical issues relating to the psychiatric diagnosis. *Monash. Bioethics Review*, (29, 4), pp.12.1-22.

[75] Giordano, S. (2014). A heaven without giants or dwarfs. *Cambridge Quarterly of Healthcare Ethics,* (23, 1), pp. 22-29.

[76] Robin McKie and Gaby Hinsliff (2008). This couple want a deaf child. Should we try to stop them? The Observer. Sunday 9 March 2008 Available at .http://www.theguardian.com/science Last accessed 11 April 2014.

[77] The Yogyakarta Principles on the Application of Human Rights Law to Sexual Orientation and Gender Identity, 2007, available at www.unhcr.org/refworld/docid/48244e602.html Last accessed 6 April 2014.

[78] www.transactivists.org Last accessed 6 April 2014.

[79] Jervis, G. (1997). Manuale critico di psichiatria. Milano: Feltrinelli.

[80] http://apps.who.int/classifications/icd10/browse/2010/en#/XXI Last accessed 6 April 2014.

[81] Stop Trans Pathologization STO, International Campaign Stop Trans PatHologization, Reflection from STP regarding the ICD revision process and publication of the DSM-5, 2014. They have made important observation on the notion of 'incongruence', among others. Communication at the WPATH conference in Bangkok, Februrary 2014.

[82] Universal Declaration of Human Rights, Preamble. Online at .http://www.un.org/en/documents/udhr/index.shtml Last accessed 6 April 2014.

In: Gender Identity   ISBN: 978-1-63321-488-0
Editor: Beverly L. Miller   © 2014 Nova Science Publishers, Inc.

Chapter 9

EVALUATING PSYCHOBIOLOGICAL AND MENTAL DISTRESS IN TRANSSEXUALISM BEFORE AND AFTER CROSS-SEX HORMONAL TREATMENT: LESSON LEARNED FROM THREE LONGITUDINAL STUDIES

Marco Colizzi, M.D., Rosalia Costa, M.D. and Orlando Todarello, M.D., Ph.D.
Department of Basic Medical Sciences, Neuroscience and Sense Organs,
University of Bari "Aldo Moro", Bari, Italy

ABSTRACT

In the past few decades, the literature has addressed transsexual patients' quality of life, satisfaction and various other outcomes such as sexual functioning after sex reassignment surgery. Instead, the role of the cross-sex hormonal treatment alone in the well-being of transsexual patients has been the subject of very little differentiated investigation. Moreover, due to their cross-sectional design, previous studies did not demonstrate a direct effect of hormonal treatment in transsexual patients' distress. To our knowledge only three recent researches studied the transsexual patients' distress related to the hormonal treatment in a longitudinal study. In light of the importance of this information, this chapter discusses a review of these three perspective studies, two of whom were performed in partially overlapping samples from the same gender unit. Although transsexualism has been described as a diagnostic entity in its own right, not necessarily associated with severe comorbid psychiatric findings, for most patients transsexualism may be a stressful situation and may cause clinical distress or impairment in important areas of functioning. This review provides information on the prevalence and/or severity of psychobiological distress, mental distress and functional impairment in untreated transsexual patients. One of these three studies revealed that, despite the majority of transsexual patients do not suffer of a psychiatric disorder, the condition is associated with subthreshold anxiety/depression, psychological distress and functional impairment. Another of these three studies achieved the same results on the psychological distress in untreated transsexual patients, using part of the methodology of the previous study in a different sample. The last study added information about the untreated transsexual patients' stress system dysregulation, revealing that these patients show hypothalamic-pituitary-adrenal (HPA) system dysregulation and appear to notably differ from normative samples in terms of mean levels of perceived stress. In particular, untreated transsexual patients showed elevated cortisol awakening response (CAR), with cortisol levels above the normal range, and elevated perceived stress. Moreover, this review reports the role of the hormonal treatment in reducing psychobiological and mental distress in transsexualism. Specifically, when treated with hormonal treatment transsexual patients reported less anxiety, depression, psychological distress and functional impairment. Also transsexual patients showed reduced cortisol awakening response (CAR) and perceived stress levels after the beginning of the cross-sex hormonal treatment. It should be added that in all the three studies the psychobiological and mental distress scores resembled those of a general population after cross-sex hormonal treatment was initiated. Finally, the review discusses the hypothesis of a direct relation versus an indirect relation between the hormone therapy itself and the patients' well-being, supporting a psycho-social meaning of the hormonal treatment (indirect relation) rather than a biological effect of sex hormones (direct relation).

INTRODUCTION

In the past few decades research has prevalently focused on the effects of sex reassignment surgery on transsexual patients' well-being and psychological parameters. In fact, previous studies have demonstrated that sex reassignment surgery positively impact on transsexual patients' personal and general satisfaction (Lothstein, 1984; Cohen-Kettenis and van Goozen, 1997; Rehman et al., 1999; Lawrence, 2003), self confidence with body image (Bodlund and Armelius, 1994; Wolfradt and Neumann, 2001; Kraemer et al., 2008; Weyers et al., 2009) and quality of life (Rakic et al., 1996; Newfield et al., 2006; Kuhn et al., 2009; Ainsworth and Spiegel, 2010). In contrast, the role of the cross-sex hormonal treatment in the well-being of transsexual patients has been the subject of very little investigation.

In a recent meta analysis carried out on twenty-eight observational studies about hormonal therapy and sex reassignment in the transsexual population, Murad and colleagues identified only five studies that specifically examined the impact of hormonal treatment on transsexual patients' well-being (2010). In particular, hormonal treatment resulted to be associated to better transformation satisfaction (Kuiper and Cohen-Kettenis, 1988), psychological profile (Leavitt et al., 1980), cognitive function (Slabbekoorn et al., 1999; Miles et al., 2006), and emotional repercussions (Slabbekoorn et al., 1999). More recently, other studies found an association between cross-sex hormonal treatment and better quality of life (Newfield et al., 2006; Gorin-Lazard et al., 2012; Motmans et al., 2012).

Although the majority of the studies concluded that hormonal treatment has a positive effect on transsexual patients' psycho-social wellbeing (Newfield et al., 2006; Murad et al., 2010; Gorin-Lazard et al., 2012; Motmans et al., 2012), when considering specifically psychiatric and psychological outcomes research revealed contradictory findings. Hormonal treatment has not been always related to better mental health. Some previous reports found an association between hormone therapy and reduced psychological/psychiatric distress levels (Gómez-Gil et al., 2012; Gorin-Lazard et al., 2013). Instead, a recent study revealed that hormonal treatment is associated to reduced body uneasiness but have no effect on transsexual patients' psychological state (Fisher et al., 2014). It should be added that transsexual patients' psychiatry comorbidity is still a matter of contention. Some research reported that transsexual patients show a high prevalence of psychiatric comorbidity (A Campo et al., 2003; Hepp et al., 2005; Heylens et al., 2013). Instead, other studies showed a low level of psychopathology (Gómez-Gil et al., 2009; Hoshiai et al., 2010; Fisher et al., 2013). The lack of consistency between studies about transsexual patients' psychiatric/ psychological comorbidity and effect of hormonal treatment on psychiatric/psychological outcomes could be partially explained by their observational or cross-sectional design. In fact, due to their designs, previous studies did not explore the role of the lack of hormonal treatment in transsexual patients' mental distress. Moreover, previous studies revealing reduced or unchanged mental distress in hormone-treated transsexual patients with respect to untreated transsexual individuals did not demonstrate a direct positive effect or an absent effect of hormonal treatment in transsexual patients' mental health (Gómez-Gil et al., 2012; Gorin-Lazard et al., 2013). Longitudinal studies, instead, conduct observations of the same subjects over a period of time and can establish sequences of events and detect changes in the characteristics of the target population.

In the current review we are interested in providing information on the same transsexual patients' psychobiological and mental distress before and after the beginning of the cross-sex hormonal treatment. With this aim, we selected from the literature the longitudinal studies which evaluated the hormonal treatment induced effect on transsexual patients well-being.

MATERIALS AND METHODS

This review identified three studies which longitudinally evaluated the role of the cross-sex hormonal treatment in the transsexual patients' distress. Two of these studies were conducted at the Gender Identity Unit of the University of Bari on samples partially overlapped (Colizzi et al., 2013; 2014). A third study was conducted at the Gender Clinic of the Ghent University Hospital (Heylens et al., 2014).

Colizzi et al., 2013

Concerning the Bari reports, the first study included only healthy transsexual patients ($n = 70$) and evaluated biological distress and subjective distress (Colizzi et al., 2013). Specifically, cortisol awakening response (CAR) was assessed taking blood samples for three consecutive days, once before the onset of hormone therapy (baseline), and once after about 12 months of hormone therapy (follow-up). Similarly, patients performed a self-reported evaluation of perceived stress, the Perceived Stress Scale (Cohen and Williamson, 1988), once at baseline, and once at follow-up. Moreover, because of the possibility to compare cortisol awakening response (CAR) values and perceived stress scores with cortisol levels normal range and perceived stress normative data (Cohen and Williamson, 1988), this study provided information on the transsexual patients' distress with respect to normal/normative values/data which are supposed to be stress levels in general population. This study included also the evaluation of the patients' attachment style (George et al., 1985) which is fundamental in stress management and hypothalamic-pituitary-adrenal (HPA) axis regulation (Bowlby, 1969; Mikulincer et al., 2003).

The attachment styles have been assessed through the Adult Attachment Interview (AAI), a semi-structured interview that explores the representation of attachment in the adult by a backward investigation in the relations between the child and the parental figures (George et al., 1985). Because of its stability during the life span (Bowlby, 1969; Mikulincer et al., 2003), patients' attachment styles have not been retested at follow-up but have been studied in association with the other stress parameters.

Colizzi et al., 2014

The second Bari study (Colizzi et al., 2014) incorporated the same longitudinal design (one year follow-up) of the previous study. All the patients attending the Gender Identity Unit were enrolled (*n* = 118), with the aims to evaluate the presence of psychiatric diagnoses/distress in a transsexual population and to compare psychiatric distress with regard to the hormonal intervention.

The study used both diagnostic clinical interviews and self-reported scales, in order to evaluate psychiatric disorders/distress according to the categorical/hetero evaluation or the dimensional/self evaluation diagnostic approach. Specifically, the Structured Clinical Interview for Diagnostic and Statistical Manual of Mental Disorders fourth edition (DSM-IV) Axis I disorders (SCID-I) was used to determine DSM-IV psychiatric comorbidity for major mental disorders and functional impairment. Zung Self-Rating Anxiety Scale (SAS; Zung, 1971), Zung Self-Rating Depression Scale (SDS; Zung, 1967) and Symptom Checklist 90-Revised (SCL-90-R; Derogatis, 1994) were used to provide a self-reported measure of current anxiety, depression and psychological status, respectively. Because of their unstable psychiatric comorbidity, which could have been a bias in the evaluation of the hormonal treatment effects, 11 patients (9.3%) were excluded from the follow-up assessment of the hormonal treatment induced changes in mental distress. Instead, they were included only in the study of the prevalence of psychiatric comorbidity among transsexual individuals. All the other 107 patients (90.7%), including 6 patients affected by a stable psychiatric comorbidity (5.1%), participated to all the phases of this research.

In both the Bari studies no patient had undergone any type of surgical intervention. Moreover, both the Bari studies collected socio-demographic data at baseline. However, this information was not revaluated at follow-up.

Heylens et al., 2014

The Ghent study included 57 transsexual patients who were evaluated by self-reported scales in a follow-up period (Heylens et al., 2014). In particular, transsexual patients were assessed at baseline, 3-6 months after the beginning of hormonal treatment and 1-12 months after sex reassignment surgery. Transsexual patients' psychological/psychiatric profile was evaluated by a self-reported scale, the Symptom Checklist 90 (SCL-90; Derogatis et al., 1973; Arrindell and Ettema, 2005). This study included also a psychosocial questionnaire, based on the biographic questionnaire patients filled out at the first treatment attendance. This questionnaire aimed at the evaluation of socio-demographic and sexual parameters according to the sex reassignment intervention. Although this study did not include an assessment of the major mental disorders psychiatric comorbidity, it measured longitudinally the transsexual patients' evolution in psychological status during both hormonal and surgical phases of sex reassignment.

Additionally, as for the first Bari study, results have been compared with those of general population. Intriguingly, this study used the Symptom Checklist 90 (SCL-90) which is quite comparable to the SCL-90-R used in the second Bari study.

RESULTS

Psychobiological and Mental Distress at Baseline

At baseline, transsexual patients' cortisol awakening response (CAR) average total level (M = 28.98 µg/dL, SD = 20.82 µg/dL) exceeded the upper limit of the given normal range (9-23 µg/dL), independently of the biological sex. Similarly, non hormone treated transsexual individuals expressed a considerably higher average total perceived stress score (M = 27.70, SD = 6.11) with respect to non clinical samples of the same age (M = 14.2, SD = 6.2). Also in this case, there were no differences in perceived stress scores according to the biological sex. Furthermore, the majority of the transsexual patients expressed an insecure attachment (70%). The percentage of insecure conditions (avoidant and anxious types) in the transsexual group was higher than that reported in non clinical samples of the same age (44%). Moreover, the study of the association between attachment style and biological/subjective stress revealed that insecure attachment styles, especially the anxious style (CAR: M = 42.94 µg/dL, SD = 33.77 µg/dL; perceived stress: M = 33.09, SD = 5.28), are prevalently responsible for the increased stress levels in transsexual individuals (Colizzi et al., 2013).

Although the second Bari study revealed that the majority of transsexual patients (94.4%) did not satisfy DSM-IV diagnostic criteria for major mental disorders due to absence or insufficient number/duration of symptoms, at baseline about one out of two patients experienced symptoms of anxiety (50%) or depression (42%). Moreover, one out of four patients expressed significant psychological symptoms (24%) or substantial functional impairment (23%). However, only a few patients expressed severe anxiety symptoms (2%) or severe depression symptoms (4%). Moreover, except for anxiety scores (SAS and SCL-90 anxiety subscale), the mean SDS and SCL-90 scores were on the normal range. There were no significant differences in the mental distress scores according to the biological sex or the patients' gender role (Colizzi et al., 2014).

In their study Heylens and colleagues (2014) found that non hormone treated transsexual patients express more psychological symptoms (overall SCL-90: M = 157.7, SD = 49.8) than a general population (overall SCL-90: M = 118.3, SD = 32.4). Specifically, all the transsexual individuals' SCL-90 subscale scores were higher than that found in a general population, including anxiety and depression.

Psychobiological and Mental Distress at Follow-Up

The first Bari study revealed a significant association between hormonal treatment and biological/subjective stress. Specifically, when treated with cross sex hormonal treatment transsexual individuals reported less cortisol awakening response (CAR) and perceived stress levels. The role of the hormonal therapy in reducing stress levels was independent of the biological sex and of the attachment style. Moreover, cortisol awakening response (CAR) levels in hormone treated transsexual patients (M = 15.72 µg/dL, SD = 6.54 µg/dL) fell within the normal range for morning cortisol levels (9-23 µg/dL). Similarly, hormone treated transsexual patients' perceived stress levels (M = 14.96, SD = 4.89) resulted similar to those found in normative samples (M = 14.2, SD = 6.2) (Colizzi et al., 2013).

The second Bari study revealed a significant association between hormonal treatment and mental distress. After one year of cross sex hormonal treatment transsexual individuals reported significant lower SAS, SDS and SCL-90 scores. When treated with hormone therapy the majority of the patients did not report any symptoms of anxiety (83%) or depression (77%). It should be added that no patients reported severe symptoms of anxiety or depression at follow-up. Furthermore, only about one out of ten patients reported significant psychological problems (11%) or functional impairment (10%) at follow-up. Finally, no patient developed a psychiatric comorbidity during the follow-up period (Colizzi et al., 2014).

The Ghent study showed that sex reassignment has a positive impact in reducing transsexual patients' global mental distress. In particular, with regard to SCL-90 subscale, sex reassignment significantly reduced anxiety, depression, interpersonal sensitivity and hostility. With the exception of sleeping problems and psychoticism after sex reassignment therapy, SCL-90 scores at follow-up were similar to the SCL-90 scores of a general population. Sleeping problems and psychoticism scores, which were comparable to a general population after the beginning of the hormonal treatment, returned to a high level after sex reassignment surgery. The main reduction of mental distress was prevalently due to the hormonal intervention. In fact, no further decrease was observed after the sex reassignment surgery. The effect of both surgical and hormonal interventions was not more pronounced than that obtained by hormonal treatment alone. Consistently, psychosocial questionnaires revealed that most patients subjectively experience the biggest progress after the beginning of the hormonal treatment (57.9%), while 31.6% report the most important changes in mental distress after sex reassignment surgery. The remaining 10.5% of the patients described the most important increase in mental health during the diagnostical phase, before of the sex reassignment interventions (Heylens et al., 2014).

CONCLUSION

This chapter aimed at evaluating previous research on the role of cross sex hormonal treatment in the transsexual patients' distress. In order to evaluate the possible positive effect of hormone therapy in reducing distress, we selected only research which specifically evaluate the association between hormonal treatment and patients' well-being in a longitudinal study. To our knowledge only three studies evaluated distress in the same transsexual population before and after the beginning of the cross sex hormonal treatment.

Results from these three researches provide important information on transsexualism related distress, including psychiatric comorbidity and hypothalamic-pituitary-adrenal (HPA) axis dysregulation. Moreover, all these studies demonstrate that hormonal treatment is associated with a significant reduction in psychobiological and mental distress. In light of the importance of this information, possible explanations for this association are discussed.

Transsexualism: A Stressful Condition

For most transsexual patients, a strong and persistent identification with the opposite sex as well as the persistent discomfort with one's own biological sex or the role assigned to it, which are core aspects of the condition (APA, 2000), may cause clinical distress or impairment in important areas of functioning (Sohn and Bosinski, 2007; Gómez-Gil et al., 2009). Consistently, all the studies evaluated in this chapter reveal that transsexual patients attending a Gender Unit express objective and subjective psychobiological and mental distress. At enrollment transsexual patients reported hypothalamic-pituitary-adrenal (HPA) axis dysregulation (Colizzi et al., 2013) and psychological/psychiatric distress (Colizzi et al., 2014; Heylens et al., 2014). More specifically, transsexual individuals not yet treated with hormone therapy showed morning cortisol levels above the normal range and elevated perceived stress if compared to normative samples, especially in the context of an anxious style of stress management (Colizzi et al., 2013). Moreover, functional impairment and psychological problems, including anxiety and depression, were reported in a large amount of transsexual patients (Colizzi et al., 2014) and were higher than that found in a general population (Heylens et al., 2014).

Transsexualism Related Distress Could be a Transient Condition

All the studies included in this review indicate a positive effect of cross sex hormonal treatment in reducing psychobiological and mental distress. In particular, when treated with hormone therapy, transsexual individuals reported lower morning cortisol levels, perceived stress, psychological/psychiatric symptoms and functional impairment (Colizzi et al., 2013; 2014; Heylens et al., 2014). When possible, distress parameters were compared to normal range values or normative data for a general population, indicating that after the beginning of the cross sex hormonal treatment transsexual patients express distress levels similar to a general population (Colizzi et al., 2013; Heylens et al., 2014).

These results are in line with the majority of the previous studies indicating that hormone therapy improves well-being among transsexual individuals and decreases the psychiatric comorbidities often associated with a lack of hormonal treatment (Murad et al., 2010; Moreno-Pérez et al., 2012; Gorin-Lazard et al., 2012; Gómez-Gil et al., 2012). Intriguingly, studies included in this chapter reveal that transsexualism related distress could be transient, also when considering biological distress. In fact, hormone therapy results to have a positive effect not only on transsexual individuals' self-reported psychological distress but also on the increased cortisol awakening response, which is a sensible parameter of biological stress (Powell and Schlotz, 2012). Although elevated cortisol levels have been reported to be a characteristic consequence of chronic stress-induced stimulation of hypothalamic-pituitary-adrenal (HPA) axis activity (Jacobson, 2005), the overriding function of the hypothalamic-pituitary-adrenal (HPA) axis resulted to be reversible.

Is transsexualism a Diagnostic Entity in Its Own Right?

The longitudinal evaluation of the transsexual patients' mental distress (Colizzi et al., 2014; Heylens et al., 2014) as well as the use of both categorical/hetero evaluation and dimensional/self evaluation diagnostic approaches (Colizzi et al., 2014) resulted to be helpful in the discussion on the transsexual patients' psychiatric comorbidity. As previously reported, research on this matter revealed contradictory finding (A Campo et al., 2003; Hepp et al., 2005; Gómez-Gil et al., 2009; Heylens et al., 2013; Hoshiai et al., 2010; Fisher et al., 2013). Instead, results from the studies included in this chapter clearly reveal that in the majority of cases psychological/psychiatric distress in transsexualism is not a stable symptomatology. Rather, distress seems to represent a transient symptomatology related to the transsexual condition which could beneficiate of the hormonal intervention. Mental distress may be considered as a reaction to the non-satisfaction connected to the transsexual individual's incongruent image. Hormone therapy induces desired changes in transsexual patients' body, which could be responsible for the patients' increased well-being. Consistently, the prevalence of mental distress in hormone treated transsexual patients was dramatically lower with respect to the evaluation at baseline (Colizzi et al., 2014). Moreover, transsexual patients' psychological symptoms, which were higher than that found in a general population at baseline, after the beginning of the cross-sex hormonal treatment decreased to levels comparable to a general population (Heylens et al., 2014). It should be added that, despite at baseline a large amount of transsexual patients reported some psychological/psychiatric symptoms, rarely these symptoms were severe and the majority of the transsexual patients did not satisfy diagnostic criteria for a major mental disorder (Colizzi et al., 2014). This result suggested that transsexualism is not necessarily associated with severe psychiatric comorbidity and that the transsexual condition could be a diagnostic entity in its own. Moreover, results from these studies indicated that inconsistencies between previous studies on the transsexual patients' comorbidity could be due to methodological procedures (categorical vs. dimensional evaluation; hetero vs. self-reported evaluation). However, both the longitudinal studies on mental distress included in this chapter (Colizzi et al., 2014; Heylens et al., 2014) underlined the suffering of non hormone treated transsexual patients which demands recognition as possible risk-factor for more severe or full-syndromal psychiatric disorders.

Direct (Biological) vs. Indirect (Psychological) Hormonal Treatment Effect on Well-Being

The association between hormonal treatment and lower psychobiological and mental distress may have several explanations. The question which arises from this finding is if sex hormones exert a direct effect on distress, implying a biological reason for the reduced distress levels in hormone treated transsexual patients. The first Bari study result of reduced cortisol serum levels in hormone treated transsexual patients is consistent with a previous research. This previous study on the relation between sex hormones and cortisol levels carried out only in Male to Female (MtF) transsexual patients found that cortisol levels are drastically reduced after one year of estrogenic therapy. The authors involved a possible biological explanation for this result, indicating that cortisol serum levels may be decreased due to estrogen induced increase in corticoid-binding globulin (Mueller et al., 2006). Conversely, although no research has been carried out on the effect of androgenic therapy in Female to Male (FtM) transsexual patients, previous studies revealed that testosterone levels are significantly associated with biological and psychological measures of stress in women, perceived stress included (King et al., 2005). Sex hormones may exert different effects on mental distress too, but inducing an opposite pattern with respect to cortisol levels. Specifically, in this case estrogens may increase mental distress, making individuals more prone to anxiety and depression (Asscheman et al., 1989). Instead, androgens can reduce mental distress, promoting feelings of euphoria and energy (Su et al., 1993). However, androgens have been related to stress and hostility too (King et al., 2005). In summary, hormonal treatment should reduce cortisol levels but increase mental distress in Male to Female (MtF) transsexual patients, because of the biological effect of estrogens. Conversely, hormone therapy in Female to Male (FtM) transsexual subjects should increase cortisol levels and have both positive and negative effect on mental distress, depending on the mental health parameters evaluated, because of the biological effects of androgens. Nevertheless, studies included in this chapter found that hormonal treatment has a positive effect on both stress levels and mental distress parameters. Moreover, the two Bari studies, which expressly included gender in the statistical analyses, did not find differences between Male to Female (MtF) and Female to Male (FtM) transsexual patients. Therefore, all these three studies do not support the hypothesis of a direct effect of hormone therapy on transsexual patients' well-being. Conversely, in accordance with Kuiper and Cohen-Kettenis (1988), the distress differences might be an indirect effect of hormone therapy. More specifically, hormonal treatment induced changes in body features and shape could translate into a better quality of life for the patient himself. Therefore, thanks to the body changes obtained, transsexual patients could experience a reduction of their distress (Kraemer et al., 2008). In this perspective, distress in transsexualism may be considered as a reaction to the non satisfaction connected to the incongruent body image, rather than a stable comorbidity. In particular, untreated transsexual individuals face difficulties in managing their gender identity and the sex reassignment procedure may reinforce the gender affirmation with a better social recognition. Finally, it should be considered that the initiation of the hormonal treatment could have a psychological meaning which per se could be fundamental in reducing distress. It is quite interesting that in the Ghent study about one out of ten patients described the most important increase in mental health at baseline, during the diagnostical phase, when hormonal treatment had not yet prescribed (Heylens et al., 2014). It is not clear if these patients had still received their eligibility for the hormonal treatment, which may have influenced their well-being. In fact, in the Bari studies the authors indicated in their conclusions that for most transsexual patients the eligibility for hormone therapy represents an acceptance of their requirement which could positively impact on the well-being. On the contrary, the hormonal treatment delay due to health problems disappoints transsexual patients and could increase their distress.

In conclusion, this chapter provides information on psychobiological and mental distress of transsexual patients. Although the majority of transsexual patients have no psychiatric comorbidity, transsexualism seems to be associated with hypothalamic-pituitary-adrenal (HPA) axis dysregulation, increased perceived stress, substantial functional impairment and frequent but not severe psychological/psychiatric symptoms. Distress in untreated transsexual individuals seemed to be higher than that found in a general population. Furthermore, there appeared to be a relationship between hormone therapy and lower psychobiological and mental distress, suggesting that distress in transsexualism could be a transient condition. Intriguingly, this association did not seem to be attributable to the biological effect of sex hormones. Conversely, hormonal treatment seemed to have an indirect effect on transsexual patients' well-being. In particular, the improved well-being could be due to the induced desired body changes, which reinforce the transsexual individuals' gender affirmation. Moreover, the initiation of the hormonal treatment could have a psychological meaning: when receiving eligibility for hormonal treatment, transsexual patients could experience a distress reduction because of their understood discomfort.

FUNDING AND DISCLOSURE

In this study there is no funding source. The authors declare that they have no conflicts of interest in the research.

REFERENCES

A Campo, J; Nijman, H; Merckelbach, H; Evers, C. Psychiatric comorbidity of gender identity disorders: a survey among Dutch psychiatrists. *Am. J. Psychiatry*, 2003; 160, 1332-1336.

Ainsworth, TA; Spiegel, JH. Quality of life of individuals with and without facial feminization surgery or gender reassignment surgery. *Qual. Life Res.,* 2010; 19 (7), 1019-1024.

American Psychiatric Association. Diagnostic and statistical manual of mental disorders: DSM-IV-TR. 4th edition. Washington, DC: APA; 2000.

Arrindell, WA; Ettema, JHM. Symptom Checklist SCL-90: Handleiding bij een multidimensionele psychopathologie indicator. Amsterdam: Harcourt Test Publishers; 2005.

Asscheman, H; Gooren, LJ; Eklund, PL. Mortality and morbidity in transsexual patients with cross-gender hormone treatment. *Metabolism*, 1989; 38 (9) 869-873.

Bodlund, O; Armelius, K. Self-image and personality traits in gender identity disorders: an empirical study. *J. Sex Marital Ther.*, 1994; 20 (4), 303-317.

Bowlby, J. *Attachment and loss*. Attachment. Vol. 1. New York: Basic Books; 1969.

Cohen, S; Williamson, G. Perceived stress in a probability sample of the United States. In: Spacapan S, Oskamp S, eds. Social psychology of health. Newbury Park, CA: Sage; 1988:31-68.

Cohen-Kettenis, PT; van Goozen, SHM. Sex reassignment of adolescent transsexuals: a follow-up study. *J. Am. Acad. Child Adolesc. Psychiatry*, 1997; 36, 263-271.

Colizzi, M; Costa, R; Pace, V; Todarello O. Hormonal treatment reduces psychobiological distress in gender identity disorder, independently of the attachment style. *J. Sex. Med.*, 2013; 10(12):3049-3058.

Colizzi, M; Costa, R; Todarello, O. Transsexual patients' psychiatric comorbidity and positive effect of cross-sex hormonal treatment on mental health: results from a longitudinal study. *Psychoneuroendocrinology*, 2014 Jan; 39:65-73

Derogatis, L. Symptom Checklist-90-R: Administration, Scoring and Procedures Manual, 3rd ed. National Computer Systems Inc., Minneapolis, MN; 1994. Derogatis, LR; Lipman, RS; Covi, L. SCL-90: an outpatient psychiatric rating scale--preliminary report. *Psychopharmacol Bull.*, 1973; 9(1):13-28.

Fisher AD; Castellini G; Bandini E; Casale H; Fanni E; Benni L; Ferruccio N; Meriggiola MC; Manieri C; Gualerzi A; Jannini E; Oppo A; Ricca V; Maggi M; Rellini AH. Cross-sex hormonal treatment and body uneasiness in individuals with gender dysphoria. *J. Sex. Med.*, 2014; 11 (3):709-719.

Fisher, AD; Bandini, E; Casale, H; Ferruccio, N; Meriggiola, MC; Gualerzi, A; Manieri, C; Jannini, E; Mannucci, E; Monami, M; Stomaci, N; Delle Rose, A; Susini, T; Ricca, V; Maggi, M. Sociodemographic and clinical features of gender identity disorder: an Italian multicentric evaluation. *J. Sex. Med.*, 2013; 10(2):408-419.

George, C; Kaplan, N; Main, M. Adult Attachment Interview. Unpublished manuscript. Department of Psychology, University of California, Berkeley; 1985.

Gómez-Gil, E; Trilla, A; Salamero, M; Godás, T; Valdés, M. Sociodemographic, clinical, and psychiatric characteristics of transsexuals from Spain. *Arch. Sex. Behav.*, 2009; 38 (3) 378-392.

Gómez-Gil, E; Zubiaurre-Elorza, L; Esteva, I; Guillamon, A; Godás, T; Cruz Almaraz, M; Halperin, I; Salamero, M. Hormone-treated transsexuals report less social distress, anxiety and depression. *Psychoneuroendocrinology*, 2012; 37 (5) 662-670.

Gorin-Lazard A; Baumstarck K; Boyer L; Maquigneau A; Penochet JC; Pringuey D; Albarel F; Morange I; Bonierbale M; Lançon C; Auquier P. Hormonal therapy is associated with better self-esteem, mood, and quality of life in transsexuals. *J. Nerv. Ment. Dis.*, 2013; 201(11):996-1000.

Gorin-Lazard, A; Baumstarck, K; Boyer, L; Maquigneau, A; Gebleux, S; Penochet, JC; Pringuey, D; Albarel, F; Morange, I; Loundou, A; Berbis, J; Auquier, P; Lançon, C; Bonierbale, M. Is hormonal therapy associated with better quality of life in transsexuals? A cross-sectional study. *J. Sex. Med.*, 2012; 9 (2) 531-541.

Hepp, U; Kraemer, B; Schnyder, U; Miller, N; Delsignore, A. Psychiatric comorbidity in gender identity disorder. *J. Psychosom. Res.*, 2005; 58, 259-261.

Heylens, G; Elaut, E; Kreukels, BPC; Paap, MCS; Cerwenka, S; Richter-Appelt, H; Cohen-Kettenis, PT; Haraldsen, IR; De Cuypere, G. Psychiatric characteristics in transsexual individuals: multicentre study in four European countries. *Br. J. Psychiatry*, 2014; 204(2):151-156.

Heylens, G; Verroken, C; De Cock, S; T'Sjoen, G; De Cuypere, G. Effects of different steps in gender reassignment therapy on psychopathology: a prospective study of persons with a gender identity disorder. *J. Sex. Med.*, 2014; 11(1):119-126.

Hoshiai, M; Matsumoto, Y; Sato, T; Ohnishi, M; Okabe, N; Kishimoto, Y; Terada, S; Kuroda, S. Psychiatric comorbidity among patients with gender identity disorder. *Psychiatry Clin. Neurosci.*, 2010; 64, 514-519.

Jacobson, L. Hypothalamic–pituitary–adrenocortical axis regulation. *Endocrinol. Metab. Clin. North Am.*, 2005; 34:271-292.

King, JA; Rosal, MC; Ma, Y; Reed, GW. Association of stress, hostility and plasma testosterone levels. *Neuro Endocrino.l Lett.*, 2005; 26:355-360.

Kraemer, B; Delsignore, A; Schnyder, U; Hepp U. Body image and transsexualism. *Psychopathology*, 2008;41:96-100.

Kraemer, B; Delsignore, A; Schnyder, U; Hepp, U. Body image and transsexualism. *Psychopathology*, 2008; 41 (2), 96-100.

Kuhn, A; Bodmer, C; Stadlmayr, W; Kuhn, P; Mueller, MD; Birkhäuser, M. Quality of life 15 years after sex reassignment surgery for transsexualism. *Fertil. Steril.*, 2009; 92 (5), 1685-1689 e3.

Kuiper, B; Cohen-Kettenis, P. Sex reassignment surgery: a study of 141 Dutch transsexuals. *Arch. Sex. Behav.*, 1988; 17, 439-457.

Lawrence, AA. Factors associated with satisfaction or regret following male-to-male sex reassignment surgery. *Arch. Sex. Behav.*, 2003; 32 (4), 299-315.

Leavitt, F; Berger, JC; Hoeppner, JA; Northrop, G. Pre- surgical adjustment in male transsexuals with and without hormonal treatment. *J. Nerv. Ment. Dis.*, 1980; 168, 693-697.

Lothstein, LM. Psychological testing with transsexuals: a 30-year review. *J. Pers. Assess.*, 1984; 48 (5), 500-507.

Mikulincer, M; Shaver, PR; Pereg, D. Attachment theory and affect regulation: The dynamics, development, and cognitive consequences of attachment-related strategies. *Motiv Emot.*, 2003; 27:77-102.

Miles, C; Green, R; Hines, M. Estrogen treatment effects on cognition, memory and mood in male-to-female transsexuals. *Horm. Behav.*, 2006; 50, 708-717.

Moreno-Pérez, O; Esteva De Antonio, I; Grupo de Identidad y Diferenciación Sexual de la SEEN (GIDSEEN). Clinical practice guidelines for assessment and treatment of transsexualism. SEEN Identity and Sexual Differentiation Group (GIDSEEN). *Endocrinol. Nutr.*, 2012; 59:367-382.

Motmans, J; Meier, P; Ponnet, K; T'Sjoen, G. Female and male transgender quality of life: socioeconomic and medical differences. *J. Sex. Med.*, 2012; 9 (3) 743-750.

Mueller, A; Binder, H; Cupisti, S; Hoffmann, I; Beckmann, MW; Dittrich, R. Effects on the male endocrine system of long-term treatment with gonadotropin-releasing hormone agonists and estrogens in male-to-female transsexuals. *Horm. Metab. Res.*, 2006; 38:183-187.

Murad, MH; Elamin, MB; Garcia, MZ; Mullan, RJ; Murad, A; Erwin, PJ; Montori, VM. Hormonal therapy and sex reassignment: A systematic review and meta-analysis of quality of life and psychosocial outcomes. *Clin Endocrinol (Oxf)*, 2010; 72:214-231.

Newfield, E; Hart, S; Dibble, S; Kohler, L. Female-to-male transgender quality of life. *Qual. Life Res.*, 2006; 15, 1447-1457.

Powell, DJ; Schlotz, W. Daily life stress and the cortisol awakening response: Testing the anticipation hypothesis. *PLoS ONE*, 2012; 7(12):e52067.

Rakic, Z; Starcevic, V; Maric, J; Kelin, K. The outcome of sex reassignment surgery in Belgrade: 32 patients of both sexes. *Arch. Sex. Behav.*, 1996; 25 (5), 515-525.

Rehman, J; Lazer, S; Benet, AE; Shaefer, LC; Melman, A. The reported sex and surgery satisfactions of 28 postoperative male-to-female transsexual patients. *Arch. Sex. Behav.*, 1999; 28 (1), 71-89.

Slabbekoorn, D; van Goozen, SH; Megens, J; Gooren, LJ; Cohen-Kettenis, PT. Activating effects of cross-sex hormones on cognitive functioning: a study of short-term and long-term hormone effects in transsexuals. *Psychoneuroendocrinology*, 1999; 24, 423-447.

Sohn, M; Bosinski, HA. Gender identity disorders: Diagnostic and surgical aspects. *J. Sex. Med.*, 2007; 4:1193–207; quiz 1208.

Su, TP; Pagliaro, M; Schmidt, PJ; Pickar, D; Wolkowitz, O; Rubinow, DR. Neuropsychiatric effects of anabolic steroids in male normal volunteers. *JAMA*, 1993; 269, 2760-2764.

Weyers, S; Elaut, E; De Sutter, P; Gerris, J; T'Sjoen, G; Heylens, G; De Cuypere, G; Verstraelen, H. Long-term assessment of the physical, mental, and sexual health among transsexual women. *J. Sex Med.*, 2009; 6 (3), 752-760.

Wolfradt, U; Neumann, K. Depersonalization, self-esteem and body image in male-to-female transsexuals compared to male and female controls. *Arch. Sex. Behav.*, 2001; 30 (3), 301-310.

Zung, WWK. A rating instrument for anxiety disorders. *Psychosomatics*, 1971; 12, 371-379.

Zung, WWK. Factors influencing the Self-Rating Depression Scale. *Arch. Gen. Psychiatry*, 1967; 16, 543-547.

In: Gender Identity
Editor: Beverly L. Miller

ISBN: 978-1-63321-488-0
© 2014 Nova Science Publishers, Inc.

Chapter 10

GENDER DYSPHORIA IN MINORS, A GROWING PHENOMENON IN OUR SOCIETY: DEMOGRAPHIC AND CLINICAL CHARACTERISTICS OF THIS POPULATION IN SPAIN

I. Esteva de Antonio[1]*, I. Prior-Sánchez[2], B. García-Bray[3], M.C. Almaraz[1], R. Yahyahouï[4], R. Fernández-García Salazar[1], E. Gómez-Gil[5] and J. Martínez-Tudela[6]

[1]Department of Endocrinology, Andalusian Gender Team. (IBIMA).
Carlos Haya Hospital, Malaga, Spain
[2]Department of Endocrinology and Nutrition. Reina Sofia Hospital, Córdoba, Spain
[3]Department of Endocrinology and Nutrition. Nuestra Señora de la Candelaria Hospital, Tenerife, Spain
[4]Department of Laboratory, Andalusian Gender Team.
Carlos Haya Hospital, Malaga, Spain
[5]Institute Clinic of Neurosciences, Department of Psychiatry, Gender Identity Unit.
Hospital Clinic, Barcelona, Spain
[6]Department of Psychology, Andalusian Gender Team.
Carlos Haya Hospital, Malaga, Spain

ABSTRACT

The demands of gender dysphoria (GD) in children and adolescents are increasing in recent years in the Spanish public health system. The complexity of the process and its clinical approach requires providing treatment by specialized units with multidisciplinary teams.

* Corresponding author: Isabel Esteva de Antonio, Hospital Carlos Haya, Servicio de Endocrinología y Nutrición. Pabellón C. Plaza del Hospital Civil s/n. 29009 Malaga, Spain. Telephone: +34951290415. e-mail: miesteva@ wanadoo.es.

The legislation relating to children with GD is not homogeneous in Spain. It currently provides health care for this population in gender teams with a non-interventionist attitude in children, and recommending pubertal suppression for adolescents in Tanner Stage above 2, in most units.

Integral care of the GD begins in the Spanish public health system in Andalusia (southern region) in 1999 (Andalusian-Gender-Team, AGT). The demand for minors has grown dramatically in recent years, having a fivefold increase in the number of applications since 2007, especially in the group of natal boys.

From 1999 through 2013, 165 subjects with a range of age (5 to 17 years) have been evaluated. 74,5% were natal males (male-to-female, MtF) and 25,5% female-to-male (FtM). 12%, were ≤ 12 years (childhood group), the rest had 12 to 17 years (adolescent group). 4 cases were excluded and 22 dropped out from the AGT. 3 boys regreted the GD in this period. Currently 136 subjetcs mantain follow up (42% in psychogical-evaluation-phase and 58% in cross-hormone-treatment, CHT). In 10 adolescents the puberty has been blocked. No alterations in the karyotype, ultrasound or analytical tests were found but basal bone mineral mass is decreased, especially in the group of MtF.

During this period, at the legal age (18 years), sex-reassignment-surgeries have been indicated in 16% of the patients (female genitoplasty in 21 MtF and hysterooforectomies in 5 FtM). 24 cases have had breast surgeries (13 mamoplasties and 10 mastectomies).

Most of the adolescents, or their parents, asked for intervention (psychological, endocrine, or surgical) at the first visit. Parents of children also requested intervention in most cases. The request at first visits in our Unit is significatively associated to the age group.

In recent years there has been an associative movement of patients and their families around social groups, which has led to increased demand for therapeutic procedures or deadlines that do not always agree with the recommendations of scientific societies. In the case of minors, sometimes these demands include not only early medical intervention, but full integration in schools according to their sexual identity. Therefore, it is essential to organize care with transgender population through specialized interdisciplinary teams, in close collaboration with the family and educational environment.

Keywords: Gender Dysphoria, childhood, adolescency, sex reassignment process

DEFINITION

Transsexuality or Gender Dysphoria (GD) can be defined as a strong and persistent cross-gender identification or discordance between gender identity and biological sex. It leads to a loss of well being and in some cases intense suffering and psychological distress. Definition of this condition can be found in DSM-V (*Diagnostic and Statistical Manual of Mental Disorders*; American Psychiatry Association, 1994), and *ICD-10* (World Health Organization, 1993) [1-2]. In children GD requires to fulfill a minimum number of criteria [1], including a 6 months period of persistent symptoms and a strong desire to belong to the other gender or a strong conviction of being of the opposite gender (see Figure 1 and 2).

Usual terminology refers in adults to transsexuals women (male to female = MtF) and transsexuals men (female to male = FtM), and in childhood and adolescents it is recommended the term of Gender Dysphoria. If we delve into the origins of the acknowledgement of this problem in minors, we find that it was first addressed in ICD-9, in 1978. After, followed its inclusion in DSM-III in 1980. This last classification system points out that a great percentage of children initially suspected to have an identity disorder don´t develop it into the adulthood. Also, it gives a great relevance in not confusing gender dysphoria with attitudes that simply are not the common ones associated to a particular gender but do not imply any identity disorder.

A. A marked incongruence between one's experienced/expressed gender and assigned gender, of at least 6 months duration, as manifested by at least 6 of the following indicators (including A1):

1. a strong desire to be of the other gender or an insistence that he or she is the other gender (or some alternative gender different from one's assigned gender)
2. in boys, a strong preference for cross-dressing or simulating female attire; in girls, a strong preference for wearing only typical masculine clothing and a strong resistance to the wearing of typical feminine clothing
3. a strong preference for cross-gender roles in make-believe or fantasy play
4. a strong preference for the toys, games, or activities typical of the other gender
5. a strong preference for playmates of the other gender
6. in boys, a strong rejection of typically masculine toys, games, and activities and a strong avoidance of rough-and-tumble play; in girls, a strong rejection of typically feminine toys, games, and activities
7. a strong dislike of one's sexual anatomy
8. a strong desire for the primary and/or secondary sex characteristics that match one's experienced gender.

B. The condition is associated with clinically significant distress or impairment in social, occupational, or other important areas of functioning, or with a significantly increased risk of suffering, such as distress or disability.

Subtypes
With a disorder of sex development
Without a disorder of sex development

Data from American Psychiatric Association. DSM-5: the Future of Psychiatric Diagnosis, 2013.

Figure 1. DSM-5 diagnostic criteria for gender dysphoria in children.

The diagnostic essential characteristic is the general and persistent desire of the individual to be of the sex opposite to the own one, with an intense rejection of the behavior, attributes and pomps of the same gender.

In girls:
An early interest often exists towards masculine forms of conduct. They are in the habit of having masculine companions of game and demonstrate an eager interest in sports and rough games. They reject or do not show interest towards games, puzzles or feminine clothes.
In strange occasions can appear a persistent rejection of the anatomical feminine structures, demonstrated by the following affirmations:
- She has a penis and it will grow.
- To reject to urinating in seated position or
- Affirmation of which she does not want that her breasts grow or that the menstruation appears.

In boys:
An early interest towards feminine forms of conduct, which one shows for a preference for dressing clothes of the opposite sex or for an intense desire to take part in the games and other girls' activities.
In strange occasions can appear a persistent rejection of the anatomical masculine structures, demonstrated by the following affirmations:
- That his somatic development will be that of a woman.
- That hispenis and testicles are disgusting or that they will disappear.
- That would be better not to have penis or testicles

The desire appears for the first time during the pre-school years. To be able to be diagnosed it must have demonstrates before the puberty.

Data from ICD (*International Classification of Diseases* – WHO, 1992).

Figure 2. ICD-10 diagnostic criteria for disorder of gender identity in children.

PUBLIC HEALTH CARE FOR GENDER DYSPHORIA IN SPAIN

The Spanish public health system integral care for gender dysphoria began in Andalusia (southern region) in 1999, having various units in the country nowadays [3]. Thus, it is a fairly young system and not fully extended to all of the Spanish territory. Other countries have similar situations, not including transgender care in their public health systems.

Nowadays, there are great limitations in the treatment for this patients in Spain. First of all, there are a lot of territories in the country without an established multidisciplinary unit for attention and treatment of this individuals. Moreover, not all of this units offer a complete treatment procedure, lacking in a lot of cases the surgical option. The first region to include all sex reassignment protocol (SRP), which includes psychotherapy, hormonal therapy and surgery, was Andalusia in 1999, having other important territories like Madrid and Catalonia to wait for the inclusion of surgical procedures until 2007 [3]. On top of that, communication between the endocrinological team and the psychological one can prove difficult, due to not being placed in the same area, needing the patient to visit different sanitary institutions to receive one kind of follow up or another. This proves hurdles to the patient and to the medical team that in some cases don't have an adequate feedback between the multiple specialities involved in this process.

Thanks to a recent study done by the Group on Identity and Sexual Differentiation, of the Spanish Society of Endocrinology (GIDSEEN Group) prevalence of this condition in Spain is estimated at around 1 in 15.000 inhabitants, having a good correlation with other European estimates, and being clearly above national sanitary agencies predictions [3].

Over 3000 applicants of all ages, were recorded in the above mentioned study. Children and adolescents with GD (which constitute 10% of the total number), have only recently been considered for care in Spain, especially since gender experts units from other countries and newer versions of the Standards of Care (SOC), have highlighted the need to initiate multidisciplinary protocols for handling [4-8] of this individuals. In recent years, demands of gender dysphoria management in children and teenagers are increasing in Spain, with a fivefold increase in the number of applications since 2007, especially in the natal boys group (ASB in press).

STANDARD CLINICAL ASSESSMENT

The diagnosis and the therapeutic procedures must be done in specialized multidisciplinary units according to the international recommendations [4-13]. Psychology or psychiatry specialists with experience in children and adolescents should make the initial diagnosis and then continue to follow up the patient through all the SRP. For the assessment it is recommended to assume the SOC [4] and *The Endocrine Society* guides [5]. This recommendations are: 1) a psychological diagnose and evaluation, at least during the first 6-12 months (with psychotherapy), 2) endocrinological study and cross-sex hormone treatment (CHT), and 3) sex reassignment surgeries at legal age.

The protocol also depends on the age of the minor. In children, successive clinical interviews and psychometrics tests are performed on parents and children by psychologists with experience in childhood. Psychological assessment is also part of the diagnostic procedure and can last for several years until the child reaches the age of 12 or achieves a pubertal stage Tanner 2. In adolescents, first of all, the diagnose and real life experience, as pointed out before, needs to be handed primarily by a mental health carer. Real life experience (RLE), now called social role transition, means socially presenting oneself as the gender of the nonbiological gender, including a cross-gender name and cross-gender clothing. The first psychological interview includes sociodemographic characteristics, evolution of gender identity, associated psychiatric comorbidities and expectations of the treatment requested in the unit for GD. The second management phase has primarily, an endocrinological perspective, but always with the appropriate psychological support. A complete medical interview has to be conducted with additional points, like previous cross-sex hormone treatment (CHT), cosmetic procedures and, very importantly, pubertal stage. Diagnostic complementary tests can include abdominal ultrasound, and blood samples to help discard possible illness such as a virilizing tumour, chromosomal anomalies or any endocrinological alterations. If no contraindications arise, the hormonal treatment will depend on the pubertal stage, in Tanner 2-3 and always in older than 12, gonadotropin-releasing hormone (GnRH) analogues can be used until the age of 16, and at this age the CHT can be started with increasing doses of estrogens in MtF or androgens in FtM, when:

1) The mental health carer provides a satisfactory report.
2) RLE, 3 months before or psychotherapy by a mental health professional.
3) Having obtained an informed assent. Patient and tutors are fully aware of therapeutic options, knowing their benefits and risks, and committing themselves to an adequate endocrine and psychological follow up. Usually, the patient is under legal age, so it is necessary to have their tutor´s consent at the time of starting hormonal therapy.
4) The patient has reached Tanner 2 puberty stage.

Hormonal therapy seeks to suppress endogenous sex hormone secretion and to substitute them with the desired sex hormones. Changes can appear up to 2 or even 3 years after treatment initiation. MtF older adolescents usually receive antiandrogenic drugs jointly with estrogens and FtM patients receive androgens, that are usually enough to suppress the female hormonal axis.

The CHT maintains the suppression of endogenous sex hormone and substitutes them with the desired sex hormones. Changes can appear up to 2 or even 3 years after treatment initiation. Finally, sex reassignment surgeries can be offered when the patient is over 18 years old and after 2 years of treatment. Legal identity change can also be achieved in Spain, after 2 years of CHT and always in people older than 18.

All the points in the previous paragraphs are only a minimal part of whole process. This can be deeply distressful, in a lot of cases having to treat a person that has been living a considerable amount of his life feeling "trapped" in a role he despises. We cannot stress enough the importance of psychological support and the need for an endocrinologist and surgeon with expertise in the field. If not, secondary effects, failure to achieve previously established objectives, or worse still, doing an irreversible procedure in a patient that does not fit in the gender dysphoria diagnostic criteria can occur. Multidisciplinary teams are essential for management of these patients.

EXPERIENCE IN ANDALUSIAN GENDER TEAM (AGT), SPAIN

The consideration of the healthcare of GD through sex-reassignment protocol (SRP), is a recent event in the Spanish public health system, since the regulations did not contemplate this therapeutic approach before 1999. In 1999, the Andalusian Gender Team (AGT), was the first public unit to incorporate the entire SRP [19]. AGT is the main and only public center in a wide geographical area (Andalusia), with more than 10 million people.

From October 1999 until October 2013, 165 minors with a range of age (5 to 17 years) requested treatment at the AGT, all of them have been included consecutively in the cohort described in this chapter.

The evaluation and approach to the subjects included was done on the basis of international protocols and performance guides [4-6], mentioned in the previous section according to the therapeutic triad: *psychological evaluation-experience of real life, cross-sex hormone treatment and finally sex reassignment surgeries.* The psychological assessment was developed by mental health specialists, who not only verify the diagnosis, detecting co-morbidities and excluding cases that did not meet the eligibility criteria, but also offered psychotherapy support throughout the entire process, especially in the group of 12 year old minors.

Once the diagnosis was confirmed, the criteria to select the most appropriate treatment method depended on the puberty stage and was discussed in a multidisciplinary clinical session. If the subject was in an initial puberty phase (Tanner phase 2-3), puberty blocking was prescribed with GnRH analogues. While if puberty was advanced, hormonal treatment was initiated with increased doses of cross-sex steroids. Monitoring of subjects by the team was carried out and recorded every 3-6 months to ensure an appropriate physical and psychic adaptation to changes and detect in advance possible side effects of the treatment.

Descriptive demographic, anthropometric (height, weight, BMI, waist/hip perimeter) and puberty stage statistics were collected, as well as the results of the basic study requested in the initial endocrinological assessment, which includes: *1) Complete analysis,* with haemogram, biochemical, lipid profile, hepatic function, serology and basal hormone tests - thyroid, gonadal and adrenal axis -, *2) karyotype, 3) abdominopelvic ultrasound and 4) Bone Mineral Densitometry (BMD).* Densitometric values are assessed in accordance with the latest recommendations stipulated at the PDC -*Pediatric Position Development Conference*-[22] (using the Z score marking for assessment).

In our series of patients, 74.5% of the requests (n=123) were from biological males and 25.5% (n=42) females. We could differentiate two groups. On one side, *Children Group,* aged ≤12 (n=20), where a conservative attitude was adopted, without carrying out any medical intervention except that of monitoring the evolutionary stages of the process. Attention in this sub-group therefore was focused especially on the parents, providing advice, support and information. And on the other hand, *Adolescents Group,* aged 13-17 (n=145), where treatment was decided on after obtaining a favourable psychological report, according to the previous premises.

Combined Sample

The average age at the first visit was 15.02, with a minimum value of 5 and maximum of 17. The sex ratio was 5.6:1 in the infant group (≤ 12) and 3:1 in adolescents. In the diagnostic assessment phase, 4 subjects (all natal males) were excluded: 2 cases, for *severe personality disorders*, another for a *psychotic disorder* and the last for a *low IQ*. During the period of the study and follow-up, 22 subjects have been lost: one had a sudden death (MtF) at 23 years of age after some years of cross-sex hormone treatment and genitoplastic surgery; the remainder (n=21) were lost because of moving to other localities or due to withdrawals; 11 of these subjects did not complete the first phase of psychological evaluation. During follow up 3 subjects were recorded as having remission of dysphoria (at 9, 12, 17 years of age). Therefore, 136 subjects are currently being monitored by the AGT, although in different phases of the process: 58% (n=78) obtained a favourable psychological report and are undergoing CHT and 42% (n=58) have still not started it, as they are in the first phase of the process yet. In 10 subjects puberty was blocked with GnRH analogues (average age 15.3 [13.4-16.8]). During the monitoring in the adolescents group, 16% of the series underwent sex reassignment surgeries: 15 female genitoplasties in AGT and six of them at private centres and 5 hysterectomies with double anexectomy in our unit. Likewise, around 14 % of breast surgery, 13 mamoplasties (at private centres since the process is not provided at AGT) and 10 mastectomies in AGT, (Figure 3).

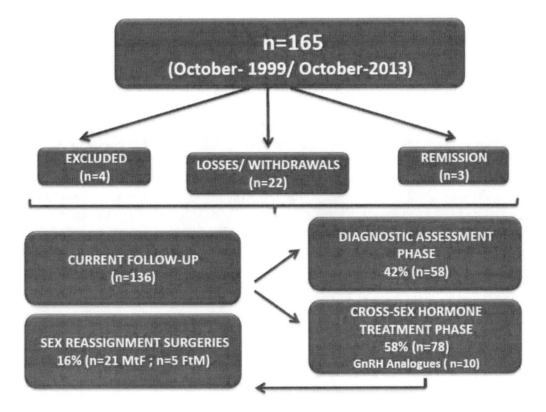

Figure 3. Evolutionary scheme of monitoring.

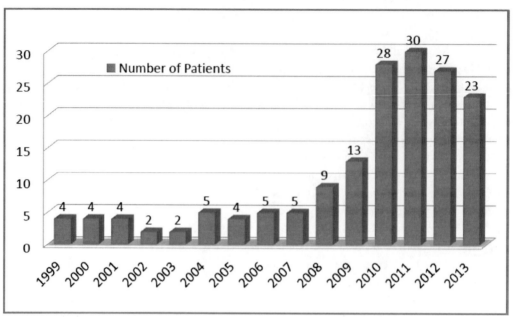

In this graph, we can observe a fivefold increase in the number of applications since 2007.

Figure 4. Annual number of demands.

The average at surgery was 20.1 [range: 18-28]. The average period from the start of diagnostic evaluation until complete eligibility criteria for hormone treatment, was in the whole sample 14.90 months [range: 6-33 months] and in children group this period has taken more than 4-5 years when the diagnostic phase was started before the age of 8-10 years.

Application requests have increased significantly in recent years as can be seen in Figure 4.

With respect to the procedure, 8.5% of the subjects (n=14) were sent from other Spanish regions; the remaining percentage (>90%) came from Andalusia. Overall, 19% of the sample had some type of substance abuse: alcohol (n=49), tobacco (n=28) or drugs (n=18), mainly cannabis; only 4 cases of the latter sub-group took cocaine and/or designer drugs. The average age for starting substance abuse was 15.27 [range: 11-17], 13.96 [range: 9-17] and 14.4 [range: 11-17] respectively. The surprising fact was in terms of gender, the relative percentage of substance abusers was higher among natal females.

With regard to the start of gender dysphoria, 55 % of the global series (n=92) located it in infancy, when they were 12 or younger; likewise, when asked about real life experience, 46 % (n=77), had already started it at the first consultation.

With regard to whether CHT had started or not when they were first treated at the AGT, most of the subjects (≈ 85%; n=141) were naive, i.e., had never taken hormones or any other type of medication. 15% (n=24) had started treatment, either under supervision (n=8) or on their own initiative (n=16). It should be noted that all cases of self-treatment were in the adolescents group, natal males and only in one subject FtM testosterone was administered but under supervision by a private endocrinologist (Figure 5).

In 10 patients, and always after a multidiciplinary clinical session, puberty has been suppressed with GnRH analogues. The clinical characteristics of these subjects are shown in figure 6.

	Natal Male Patients n(%)	Natal Female Patients n(%)	Total n(%)
Patients	123(74,5%)	42(25,5%)	165(100%)
Age first contact			
≤12 years	17(13,8%)	3(7,1%)	20 (12,1%)
>12 yearas	106(86,2%)	39(92,9%)	145(87,9%
Referred place			
Andalusía	112(91,1%)	39(92,9%)	151(91,5%)
Other Spanish regions	11(8,9%)	3(7,1%)	14(8,5%)
Toxic habits			
Alcohol	36(29,3%)	13(31%)	49(29,7%)
Smoking	19(15,4%)	9(21,4%)	28(17%)
Drugs	11/8,9%)	7(16,7%)	18(10,9%)
Tanner Stage*			
II	5(7,8%)	0(0%)	5(5,7%)
III	2(3,1%)	1(4,2%)	3(3,4%)
IV	48(75%)	19(79,2%)	67(76,1%)
V	9(14,1%)	4(16,7%)	13(14,8%)
Onset of Gender Dysphoria			
Childhood	67(54,5%)	25(59,5%)	92(55,7%)
>12 years	39(31,7%)	10(23,8%)	49(29,7%)
No Data	17(13,8%)	7(16,6%)	24(14,54%)
Started the RLE• at first visit			
Yes	63(51,2%)	14(33,3%)	77(46,7%)
No	50(40,7%)	25(59,5%)	75(45,5%)
No data	10(8,1%)	3(7,1%)	13(7,9%)
Treatment Group at first visit			
Naive	100(81,3%)	41(97,6%)	141(85,5%)
Supervised	5(4,1%)	1(2,4%%)	6(3,6%)
GnRH	2(1,6%)	0(0%)	2(1,2%)
Autotreatment	16(13%)	0(0%)	16(9,7%)
Start treatment at the AGT			
Yes	64(52%)	24(57,1%)	88(53,3%)
No	59(48%)	18(42,9%)	77(46,7%)
Exclusion	4(3,3%)	0(0%)	4(2,4%)
Losses/withdrawals	20(15,4%)	2(4,8%)	22(12,7%)
Regression G.Dysphoria	2(1,6%)	1(2,4%)	3(1,8%)

* There has not been reflected the Tanner Stage of subjects who have not been yet evaluated by an endocrinologist and those less than twelve years old neither.

• Real Life Experience.

Figure 5. Demographic and clinical characteristics in AGT.

The physical examination (weight, height, *BMI, blood pressure, waist/hip perimeter, puberty stage*) and analytical data was only collected from subjects aged >12, once the endocrinology examination assessed the start of treatment and after an informed consent form was signed by the tutor/s (n=107). Figure 7 displays the somatometric data obtained.

The global overweight (BMI >25 kg/m2), obesity (BMI>30 kg/m2), as well as low weight (BMI<18.5 kg/m2) percentages were 12.14%, 4.6% and 14.01%, respectively. Overweight and obesity were more prevalent among natal females while the percentage of low weight was greater among biological males.

Patient	Treatment group	Starting date of blockade	Starting age	Duration of blockade	Tanner Stage	SRS*	BMD (g/cm2)	Other information
MtF	Self-treatment	16-Oct-98	16,8	21 months	3	Yes	1,204	Loss/withdrawals in 2005
MtF	GnRH	01-Dec-11	15,1	9 months	3	No	–	Treatment with Decapeptyll® in private center
MtF	GnRH	15-Aug-97	16,8	12 months	3	Yes	0,962	Self-treatment with Androcur® for 1 year
MtF	Naive	01-Jun-99	17,3	8 months	3	Yes	1,215	
MtF	Naive	14-Jan-13	16,6	6 months	2	No	0,879	She has not initiated the CHT**
MtF	Naive	08-Mar-05	15,6	4 months	2	Yes	1,045	
MtF	Naive	15-Mar-11	15,3	24 months	2	No	1,106	
FtM	Naive	19-Jun-12	15,2	9 months	3	No	1,067	
MtF	Naive	26-Jun-12	13,4	17 months	2	No	0,770	She has not initiated the CHT
MtF	Naive	16-Feb-10	14,4	39 months	2	No	0,969	Loss/withdrawal in 2005

In only 10 cases puberal blockade has been carried out. The average age of starting treatment with GnRH analogues has been ≈15 years.

* SRS: Sex Reassignment Surgery throughout follow up in AGT.

** Cross-sex Hormone Treatment.

Figure 6. Clinical characteristics of the patients selected for puberty suppression with GnRH analogues.

	Natal Male Patients (n=80)				Natal Female Patients (n=27)			
	Min.	Max.	Mean	±SD	Min.	Max.	Mean	±SD
Weight (Kg)	46,0	127,2	63,25	12,27	41,2	86,6	61,25	13,13
Height (m)	1,56	1,84	1,715	0,06	1,48	1,68	1,59	0,05
BMI (Kg/m2)*	16,0	37,6	21,63	3,66	17,5	37,0	23,96	4,87
BMI >25kg/m²		n=7 (8,7%)				n=6(22,2%)		
BMI >30kg/m²		n=2 (2,5%)				n=3 (11,1%)		
BMI <18.5kg/m²		n=13 (16,2%)				n=2 (7,4%)		
SBP** (mm Hg)	90	156	123,44	13,48	93	140	114,70	12,85
DBP***(mmHg)	40	98	72,64	11,56	60	90	72,19	9,91
Waist (cm)	62	115	74,58	9,25	57	101	75,89	12,31
Hip (cm)	76	133	92,56	8,54	82	125	97,85	10,60

* BMI: Body Mass Index. Overweight: BMI >25kg/m2, Obesity: BMI >30kg/m2 and Underweight: BMI<18,5kg/m2.

** Systolic Blood Pressure.

*** Diastolic Blood Pressure.

Figure 7. Somatometric and physical examination data.

	Biological Male Patients (n=71)		Biological Female Patients (n=26)	
	Mean	±SD	Mean	±SD
Hemoglobin (g/dl) *	15,31	3,28	13,30	0,90
Haematocrit (%)	44,11	3,95	40,22	2,74
Glucose (mg/dl) **	88,18	7,87	84,52	8,82
Creatinine (mg/dl)	0,79	0,13	0,72	0,13
Uric acid (mg/dl)	4,90	1,07	4,22	1,28
Total Cholesterol (mg/dl)	144,43	25,33	154,36	22,10
LDL_c (mg/dl)	83,75	22,20	90,32	17,03
HDL_c (mg/dl)	47,423	10,14	53,16	12,50
Triglycerides (mg/dl)	69,72	35,43	64,64	28,35
Prolactin (ng/ml)	12,23	6,85	18,01	14,54
TSH (mcUI/ml)***	2,63	1,27	5,08	9,15
FSH (mUI/ml)	4,28	3,05	5,80	3,21
LH (mUI/ml)	4,88	2,48	11,05	14,73
Total Testosterone (ng/ml)	5,68	1,79	0,47	0,25
Estradiol (pg/ml)	31,94	13,68	127,17	107,44
SEROLOGY: HBV, HCV, HIV	N E G A T I V E (Only three cases were positive for the HBV, but none was presenting active viral replication)			
KARYOTYPE	46(XY)****		46(XX)	
ABDOMINOPELVIC ULTRASOUND	W I T H O U T R E L E V A N T F I N D S			

* Minimal value of hemoglobin 7,8 g/dl: in biological male patiens who suffered from thalassemia.

** Maximum value of Glycemia 109 mg/dl: in biological male subject with debut of diabetes mellitus type 1 confirmed in the follow-up.

*** TSH's level altered in 5 subjects (two biological males and 3 with natal female sex): Only three cases with later confirmation of hypothyroidism.

**** Only an alteration has been detected in the Karyotype: fragile point on the short arm of the chromosome16 [16p (12)].

Figure 8. Results of the baseline study requested in the initial endocrinological assessment.

With regard to additional examinations (Figure 8) the following were collected and recorded: *1) basal analytical data*: haemogram, general biochemical, lipids, hormonal axes, serology; *2) Karyotype*, which were normal in all cases, except in 1 subject who had a weak point in the short arm of pair 16[16p(12)], without pathological meaning; *3) abdominal ultrasound, which did not display relevant results and 4) BMD*. It should be highlighted that the densitometric values in the 97 BMD carried out showed that 44% of bone mass values were low for the age and gender range ("Z" score marking -1.0 DS). 12.4% (n=12) of these subjects had a Z score value of -2DS. By gender this percentage is significantly higher in natal males; only 4 natal females had a reduced BMD compared to the reference population (figures. 9 and 10).

Diagnostic approach must be extremely cautious at this age due to a relatively high chance of gender dysphoria regression. The legislation related to children with gender dysphoria is not homogeneous in the world. Currently, it provides health care for this population in gender teams with a non-interventionist attitude. Treatment criteria with CHT are similar to those of adults, but adding the necessity of at least a Tanner 2 pubertal stage and a solid psychological and social backup. Nevertheless, delaying treatment and not avoiding the appearance of secondary sexual characters could unleash great harm on the individual, thus blocking puberty with gonadal axis suppression is usually the option of choice, taking also into account its reversibility. Close follow up must be granted. CHT can be started at the age of 16, combining it with puberty suppression ideally up to the age of 18(6-15).

Secondary effects in this group of patients are largely unknown, it is necessary to consider during the long term follow up a possible increase in cardiovascular risk. Also, puberty suppression could have a negative impact on bone density, but no studies are available at this point to back up this hypothesis. The Amsterdam Gender Identity Clinic tried to study possible secondary effects on transgender minors, but an article published in Nature in 2011(15), admits not having enough data to take concrete conclusions. Taking all of this into account, there are arguments for and against treatment at this age. Suppression of sexual development can alleviate patient's suffering. Also, future surgery may obtain better results if puberty is suppressed. Also, this treatment is reversible. On the other hand, puberty blockage prevents the normal sexual development under the influence of the native sex hormones and this could prevent the complete development of gender identity.

Commentaries About Clinical and Demographic Data in AGT

Requests for gender dysphoria in children and adolescents increased in the Spanish socio-health context [20]. This data matches the situation of other health systems, both in Europe and in North America [11-13, 16-18]. Nevertheless, it is still not possible to deduce if this increase truly reflects an increase in incidence/prevalence or is a consequence of socio-cultural factors, such as the pull effect of the media or the creation of centralised functional units focusing on the number of cases [21]. It is noteworthy that despite the small infant group its incidence accumulates mainly in the later years of this study.

A distinctive aspect of this cohort is the gender ratio for each age group, with a clear predominance of the male natal gender both in pre-pubescents (5.6:1) and in adolescents (3:1). In the Canada [18] series, the children population male/female ratio fluctuated between 2.02:1 and in adolescents 1.01:1. Similar results in adolescents (ratio 1:1) were obtained in the North American study of Spack et al. [12], and in the Netherlands series "The Dutch Approach" [13].

Another interesting aspect to be commented on is the delay in the request for health care; although over 50% of the individuals said they had started their gender dysphoria as infants, the majority did not come for a consultation until they had an advanced puberty stage (76%, Tanner stage 4). This delay in starting medical treatment is similar to other series [11-13]. Nevertheless, the recent tendency is that of consulting at earlier ages, which will enable if necessary, blocking puberty with GnRH analogues. Early treatment of adolescents will also prevent the observed self-treatment, especially in the MtF group.

Other results to highlight are the basal values of bone mineral density obtained in our series showing a striking percentage of low bone mass (≈44%) mainly in natal male subjects. There is little data published in the scientific literature showing the basal densitometric status of subjects with gender dysphoria and much less in the infant-juvenile population. Most of them analyse the BMD status during hormonal treatment, observing its maintenance and even an increase after 2 years of treatment [24-25].

A Belgian study by Van Caenegem [26], concluded that MtF subjects had a greater prevalence of osteopenia and less muscular mass before initiating treatment in comparison with healthy controls (males); its results are similar to those of our cohort but this study was carried out on adult subjects, once the bone mass peak has been reached (age range 26-46). In a child and adolescent population osteopenia or osteoporosis have been defined [22-23], with the latter being diagnosed only in cases where a Z-score lower than -2DE and previous history of fracture co-exist.

The factors described in the literature to explain this greater prevalence of a low bone mass in the MtF are avoidance of sports activities, less exposure to sunlight, low levels of vitamin D and greater substance abuse [26]. It is known that puberty blocking and CHT initially stop bone mineralisation, requiring more prospective studies to assess the BMD of this population as adults.

DXA* values	Natal Male Patients (n=71)	Natal Female Patients (n=26)	Total	p**
Z-score ≥ -1SD	32(45,1%)	22(84,6%)	54(55,7%)	0,002
Z-score between -1SD/-2SD	28(39,4%)	3(11,5%)	31(3,0%)	0,001
Z-score ≤ -2SD	11(15,5%)	1(3,8%)	12(12,4%)	0,002

* DXA: Dual-energy X-ray Absorptiometry.
** Comparison of Z-score values categorized according to natal sex (Chi-square Test).

In agreement with the last guides [14,15], bone mass in paediatric age should be evaluated measuring the area of bone mineral density (g/cm^2) in lumbar spine. These values are compared with reference values from healthy youth of similar age, gender, and, if possible, race/ethnicity to calculate a Z-score.

Figure 9. Bone mineral density (BMD) values according to Z-scores.

Classification for biological sex	Area of BMD (L2-L4) g/cm2 Mean (minimum – maximum value)	p*
Natal Male Patients (n=71)	1,056(0,635-1,388)	<0,001
Natal Female Patients (n=26)	1,171(0,897-1,446)	

* Comparison of BMD's average values measured in L2-L4 (g/cm2) attending to natal sex (T-Student for independent samples).

Figure 10. Bone mineral density (BMD) values in g/cm2.

With regard to the remaining analytical parameters, our data reflects the fact that subjects with gender dysphoria are biologically healthy and their state of health is comparable to the rest of the infant-juvenile population.

ABOUT THE TREND OF WORLDWIDE DEPATHOLOGIZATION

In recent years there has been an associative movement of patients and their families around social groups, which has led to an increased demand for therapeutic procedures or deadlines that not always agree with the recommendations of scientific societies. In the case of minors, sometimes these demands include not only early medical intervention, but full integration in schools according to their sexual identity.

Nowadays, numerous claims trying to classify gender dysphoria out of a pathological context are increasing. These movement has been seen worldwide in an increasing manor. This dilemma can be tackled from a pure philosophical or anthropological point of view, but the consequences it can produce, especially in minors, have to be taken into account. Hormonal treatment needs of a close follow up, not only from an endocrine point of view, but with a psychological support, being this a necessity not an option. Also, experience in this field is a must have for the professionals that deal with this entity, not only for treatment and follow up, but also for the initial selection of cases, always taking into account that we can produce irreversible and disastrous consequences if a wrong diagnose has been made.

Therefore, it is essential to organize care for the transgender population through specialized interdisciplinary teams, in close collaboration with the family and the educational environment.

CONCLUSION

Between 1999-2013 the AGT has attended 1550 people with GD, the minors population has supposed a 10,6%. The children infant group is still limited but has increased in recent years and cases of dysphoria regression have been observed. The infant-juvenile population with gender dysphoria does not have a different health profile from the general population except in the state of its bone mass. During the period studied, the adolescent group came to the AGT already in an advanced stage of puberty. In the last guidelines, no medical intervention is recommended in pre-puberty stages, so an attitude of evolving supervision of the process was adopted. Puberty blocking was performed only in cases that reached the Tanner 2 stage. The complexity of the diagnostic-therapeutic approach of child and adolescent patients with gender dysphoria requires their supervision in specialised multidisciplinary units that respond with health care quality and to increasing application requests.

The prospective monitoring of this series will allow anthropometric, biochemical and densitometric changes to be established and analysis of possible adverse events due to CHT as well as the use of GnRH analogues and evaluation of the persistence or not of dysphoria in the children group.

✦*GIDSEEN* **Group** (Gender Identity and Sexual Development Disorders Spanish Group), Spanish Endocrine Society: *Almaraz MC (Andalucía), Álvarez-Diz JA (Asturias), Asenjo N (Madrid), Audí L (Cataluña), Becerra A (Madrid), Castaño L (P.Vasco), Esteva I (Andalucía), Fernández Sánchez-Barbudo M (I.Canarias), Gómez-Balaguer M (C. Valenciana), Gómez-Gil E (Cataluña), Hurtado F (C. Valenciana), López-Siguero JP (Andalucía), Martínez-Tudela J (Andalucía), Moreno-Pérez O (C. Valenciana), Rodríguez-*

Molina JM (Madrid), Sanisidro C (Aragón), Toni M (Navarra), Vázquez-San Miguel F (P. Vasco), Vidales A (Castilla-León).

REFERENCES

[1]   American Psychiatric Association. *Diagnostic and statistical manual of mental disorders*: DSM-5. 5th ed. Washington, D.C: American Psychiatric Association, 2013, 947p.

[2]   World Health Organization. *International statistical classification of diseases and related health problems*. 10th revision, 2nd edition. Geneva: World Health Organization, 2004. 3p.

[3]   Esteva de Antonio, I; Gomez-Gil, E; Almaraz, MA; Martinez-Tudela, J; Bergero, T; Olveira, G; Soriguer, F; GIDSEEN Group. Organization of healthcare for transsexual persons in the Spanish national health system. *Gac Sanit*, 26(3), 203-209, 2012.

[4]   Coleman, E; Bockting, W; Botzer, M; Cohen-Kettenis, P; DeCuypere, G; et al. Standards of Care for the Health of Transsexual,Transgender, and Gender-Nonconforming People, Version 7. (2011). *International Journal of Transgenderism*, 13, 165-232.

[5]   Hembree, WC; Cohen-Kettenis, P; Delemarre, HA; Gooren, LJ; Meyer III, WJ; Spack, NP; et al. Endocrine treatment of transsexual persons: An Endocrine Society Clinical Practice Guideline. *JClin Endocrinol Metab.*, 2009, 94, 3132-54.

[6]   Moreno-Pérez, O; Esteva De Antonio, I. y Grupo de Identidad y Diferenciación Sexual de la SEEN (GIDSEEN). Clinical Practice Guidelines for Assessment and Treatment of Transsexualism. *Endocrinol Nutr.*, 2012, 59(6), 367-82.

[7]   Zucker, KJ. Gender identity disorder in children and adolescents. *Annu Rev Clin Psychol*, 2005, 1, 467-92. Review.

[8]   Delemarre-van de Waal, H; Cohen-Kettenis, P. Clinical management of gender identity disorder in adolescents: a protocol on psychological and paediatric endocrinology aspects. *European Journal of Endocrinology*, 2006, 155 (Suppl.), 8.

[9]   de Vries, AL; Cohen-Kettenis, PT; Delemarre-van de Waal, HA. Clinical management of gender dysphoria in adolescents. *International Journal of Transgenderism*, 2007, 9, 83–94.

[10]   Shumer, DE; Spack, NP. Current management of gender identity disorder in childhood and adolescence: guidelines, barriers and areas of controversy. Curr *Opin Endocrinol Diabetes Obes*, 2013, 20, 69–73.

[11]   Cohen-Kettenis, PT; Steensma, TD; et al. Treatment of adolescent with Gender Dysphoria in the Netherlands. *Child Adolesc Psychiatric Clin N Am*, 20 (2011), 689–700.

[12]   Spack, NP; Edwards-Leeper, L; Feldman, HA; et al. Children and Adolescents With Gender Identity Disorder Referred to a Pediatric Medical Center. *Pediatrics*, 2012 Mar, 129(3), 418-25.

[13]   de Vries, ALC; Cohen-Kettenis, PT. Clinical Management of Gender Dysphoria in Child and Adolescents: The Dutch Approach. *J Homosex*, 2012, 59(3), 301-20.

[14] de Vries, AL; Steensma, TD; Doreleijers, TA; et al. Puberty suppression in adolescents with gender identity disorder:a prospective follow-up study. *J Sex Med*, 2011, 8, 2276-83.

[15] Kreukels, BPC; Cohen-Kettenis, PT. Puberty suppression in gender identity disorder: the Amsterdam experience. *Nature Reviews Endocrinology*, 2011 May 17, 7(8), 466–72).

[16] Steensma, TD; Biedmond, R; de Boer, F; Cohen-Kettenis, PT. Desisting and persisting gender dysphoria after childhood: a qualitative follow-up study. *Clin Child Psychol Psychiatry*, 2011, 16, 499–516.

[17] Reed, B; Rhodes, S; Schofield, P; Wylie, K. Gender variance in the UK: Prevalence, incidence, growth and geographic distribution, 2009. Retrieved June8, 2011, from http://www.gires.org.uk/assets/MedproAssets/GenderVarianceUK-report.pdf.

[18] Wood, H; Sasaki, S; Bradley, SJ; Zucker, KJ; et al. Patterns of Referral to a Gender Identity Service for Children and Adolescents (1976–2011): Age, Sex Ratio, and Sexual Orientation, *Journal of Sex & Marital Therapy*, (2013) 39, 1, 1-6.

[19] Gómez-Gil, E; Esteva de Antonio, I. Ser transexual: dirigido al paciente, a su familia y al entorno sanitario, judicial y social: GLOSA. : (2006). ISBN 84-7429-267-0.

[20] Gómez-Gil, E; et al. La atención a la transexualidad por la unidad de salud mental del Hospital Clinic de Barcelona en los últimos años. C. Med. Psicosom, n°78, 2006.

[21] Esteva de Antonio, I; Gomez-Gil, E; GIDSEEN Group. Coordination of Health Care for Transsexual Persons: A Multidisciplinary Approach. Current Opinion in Endocrinology and Diabetes (*Endocrinology reproductive*), 20 (6), 585-591, 2013.

[22] Gordon, CM; Bachrach, LK; Carpenter, TO; el al. Dual energy x-ray absorptiometry interpretation and reporting in children and adolescents: the 2007 ISCD pediatric official positions. *J Clin Densitom*, 2008, 11(1), 43-58.

[23] American Academy of Pediatrics. Clinical Report- Bone Densitometry in Children and Adolescents-. *Pediatrics*, 2011, 127, 189-94.

[24] Mueller, A; Zollver, H; Kronawitter, D; Oppelt, PG; Claassen, T; Hoffmann, I; et al. Body composition and bone mineral density in male-to-female transsexuals during cross-sex hormone therapy using gonadotrophin-releasing hormone agonist. *Exp Clin Endocrinol Diabetes*, 2011, 119, 95–100.

[25] Van Kesteren, P; Lips, P; Gooren, LJ; Asscheman, H; Megens, J. Long-term follow-up of bone mineral density and bone metabolism in transsexuals treated with cross-sex hormones. *Clin Endocrinol* (Oxf), 1998, 48, 347–54.

[26] Van Caenegem, E; Taes, Y; Wierckx, K; et al. Low bone mass is prevalent in male-to-female transsexual persons before the start of cross-sex hormonal therapy and gonadectomy. *Bone*, 54 (2013), 92-97.

In: Gender Identity
Editor: Beverly L. Miller

ISBN: 978-1-63321-488-0
© 2014 Nova Science Publishers, Inc.

Chapter 11

SUBSTANCE USE AND EXPOSURE TO VIOLENCE DURING CHILDHOOD AND ADOLESCENCE IN TRANSSEXUALS

T. Bergero-Miguel[1], P. Paulino-Matos[2], J. Guzmán-Parra[1], Y. de Diego-Otero[3], N. Sánchez-Álvarez[4] and L. Pérez-Costillas[5,6]*

[1]Clinical Psychologist, Department of Mental Health, Regional University Hospital.
Malaga Biomedical Research Institute (IBIMA), Malaga. Spain
[2]Internal Medical Resident on Psychiatry, Department of Mental Health,
Regional University Hospital), Malaga. Spain.
[3]Biologist, PhD. Department of Mental Health, Regional University Hospital,
Malaga Biomedical Research Institute (IBIMA), Malaga. Spain
[4]Psychologist, Department of Mental Health, Regional University Hospital.
Malaga Biomedical Research Institute (IBIMA), Malaga. Spain
[5]Psychiatrist, PhD, Department of Mental Health, Regional University Hospital,
Malaga Biomedical Research Institute (IBIMA), Malaga. Spain
[6]Department of Psychiatry. University of Malaga. Malaga. Spain

ABSTRACT

Objective: We aim to study the relation between exposure to violence during childhood and adolescence and substance consumption in adulthood in a population of transsexuals.

Material and Methods: Descriptive study of 209 transsexual subjects, based on the ICD-10 diagnostic criteria (109 male-to-female, and 100 female-to-male), followed at the Transsexuality and Gender Identity Unit of the General University Hospital of Malaga (Spain).

* Corresponding author: Trinidad Bergero Miguel. UGC Salud Mental, Hospital Regional Universitario de Málaga. Pabellón 2. Planta baja, Hospital Civil. 29009 Málaga. E-mail: berg7679@hotmail.com

The Social-demographic structured questionnaire and Exposure to Violence Questionnaire (EVQ) were used during the psychological evaluation phase of the gender reassignment process.

Results: The highest score of direct violence experienced in childhood and adolescence was obtained from when the subjects were at school, the lowest score was obtained at home, and direct violence in the neighbourhood came second.

The average score of the EVQ questionnaire (Violence in the neighbourhood) was significantly higher in those who had consumed cannabis in the past compared to those who hadn't ($p<0.05$). Differences were not observed either in the total direct score of EVQ nor in the other EVQ scores for active *cannabis* consumers.

The average of the EVQ direct score in those who had consumed cocaine in the past ($p <0.05$) were higher. Specifically, higher scores of violence were experienced at home, both among current and past consumers of cocaine.

The differences between consumers and non-consumers of designer drugs in the past were significant within the scores of exposure to violence at home ($p<0.05$) but not on the total questionnaire score.

Conclusions: In accordance with the data, violence experienced during childhood and adolescence may play a role in substance abuse in adult transsexuals. In addition, some characteristic patterns are observed between exposure to violence and the type of drug consumed.

In an attempt to prevent early exposure to violence and its consequences on mental health and influence the psychosocial adjustment in transsexuals, early interventions are imperative.

INTRODUCTION

Transsexualism is defined, in the *International Classification of Diseases*, in its 10th *version* (ICD-10), as an intense manifestation of the spectrum of gender dysphoria (GD) (APA, 2000; 2013). It is considered as:

The desire to live and be accepted as a member of the opposite sex, usually, accompanied by the wish to make/change his or her body as congruent as possible with the preferred sex through hormonal and/or surgical treatment. This feeling of incongruence should be present for at least two years and not a symptom of another mental disorder or a chromosomal abnormality or intersexual state (WHO, 1992).

The existence of a strong and persistent identification with the opposite sex, and the discomfort with one's own anatomical sex, besides being a life challenging situation, often produces psychological distress and carries potential stigmatization (Bergero et al., 2004; Gómez-Gil, Esteva, & Bergero, 2006; Hoshiai, Matsumoto, & Sato, 2009; Terada, Matsumoto, Sato et al., 2011; 2012).

Recent literature suggests that people who are not in accordance with heteronormative societal values are at risk of victimization during adolescence (Bergero et al., 2008; Gordon & Meyer, 2007; Meyer, 2003; Oswald, Blume, & Marks, 2005), which could lead to a negative/poor psychosocial adjustment in adulthood (e.g.: anxiety disorders, social anxiety, depression, suicidal attempts, substance misuse) (D'Augelli, Grossman, & Starks, 2006; Pilkington & D'Augelli, 1995; Toomey, Ryan, Diaz et al., 2010), parental and peer rejection (Landolt, Bartholomew, Saffrey et al., 2004), and as individuals are expected to assume the roles and characteristics socially associated and accepted within their respective biological sex (Lombardi et al., 2001; D'Augelli, Grossman, & Starks, 2006). Lesbians, Gays, Bisexuals and Transgenders (LGBT) and gender-nonconforming youths have an increased risk of experiencing victimization (O'Saughnessy et al., 2004; Kosciw, Diaz, & Greytak, 2008), which normally starts before the age of 18 (the average age is 13 years) (D'Augelli, Grossman, & Starks, 2006). School is reported to be the placement of the first physical victimization experience, more so than home or within the community (D'Augelli et al., 2006). Another recent study found that at school, nearly two thirds of gender nonconforming youths reported verbal harassment and nearly one third were exposed to physical violence (Kosciw et al., 2008; Toomey et al., 2010).

The lack of social knowledge regarding this problem including social stereotypes produce discriminatory attitudes, harassment and exclusion in different areas, such as, for example, at school and in the workplace (Kosciw et al., 2008; Terada et al., 2012; Toomey et al., 2010). An important part of the transsexuals' suffering is in part related to the refusal perceived by society, oppression and discrimination (Bergero et al., 2008). As reported by Lombardi et al., over half of transgenders individuals experience some form of harassment or violence within their lifetime (Lombardi et al., 2001).

Drug use/abuse and alcohol consumption has a higher prevalence in the LBGT collective when compared to the general population (Marshal et al., 2008). Within the transsexual population, disorders relating to substance use/abuse and/or dependence are frequent, at 16%, it is the third most common morbidity in this group, behind anxiety related disorders (18.6%) and major depression (17.4%) (Haraldsen & Dahl, 2000).

In several studies, a significant and positive relation was found between substance use in adult life and the exposure to violence at home also related to aggressive behavior in children and adolescents in the general population (e.g. Baldry, 2003; Calvete, 2007), both reactive and proactive (e.g., Orue & Calvete, 2010). Research shows that various forms of early adversity, including violence, can carry long-term developmental consequences for children and their relation to substance misuse (Herrenkohl, Hong, Bart et al., 2013). However there is little information on the effect of violence in different settings and their effects on consumption patterns and type of substance.

With this work we aim to study if there is a relation between exposure in different contexts (neighborhood, school and home) to violence during childhood and adolescence and substance misuse in adulthood in a group of transsexuals attended by the Transsexuality and Gender Identity Unit (TGIU).

METHODOLOGY

Participants

Descriptive study with 209 patients (M = 28.01; SD = 9.45; Range 13-56 years): 109 in the male-to-female group (MtF) (M = 28.96; SD = 10.99; Range 14-56) and 100 in the female-to-male group (FtM) (M = 26.98; SD = 7.34; Range 13-48). Patients diagnosed of Transsexualism (F64), based on the ICD-10 diagnostic criteria that did not meet any of the exclusion criteria (presenting a basal psychotic disorder or a severe personality disorder) were selected from patients attending the TGIU.

Instruments

Sociodemographic Structured Questionnaire: with other sociodemographic varialbles, substance use was considered (Cannabis, Cocaine and Designer Drugs). Each participant was asked about substance use and consumption, both in the past ("lifetime consumer") and if they currently consumed ("active consumer") (Bergero et al., 2004). This interview was developed by the Unit and designed to be used during the psychological evaluation phase.

Exposure to violence questionnaire (EVQ) [Cuestionario de exposición a la violencia], Elaborate for Orue and Calvete, and validated for the Spanish-scholar population (Orue & Calvete, 2010). This questionnaire consists of 21 items that explore exposure to violence during childhood and adolescence, where 9 items evaluate direct exposure or victimization and 12 items indirect exposure in four different contexts (school, neighborhood, home and television). We used only direct scores.

Procedure

In order to confirm the diagnosis, prior to initiating hormonal therapy controlled by the Endocrinology Service, data was received during the psychological diagnostic evaluation phase of the gender reassignment process, either by individual or family interviews on a monthly basis. The protocol was approved by the *GIDSEEN group* (Moreno-Pérez et al., 2012) following the International Standards of Care (SOC) guidelines as proposed by the *World Professional Association for Transgender Health* (WPATH, former *Harry Benjamin International Gender Dysphoria Association*, HBIGDA) (SOC, 7th edition). Patients that requested sex reassignment were attended and followed at the outpatient Transsexuality and Gender Identity Unit (TGIU), included within the Andalusian Public Healthcare System (located at the General University Hospital, in Malaga). This unit is a National Reference Centre for Transsexuals since the service started its activity in 1999 (Consejería de Salud, Junta de Andalucía, 1999; Gómez-Gil et al., 2011). All patients gave their informed consent for the study (approved by the Hospital Ethics Committee). Parents also had to give their informed consent for the participation of minors in the study.

The patients were evaluated and data were analyzed according to substance use (*cannabis*, cocaine, design drugs, excluding tobacco and alcohol) and the consumption pattern (current and past). Groups were formed accounting for each drug independently. First, active consumers were compared with those who were not current consumers. Later, a second analysis was performed, where two groups were analysed for each substance, comparing those who had been past consumers and those who had never consumed (excluding active consumers). Results were compared to scores obtained by the EVQ questionnaire. An in depth analysis regarding the different subscales of the questionnaire and its relation to substance use was also carried out.

Statistical Analyses

The Shapiro-Wilks test was used to confirm a normal distribution for the data of direct violence suffered in childhood and adolescence. When data did not adjust to normality, the

Mann-Whitney non parametric and the Kruskal-Wallis tests were used to compare two and three groups, including new variables such as age and educational level, respectively.

Finally, a multiple logistic regression analysis was conducted using those variables giving significant results in the bivariate analysis, in order to study confounding factors (sex and educational status) related to exposure to early life violence and substance abuse. Statistical analysis was performed using R version 3.0.2 and R commander version 2.0-0 for Windows. The confidence level was adjusted at 95%.

RESULTS

In order to study the relation between violence and substance use in transgenders we performed analysis of the recorded data. The average scores for perceived violence were higher for violence suffered at school ($M = 5.13$ $SD = 3.38$), followed by violence in the neighborhood ($M = 4.52$ $SD = 3.20$) and violence at home ($M = 3.04$ $SD = 3.52$) (Total score: $M = 12.68$ $SD = 7.89$).

The results of the sociodemographic aspects and its violence relation are shown in Table 1. Gender was related with higher violence in the total score and in the school score, being the MtF group the most affected. The education level was negatively associated with the total score of violence exposure, mainly in the neighborhood and at school.

Table 1. Socio-demographic variables

Socio-demographic/Violence(Mean)	Total Violence (Mean)	Violence in neighborhood (Mean)	Violence at School (Mean)	Violence at Home (Mean)
Age (N)				
<24 (76)	12.44	4.35	5.22	2.56
24-35 (93)	13.61	4.83	5.51	3.25
>35 (40)	11.5	4.07	4.05	3.42
Biological Sex				
Male (109)	14.01*	4.93	5.79**	3.29
Female (100)	11.23	4.04	4.41	2.76
Nationality				
Spanish (192)	12.62	4.47	5.14	3.01
Non Spanish (17)	13.35	5	5	3.35
Education				
Elementary	15.58*	5.54*	5.88*	4.16
Secondary	12.14	4.36	5.09	2.67
University	10	3.46	3.84	2.68
Civil Status				
Married or couple	12.67	4.34	5.21	3.10
Single	12.78	4.61	5.10	3.05
Employment				
Unemployed (69)	13.29	4.77	5.40	3.11
Employed (140)	12.38	4.39	4.99	3

*p<0.05.

**p<0.01.

Table 2. Relation between scores in EVQ and substance consumption

Substance Use/Violence	Total Violence EVQ (Mean)	Violence in neighborhood (Mean)	Violence at School (Mean)	Violence at Home (Mean)
Cannabis Actual (Yes N=33/No N=176)	14.36/12.36	4.96/4.43	5.57/5.04	3.81/2.89
Cannabis Lifetime (Yes N=41/No N=135)	14.12/11.83	5.41/4.13*	5.07/5.04	3.63/2.66
Cocaine Actual(Yes N=6/No N=203)	20.06 /12.46	6.83/4.44	6.83/5.07	6.5/2.93*
Cocaine Lifetime (Yes N=26/No N=177)	17.92/11.66**	6/4.22**	5.92/4.95	6/2.48**
Design Drugs Lifetime (Yes N=9/No N=200)	16.70/12.50	5.77/4.46	4.88/5.14	6.11/2.90**

*p<0.05.
**p<0.01.
EVQ: Exposure to violence questionnaire.

Table 3. Adjusted OR for Sex and educational level

Independent V.	Adjusted OR	Wald	P Value	Dependent V.
Violence in Neighborhood	1.15	5.50	<0.05	Cannabis Lifetime
Violence at Home	1.19	2.68	0.10	Cocaine Actual
Violence Total	1.11	12.60	<0.01	Cocaine Lifetime
Violence in Neighborhood	1.19	6.32	<0.05	Cocaine Lifetime
Violence at Home	1.28	17.47	<0.01	Cocaine Lifetime
Violence at Home	1.30	7.45	<0.01	Designer Drugs Lifetime

OR: Odds Ratios. V: Variable.

As resumed in Table 2, the average score of the EVQ questionnaire (violence in the neighborhood) was significantly higher for those who had consumed lifetime cannabis compared to those who hadn't (p < 0.05). Differences were not observed between those who were active cannabis consumers. The average EVQ score in those who had consumed lifetime cocaine was statistically superior to those who hadn't ($p < 0.01$), specifically violence in the neighborhood and at home. Also the difference was statistically significant when we measured active consumption of cocaine in violence at home ($p < 0.05$). The differences between lifetime consumers and non-consumers of designer drugs were significantly higher respective to violence at home ($p < 0.01$).

In the logistic regression analysis the variables remained significantly related, except for exposure to violence at home and current cocaine consumption (Table 3).

DISCUSSION

This study was conducted in order to ascertain if there is a relationship between exposure to early life violence in different contexts (neighborhood, school and home) and substance misuse in the transsexual population. The study shows an association between exposure to violence in childhood and *cannabis* use and, especially, with current and past consumption of cocaine. Violence experienced during childhood and adolescence seems to have an impact on the misuse of substances in adulthood. A growing body of research has exposed discrimination and violence victimization targeted toward gender nonconformity and its possible mental and physical health problems. Gender was related with the level of exposure to violence during childhood and adolescence, being the female transgender (MtF) the group with higher scores for exposure to violence at school, according to other published studies (D'Augelli et al., 2006). In general, this group faced more harassment from their peers and perceived their schools as more dangerous compared with the FtM group (Kosciw, Diaz, & Greytak, 2008), starting at a younger age than FtM transgender youths (Grossman, D'Augelli, Salter, & Hubbard, 2005).

We also observed that the level of education is negatively related with experienced levels of violence, suggesting that those who have experienced violence may have more risk of educational difficulties (reducing educational attainment by increasing the risk of school dropout) and are caused either directly or through indirect mechanisms or otherwise related with the presence of a more favorable social environment or better personal adaptive resources (Baldry et al., 2003; Kosciw et al., 2008; O'Shaughnessy et al., 2004).

Although data were not significantly different, there seems to be a slight tendency to suffer higher levels of violence at home at a greater age, whereas the opposite occurs regarding to exposure to violence at school. This could be a consequence of a high collective visibility and major social acceptance; it paradoxically contributes to an early exposure to bullying, although a reduction in violence at home is also observed.

Although further studies should be considered, we didn´t find a significant relation between the EVQ subscale values in violence experienced at school with substance use. Our analyses suggested that exposure to violence at home (or perpetrated by a family member or relative) has a significant correlation to substance use (results observed for present and past use of cocaine and design drugs). This conclusion is in accordance with similar works studying exposure to interparental violence and its positive association with bullying and victimization in school, as violence within the family may have detrimental effects on the adolescent's or child's behavior (Baldry et al., 2003; D'Augelli et al., 2005; 2006; Grossman et al., 2005; Pilkington & D'Augelli, 1995; Calvete, 2007; Orue & Calvete, 2010).

It appears that exposure to violence at an early age is significantly related with cocaine consumption and to a lesser extent, with cannabis use, perhaps because cannabis is more widespread , more frequently consumed and socially accepted. On the other hand, the existence of a smaller relation within active consumers compared to past consumers suggests the possible presence of other aspects that may influence current consumption, so further studies should be considered in this population to assess risk and factors related to consumption.

From this work, various clinical implications can be assessed. It is important to develop preventive and active interventions that attend to early exposure to violence and its consequences on mental health and psychosocial adjustment in transsexuals, preferably carried out at specific clinical units (Bergero et al. 2004; Gómez-Gil et al., 2011; HBIGDA, 2011). As clinicians, we should be able to recognize the importance of violence experienced during childhood and adolescence, the prejudice associated with gender nonconformity and integrate this aspect within the evaluation and treatment of addictions in those with gender dysphoria.

These results should be considered in light of the limitations faced by this study. First, the cross-sectional nature of the design doesn't allow for the realization of causal relationships. Second, the sample may not be representative of the entire transsexual population. Third, at present, there is no specific questionnaire to study exposure to violence during childhood and adolescence in the Spanish transsexual population and the adaptation to this particular population may be burdened by limitations. This questionnaire was used as it analyzes victimization and exposure to discrimination and harassment situations in various settings. Fourth, consider the reliance on subjective appraisal of discrimination and self-report. Finally, minority group members often tend to minimize discrimination (either of perception or articulation) to protect their self-esteem from vulnerability and against both recrimination and reinforcement of social and natural cultural stereotypes.

This study provides empirical data regarding the relation between exposure to violence during childhood and adolescence and major substance use, and is especially significant when originating within the family environment. In addition, a differential pattern seems to appear depending on the substance studied, especially for cocaine and designer drug consumption being associated with violence at home, however cannabis use is associated with violence in the neighborhood.

ACKNOWLEDGMENTS

We would like to acknowledge the cooperation of all the participants in this study as well as to all members of the TGIU. The authors wish to thank David W.E. Ramsden for valuable assistance correcting the English version of the manuscript, and also the technical assistance of L. Sanchez. Part of this work was presented at the III International Congress of Dual Pathology. Addictions and other mental disorders (23-26 October, 2013; in Barcelona).

FUNDING

This study is part of an ongoing project initiated in the year 2000: "Transsexualism in Andalusia: psychiatric, endocrinological and surgical morbidity and evaluation of the therapeutic intervention process: experiences of the first reference Unit in Spain"

This study was supported by Projects PI01-0447 and PI06-1339, funded by the Carlos III Health Institute. Ministry of Health, Social Affairs and Equality, Spain. Project PI07-0157 was funded by the Ministry of Health and CTS546 by the Ministry of Innovation of the Andalusian Regional Government, Spain. YDDO is recipient of a 'Nicolas Monarde' contract from the 'Servicio Andaluz de Salud. Consejeria de Salud. Junta de Andalucia'

DISCLOSURES

The authors declare that there are no conflicts of interest.

REFERENCES

American Psychiatric Association (2000). *Diagnostic and Statistical Manual of Mental Disorders IV-TR (Fourth ed. revised).* American Psychiatric Publishing. Washington, DC

American Psychiatric Association (2013). *Diagnostic and Statistical Manual of Mental Disorders - V (Fifth ed.).* American Psychiatric Publishing. Arlington, VA

Baldry, A. C. (2003). Bullying in schools and exposure to domestic violence. *Child Abuse & Neglect, 27,* 713–732. doi:10.1016/S0145-2134(03)00114-5

Bergero, T., Asiain, S., Gorneman, I., Giraldo, F., Lara, J., Esteva, I. & Gómez, M. (2008). Una reflexión sobre el concepto de género alrededor de la transexualidad. *Revista de la AEN, , 101,* 211–226.

Bergero, T., Cano, G. et al. (2004). La transexualidad: asistencia multidisciplinar en el sistema público. *Revista de la AEN, 90,* 28–38.

Calvete, E. (2007). Justification of violence beliefs and social problem-solving as mediators between maltreatment and behavior problems in adolescents. *Spanish Journal of Psychology, 10,* 131–140.

Consejería de Salud, Junta de Andalucía (1999). *Informe preliminar. Problemática de salud ligada a la transexualidad en Andalucía. Posibilidades de abordaje e inclusión entre las prestaciones del sistema sanitario público de Andalucía.*

D'Augelli, A. R., Grossman, A. H., & Starks, M. T. (2005). Parents' awareness of lesbian, gay, and bisexual youths' sexual orientation. *Journal of Marriage & Family, 67,* 474–482.

D'Augelli, A. R., Grossman, A. H., & Starks, M. T. (2006). Childhood gender atypicality, victimization, and PTSD among lesbian, gay and bisexual youth. *Journal of Interpersonal Violence, 21,* 62–82.

Gómez-Gil, E., Esteva, I., Almaraz, M. C., Godás, T., Halperin, I., & Soriguer, F. (2011). Demanda de atención sanitaria en las Unidades de Identidad de Género de Andalucía y Cataluña durante la década 2000 a 2009. *Revista Clinica Española, 211,* 233–239. doi:10.1016/j.gaceta.2011.10.021

Gómez-Gil, E., Esteva, I., & Bergero, T. (2006). La transexualidad, transexualismo o trastorno de la identidad de género en el adulto: Concepto y características básicas. *C. Medicina Psicosomatica, 78,* 7–12.

Gordon, A. R., & Meyer, I. H. (2007). Gender nonconformity as a target of prejudice, discrimination, and violence against LGB individuals. *LGBT Health Res. 3(3),* 55–71.

Grossman, A. H., D'Augelli, A. R., Salter, N. P., & Hubbard S. M. (2005). Comparing gender expression, gender nonconformity, and parents' responses of female-to-male and male-to-female Transgender youth: Implications for counseling. *Journal of LGBT Issues in Counseling, 1,* 41–59.

Haraldsen, I. R., & Dahl, A. (2000). Symptom profiles of gender dysphoric patients of transsexual type compared to patients with personality disorders and healthy adults. *Acta psychiatrica Scandinavica, 102(4),* 276–81.

Herrenkohl, T., Hong, S., Bart, J., Herrenkohl, R., & Jean, M. (2013). Developlmental impacts of child abuse and neglect related to adult mental health, substance use, and physical health. *Journal of Family Violence, 28(2).* doi:10.1007/s10896-012-9474-9

Hoshiai, M., Matsumoto, Y., Sato, T., Ohnishi, M., Okabe, N., Kishimoto, Y., Terada, S., & Kuroda, S. (2010). Psychiatric comorbidity among patients with gender identity disorder. *Psychiatric and Clinical Neurosciences, 64,* 514–519.

Kosciw, J. G., Diaz, E. M., & Greytak, E. A. (2008). *The 2007 national school climate survey: the experiences of lesbian, gay, bisexual and transgender youth in our nation's schools.* New York, NY: Gay, Lesbian and Straight Education Network

Landolt, M. A., Bartholomew, K., Saffrey, C., Oram, D., & Perlman, D. (2004). Gender nonconformity, childhood rejection, and adult attachment: a study of gay men. *Archives of Sexual Behaviour, 33(2),*117–128.

Lombardi, E. L., Wilchins, R. A., Priesing, D., & Malouf, D. (2001). Gender violence: transgender experiences with violence and discrimination. *Journal of Homosexuality. 42(1),* 89–101.

Marshal, M. P., Friedman, M. S., Stall, R., King, K. M., Miles, J., Gold, M. A., Bukstein, O. G., & Morse, J. Q. (2008). Sexual orientation and adolescent substance use: a meta-analysis and methodological review. *Addiction, 103(4),* 546–556. doi:10.1111/j.1360-0443.2008.02149.x.

Meyer, I. H. (2003). Prejudice, social stress, and mental health in lesbian, gay and bisexual populations: Conceptual issues and research evidence. *Psychological Bulletin, 129,* 674–697.

Moreno-Pérez, O., Esteva, I., Grupo de Identidad y Diferenciación Sexual de la SEEN (GIDSEEN) (2012). Clinical practice guidelines for assessment and treatment of transsexualism. SEEN Identity and Sexual Differentiation Group (GIDSEEN). *Endocrinologia y Nutrición. 59(6),* 367–82. doi: 10.1016/j.endonu.2012.02.001. Epub 2012 Apr 26.

Orue, I., & Calvete, E. (2010). Development and validation of a questionnaire to measure exposure to violence. *International Journal of Psychology and Psychological Therapy, 10(2),* 279–292.

O'Shaughnessy, M., Russel, S., Heck, K., Calhoun, C., & Laub, C. (2004). *Safe place to learn: consequences of harassment based on actual or perceived sexual orientation and gender non-conformity and steps for making school safer.* San Francisco, CA: California Safe Schools Coalition.

Oswald, R. F., Blume, L. B., & Marks, S. R. (2005). Decentering heteronormativity: A model for family studies. In V.L. Bengston, A.C. Acock, K.R. Allen, P. Dilworth-Anderson, and D.M. Klein (Eds.), *Sourcebook of family theory and research*, 143–165.

Pilkington, N. W., & D'Augelli, A. R. (1995). Victimization of lesbian, gay and bisexual youth in community settings. *Journal of Community Psychology, 23,* 34–56.

The Harry Benjamin International Gender Dysphoria Association (HBIGDA) (2011). *The Standards of Care for Gender Identity Disorders. (Seventh version).*

Terada, S., Matsumoto, Y., Sato, T., Okabe, N., Kishimoto, Y., & Uchitomi, Y. (2011). Suicidal ideation among patients with gender identity disorder. *Psychiatry Research, 190,* 159–162. doi: 10.1016/j.psychres.2011.04.024

Terada, S., Matsumoto, Y., Sato, T., Okabe, N., Kishimoto, Y., & Uchitomi, Y. (2012). School refusal by patients with gender identity disorder. *General Hospital Psychiatry, 34,* 299–303. doi: 10.1016/j.genhosppsych.2011.11.008

Toomey, R. B., Ryan, C., Diaz, R. M., Card, N. A., & Russel, S. T. (2010). Gender-Nonconforming Lesbian, Gay, Bisexual and Transgender Youth: School Victimization and Young adult Psychosocial Adjustment. *Developmental Psychology*. Advance online publication. doi: 10.1037/a0020705

World Health Organization (1992). *International Classification of Diseases (ICD-10): Classification of Mental and Behavioural Disorders, Diagnostic criteria for research.*

In: Gender Identity
Editor: Beverly L. Miller

ISBN: 978-1-63321-488-0
© 2014 Nova Science Publishers, Inc.

Chapter 12

REPRESENTATIONS OF TEACHERS ABOUT THE RELATION BETWEEN PHYSICAL EDUCATION CONTENTS AND GENDER IDENTITIES

Fabiano Pries Devide, Juliana Pelluso Fernandes da Cunha and Sebastião Josué Votre*

[1]PhD in Physical Education and Culture,
researcher on Gender Studies in Sport and Physical Education.
Teacher at Fluminense Federal University, Rio de Janeiro, Brazil
[2]Graduated in Physical Education by Fluminense Federal University,
Rio de Janeiro, Brazil. FAPERJ sponsorship for scientific initiation
[3]PhD in Linguistics, researcher on language and gender.
Teacher at Fluminense Federal University, Rio de Janeiro, Brazil

ABSTRACT

This study aims to investigate how Physical Education (P.E.) teachers of elementary/middle schools from Municipal Education Foundation of Niterói (FME) represent the relationship between course content and the construction of gender identities. The study was developed in three stages: i) document research on the FME Curriculum; ii) a structured questionnaire with all 55 P.E. teachers from FME-Niterói to analyze their professional profiles; iii) ten structured interviews with teachers who have five or more years of experience in teaching P.E. in elementary/middle school. After documental analysis, general questions of gender were identified in the P.E. Curriculum of FME, leading us to the conclusion that FME teachers should be knowledgeable about this subject. Literature Research on the subject of gender was completed about gender identities, co-education and course content. The group of teachers interviewed was composed of 59% women, and 41% men, and the average age was 40 years old. Most of them (86%) were born in Rio de Janeiro. Regarding their higher education background, 79% came from public universities and 24% from private institutions. The average time experience teaching P.E. was 14 years. All teachers work in public schools, and four of

---

* e-mail: fabianodevide@uol.com.br.

them also teach in private schools. The Content Analysis of interviews resulted in six categories: "misunderstanding about the concept of gender identity"; "teacher's program versus FME curriculum"; "students' resistance to mixed gender classes"; "lack of knowledge about Co-Education"; "sports as a factor for gender exclusion"; and "course content and identity". We concluded that most of the teachers don't know concepts about gender and Co-education, and don't follow the learning objectives related to the gender issues presented in the curriculum orientation of FME. The teachers interviewed have a tendency to teach the P.E. content in a gendered way, reproducing gender stereotypes and/or separating students by gender during the class activities. We believe that P.E. class is a moment of learning relevant questions related to diversity and gender, creating a sense of inclusion for every student. Teachers need to select their content that encourages gender-related discussions, allowing students to question their gender representations. In this way, they could recreate themselves in a non-stereotypical way, being free to construct their identities and participate in any activities in P.E. classes. To achieve this objective, teachers must be better prepared by the universities to face this important question. Unfortunately, in Brazil, universities rarely or poorly discuss gender topics in P.E. undergraduate courses.

Keywords: Physical Education, Gender, Contents, Social Representations

INTRODUCTION AND METHODOLOGICAL DECISIONS

Physical Education classes that present gendered content can create conflicts between students of opposite sexes and influence the formation of roles[1] related to the gender identities of these learners. (Altmann, 1998; Saraiva, 1999; Sayão, 2001, 2002). Such roles are reinforced by teachers with a pedagogical approach that describes a sexist criteria in the selelction of course content and design of class activities with students separated by gender. (Abreu, 1995; Louzada De Jesus, Votre, Devide, 2007; 2008).

Being a man or a woman does not necessarily mean to be feminine or masculine. Gender identities are changeable and flexible as they relate to how individuals identify themselves with their actions and behaviors, which are shaped by culture and defined as sexual identity (Louro, 2001)[2]. Children internalize sexist patterns about what boys and girls should do for fun, as boys play with cars and wear the color blue and girls play with dolls and dress up in pink. Those who don't fit in to these standards are crossing a boundary of gender and are considered different. They are kept under watch by family members and school staff because their identity is considered "deviant" from the norm usually associated with the heterosexist model.

> "The affirmation of identity always implies the demarcation and the denial of its opposite, which is constituted as different. This "difference", however, remains indispensable. The identity denied constitutes the individual and provides consistency and limits at the same time, but creating instability" (Louro, 2008, p. 45).

---

[1] Roles are interpreted as patterns or rules imposed arbitrarily by society as suitable and appropriate behaviors in men and women (Louro, Felipe, Goellner, 2010). 3 We understand as coed classes the lectures where male and female students share the same space without necessarily interacting. Therefore, gender issues are not questioned, reinforcing the gender inequalities (Louzada De Jesus, 2006).

[2] Sexual identities are associated with the desires and pleasures that the individual directs to the opposite sex, at the same sex or towards both sexes, differing from gender identity (Goellner, 2001).

Men have historically been regarded as naturally stronger, agile, skillful and violent; women have been viewed as delicate, fragile and less skilled (Devide, 2005). During Physical education classes in schools these differences become evident when girls participate less in coed classes[3], feeling excluded by the boys because they posses less strength and motor skills to play. However, the exclusion in PE classes does not happen only by gender, but by a "tangle of exclusions", such as age, strength and skill, which in the case of girls maybe due to the lack of motor experiences during childhood and adolescence (Altmann, 2002). Thus, girls are not the only ones being excluded; some boys also experience situations of exclusion because they are less skilled, shorter, younger and/or weaker (Souza, Altmann, 1999). Therefore, even when the classes are separated by gender there is still exclusion and differences[4] between the students according to research conducted by Devide et al. (2010), especially amongst girls where friendship ties can become the main factors for exclusion from games and activities.

Therefore, "gender" is just another criterion for exclusion in Physical Education classes. For example, soccer in Brazil tends to be labeled as a masculine game, because of the contact, motor skills and behaviors that are associated with this sport and constitute the norm (Faria Júnior, 1995). Therefore, girls who are skilled in soccer tend to be discriminated and have their sexual identity questioned constantly because the way they play the game is compatible with masculine identity.

According to Robert Connell (1995), masculinity is complex and appears permeated by power relations. The author states that there exist different forms of masculinity within the same social context; there is a hegemonic form of masculinity and other marginal forms of expressing masculinities, creating exclusions between groups of boys in P.E Classes.

When a child arrives at schools and Educational institutions, gender differences tend to be reinforced, because besides the classroom content we also learn how to behave as men and women and follow the roles that are imposed on us by society. While the school reinforces the heterosexist norm, it suppresses sexuality as an important topic in the educational field:

> "Those students who dare to express their sexuality more clearly become immediate targets of increased adult supervision and are "labeled" as individuals that deviate from the expected norm, by adopting attitudes or behaviors that are not consistent with the school environment"(Louro, 2001, p. 26).

This way, the school is characterized as a place where there are clear limits in expressing and discussing sexuality. It is a subject approached very timidly only covering topics such as sexually transmitted diseases, teen pregnancy, contraceptive methods, abortion, AIDS, and the biological and psychological changes of adolescence (Navarro, 2006).

In the school setting, Physical Education classes are historically an environment where the bodies and personal expressions are more exposed (Louro, 1997), because they normally take place in open spaces, unlike other classes, where the students' bodies are "protected" by

---

[3] We understand as coed classes the lectures where male and female students share the same space without necessarily interacting. Therefore, gender issues are not questioned, reinforcing the gender inequalities (Louzada De Jesus, Devide, 2006).

[4] The processes of student exclusion in non-coeducational classes occurs similarly to what happens in coed classes, the differences in the levels of motor skill being determinants in these processes, because students have difficulties in dealing with this aspect (Devide et al, 2010).

tables, chairs and walls. In these classes, the virility of boys and the desire to show that they are superior (as males), becomes evident not only in relation to girls, but also in relation to boys who are weaker and less skilled (Bourdieu, 1998).

When a boy shows no interest in activities that are considered masculine he also becomes excluded and discriminated against by other students. In Brazil "playing soccer is very much considered a 'must' for any boy who is 'normal' and 'healthy'" (Louro, 1997, p 75.); In England rugby is part of the ritual in constructing manhood for boys (Dunning, 1992; Messner, 1992). The same scenario happens with girls who are interested in sports and activities that are considered masculine, instead of rhythmic-expressive activities, such as dance. These youngsters who cross the borders of their gender are considered "out of the ordinary (...), ultimately analyzed as exceptions." (Silva, 2004, p. 86).

Among the problems faced by male and female students who experience discrimination because of gender identity and/or homophobia[5] identified within the school are symbolic violence (Bourdieu, 1998) and physical aggression. Another recurring problem is homophobic bullying[6] (Pecanha, Devide, 2010), when boys and girls are discriminated against because of their sexual identity or gender identity and are considered deviant from the norm. They are victims of prejudiced nicknames as well as gestural and verbal aggression, which leads to uneasiness and discomfort and could result in emotional and social problems. As an example, students who are less skilled in ball games end up being discriminated against by others and nicknamed "sissy" and/or "little girl", because playing sports is an important element in the process of socialization and construction of masculine identity (Messner, 1992; Figueiredo Da Silva, Devide, 2009). Similarly, girls who exhibit skills in sports or activities that are stereotyped as masculine are considered manly and are also labeled as "lesbians".

Gender identities are not fixed, in fact, they are under construction throughout the socialization process of the individuals. Therefore, students cannot abandon their identities when they enter the walls of the school or participate in P.E classes. The school cannot be omitted as part of the construction process of affirmative identities of its students and must stand against discriminatory practices and prejudices.

Considering this problem, it is important to investigate how Physical Education teachers find ways to relate gender identities to the content of their classes. Teachers must reconsider their pedagogical practice and provide students with the opportunity to discuss this topic while promoting a greater understanding by respecting these differences, whether related to gender or sexual identity, to aesthetic patterns, cultural or social standards (Cruz, Palmeira, 2009).

The Course content is a set of knowledge, customs, values, social activities, organized and planned didactically and pedagogically (Libâneo, 1994). Such knowledge must be available to all students and point to a broader, more critical approach to education and take into consideration the cultural background of the individuals, regardless of gender. Darido (2012) adds that this knowledge must be used to working in teams, to show solidarity towards

---

[5] For the purpose of this study, we interpret homophobia as a prejudice against homosexuals, characterized by an unreasonable fear or hatred of this group (Nunan, 2003).

[6] Phenomenon characterized by cruel behavior where weaker, younger and less powerful individuals become objects of pleasure and enjoyment by acts of mockery and ridicule created by a stronger, older, more powerful set of individuals where the victims are intimidated and become excluded from their social groups (Oliveira, Votre, 2006).

colleagues, respect and value the work of others and never discriminate against people based on gender, age or other individual characteristics.

The elements of a Culture based on physical activity taught in P.E classes should relate to the socio-cultural reality these students come from, allowing them to make a critical analysis about what the P.E Classes propose and its relation to the real world (Coletivo De Autores, 1992). In this respect, although permeated by critics (CBCE, 1997) the document of the National Curriculum Guidelines also mentions combating sex discrimination, noting that students must:

> "Participate in physical activities establishing balanced and constructive relationships with others by recognizing and respecting physical characteristics, without judgment of performance and never discriminating on personal, physical, sexual or social characteristics" (Brazil 1997, p. 33).

However, despite these guidelines teachers face resistance from students when teaching content that is considered masculine or feminine such as team sports: football, volleyball, handball for females; and rhythmic and expressive activities: dancing and gymnastics for males. This labeling of activities by sex reproduces gender stereotypes in P.E. classes and contributes to a deficiency in the organization and execution of course content. It also perpetuates prejudices particularly when teachers separate male and female students in PE classes. These lesson formats meet the expectations of teachers and students: students classify same-sex classes as more homogeneous, less violent, stimulating positive socialization and greater participation with greater emphasis on the motor performance. At the same time, for teachers the justification is that this type of class is "easier", specifically with the girls, because they are less skilled. (Louzada De Jesus, Devide, 2006).

Given the problems in the scenario of Physical Education classes in Brazil, the *general objective* of this research is to investigate how elementary/middle school P.E. teachers establish the relationship between course content and the construction of gender identities. The *specific objectives* of the study are: i) reflect on the teachers representations and the relationship between course content and gender identity in P.E.; ii) investigate the knowledge of teachers about gender and coeducation; and iii) identify how teachers deal with gender conflicts that are motivated by discrimination of students in relation to the course content.

The study has a qualitative, exploratory and documentary design (Minayo, 2000; Thomas; Nelson, 2002; Richardson, 2009). We seek to answer questions related to the significance, value, direction and beliefs about our object of study: the representations of teachers about the relationship between teaching content and gender identities in P.E. classes. This research is exploratory because it looks within the field for data from a percentage of "generic individuals" (Spink, 1995), who are the spokespeople for a group of teachers from Municipal Education Foundation of Niterói (FME-Niterói). It is a documentary research because it examines the Curriculum frameworks of FME/Niterói (Niterói, 2010).

The research was conducted at FME/Niterói, in the State of Rio de Janeiro, and it was organized in three stages. First we visited the FME/Niterói, in order to meet with the Director of the Physical Education department and gain access to the documents including "Curriculum frameworks" for P.E. (Niterói, 2010), with the intent to analyse the presence or absence of discussion on gender issues in PE content. The second stage of the study was a structured questionnaire administered to 55 P.E. teachers enrolled in FME/Niterói, with the objective of tracing a professional profile of the group. Finally in the third stage, we selected ten teachers who have acquired five or more years of experience lecturing P.E., constituting a group of ten interviews. The exact number of interviewees[7] was reached by following the research saturation criterion in order to complete the data collection (Alves-Mazzotti, 2002).

The study used a structured interview script, validated by Ramos (2012), when applied to a similar group during research on the same subject matter. We understand that this instrument for data collection facilitates the interviewer-interviewee dialogue in order to interpret a given reality and describe the phenomena investigated when approaching complex issues. The interview method provides a sense of freedom to the interviewee in answering the questions, helping us meet the goals established for the research (Duarte, 2008; Richardson, 2009).

The Data collection procedure began by scheduling the interviews. The time and locations were determined by the teachers from the schools surveyed. At the start of each interview, the researcher requested permission to record the interviewee for the purpose of later transcription and analysis. They signed a term of consent and freedom of research (TCLE), authorizing the use of the data for academic[8] purposes.

For analysis and interpretation of data, the theoretical and methodological frameworks of Content Analysis (CA) (Bardin, 2008) was utilized and the Gender Studies (SCOTT, 1995, 2005; Faria Júnior, 1995; Altmann, 1998; Bourdieu, 1998; Souza, Altmann, 1999; Louro, 2001, 2008; Butler, 2003; Silva, 2004; Gomes, Silva, QUEIRÓS, 2004; Devide, 2005; Louzada De Jesus, Votre, Devide, 2007; Ferretti, Knijnik, 2007; Goellner, 2008; Uchoga, 2010) were used.

The CA is a set of techniques that investigates communication. It is a research technique that through objective and systematic description of the content of the responses and looks to interpret them through inferences about the messages (Bardin, 2008; Richardson, 2009). The taxonomic method builds categories that order and organize the material in different stages: pre-analysis, material exploration, treatment results, inference and interpretation.

In the *pre-analysis* stage the documents that are going to be analyzed are organized and systematized, in this particular research being represented by the "Curriculum Frameworks" of FME/Niterói (Niterói, 2010) and the responses from the ten interviews. In this phase there is a scanning of the material to establish a first contact and formulate the hypotheses, objectives and indicators that underpin the interpretation of the same. In the *material exploration* phase, the data is encoded to reach the full comprehension of the text based on their discursive marks meaning those recurring characteristics in the group's responses. In the *interpretation* phase, there is a classification of each of the samples according to their similarities or differences followed by a categorization[9] of the samples (Bardin, 2008).

---

[7] 55 questionnaires were distributed to P.E. teachers who taught classes at different poles of FME / Niterói, in order to guarantee the representativeness of the group. 29 informants (55%) returned the questionnaires, and after we mapped out the group we found that 93.1% of the teachers had five or more years of experience in teaching P.E in basic education. In this sense, by lottery, we selected 10 of those teachers.

[8] Each informant was contacted to clarify the objectives of the study and guaranteed the assurance of information, confidentiality as well as privacy and identity, with the formal consent of the participants.

[9] To Bardin (2008) a set of categories must obey the criteria for mutual exclusion (each element cannot exist in more than one category); homogeneity (a single principle of classification should direct your organization); pertinence (must be adapted to the content of analysis , reflecting the objectives of the study); objectivity and fidelity (the different parts of a *corpus* should be categorized in the same manner and the criteria for defining the variables and indexes must be the same for all analysts); and productivity (categories should provide productive results related to the objectives of the study).

RESULTS AND DISCUSSION

Analisys of FME Curriculum

The "Curriculum Frameworks" FME/Niterói (2010) document was constructed with the participation of the school community. It operates under the concept of multiculturalism which respects diversity and overcoming prejudice and discrimination of any kind. These principles must be addressed in every aspect of the curriculum, from topics such as gender, sexuality and cultural plurality. This document interprets the curriculum as an instrument of combating different objectives with the intent of building a "School of ideal Citizens and Cultural Diversity" (Niterói, 2010, p. 12).

In this perspective the curriculum of FME/Niterói seeks to integrate plural identities (ethnic racial cultural and others) that make up the school environment giving voice to marginalized identities. It seeks to provide reflections on hegemonic discourses in order to value cultural diversity, introducing male and female students to both familiar and unfamiliar cultures, expanding awareness and fighting prejudice and discrimination.

"The curriculum is seen as a document that brings forth socially and economically marginalized identities and gives them a chance to be heard, which is particularly relevant in the plural context of our schools" (Niterói, 2010, p. 13).

The "Curriculum Frameworks" articulate two different dimensions: *the individual* and *the citizen*. The first dimension addresses work by axels[10] and cycles, composed from the curricular content, oriented by national, state and municipal curricular documents and redesigned in the light of the perspective of the citizen and of diversity. The *citizen* dimension focuses on cultural diversity and includes all axes and cycles, and consists of skills that underlie these contents and impart coherence to the curriculum axis.

It was possible to identify the theme of gender in some integrating components of the "Curriculum Frameworks". Out of the seven components, we identified three that address the issue of gender directly or indirectly, as seen in the following excerpt:

"A) appreciation of cultural, ethnic, racial, linguistic, generational, *gender*, religion, *sexual* and other types of diversity, recognizing their contributions to the enrichment of local, national and global society; B) combating prejudices, discrimination, harassment of any form including violence and intolerance against others, seeking to acknowledge its origins and report its manifestations (...) G) Participate in activities that promote ethical attitudes, cooperation, respect and solidarity towards others" (Niterói, 2010, p. 20-21).

In Physical Education (axis of Languages) the theme is presented directly and indirectly in the objectives of the "Skills/Citizen Practices" theme. Gender appears explicitly in the objective which concerns interaction "with colleagues without stigmatizing or discriminating on physical, social, cultural or gender grounds" (Niterói, 2010, p. 28), which appears in the arrays of the first (1st to 3rd grade) and second cycles (4th and 5th grade) of elementary school, being absent in the third (6 and 7 grade) and fourth cycles (8th and 9th grade).

---

[10] Languages, Time and Space, Sciences and Sustainable Development.

We also identified other objectives where the theme of gender is present indirectly such as respect, cooperation, inclusion and solidarity as well as adopting a non-prejudicial or discriminatory attitude and other objectives present in all cycles as the following passage describes:

> "Develop respectful, cooperative and supportive relationships to one another and incorporate that into their performance in physical activities with the goal of favoring inclusion (G)" (NITERÓI. 2010, p. 28).
> "Respect the physical and moral integrity of the others (B)" (Niterói, 2010, p. 70).

The disappearance of the gender theme in the third and fourth cycles (which is exactly at the age where boys and girls reach puberty, a period where significant changes related to the construction of identities and interests for the content of P.E. lessons occur) allows us to interpret the school as a place where gender relations are usually silenced. This is because they tend to be linked to sexuality, a subject that schools treat as something alien to this universe (Louro, 1997), collaborating to the reproduction and imposition of the heterosexual matrix. Thus, the school is characterized as an institution where the discussion on gender and sexual identities is still scarce.

> "At schools, pedagogy of sexuality is encouraged that legitimizes certain sexual identities and practices and suppresses and marginalizes others by affirmation or by silencing. The same happens in recognized public areas or in private hidden corners" (Louro, 2001. p. 31).

We identify the gender theme as part of the content in the "Curriculum Frameworks" of FME/Niterói, which is also mentioned in the national[11] curriculum documents, cited as reference for the construction of these frameworks. Therefore we assume that all teachers in the public school sector are familiar with this theme. This allows us to infer that the group of interviewees' posses understanding about the relations between gender identities and the course content of Physical Education. Such educational intervention has an important role in combating prejudices and gender stereotypes so that the curricula, through the organization and selection of content, can serve as an instrument of legitimization or disqualification of individuals (Louro, 1997), anchored in physical practices and reproduced in the context of PE classes.

Interviewees' Group Profile

From the structured surveys returned (n=29, 55%), we can infer that the group of teachers from FME-Niterói consists of 17 (58, 6%) women and 12 (41,4%) men. The average age of the teachers is 40,9 years old, 19 (65,5%) are married, 4 (13,8%) are single, 1 (3,4%) is widowed, 3 (10,3%) are divorced and 1 (3,4%) is in a stable relationship. The majority of teachers (n=25, 86,2%) are from the State of Rio de Janeiro. The other teachers are from the

---

[11] National Curricular Parameters (Brasil, 1997).

state of Espírito Santo (n=1, 3,4%), Minas Gerais (n=1 3,4%) e São Paulo (n=1 3,4%). One teacher did not inform his Birth place. The average number of children per teacher is 1.7.

Concerning the teachers educational background, 22 teachers (75, 9%) graduated from public universities and 7 (24, 1%) graduated from private universities. The group presented an average of 14.2 years of experience in teaching PE, meaning that 27 (93.1%) of the 29 teachers have 5 or more years of experience in the field. In addition to teaching in public schools, four teachers also lecture in private schools. Eight teachers have degrees in other areas. Out of 29 teachers, 19 (65.5%) have specialization courses in the field of Physical Education and 3 (10.3%) have a masters degree.

THE DISCOURSE OF PHYSICAL EDUCATION TEACHERS

The Content Analysis (BARDIN, 2008) of the ten interviews resulted in the construction of six categories: "misunderstanding about the concept of gender identity"; "teacher's program versus FME curriculum"; "students' resistance to mixed gender classes"; "lack of knowledge about Co-Education"; "sports as a factor for gender exclusion"; and "course content and identity".

MISUNDERSTANDING ABOUT THE CONCEPT OF GENDER IDENTITY

The respondents demonstrated difficulties in conceptualizing the term gender, possibly showing that this topic is not part of the group's class planning, although referred to in the "Curriculum Frameworks" FME/Niterói document. The group associated the term gender with sex and showed evidence of conceptual confusion between the meanings of gender identity and sexual identity (Goellner, 2001, 2005), according to the discourse of respondent 2:

> "(...) Gender, you mean, male and female, right? (...) Gender Identity (...) it's admitting about your sexuality. Am I right or wrong? I think it's about coming out about your sexuality (...)" (R2)

In the speech of R2 the conceptual confusion between gender identity and sexual identity is made explicit when the teacher mentions that gender identity is related to the act of admitting to your sexual orientation, when they are two distinct concepts. According to the literature, gender identity relates to the way that individuals - men and women - are identified based on actions and behaviors constructed culturally and socially (Louro, 2001); while sexual identity is related to desires and pleasures that the individual directs to the opposite sex, to the same sex or both sexes (Goellner, 2001).

The majority of the group tends to conceptualize gender from a common sense understanding, designating it as a category associated with "masculine" and "feminine", never referring it to its social, cultural, historical and relational dimensions (Scott, 1995), in accordance to the discourse of respondent 9:

"Yeah (...) I learned that (...) (laughs) Initially, there are feminine and masculine genders. But today I don't see it this way any longer (...) Let's say, there are kids (...) at least I think (...) for example girls that have a homosexual tendency (…) I don't know what you would call this (…) Let's say (…) but girls that like girls (…) or kids that are not attracted to the opposite sex." (R9)

The presence of laughter in R9's response besides the words "Let's say" being used twice attests to the difficulty of explaining what this informant meant by gender. Despite that gender issues are listed in the objectives of the "Curriculum Frameworks" of FME/Niterói for Physical Education in elementary/middle school, ignorance concerning this theme was identified from the content analysis of teacher discourses indicating a potential difficulty for the group, to discuss these issues in P.E. classes. Such results were also found in studies by Correia (2008) and Silva, Peçanha Devide (2010) while investigating the presence of gender issues in vocational training in Physical Education.

Correia (2008), in a study which examined the curriculum, the syllabus of disciplines, as well as interviewed teachers and students graduating with a Bachelor's Degree in P.E., found no specific content to indicate the approach of the theme of gender in vocational training. The author identified the possibility to approach this theme in other subjects, which may vary according to interests and objectives of teachers, with the possibility of repetitive and outdated responses. The author confirms that gender is not a theme that is a part of the professional training in the institutions investigated, which interferes with teachers' pedagogical practice of P.E, because the lack of knowledge about gender issues leads them to elaborate a thought pattern based on common sense to resolve gender conflicts in P.E. classes, sometimes in a discriminatory manner recreating inequalities.

In order for the teacher to pass on to the students an awareness about the issues of gender and sexuality, he or she must first understand it (Cembranel, 2000; Saraiva, 2002; Costa, Silva, 2002; Louzada De Jesus, Devide, 2007), a process that should begin in higher education within the context of undergraduate courses. The teacher must be aware of the way physical activities are experienced by boys and girls as cultural processes, and that they result in different social representations for men and women in relation to these practices. Boys and girls develop in cultures differentiated by gender, preventing intercultural learning and limiting what and to whom certain activities are available. Rhythmic and expressive activities such as dance serve as a prime example of how the cultural process can limit an activity due to a sexist approach, as dancing is for males. Physical Education can seek educational alternatives that enable changes in power relations between males and females, liberating boys and girls from these limitations, according to Saraiva (2002).

Starting from the understanding that the school plays a key role in the education process of individuals and that besides course content, it must teach people how to live in society, the teacher's intervention in the questioning of gender issues becomes essential. Male and female students come to schools impregnated by erroneous representations of gender relations, most often, stereotypical and prejudiced. It is up to the school and the P.E. teachers to intervene in a way to questions these issues in class, providing equal opportunities without gender differentiation.

TEACHER'S PROGRAM VERSUS FME CURRICULUM

From the analysis of the interviews, it is possible to deduce that Physical Education does not appear to have a pedagogical planning and curriculum to be followed with methodology objectives, rationale, and content to be taught in elementary/middle schools. Many teachers justify the selection criteria for the course content according to the interests of the students in the class; rather than following the criteria stated in the "Curriculum Frameworks" FME-Niterói and in the literature in this field (Libâneo, 1994; Coletivo De Autores, 1992), according to this speech:

"It's the (...) Acceptance of the students. It's about what they want! their request (...) They do not want other things (...)" (R2)

When asked about the criteria for selecting the content of their classes, we can notice in the speech above that the teacher considers the students wishes when selecting the content, rather than following criteria such as social relevance, simultaneity of content, adaptation to cognitive and motor skills of the group, availability of materials and physical space, among others.

In the following quote, respondent 8 tends to choose the activities for the class based on an understanding of the level of interest of the students in the activity or game, confirming the argument of R2. Furthermore, the teacher interprets dance as content gendered towards females, but does not seem to address the theme of gender as part of a plan to be discussed during the Physical Education classes, despite showing some knowledge about the "Curriculum Frameworks" during the course of the interview.

"Yeah, well, my experience tells me that they like playing ball games (...) right? Yeah, I use dance as well. But, girls like dancing more. You know?" (R8).

It is Important to emphasize that the speech above justifies the gendering of content suitable for boys and girls, such as ball game and dance, especially when these teachers tend to divide the class and offer distinct content interpreted as appropriate to boys and girls, depriving them of an intercultural experience when practicing physical activities, guided by an argument based on biology (Souza, Altmann, 1999; Louzada De Jesus, Devide, Votre, 2007; Louzada De Jesus, Devide, 2008).

The speech of another respondent is prototypical and exemplifies the lack of experience in using the "Curriculum Frameworks" of FME/Niterói by P.E. teachers in public schools:

"Well, The standards are not decided by the school, I determine what I am going to do (...) So (...) Yeah (...) for example, I use certain festive dates (...) like in the beginning of the year (...) we talk about the Carnaval (...) And then I use that to teach dance (...) we talk about Samba, and even a little Frevo dance (...) And so on (...)" (R29)

The distance between the discourse of the respondents regarding the selection criteria of the course content and the propositions contained in the official document of "Curriculum Referentials" FME/Niterói (2010) indicates that teachers do not use this document to guide the construction of their annual class planning, letting the topics of their classes be defined according to a criteria different from those recommended by the official document; going against the interests of the students, which makes us think about the autonomy of teachers in following the curriculum component process when selecting content.

Within the group of ten informants interviewed, only one teacher mentioned the document of "Curriculum Frameworks" directly in relation to the selection of teaching content as described below:

"(...) there is a basic orientation, which is the course planning (...) right? (...) For us who work for the city (...) This is the basic guidance (...) along with compliance with the characteristics of the class" (R9)

During his speech, this respondent presents an understanding about the existence of the "Curriculum Frameworks" as a "basic guideline". During the course of this interview, it was possible to notice that the teacher recognizes the separation of male and female students as an aspect that is culturally and socially constructed and that it must be addressed, since some activities can leverage the division of boys and girls:

"Culturally (...) Boys have less affinity with certain activities (...) like singing and dancing (...) But there is an issue to be tackled here (...) as we are oriented (...) so there is no difference between boys and girls (...) But these issues are outside the classroom. They come from the student's culture. To some boys, holding hands and singing (...) it is something that depreciates their masculinity (...)" (R9)

The same informant emphasizes that activities of extreme competitive nature can contribute to the process of exclusion (Ferreira, 2000; Devide 2003) of girls in addition to creating a scenario of rivalry between the sexes, which can be minimized by the teachers intervention, by organizing and planning coed activities for the class.

"(...) Some activities, actually, if applied incorrectly, encouraging, for example, greater competition (...) And allowing that to take place ,differentiating a group of girls and a group of boys (...) By a process of exclusion of girls (...) a rivalry between the two groups can happen (...) But this is easily broken by planning coed activities for the group (...)" (R9)

It should be emphasized that the document of "Curriculum Frameworks" FME/Niterói (Niterói, 2010) mentions gender issues in objective "A", and indirectly in two other objectives, as can be seen below:

"A) the value of diversity in linguistic, generational, ethnic, racial, cultural, gender, religion, sexuality and other, recognizing their contributions to the wealth of local, national and global society; B) combating prejudices, discrimination, harassment of all forms of intolerance and violence against each other, trying to recognize its origins and report its manifestations, (...) G) Participate in activities that promote ethical attitudes, cooperation, respect and solidarity with others" (Niterói, 2010. p. 20-21).

Moreover, with regard to the specific objectives of Physical Education, in the "Skills/Citizen practices", the document states that students must interact without stigmatizing or discriminating colleagues by physical, social, cultural or gender reasons, within the context of Physical Education classes. Despite the "Curriculum Frameworks" suggesting the planning of content and approach to different issues in their teaching objectives, including, gender relations, as previously mentioned in this text, we identify that the discourse of the majority of the teachers in this study, with the exception of R9, allows us to infer ignorance or non-alignment with the propositions of the official document. This contributes to teachers not considering gender issues in the selection of content, teaching in gendered fashion, differentiating activities for boys and girls, impacting the construction of hegemonic masculine and feminine identities. This is in accordance to what Connell (1995) proposes to discuss the policies of masculinities, which keeps other forms of masculinities marginalized; over the possibility of individuals assuming plural identities, according to what Louro (2008) points in a discussion of sexuality from Queer Theory.

STUDENTS' RESISTANCE TO MIXED GENDER CLASSES

The preference of students for activities separated by gender marked the responses from the group, who claim to endure resistance from students in relation to the coed format for P.E. classes according to studies from Louzada de Jesus and Devide (2006). This resistance is related to aspects of identity, associated with hegemonic masculinity and femininity (Connell, 1995), i.e., students inserted into schools impregnated with standards of stereotypical representations of identity for what it means to be male and female, as well as patterns of behavior for both sexes, for example, the practice of certain sports distinguished by gender, regardless of the multiple identities that this biological sex, enrolled in a culture may assume. Therefore, they naturally participate in different types of physical activity, often separated in a gendered form, according to evidence from teachers in the following narratives:

"If you go over to the court now, you will realize that the boys are playing soccer and the girl's dodgeball (...)" (R7)

"But we see that they sort of separate themselves on their own (...) They think Soccer is for boys and a lot of times boys don't want girls to participate. And the jump rope is for the girls and they also do not want the boys there (...) because it's for girls" (R29)

Both quotes demonstrate how the lack of a mediator, or teacher intervention, contributes to a framework for the reproduction of these gender stereotypes, perpetuating the representations that certain activities, such as soccer and rhythmic activities are, respectively, masculine and feminine, causing conflicts between students and creating didactic difficulties for teaching classes within Physical Education (Souza, Altmann, 1999).

The separation between boys and girls in activities is common, both independently and directed[12]. In the case of the P.E. classes, gender-related problems occur during the activities,

---

[12] We understand as free activities those in which students opt to practice without the intervention of their teachers or other professionals in the school environment, for example, playing in the courtyard during recess. In the Physical Education classes, the activities must be directed by the teacher with objectives to be achieved. However, we identified "free" classes when teachers allow the students to choose the activities they prefer, without direct intervention.

when, for example, boys want to participate in activities recognized as feminine and are discriminated against by both girls and boys. The same thing happens with girls in case they wish to participate in activities considered masculine. Both boys and girls tend to suffer from prejudices and discriminatory practices, through metaphor, as we find in the study by Figueiredo da Silva and Devide (2009).

Some teachers said that the separation between boys and girls happens because of cultural preferences for different activities. This way, we can perceive that although most teachers do not understand the concept of gender and probably don't question these issues in a planned way during their classes, some recognize the influence of culture on students' preference for certain course content, as indicated below:

> "There is of course the students' affinity with certain activities that are proposed. For example, it is obvious that dance (...) For cultural reasons (...) it is more accepted by girls. So (...) The same happens with soccer for boys" (R1)

> "For the sake of organization it becomes easier to separate girls and boys. (…) There is a correlation of affinities. We cannot disregard that culturally young girls, have preference for certain activities, and consequently they are better organized that way... (…) From time to time I teach a class called free class... Students choose the activities they want to do. So the boys eventually get together and figure something out (…). The natural tendency is that boys decide for a particular activity and girls opt for other activities, but this separation in not induced by the teacher, the boys go to one side, the girls go to another side. But there are always a couple girls that go over to the boy's side…By their own cultural orientation, right?" (R9)

Despite recognizing the cultural bias in the establishment of preferences of the students for certain content in P.E., teachers tend to not intervene in a coeducational way to question the social construction of these differences, in the direction of a Physical Education that respects diversity and creates less exclusion. Thus, despite recognizing the influence of culture in certain gendered content, the respondents tend to see it as a natural phenomena, reinforcing aspects recognized as feminine for some content, like when R1 talks about dance (Saraiva, 2002); or masculine, such as ball games like soccer. This natural influence is made explicit in the speech of R1 when he says that Physical Education teacher treat dance as a feminine content. In the speech of respondent 9, in addition to supporting this natural tendency, it is clear that the separation of boys and girls emerges as a strategy to facilitate the development of class activities; again, justifying the separation by the interests of boys and girls, that are culturally constructed, but labeled as natural in P.E. classes when they are not questioned by teachers (Louzada De Jesus, Votre, Devide, 2007). Finally, during the speech of R9, it is stated that some female students prefer to play with boys due to their own "cultural orientation" implying a prejudice in relation to the suspicion that women who insert themselves in areas of male predominance have a homosexual tendency (Cahn, 1995; Griffin, 1998; Devide, 2005; Rodrigues De Almeida 2013).

Teachers apparently believe that the separation by gender in classes occurs due to the affinities of boys and girls to certain content, disregarding the fact that this often occurs because of differences in motor skills developed by boys and girls throughout life, according to what the literature on Gender Studies in Sports indicates (Gomes, Silva, QUEIRÓS, 2004; Gomes et al., 2010; Zuzzi, Knijnik, 2010; Casco, 2010).

The sexist practice in Physical Education classes carry heavy implications. The lack of Physical activity opportunities available for girls harms their motor development and affects their psychological and social fields (Saraiva, 1999). In the psychological field, the girls, starting from the acceptance of the physical superiority of boys, tend to naturalize their position of inferiority and dependence, developing what Louro (1997) calls a "corporal timidity". In the social field, women cease to have aspirations and expectations of achievement in the public sphere. It is worth noting that most of the teachers interviewed used the Portuguese male plural – "alunos" - to make mention of male and female students in Physical Education classes , reinforcing a process of female invisibility in these classes, through language, establishing power relations, producing and securing differences between the sexes (Louro, 1997; Butler, 2003).

In this unequal context, the competitive activities, the belief in the supposed female weakness and male brutality appear as justifications given by teachers for the separation of male and female students in P.E. class activities:

> "(...) It becomes very hard, so that the coed activities become consistent (...) Sometimes a boy will say (...) - coach, I am stronger (...) I want to kick it on goal (...) And if she is the goalie (...) I might hurt her" (R4)
>
> "(...) in some activities, (...) if we encourage greater competition (...) And actually allow that to happen (...) the differentiation of a group of girls and a group of boys (...) can lead to a process of exclusion of girls (...) and even (...) Rivalry between the two groups" (R9)

In analysis of the interviews, we noticed that despite that teachers could identify the separation students, the majority seems to question it from a coeducational approach, leading teachers to understand what forms the construction of these differences often labeling it as natural and reinforcing stereotypes such as female fragility male brutality or the difference in motor skills between boys and girls (Louzada De Jesus, Votre, Devide, 2007). This aspect is aggravated when, as researched by Correia (2008), we do not identify the reflection on gender issues in professional training in P.E., which hinders the capacity of these future teachers to deal with this issue in the teaching and learning process during the years of elementary education.

The argument of the separation by gender in class due to characteristics such as fragility and brutality occurs because of the naturalization of these stereotypes, these features being stimulated by the socialization process of men and women, in a biology guided discourse denying the cultural, historical and Relational concepts of gender (Scott, 1995). Therefore, sexual stereotyping, which generates inequalities, needs to be comprehended by teachers as historical and culturally developed, understanding the roles of men and women in society are based on a historically-hegemonic discourse (Connell, 1995), so that teachers will become able to discuss this topic in order to demystify it, while constructing new social relations between women and men (Saraiva, 1999).

Competition and how it has been approached under PE, also appears as an argument for this separation between sexes, as linked to the traditional model, and emphasizes disputes while utilizing official and rigid rules separating men and women, and presenting winning as the ultimate goal, away from the values that you want to develop within the framework of Physical Education (Ferreira, 2000; Devide, 2003). In this context, boys and girls choose to separate themselves because they feel safer in the case of girls; and more motivated to play as equals, in the case of boys (Louzada De Jesus, Devide, 2006), reproducing the model of Sports "in" schools approached by VAGO (1996) and a brand of Physical Education that tends to support a model of competition to the detriment of a model of Physical Education "for" the School (Caparroz, 2005).

So despite PE classes being coed, the students prefer being separated in these classes, offering resistance. In this scenario, teachers end up separating boys and girls, based on a biologicist criterion that naturalizes culturally constructed differences, reinforcing stereotypes for each sex, for the sake of facilitating the development of the activities planned for the class. Ultimately, we interpret that such routine practice of intervention in teacher pedagogy withdraws their autonomy in directing the educational process, submitting to the interests of students in relation to the content of their preference, given sometimes as "free lessons", as already mentioned above. This causes a separation of male and female students, in addition to an imbalance in the occupation of physical space of the class, according to a study by Helena Altmann (2002).

LACK OF KNOWLEDGE ABOUT CO-EDUCATION

Most teachers appeared to be unaware of the concept of Coeducation or demonstrated to understand it as a synonym for mixed classes, as evidenced by Louzada de Jesus, Votre e Devide (2007). This way, gender issues are not likely to be questioned, so that they follow what is recommended in the "Curriculum Frameworks" (Niterói, 2010) document, hindering a concrete proposal for coeducational classes. Costa e Silva (2002) suggests the adoption of a coeducational model for P.E. classes:

> "Coeducation considers equal opportunities between genders; however, it is important to note that the coed school does not have the same meaning of coeducational school. (...) this discipline does not cover gender equality, but equity, aiming to create a climate that permits integral development: emotional, social, intellectual, motor, psychological, without prejudice concerning gender, i.e., a school for training girls and boys who value the different contributions and independent skills of each sex" (p. 48).

According Auad (2004), Coeducation can be interpreted as a way to manage gender relations in the school environment, questioning and reconstructing representations of the feminine and masculine. Costa e Silva (2002) also point out the importance of awareness that girls need a pedagogical support that could help them confront problems related to their gender. According to the authors, this practice will enable the female student to reflect on a process that also "victimizes" boys, facing discrimination when they break away from social standards of masculinity, such as when they have less ability to participate in team sports like soccer, also emphasized by Louro (1997).

In these cases, considering the lack of pedagogical tools, teachers tend to adopt strategies that include girls as well as boys with lower motor skills. However, such strategies can make less skilled girls and boys feel forced to participate, so there is no damage to the group, feeling pressured and playing without pleasure, which makes the classes traumatic at times (Uchoga, 2010).

In the context of this research, many teachers said they "talk" about these issues when problems related to discrimination between male and female students appear in class. However, we realize that teachers decide for the separation of boys and girls in their classes in order to avoid situations of conflict, jeopardizing a possible debate on gender. According to the statements of informants R1, R4 and R29, the theme of "gender" is only addressed when conflicts emerge in the classroom, and not as a previously planned topic to be discussed with the students, according to the objectives listed in the "Curriculum Frameworks" document of FME/Niterói (Niterói, 2010):

> "(...) In general, I only talk about this topic, when something related to this happens in my class (...)" (R29)

> "When it happens, a student asks me: 'Coach, but why do I have to jump rope?' At that moment, I reflect with him and show him that (...) It is not only for girls (...) Certain activities are for girls and boys too" (R1).

> "I will not tell you (...) that is a lesson that I had planned specifically (...) But today I'll do some planning (...) Considering coeducation. That's a Lie. (...), I do not take that into account when I plan my classes, because it's not important to me (...)" (R4).

On the other hand, some teachers understand the importance of questioning these issues, and they intervene in a way to combat the prejudices related to sexual stereotypes. However, the lack of concepts relating to gender and Coeducation indicate that teachers do not possess tools to deal with these issues in a broad and reflective way, as the following quote describes:

> "There was an issue at the beginning of one of my classes (...) I do not quite remember with who or how it started, but someone said: 'A girl will not be a fighter, she will dance ballet. If you are a guy, will you dance ballet? Only faggots will'. We cannot accept this kind of comments in class" (R3)

Clearly, teaching situations such as the one reported above are recurrent and may serve for a broader questioning about the contents of gender, body, identity, among other aspects. However, investigations regarding gender issues still occur irregularly and superficially and are dependent to the emergence of conflicts, not being a part of the course planning, lacking opportunities for a debate on this issue within P.E. classes.

Considering the numerous inequalities and prejudices related to this matter in the school environment, especially in P.E. classes, when the bodies are more exposed, on the move and in contact with one another, expressing themselves more freely and sometimes crossing gender boundaries, such as the boy who does not want to play ball games and prefers to participate in activities with girls and vice versa (Louro 1997).

The lack of awareness about the concept of Coeducation (Saraiva, 1999), associated to the conceptual confusion about the concept of gender (Scott, 1995; Goellner, 2005), hinders the questioning of these issues in P.E. classes, with the aim of promoting the intercultural development of male and female students in the activities experienced in the classroom, without differences in respect to gender.

In this scenario, the school and the P.E. department need to contribute to the formation of students who experience possibilities of activity, not limited to their biological gender or interpreted as activities only fit for men or women. To do this, teacher training in P.E. needs to be more critical and sensitive in relation to gender (Correia, 2008). Future teachers need to deepen their studies in order to become more aware of the representations of stereotypes continuously reinforced in their classrooms based on sexual differences grounded in the notion of hegemonic masculinity and femininity (Connell, 1995).

Cembranel (2000) stresses that teachers must know the importance of Coeducational classes, other than just accepting to work with boys and girls together in integrated classes. Such lesson formats proposes that students are together in the same classroom and performing the same activities, but this junction does not necessarily promote interaction between them.

Although not based upon a natural separation, as in the case of classes segregated by gender, integrated classes can contribute to the reproduction and naturalization of the differences between boys and girls when teachers propose erroneous strategies to include girls or boys in the activities, starting with changes in the activities that generate inhibition and that which Souza and Altmann (1999) denominated as "double exclusion" (Louzada De Jesus, Votre, Devide, 2007).

Coeducation, on the other hand, provides equal opportunities for students to experience diversified physical practices, with the objective of promoting critical awareness of the social construction of differences, making them sympathetic citizens who value the opposite sex (Devide et al., 2010). To Louzada de Jesus and Devide (2006), this class format tackles the sexism still present in P.E. classes, contributing to a better coexistence between the sexes, and to better organization and more socialization during the classes.

It is up to the school community to work so that gender differences are investigated in the school as a whole, not only in PE classes. The awareness of students about gender issues will only be reflected in their daily lives if they are questioned in the numerous spaces of socialization, among which we find the school.

Sports As a Factor for Gender Exclusion

A Large number of teachers interviewed characterized sports, especially soccer, as the main content generating exclusions between boys and girls in P.E. classes, justifying differences of cultural, social, motor skills, or the dimension of competition.

> "(...) within a few activities (...) For example, track & Field (...) (...) Boys do better than girls (...) In the matter of strength, right? Or agility (...) And sometimes it ends up excluding girls. Some girls sometimes do not want to participate (...)" (R7)

Respondent 7 comprehends that certain physical qualities like strength and agility are more natural to boys, causing the exclusion of girls in activities such as track and field, because they do not feel capable of participating, ignoring the cultural dimensions that generate differences in motor skills between genders during childhood and adolescence, because of the different motor experiences of boys and girls. Gomes, Silva and Queirós

(2004) affirm that the curriculum of P.E. classes is designed as "masculine", favoring male's success in activities such as team sports; to the detriment of the experience and contributing to the frustration of girls, who tend to withdraw from classes to avoid being considered awkward for sports. In this sense the authors propose a coeducational approach regardless of the valence between physical and motor skill and suggest that the activities should be presented in a playful manner and didactically shaped (Kunz, 2002), providing an enjoyable experience between students.

Respondent 3 states that there is a process of self-exclusion related to certain contents, something that is also identified in the research of Altmann (2002), which found that self exclusion of some students happens because of fear of making mistakes and exposing themselves to mockery for not knowing how to play. In this same speech, the respondent claims that the process of self-exclusion takes place "naturally" from the gendering of content as masculine (soccer) and feminine (dance), which contributes to the resistance from male and female students in participating in these activities during P.E. classes.

> "But of course soccer (...) and other activities. Like dance it also (...) boys and girls exclude themselves, believing that certain activities are only for boys or girls. And then you have to do some work to articulate all of this (...)" (R3)

It is still common to find teachers who legitimize content as masculine or feminine, reinforcing stereotypes and building barriers to teaching Physical Education. This attitude hampers the integrated practice of boys and girls within the same activities as in the case of soccer reported by respondent 9:

> "soccer is a better fit for boys (...) But there are some girls who really like soccer (...) Then they play and participate in the classes (...) They want to play soccer, boys don't necessarily want them to (...) But I have to control this pressure (...)" (R9)

When considering that soccer is "a better fit for boys", the teacher tends to offer different activities for boys and girls separating them by gender; unless there are skilled girls who ask to play soccer with the boys, who in turn tend to offer resistance to their participation because they may feel unmotivated or threatened. In this scenario the teacher's intervention reinforces gender stereotypes by teaching certain activities separately for both genders, rather than promoting debates about gender issues from a coeducational approach (Saraiva, 1999), perpetuating a masculinization of team sports and a feminization of the rhythmic and expressive activities in Physical Education (Saraiva, 2002).

Respondent 4 highlights sports and exacerbated competition as factors contributing to the exodus of students who are less skilled from Physical Education classes. As indicated by Devide (2003) and Ferreira (2000), competition can assume a motivational nature in P.E. classes provided that it assumes a suitable guise for the school setting, for example, the emphasis on the pursuit of excellence or overcoming of the students own limits, encouraging kids to set goals and personal challenges; to the detriment of competition while disputing with one another, where there is only one winner.

> "(...) Girls come from home with a feeling that soccer is for boys only (...) and they cannot participate" (R5)

Likewise, respondent 5 demonstrates how students already come to school with gendered opinions about the content of P.E. classes, such as sports, as in the case of girls who do not feel at ease playing soccer in the Brazilian context, where this sport is still mostly reserved for men (ROodrigues, Devide, 2009; Batista, Devide, 2009).

> "I think this is very strong in the sports context (...) Because (...) in sports we play to win, right? Everybody wants to win and they will do whatever it takes to win" (R4)

Just like it occurs with soccer, some teachers have also indicated difficulties in teaching other contents qualified as gendered, like dancing, which in addition to bringing conflicts related to gender issues, causes insecurity in teachers, which is why this content has been kept out from the curriculum of Physical Education in Brazil (Tenório Brasileiro, 2003), being often just associated with festive folklore and special dates as the following statement describes:

> "(...) We work more With Dance in the months of June, July, because we have the June festivals (...) And sometimes in August because of folklore festivals. (...) They react without wanting to dance (...) But after we talk (...) a lot (...) some of them end up (...) Dancing. And others do not really want to dance at all (...) They say dance is a girly thing, they will not dance (...)"(R5)

It is consistent in the speech of teachers that students associate the contents of dance to feminine identity, contributing to conflicts that occur during the integrated classes, hindering the participation of boys and girls in the same activity, preventing the progress of the class. A Study by Fonseca Júnior and Devide (2010) also indicates that students participate discreetly in P.E. classes when the proposed activity is dance, representing a feminine physical practice.

Overall, most participants recognized that the gendering of certain content is something culturally constructed, and is constituted as a factor of exclusion, restricted by the dimension of the differences in motor skills between boys and girls, by virtue of its processes of socialization in relation to diverse experiences with sports, as the speech of R9 about boys playing soccer outside of the school environment.

> "(...) The boys Themselves are very discriminating towards each other. I mean, why not, it's their culture, its soccer (...) Where they live (...) there are many more boys playing soccer than girls (...) girls rarely play (...)" (R9)

In this context, it is important to recognize that sports such as soccer, wrestling, and dancing, for example, arrive at schools already interpreted in a gendered form, that is often reinforced by the family nucleus when they play sports together with their kids, during leisure time outside of the school, as well as the experience gained by students in their first years of P.E. classes in the school system. However, teachers need to understand that these differences in motor skills between boys and girls derive from this perspective of reality, which creates the need for a coeducational approach to teaching P.E., with the aim to provide students with an understanding of how the social construction of such differences comes about. They should also allow it to improve students' chances of working together during activities in P.E. classes, by respecting these differences and gaining a new awareness of how it manifests.

Class content, as well as sports, need to be reinterpreted by the lecturers so that students may perceive them as part of a neutral culture according to gender (Coletivo De Autores, 1992), interpreted as a relational category and not binary (Scott, 1995).

Course Content and Identity

Many teachers associated content in Physical Education to gender identities and sexual identities, reinforcing stereotypes and gender prejudices. A prototypical example is the association of Dance with femininity and male homosexuality; and soccer with masculinity and female homosexuality, as the following describes:

> "There are girls who play soccer (...) And have homosexual tendencies, or are lesbians, I mean (...) They like other women. But that does not mean it's because they play soccer, I don't think (...) Like dancing, for example. There are some boys who have the ability to dance (...) they will not necessarily (...) be gay (...) or like other boys (...)" (R9)

In the speech above while the informant demonstrates understanding that gendered content like dancing does not necessarily influence the sexual identity of boys, looking to defend the lack of causal relationship between experiencing an activity and the construction of sexual identity; presents a counter-argument when referring "to girls playing soccer (...) who have homosexual tendencies (...) or are lesbians" as if the involvement with this sport determines their sexual identity. Meanwhile, studies such as the one by Cahn (1994) indicate that lesbian women choose certain sports where they know they will find an atmosphere of freedom, with other women of the same sexual identity, being able to play the sport without facing prejudice, while also building social and affective ties which contradicts the a priori notion that the practice of a specific sport could determine sexual identity.

The conceptual confusion indicated by Luz Júnior (2003) and Devide et al. (2011) between sexual identity and gender identity is representative in the speech of respondent 29 and brings us to the argument of Butler (2003) on the construction of identities around the male/female binarism by constructing delimited social spaces for men and women. The teachers speech emphasizes the existence of identities that are deviant from the norm, which is explicit in the context of P.E., when boys and girls are engaging in sports considered gendered as masculine or feminine.

Butler (2003) and Louro (2008) emphasize that the discourse on gender must deconstruct the understanding guided by binarism between male and female, because men and women are constructed and express masculinity and femininity of diverse hegemonies, preventing the experience with some activities considered masculine or feminine that might lead to confusion about gender relations and sexuality, as it occurs with boys who do not like soccer and girls who have no interest in rhythmic activities in P.E., preferring team sports or wrestling. This polarization between the sexes, characteristic of western heterosexist culture, ignores the complex processes that constitute plural identities, existing within the walls of schools and classes.

The normative, binary and Manichean understanding of hegemonic masculine and feminine identities that some teachers take into their pedagogical practices, makes other possibilities of experiencing gender identities impossible, defining socially accepted behaviors and attitudes for men and women that are not shared by all students in the classroom the same way, making the Physical Education experience traumatizing for some, by facing discrimination such as homophobic bullying, being interpreted as deviant from the norm by others (Peçanha, Devide, 2010) and invalidating inclusive actions in the classroom as they relate to gender.

In the discourse of the respondents it is clear that content influences the P.E. classes, because teachers perceive discriminatory practices between students as respondent 29 describes:

> "If a boy is interested in ballet in my Physical Education class, he will be labeled a homosexual (...)" (R9)

A study by Figueiredo da Silva and Devide (2009) identified a large number of discriminatory metaphors, some of sexual connotation, used to exclude colleagues of certain activities, such as "faggot" for the boy who likes another boy; "Girly" to the boy who talks like a girl; or "little boy" for the girl who hangs with the boys and likes to play soccer. In this scenario, it is essential that the teachers intervene and discuss such practices towards a less exclusionary, discriminatory and homophobic style of Physical Education.

Very few respondents mentioned that students have social representations guided by common sense, built day to day, about gender and sexual identities. These recognize the cultural and historical dimension of the concept of gender, undermining the differences that have been legitimized to separate boys and girls in classes or to teach different contents to each group, which complicates the teaching of content because of the resistance of students to participate in certain activities. The following speech recognizes the importance of transforming the scenario of Physical Education with respect to gender relations between the students and the class content, modifying current stereotypes in society.

> "When I play music in class (...) the girls just want to dance. They want to show that they can dance (...) they are more (...) willing to expose themselves in dance (...) than boys are. Boys are more usually ashamed (...) But this is because of the way they are brought up. (...) what boys can do and what they cannot do. (...) like jump rope (...) or like soccer, the boys always say: soccer is for men (...) and dance and jump rope for girls (...) And if I accept that (...) and divide the class (...) I will be automatically reaffirming what society determines (...) And I wouldn't be changing the way they think" (R8)

Other respondents stressed the unpreparedness of the school in questioning these issues, only reproducing stereotypes, even though the "Curriculum Frameworks" of FME/Niterói make mention of gender issues in three of its components, as the analysis presented in this study; besides being predicted in the planning of P.E. classes in the first cycle of elementary education.

> "(...) sometimes the school does the opposite of what it is supposed to. Sometimes, us teachers, we are the ones who create exclusion (...) For example: some teachers will organize the students into two lines, one of boys and another of girls. Sometimes we create a dispute among the genders (...)" (R7)

The quote above demonstrates a pattern of personal organizational in relation to the historical division of male and female students in lines during classes, rather than the school as an institution being responsible for this separation, stating that "the teacher always makes those lines of boys and girls". In the History of Physical Education in Brazil, we find different treatment for boys and girls in classes. In 1882, the Reform of Elementary Education suggested different physical activities for boys and girls (Soares, 1994). After World War II, the Generalized Method of Physical Education and Sports became predominate in this field and it recommended the separation of boys and girls, having as objective greater performance and physical fitness. In 1971, Federal Law mentions explicitly the separation of students by sex in P.E., according to Decree 69,450, from November 1st, 1971, article 5, item 3, which legitimized the separation of students by gender in different groups, recommending "the arrangement of classes by fifty students of the same sex, preferably selected by level of physical fitness" (Brasil, 1971).

However, starting from the Gender Studies in Physical Education in the 1980s (Devide et al., 2011) there was an increase in the debate about the dichotomy of integrated and/or separate classes by gender, with a tendency to defend the coed P.E. classes, predominant in schools today, refusing to blame the schools for the division of students by gender in P.E. classes. This was because studies show that teachers have been responsible for this action by arguing, among other things, that it is easier to teach the course contents to classes divided by gender (Louzada De Jesus, Votre, Devide, 2009).

Students sometimes arrive at the school setting with stereotyped representations of the course content in Physical Education and its relationship with gender identities and sexual identities. The teacher's intervention should be as a critical mediator of the relationships between biological sex, gender identity and sexual identity. This intervention should try to break this linear representation and heterosexist order that prevents the manifestation of plural, distinct identities from the distinct hegemonic ones already being imposed by society (Butler, 1993; Connell 1995), guaranteeing equal rights of participation and opportunities to all, regardless of the ways they express their identities or how much they approach or move away from the normative social order.

CONCLUSION

Although the Gender Studies in Brazilian P.E have started in the 1980s (Luz Júnior, 2003, Devide et al. 2011), there are several publications that address the gender relations in teaching Physical Education.

However, data arising from the document analysis and the analysis of content in the interviews with the group of teachers from FME/Niterói, indicate that there are difficulties in teaching the content of Physical Education in regards to managing gender relations, especially when the debate concerns the relationships between the course content and gendered identities.

Despite the theme of "gender" being present in the contents of the "Curriculum Frameworks" for FME/Niterói, the discourse of P.E. teachers in public schools indicated a lack of knowledge about the concept of gender (Scott, 1995), generally speaking, and of the concept of coeducation (Saraiva, 1999; Cembranel, 2000; Gomes, Silva, Queirós, 2004), as a methodological approach to teaching the contents of Physical Education in order to create opportunities for all boys and girls and provide the experience of the elements of a Culture of physical activity (Coletivo De Autores, 1992). This allows for combating prejudices and stereotypes that place gender labels in certain activities as masculine or feminine, creating resistance to the participation of boys and girls in coed classes, something also found in the study of Louzada de Jesus e Devide (2006); and at times discriminatory practices and exclusion practices (Altmann, 2002; Figuueiredo Da Silva, Devide, 2009). We also identified a lack of planning about gender issues in Physical Education at FME/Niterói, which undermines the teachers' intervention toward a more Coeducational practice. The majority of respondents only address the theme of gender in the event of a conflict between boys and girls during P.E. classes. Otherwise, the subject is disregarded.

Such a scenario makes it difficult to build a practical teaching style of Physical Education engaged in questioning gender relations within the course content, focusing on the establishment of an inclusive environment for boys and girls to experience physical practices according to their interests, with freedom and without discrimination. The lack of knowledge related to gender issues can contribute to a sense of exclusion, reproducing and reinforcing stereotypes and prejudices, rather than making the environment of Physical Education classes a place which favors contesting these same issues.

The teachers tend to reflect on the differences, inequalities, discriminations and prejudices of gender circulating in Physical Education classes from a place of common sense, confirming the results of Correia (2008) arguing that this subject is scarce in professional training in Brazilian Physical Education. The lack of tools to deal with gender issues present in the course content in Physical Education classes, makes most teachers assume practices that do not advance in the direction of emancipation and transformation of an exclusionary school setting in relation to students who are considered deviant from the heterosexist order (for example, by choosing activities considered inadequate to the their gender identity).

In this respect, the group's discourse also indicates conceptual confusion between gender identity and sexual identity, according to studies by Goellner (2001, 2005) e Devide et al. (2011). Such concepts are relevant to a transformative didactic intervention that seeks to create equal opportunities and experiences to all students, in a Coeducational perspective, combating a representation that the biological sex should be aligned with a gender identity, according to gender roles imposed by a society governed by a heterosexist order (Butler, 2003; Louro, 2008). This order interprets as diversion and establishes cause-effect relationships between social practices and identities, such as that associated with playing soccer or wrestling by women, as responsible for the construction of a male gender identity and necessarily a homosexual identity.

While recognizing the differentiation in the socialization process of boys and girls, and enunciating that there is no cause-effect relationship between course contents and the construction of sexual identities, a large proportion of teachers associates learning content to gender identity and sexual identity in a linear fashion, from the heterosexist order, disregarding the possibility of interpreting the concept of identity from an unfixed, changeable, perspective, as suggested by gender Studies (Louro, 2008).

In this context, "sports" were presented as a factor of exclusion and a content that anchors the representation that certain sports are masculine (soccer) or feminine (dance), present in the responses of the group, in order to naturalize such representations by reinforcing the gendered content. Teachers need to tackle this representation, opening new insights into plural identities, possibly to be expressed within the P.E. classes, from the experience of the contents, regardless of biological sex.

We believe, finally, that although some teachers recognize the importance of discussing gender issues in P.E. classes, standing against the separation of boys and girls and against the discrimination and prejudices related to the topic, and also superficially understand the influence of culture regarding the gendering of some of the content of P.E. and its relation to the identities, these teachers are not prepared, from the didactic and methodological point of view, to question this topic with their students.

REFERENCES

Abreu, N. G. (1995). Análise das percepções de docentes e discentes sobre turmas mistas e separadas por sexo nas aulas de Educação Física Escolar. In Romero, E. (Ed.), Corpo, Mulher e Sociedade (pp. 157-176). São Paulo: Papirus.

Altmann, H. (1998). Rompendo fronteiras de gênero: Marias (e) homens na educação física. Dissertação (Mestrado em Educação) Belo Horizonte, MG: UFMG.

Altmann, H. (2002). Exclusão nos esportes sob um enfoque de gênero. *Motus Corporis*, v. 9 (n. 1), pp. 7-8.

Alves-Mazzotti, A. J. (2002). O Planejamento de Pesquisa Qualitativa. In.: Alves-Mazzotti, A. J. & Gewandsznajder, F. (Eds.), *O Método nas Ciências Naturais e Sociais* (2 ed), São Paulo: Thompson.

Auad, D. (2004). Relações de gênero nas práticas escolares e a construção de um projeto de co-educação. Caxambu, MG. http://27reuniao.anped.org.br/ge23/t233.pdf.

Bardin, L. (2008). Análise de Conteúdo. Lisboa: Edições 70.

Batista, R. & Devide, F. P. (2009). Mulheres, futebol e gênero: reflexões sobre a participação feminina numa área de reserva masculina. EFDeportes, v. 14 (n. 137). http://www.efdeportes.com/efd137/mulheres-futebol-e-genero.htm

Bourdieu, P. (1998). A dominação masculina. Rio de Janeiro: Bertrand Brasil.

Brasil. (1997). Parâmetros curriculares nacionais: introdução aos parâmetros curriculares nacionais. Secretaria de Educação Fundamental. Brasília, DF: MEC/SEF.

Brasil. (1971). Decreto nº 69.450, de 1º de novembro de 1971. In BRASIL, Diário Oficial da República Federativa do Brasil. Brasília, DF: D.O.

Butler, J. (2003). Problemas de Gênero: feminismo e subversão da identidade. Rio de Janeiro, RJ: Civilização Brasileira.

Cahn, S. K. (1995). Coming on Strong: gender and sexuality in twentieth-century women´s sport. Cambridge: Harvard.

Casco, P. (2010) Mais e melhores práticas de inclusão de meninas na Educação Física escolar. In Knijnik, J. D. & Zuzzi, R. P. (Eds.) Meninas e Meninos na Educação Física: gênero e corporeidade no século XXI. (pp. 73-85). Jundiaí, SP: Fontoura.

Caparroz, F. E. (2005). Entre a Educação Física na Escola e a Educação Física da Escola: a Educação Física Como Componente Curricular (2 ed). Campinas, SP: Autores Associados.

CBCE. (Ed.). (1997). Educação física escolar frente à LDB e aos PCNs: Profissionais analisam renovações, modismos e interesses. Ijuí, RS: Sedigraf.

Cembranel, C. (2000). Aulas co-educativas: o que mudou no ensino da Educação Física. *Motrivivência*, v. 11 (n. 14), pp. 199-219.

Coletivo De Autores. (1992). Metodologia de Ensino da Educação Física. São Paulo: Cortez.

Connell, R. W. (1995). Políticas da Masculinidade. *Educação e Realidade*, v. 20 (n. 2), pp. 185–206.

Correia, M. M. (2008). Representações sociais sobre gênero na licenciatura em educação física. Dissertação (Mestrado em Educação Física). Niterói, RJ: Universidade Salgado de Oliveira.

Costa, M. R. F. & Silva, R. G. da. (2002). A Educação Física e a Co-educação: Igualdade ou Diferença? RBCE, v. 23 (n. 2), pp. 43-54.

Cruz, M. M. S. & Palmeira F. C. C. (2009). Construção de identidade de gênero na Educação Física Escolar. *Motriz,* v.15 (n. 1), pp.116-131.

Darido, S. C. (2012). Os conteúdos na Educação Física escolar. http://www.cvps.g12.br /centropedagogico/Centro%20Ped%202009/pdf/cursos%20e%20assessorias/Ed%20Fisic a/Capitulo5conteudos.pdf

Devide, F. P. (2003). Possíveis sentidos da competição: uma reflexão sobre o esporte máster. Motus Corporis, v. 10 (n. 2), pp. 43-62.

Devide, F. P. (2005). Gênero e Mulheres no Esporte: História das Mulheres nos Jogos Olímpicos Modernos. Ijuí, RS: Unijuí.

Devide, F. P. et al. (2010). Exclusão intrassexo em turmas femininas na Educação Física escolar: quando a diferença ultrapassa a questão de gênero. In Knijnik, J. D. & Zuzzi, R. P. (Eds.), Meninos e meninas na Educação Física: gênero e corporeirdade no século XXI (pp. 87-105). Jundiaí, SP: Fontoura.

Devide et al. (2011). Estudos de Gênero na Educação Física. Motriz, v.17 (n.1), pp. 93-103.

Duarte, J. (2008). Entrevista em Profundidade. In Duarte, J. & Barros, A. (Eds.), Métodos e Técnicas de Pesquisa em Comunicação. (2.ed., pp. 56-60). São Paulo, SP: Atlas.

Dunning, E. (1992). O desporto como uma área de reserva masculina: notas sobre os fundamentos sociais n identidade masculina e suas transformações. In Elias, N. (Ed.), A busca de excitação (pp. 389-412). Lisboa, PT: Difel.

Faria Júnior, A. G. de. (1995). Futebol, Questões de Gênero e Co-educação. Pesquisa de Campo, n. 2, p.17-39.

Ferreira, M. S. (2000). A Competição na Educação Física escolar. *Motriz,* v. 6 (n. 2), pp. 97-100.

Ferretti, M. A. C. & Knijnik, J. D. (2007). Mulheres podem praticar lutas? Um estudo sobre as representações sociais de lutadoras universitárias. *Movimento*, v. 13 (n. 1), pp. 57-80.

Figueiredo Da Silva, C. A. & Devide, F. P. (2009). Linguagem discriminatória e etnométodos de exclusão nas aulas de educação física escolar. *RBCE*, v. 30 (n. 2), pp. 181-197.

Fonseca Júnior, J. C. O. da. & Devide, F. P. (2010). Representações dos alunos do sexo masculino sobre o conteúdo dança nas aulas de Educação Física escolar. EFDeportes, v. 15 (n. 144). http://www.efdeportes.com/efd144/conteudo-danca-masculino-nas-aulas-de-educacao-fisica.htm

Griffin, P. (1998). Strong women, deep closets: lesbians and homofobia in sport. Champaign: Human Kinetics.

Goellner, S. V. (2001). Gênero, educação física e esportes. In Votre, S. J. (Ed.). Imaginário e representações sociais em educação física, esporte e lazer (pp. 215-227). Rio de Janeiro: UGF.

Goellner, S. V. (2005). Gênero. In Gonzalez, F. J & Fensterseifer, P. E. (Ed.). Dicionário Crítico de Educação Física. (pp. 207-209). Ijuí: Unijuí,

Goellner, S. V. (2008). (Ed.) Corpo, Gênero e Sexualidade: um debate contemporâneo na educação (4 ed., pp.28-40). Petrópolis, RJ: Vozes.

Gomes, P.B., Silva, P. & Queirós, P. (2004). Para uma estrutura pedagógica renovada, promotora da Co-Educação no desporto. In Simões, A. C. & Knijnik, J. D. (Eds.). O Mundo Psicossocial da Mulher no Esporte: Comportamento, Gênero, Desempenho (pp. 173- 189). São Paulo, SP: Aleph.

Gomes, P. et al. (2010). Na busca de indicadores promotores ou inibidores do desenvolvimento da prática desportiva em jovens. In Knijnik, J. D. (Ed.). Gênero e Esporte: masculinidade e feminilidades (pp. 213-229). Rio de Janeiro, RJ: Apicuri.

Kunz, E. (2002). Transformação didático-pedagógica do esporte. Ijuí: Unijuí.

Libâneo, J. C. (1994). Didática. São Paulo: Cortez.

Louro, G. L. (1997). A construção escolar das diferenças. In Louro, G. L. Gênero, sexualidade e educação: uma perspectiva pós-estruturalista (6 ed., pp. 57-87). Petrópolis: Vozes.

Louro, G. L. (2001). O Corpo Educado: Pedagogia das sexualidades. Rio de Janeiro, RJ: Bertrand Brasil.

Louro, G. L (2008). Um corpo estranho: ensaios sobre sexualidade e Teoria Queer. Belo Horizonte, MG: Autêntica.

Louro, G. L., Felipe, J. & Goellner, S. V. (Eds.). (2010). Corpo, Gênero e Sexualidade: um debate contemporâneo na educação. Petrópolis, RJ: Vozes.

Louzada De Jesus, M. & Devide, F. P. (2006). Educação física escolar, co-educação e gênero: mapeando representações de discentes. Movimento, v. 12 (n. 3), pp. 123-140.

Louzada De Jesus, M., Votre, S.& Devide, F. P. (2007). Representações de docentes acerca da distribuição dos alunos por sexo nas aulas de Educação Física. RBCE, v. 28 (n. 2), pp. 55-68.

Louzada De Jesus, M., Votre, S. & Devide, F. P. (2008). Apresentação e análise de trabalhos acerca da distribuição dos alunos por sexo nas aulas de Educação Física escolar. Movimento, v. 14 (n. 02), pp. 83-98.

Luz Júnior, A. (2003). Educação Física e Gênero: olhares em cena. São Luís, MA: Imprensa UFMA/CORSUP.

Messner, M. A. (1992). Power at Play: sports and the problem of masculinity. Boston: Beacon Press.

Minayo, C. de S. (1994). Pesquisa social: teoria, método e criatividade. Petrópolis, RJ: Vozes.

Navarro, R. T. (2006). A formação da identidade de gênero: um olhar sobre a Educação Física.
http://www.fazendogenero.ufsc.br/7/artigos/R/Rodrigo_Tramutolo_Navarro_07_B.pdf

Niterói, Fundação Municipal de Educação de Niterói/Rede Municipal de Educação de Niterói. (2010). Referenciais Curriculares para a Rede Municipal de Niterói: Ensino Fundamental.

Nunan, A. (2003). Homossexualidade: do preconceito aos padrões de consumo. Rio de Janeiro: Caravansarai.

Oliveira, F. F., & de Votre, S. J. (2006). Bullying nas aulas de educação física. Movimento, v. 12 (n. 2), pp. 173-197.

Peçanha, M. B. & Devide, F. P. (2010). O discurso dos docentes do primeiro segmento do ensino fundamental sobre o bullying homofóbico na Educação Física escolar. EFDeportes, ano 15 (n. 146). http://www.efdeportes.com/efd146/o-bullying-homofobico-na-educacao-fisica-escolar.htm

Ramos, M. R. F. (2012). Representações sociais de docentes de Educação Física escolar sobre as relações entre conteúdos de ensino e as identidades de Gênero. Dissertação (Mestrado em Educação Física) Niterói, RJ: Universidade Salgado de Oliveira.

Richardson, R. J. (2009). Pesquisa Social: métodos e técnicas. São Paulo: Atlas.

Rodrigues De Almeida, T. (2013). Mulheres e esporte: feminilidades em jogo. In Dornelles, P. G., Wenetz, I. & Schwengber, M. S. V. (Ed.) Educação Física e Gênero: desafios educacionais. (pp. 141-165) Ijuí, RS: Unijuí.

Rodrigues, F. S. J. & Devide, F. P. (2009). Inserção de mulheres em uma área de reserva masculina e o uso da co-educação para o ensino do futebol na Educação Física Escolar. EFDeportes, ano 14 (n. 138). http://www.efdeportes.com/efd138/insercao-de-mulheres-em-uma-area-de-reserva-masculina.htm

Saraiva, M. do C. (1999). Co-educação física e esportes: quando a diferença é mito. Ijuí, RS: Unijuí.

Saraiva, M. do C. (2002). Por que investigar as questões de gênero no âmbito da Educação Física, Esporte e Lazer? *Motrivivência*, v. 13 (n.19), pp. 79-85.

Sayão, D. T. (2002). A construção de identidade e papéis de gênero na infância: articulando temas para pensar o trabalho pedagógico da educação física infantil. *Pensar a Prática*, v. 5, pp. 1-14.

Soares, C. (1994). Educação física: raízes européias e Brasil. Campinas, SP: Autores Associados.

Scott, J. W. (1995) Gênero: uma categoria útil de análise histórica. *Educação & Realidade*, v. 20, n. 2, p. 71-99.

Scott, J. W. (2005). O enigma da igualdade. *Estudos Feministas*, v.13 (n.1) pp. 11-30.

Silva, R. A. da. (2004). O ponto fora da curva. In Meyer, D. E. & Soares, R. F. R. (Eds.) Corpo, gênero e sexualidade. Porto Alegre: Mediação (pp. 85-96).

Silva, I., Peçanha, M. B. & Devide, F. P. (2010). Representações da formação profissional em educação Física sobre as questões de gênero: reflexões sobre a graduação no Centro Universitário Augusto Motta. XIII Encontro Fluminense de Educação Física Escolar. Anais... Niterói: UFF.

Sousa, E. S. de & Altmann, H. (1999). Meninos e meninas: expectativas corporais e implicações na educação física escolar. *Caderno CEDES*, v. 19 (n. 48), pp. 52-68.

Spink, M. J. (1995). O estudo empírico das representações sociais. In Spink, M. J. (Ed.). O conhecimento no cotidiano: as representações sociais na perspectiva da psicologia social. (pp. 85-108) São Paulo, SP: Brasiliense.

Tenório, B. L. (2003). O conteúdo "dança" em aulas de educação física: temos o que ensinar? *Pensar a Prática*, v. 6, pp. 45-58.

Thomas, J. R & Nelson, J. K. (2002). Métodos de pesquisa em atividade física. Porto Alegre: Artmed.

Uchoga, L. (2010). Relações de gênero nos diferentes conteúdos da educação física escolar. http://www.fazendogenero.ufsc.br/9/resources/anais/1277822933_ARQUIVO_uchoga_liane.pdf

Vago, T. M. (1996). O "esporte na escola" e o "esporte da escola": da negação radical para uma relação de tensão permanente: um diálogo com Valter Bracht. *Movimento,* v. 3 (n. 5), pp. 4-17.

Zuzzi, R. P. & Knijnik, J. D. (2010). Do passado ao presente: reflexões sobre a história da Educação Física a partir das relações de gênero. In Knijnik, J. D. & Zuzzi, R. P. (Ed.) Meninas e Meninos na Educação Física: gênero e corporeidade no século XXI. (pp. 59-70) Jundiaí, SP: Fontoura.

In: Gender Identity
Editor: Beverly L. Miller

ISBN: 978-1-63321-488-0
© 2014 Nova Science Publishers, Inc.

Chapter 13

COMMON HYPOTHETICAL ETIOLOGY OF EXCESS ANDROGEN EXPOSURE IN FEMALE-TO-MALE TRANSSEXUALISM AND POLYCYSTIC OVARY SYNDROME

Tsuyoshi Baba*, Toshiaki Endo, Keiko Ikeda and Tsuyoshi Saito
Department of Obstetrics and Gynecology,
Sapporo Medical University, Sapporo, Japan

ABSTRACT

Gender identity disorder is recognized as a rare disease. The prevalence of this disorder is different among regions and races. In Japan, the prevalence of female-to-male transsexual (FTM-TS) patients is estimated to be 1 in 12,500 women, which is approximately twice as many as male-to-female transsexual patients.

There are two interesting facts in association with FTM-TS: 1) the complication rate of polycystic ovary syndrome (PCOS) is high among FTM-TS patients; and 2) natal female patients with congenital adrenal hyperplasia (CAH) tend to have gender identity problems more often than the normal population. PCOS is a common disease and it affects 5–10% of women of reproductive age. PCOS is characterized by ovulation disorder, hyperandrogenism, and polycystic ovarian morphology. Additionally, PCOS is correlated with insulin resistance, and predisposes to type 2 diabetes mellitus, atherosclerosis, and metabolic syndrome. The etiology of PCOS is still obscure, but excess androgen exposure during the fetal period is considered to be a dominant hypothesis. CAH is an autosomal recessive disorder impairing adrenal steroid metabolism, which causes excess androgenemia from the fetal period. A review on 250 natal female cases with CAH showed that 13 (5.2%) of the patients had serious gender identity problems. Surprisingly, the occurrence of FTM-TS in CAH is extremely high. The pathogenesis of FTM-TS is still uncertain. However, excess androgen exposure may be related to FTM-TS according to the above-mentioned findings.

In humans, experimental androgen administration to women is impossible. However, cross-sex hormone administration to FTM-TS patients is not associated with any

---

* Correspondence to: Tsuyoshi Baba, M.D., Ph.D., Department of Obstetrics and Gynecology, Sapporo Medical University, South 1 West 16, Chu-o-ku, Sapporo, Hokkaido, 060-8543 Japan. E-mail: tbaba@sapmed.ac.jp

problems because it is a standard tactic for treatment. If excess androgen exposure is a cause of PCOS, androgen-treated FTM-TS patients may be a disease model of PCOS. Assessment of the effects of androgen administration on metabolic parameters is informative because FTM-TS patients with PCOS may have potent insulin resistance.

In this chapter, we discuss endocrinological aspects of FTM-TS, the effect of cross-sex hormones, and the hypothetical etiology in FTM and PCOS.

INTRODUCTION

Gender identity disorder (GID) is recognized as a rare disease, with an estimated prevalence of 1:12,500 for female-to-male transsexual (FTM-TS) patients and 1:25,000 for male-to-female transsexual (MTF-TS) patients in Japan [1]. However, it is difficult to determine the precise epidemiologic characteristics of this population because there may be many people who have not undergone diagnostic evaluation. In fact, a recent report suggests that GID is more common than previously thought [2]. Therefore, the reported prevalence of GID may be underestimated. The prevalence of GID seems to be somewhat different among regions and races. In Western Europe, some epidemiological data on transsexualism indicate that MTF-TS is more prevalent than FTM-TS [3], which is contrary to our data in the Japanese population. The precise reasons for this difference are unknown. The difference could be explained by the different social attitudes towards transgender behavior in male and female individuals. Masculine behavior in female individuals is considered more acceptable than feminine behavior in male individuals in European society. Therefore, MTF-TS individuals may seek to protect themselves from negative social attitudes by having a diagnosis of GID. Ethnicity differences reflecting different genetic backgrounds also may contribute to susceptibility to transsexualism. Other genetic factors and environmental factors may partially influence GID, as well.

It is thought that gender identity is the result of both psycho-social and biological factors. Several studies indicate that GID is a multidimensional disorder that is associated with the neurodevelopment of the brain, although there is no definitive evidence [4-6]. Indeed, almost all FTM-TS patients report that they have felt discomfort with their own sex and have identified with the opposite sex for as long as they can remember. It is possible, therefore, that FTM-TS may originate during prenatal and neonatal periods, so that FTM-TS patients may be destined to develop their disorder early in life. Interestingly, studies on the association between congenital adrenal hyperplasia (CAH) and GID offer curious insights. Natal female patients with CAH, which is known to cause antenatal hyperandrogenemia because of excess production of adrenal androgen, are prone to develop FTM-TS compared with the normal population [7]. Other research indicates that natal female patients with CAH tend to show male gender-stereotyped behaviors [8]. These findings suggest that excess androgen exposure during the prenatal period may cause FTM-TS.

We have performed physical and endocrinological examinations of more than 200 FTM-TS patients, and noticed that FTM-TS patients often have comorbid polycystic ovary syndrome (PCOS). PCOS is recognized as a common heterogeneous disorder characterized by an ovulation disorder, hyperandrogenism, and polycystic ovarian morphology. A subtype of PCOS was first reported in 1935 in seven cases with amenorrhea, hirsutism, and enlarged polycystic ovaries, which was later called Stein-Leventhal syndrome [9]. Since then, PCOS has been a mysterious disorder. Diagnostic criteria for PCOS have been offered by several societies, which are summarized in Table 1 [10-13].

Table 1. Several major diagnostic criteria for PCOS

NIH 1990 (both 1 and 2)
  1) chronic anovulation
  2) clinical/ biochemical hyperandrogenism

Rotterdam 2003 (2 out of 3)
  1) oligo-/ anovulation
  2) clinical/ biochemical hyperandrogenism
  3) polycystic ovarian morphology

AE-PCOS 2006 (both 1 and 2)
  1) clinical/ biochemical hyperandrogenism
  2) Ovarian disorders (oligo-/ anovulation and/or polycystic ovarian morphology

JSOG 2007 (3 out of 3)
  1) oligo-/ anovulation
  2) polycystic ovarian morphology
  3) Hyperandrogenemia and/or hypersecretion of LH and normal FSH

NIH, National Institute of Health; Rotterdam, Rotterdam ESHRE/ASRM-Sponsored PCOS Consensus Workshop Group; AE-PCOS, The Androgen Excess and PCOS Society; JSOG, Japan Society of Obstetrics and Gynecology

The prevalence of PCOS varies depending on which criteria are used to make the diagnosis, and is about 6–7% in the general population when the National Institute of Health (NIH) 1990 criteria are used [14, 15]. Other pathognomonic characteristics of PCOS include insulin resistance and hypersecretion of the luteinizing hormone (LH), which are closely associated with the pathogenesis of PCOS. This means that not a small number of FTM-TS patients may be susceptible to diseases related to insulin-resistance, such as type 2 diabetes mellitus (DM), dyslipidemia, and hypertension. The exact mechanism of developing PCOS is not well known; however, excess androgen exposure during the fetal period is thought to be its likely cause. Studies with rhesus monkeys show that testosterone administration during the fetal period causes the typical features of human PCOS [16].Hence, FTM-TS and PCOS may have a common etiology, that is, an excessive exposure to androgen during the fetal period.

Almost all FTM-TS patients eventually undergo cross-sex hormone treatment to acquire the secondary sex characteristics of the opposite sex. However, the long-term consequences of androgen administration in FTM-TS patients are unclear. The effects of androgens are different between men and women. Generally, testosterone is believed to remedy the risk of metabolic syndrome and mortality in hypogonadal men [17, 18]. Contrary to its effects in men, hyperandrogenism is an exacerbating factor for metabolic syndrome and vascular dysfunction in biological women [19, 20].Therefore, it is important to examine whether androgens and PCOS synergistically worsen metabolic disorders in FTM-TS patients. Moreover, androgen treatment in FTM-TS may reflect a disease model of a hyperandrogenic disorder, such as PCOS. Thus, it is worth examining the ovarian morphology in androgenized FTM-TS patients.

In this article, we validate the hypothetical etiology of excess androgen exposure and the relationship between FTM-TS and PCOS. In addition, we describe the effects of cross-sex hormone treatment and discuss the potential advantages and disadvantages of comorbid PCOS in FTM-TS patients.

A Ten-Year Follow-Up Study of FTM-TS Patients at a Single Japanese GID Clinic: PCOS is a Common Finding in Untreated FTM-TS

Our institution, Sapporo Medical University Hospital, established a GID clinic in May 2003, and 342 biological female patients with gender dysphoria had visited the hospital by December 2013.

We performed a retrospective study of the patients regarding their menstruation, hormonal status, and ovarian morphology. Psychological, physical, and endocrinological examinations are generally required for diagnosing GID. Physical, endocrinological, and chromosomal evaluations are performed for candidate patients at our institution after a thorough psychological evaluation. After psychological and physical assessment is performed, an institutional review board approves cross-sex hormone therapy, mastectomy, and sex-reassignment surgery (SRS) based on the institution's formulated GID guidelines. Of the 342 patients, 249 (72.8%) patients received physical, endocrinological, and chromosomal evaluations.

As found in previous studies [21, 22], all of the patients were chromosomally normal female karyotype (46,XX) and developed secondary female-sex characteristics as evaluated using the Tanner scale. Of the 249 patients, eight patients were eliminated from the study because appropriate hormonal tests could not be performed for the following reasons; the patients already had SRS (five cases), the medical record was deficient (one case), hyperandrogenemia was untreated because of CAH (one case), and menopause (one case) (Figure 1). Of the remaining 241 patients, 57(23.7%) had received cross-sex hormones (self-administration group), and 184 (76.3%) had not (no prior treatment group) before their initial visit.

We investigated the complication rates of menstrual irregularity, ovarian morphology, and hormonal profiles in the no prior treatment group because exogenous androgen affects endocrinological activity, menstruation, and ovarian morphology. Of the 184 cases in the no prior treatment group 59 (32.1%) had menstrual irregularity, 65 (35.3%) had polycystic ovarian morphology, and 66 (35.9%) had hyperandrogenemia.

The prevalence of PCOS in FTM-TS patients was 16.8% (n=31) using the NIH 1990 criteria and 30.4% (n=56) using the Rotterdam 2003 criteria, which is about three times higher than the rate of PCOS in the normal population.

Effects of Prenatally Exposed Androgens (E.G., Congenital Adrenal Hyperplasia) on Gender Identity and Behavior

CAH is an autosomal recessive disorder caused by genetic mutations in one of six different enzymes of steroidogenic pathways in the adrenal cortex (Figure 2). Over 90% of CAH cases have 21-hydroxylase deficiency (21-OHD). The time of onset and the severity of the disease in CAH female individuals vary, depending on the degree of impairment in enzymatic activity.

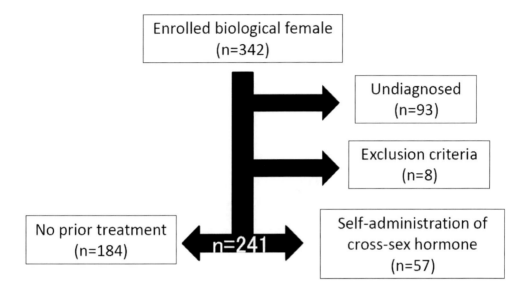

Figure 1. Study subject selection in FTM-TS. Three hundred and forty-two female patients visited the GID clinic at Sapporo Medical University Hospital. In these women, 93 patients did not fulfill the diagnostic criteria for GID because they did not undergo physical and endocrinological studies. In addition, eight patients were eliminated from the review study because they could not perform appropriate hormonal studies for various reasons. Of the remaining 241 patients, 184 patients were not taken exogenous androgens previously, and 57 patients had undergone prior androgen administration.

The genotypes of cytochrome P450 21A2 (CYP21A2) gene, which encodes21-hydroxylase, define enzymatic activity and several phenotypes. Classical CAH is known to cause endogenous hyperandrogenism during the prenatal period. The manifestations of classical CAH are various, from simple virilization of external genitalia, through to virilization with neonatal salt-wasting crisis. Conversely, non-classical CAH rarely manifests in neonatal virilization and develops signs of hyperandrogenism during the peripubertal period or later.

Studies on gender behavior in female patients with classical CAH showed that they exhibited masculinized behavior [23-25]. Another study indicated the prevalence of GID was higher in natal female patients with classical CAH than in a control sample [7]. Judging from these findings, prenatal exposure to excessive androgen by CAH may lead to a higher degree of brain masculinization and affect gender identity in female individuals. However, patients with serious gender identity problems are seen in only 5.2% of CAH patients. Several studies found that genetic female individuals exposed to prenatal androgen show marked behavioral masculinization, but this did not necessarily lead to gender dysphoria [26, 27]. That is, exposure to excess androgen in women during their fetal period does not always mean a change of gender identity and it is possible to have behavioral masculinization independent of gender identity.

Non-classical CAH is a mild form of CAH, and it is a representative model for postnatal hyperandrogenism in humans. In non-classical CAH, gender problems are not reported, contrary to the reports of classical CAH. This indicates that programming of the development of FTM-TS by androgens occurs only during specific time windows, that is, the prenatal period. As a follow-up note, gender problems in FTM-TS are usually recognized before puberty.

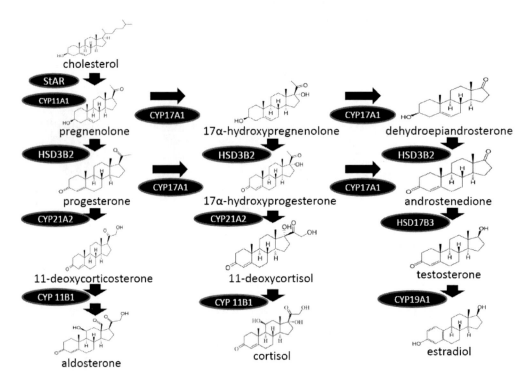

Figure 2. Biosynthesis of steroid hormones in adrenal glands and gonads. Mutations of the following genes (CYP21A2, StAR, CYP11A1, HSD3B2, CYP17A1, or CYP11B1) cause deficient cortisol secretion and compensated hypersecretion of adrenocorticotropic hormone, and subsequently develop adrenal hyperplasia. Almost all the cases with congenital adrenal hyperplasia have mutated CYP21A2 gene. Several polymorphisms of gene encoding steroid-metabolizing enzymes are associated with hyperandrogenism. StAR, steroidogenic acute regulatory protein; CYP11A1, cholesterol side chain cleavage; CYP17A1, 17α-hydroxylase/ 17, 20 lyase; HSD3B2, 3β-hydroxysteroid dehydrogenase; CYP21A2, 21-hydroxylase; HSD17B3, 17β-hydroxysteroid dehydrogenase; CYP11B1, 11β-hydroxylase; CYP19A1, aromatase.

Intriguingly, about 80% of women with the severe type of classical CAH (less than 1% of 21-hydroxylase activity) had never tried to have children [28]. However, more than half of patients with moderate types of CAH (more than 1% of enzymatic activity; i.e., both simple virilizing and non-classical types) had tried to have children. Of course, age is an important factor in the desire to become pregnant and the age distribution was statistically similar in both types of disease. That suggests that gender-related behaviors in patients with CAH may be affected by disease severity or an underlying genotypic difference.

The Association among PCOS, CAH and FTM-TS

We have noticed from previous studies that excessive androgen exposure during the prenatal period masculinizes the brain in some individuals, although it is not a major event. Furthermore, the association between FTM-TS and PCOS is highly credible [29-31] and, as mentioned previously, CAH may be one of the causes of FTM-TS. So, what common traits can we discover between PCOS and CAH? Previous studies indicated that women with classical CAH develop PCOS in adulthood, even though corticosteroid treatment is successful in early life [32]. Interestingly, other studies reported that several characteristics of PCOS were recognized in women with non-classical CAH [33, 34]. Moreover, both CAH and PCOS are thought to originate from excessive androgen exposure during fetal to prepubertal periods. Therefore, it is speculated that excessive androgen are associated with FTM-TS, PCOS, and CAH.

The hypothetical etiology of excessive androgen exposure in FTM-TS and PCOS raises questions about the considerable differences in the occurrence rates of FTM-TS and PCOS. Additionally, it should be mentioned that only a small number of patients with classical CAH develop FTM-TS, even though their androgen levels during the prenatal period were high enough to virilize their external genitalia. It is possible, therefore, that variations in the sensitivity to androgens may alter susceptibility to GID and PCOS. Factors other than the level of excessive androgen exposure may modulate the development of gender identity. Gender identity development in patients with classical CAH may depend on the severity of the disorder because patients with the salt-wasting type of CAH are likely to have gender dysphoria compared with patients with the simple virilizing type of CAH [23]. However, both the simple virilizing type and the salt-wasting type of classical CAH cause hyperandrogenemia during the prenatal period and produce similar virilization of the external genitalia. Hence, the androgen levels during the prenatal period are comparable, although the development of gender identity is quite different between the simple virilizing and salt-wasting types of CAH. Therefore, we propose a "critical period" of androgen exposure that programs the disorder, as a possible solution to these questions. Brain masculinization and gender dysphoria are suspected to occur during the short prenatal period in FTM-TS, but the period of susceptibility to excess androgen is presumed to be wider, so the chance of PCOS is higher.

Epigenetic Mechanisms as a Possible Contributing Factor of Developing FTM-TS

Curiously, untreated FTM-TS cases with PCOS tended to show an exaggerated increase in serum androstenedione levels in our study. In natal female with PCOS, testosterone levels were usually elevated but androstenedione levels were slightly elevated, at most. Generally, cross-sex hormone treatment for FTM-TS does not increase androstenedione because testosterone is hardly converted to androstenedione, and therefore, the effect of exogenous androgens is unlikely. This phenomenon, PCOS with high serum levels of androstenedione, is also observed in patients taking valproate. Valproate is used in the treatment of epilepsy, bipolar disorders, and migraines, and it is known to cause PCOS-like conditions [35]. That is, some FTM-TS patients and most patients taking valproate have identical features. Moreover, autism spectrum disorder is associated with prenatal testosterone and valproate exposure, and both of these factors are also related to FTM-TS and PCOS. Many studies indicate that elevated fetal testosterone is a potential risk factor for autism spectrum disorders [36]. In utero exposure to valproate causes neurodevelopmental abnormalities in rodents and this is an important model of autism spectrum disorders [37]. In humans, prenatal valproate exposure is associated with a seven-fold increased risk of developing autism spectrum disorders [38]. Valproate is a component of histone deacetylase inhibitor modifying epigenetic gene transcription, and, therefore, epigenetics may be one of the causes of FTM-TS, PCOS, and autism spectrum disorders. Such an epigenetic modification may explain another cause of FTM-TS.

Socio-Demographic Differences of FTM-TS: Another Consideration of the Factors for Developing GID

Although transsexualism is a universal phenomenon, its prevalence is different among various countries and regions. In western countries, MTF-TS is more prevalent than FTM-TS. Conversely, we have reported that FTM-TS is more prevalent than MTF-TS in Japan [1]. Social attitudes in Europe, which are less receptive to male homosexuals, may encourage male-homosexuals to seek a diagnostic of heterosexual MTF-TS (sexual orientation against male individuals that seems homosexual from a standpoint of biological sex) and affect the prevalence of transsexualism. Moreover, confirmed cases with GID may represent a partial segment of the whole population. A previous study in Belgium suggested that the prevalence is partially dependent upon the chance of accessing a GID clinic in various regions [39].Thus, the diagnosis of GID is quite complicated, and socio-demographic factors may affect its incidence.

It could be that ethnic differences in prevalence rates are attributable to genetic variations. The research of Coolidge and colleagues on parents of twins found the heritability of GID was 62% [40]. Heylens and colleagues reported that 39.1% of monozygotic twins were concordant for GID, contrary to the finding in dizygotic twins (none were concordant for GID) [41]. Several studies on the concordance for GID in twin cases indicate that GID has strong elements of heritability. However, twin studies cannot completely exclude the influences of shared environmental factors. However, the familial study of concordance for GID within a sibling may explain the independent genetic risk more precisely. Previous research indicated that the prevalence of transsexualism in siblings of transsexual probands (0.47%) was much higher than that of the general population [42]. Interestingly, this study also showed that MTF-TS siblings are about four times more likely to be transsexual than FTM-TS siblings. Therefore, it is thought that gender identities in biological male individuals are more susceptible to genetic alterations.

Genetic polymorphisms are variations in DNA sequences and one of the contributing factors to racial differences. These genetic variations affect gene expression levels that modify enzymatic activities, binding efficiencies to specific targets, and subsequently defining disease susceptibility. It is thought that genes encoding enzymes of steroidogenic pathways and steroid hormone receptors are associated with GID, because androgens and estrogens may affect the sexual development of the human brain. A single nucleotide polymorphism of the CYP17A1 gene, which regulates 17 alpha-hydroxylase/ 17, 20 lyase (Figure2), may be related to FTM-TS [43]. The estrogen receptor beta gene also is presumed to be a candidate for FTM-TS [44]. In MTF-TS, polymorphism of the androgen receptor gene is associated with the disorder [45]. These studies indicate that certain genetic factors partially affect the development of transsexualism.

Potential Problems Related to the Complication of PCOS in FTM-TS

It is known that PCOS often complicates lifestyle diseases and it may negatively affect the lives of FTM-TS patients. PCOS is associated with an increased incidence of type 2 DM and metabolic syndrome. A meta-analysis showed that women with PCOS have an increased prevalence of impaired glucose tolerance (BMI-matched studies, odds ratio (OR) = 2.54, 95% confidence interval (CI) = 1.44–4.47), type 2 DM (BMI-matched studies, OR = 4.00, 95% CI = 1.97–8.10), and metabolic syndrome (BMI-matched studies, OR = 2.20, 95% CI= 1.36–3.56) [46]. PCOS women have been found to have a significantly higher prevalence of risk factors for cardiovascular disease (CVD), such as hypertension and higher triglyceride levels than controls. However, the actual incidence of CVD later in life was statistically similar among PCOS women and controls, and uncertainty remains regarding the development of CVD in PCOS women [47].

In addition, patients with PCOS manifest skin complications, such as acne and hirsutism owing to hyperandrogenism. Therefore, multi-disciplinary approaches are needed, including dermatology, endocrinology, diabetology, and cardiology, because PCOS is a condition requiring life-long attention.

PCOS poses another problem; it is a burden on a nation's healthcare system. Azziz and colleagues estimated the mean annual cost of PCOS-associated DM to be 1.77 billion dollars in the United States [48]. Because hyperandrogenemia is thought to exacerbate metabolic problems in PCOS women, androgen treatment in FTM-TS patients may increase the cost of medical care, as seen for hyperandrogenic PCOS.

If PCOS has a genetic basis, it may be reasonable to predict that MTF-TS patients with the putative genes responsible for PCOS are also affected by other lifestyle diseases. However, the male phenotypes corresponding to PCOS in women are not recognized and, therefore, it is unclear whether the subset of MTF-TS patients is susceptible to lifestyle diseases or not.

The Effects of Exogenous Androgen on Ovarian Morphology and Endocrinological Profiles: Is Cross-Sex Hormone Treatment in FTM-TS Patients a Model of PCOS?

Cross-sex hormone therapy is a standard treatment for GID, and many FTM-TS patients had administered androgens themselves. Unfortunately, we were unable to conduct a follow-up study on the effects of hormonal treatment on these individuals because most of the patients left the hospital after the diagnosis. Instead, we compared the no prior treatment at initial visit group and the self-administration group to estimate the effect of androgen administration. Table 2 summarizes the hormonal profiles of both groups. Compared withthe no prior treatment group, the self-administration group had significantly lower LH levels and a lower insulin resistance index [1]. These findings are not consistent with PCOS, possibly because the effect of endogenous hyperandrogenism in PCOS may be different from that of exogenous excess androgen with regard to hormonal profiles.

Table 2. Hormonal profiles of FTM-TS

	No prior treatment	Self-administration
Age	23 (20, 27)	25 (22, 31)
BMI	21.8 (19.6, 24.7)	21.2 (20.3, 24.7)
	≧25: 24.5%	≧25: 22.8%
LH	5.86 (4.17, 9.19)	3.91 (2.19, 7.82)
FSH	5.72 (4.04, 6.92)	5.42 (3.40, 6.86)
Estradiol	46.77 (34.76, 80.34)	38.26 (31.73, 57.77)
Total testosterone	0.44 (0.31, 0.60)	6.33 (2.53, 10.89)
Free testosterone	<0.6 (<0.6, 1)	13.8 (7.7, 30.6)
Androstenedione	2.5 (1.9, 3.1)	2.7 (2.1, 3.5)
DHEAS	220 (159, 287)	208 (159, 279)
HOMA-IR	1.61 (1.01, 2.30)	1.14 (0.77, 1.78)

Data are expressed as medians (25th and 75th percentiles).
BMI, body mass index; DHEAS, dehydroepiandrosterone sulfate; HOMA-IR, homeostasis model assessment of insulin resistance

Several patients had undergone additional SRS, including total abdominal hysterectomy and bilateral salpingo-oophorectomy. Androgen-exposed ovaries resected by SRS may be a pathological model of PCOS ovaries because hyperandrogenemia is thought to yield polycystic ovarian morphology in PCOS. Therefore, we evaluated the androgen-exposed ovaries histologically [49]. From May 2007 through March 2011, 20 FTM-TS patients underwent SRS in our hospital. Of these 20 FTM-TS patients, nine patients were eliminated because the pathological specimens of their ovaries were in a poor state of preservation. The remaining 11 patients had been administered 125–250 mg testosterone enanthate intramuscularly every 2 weeks for periods from 17 months to 14 years (median: 38 months). All of the FTM-TS patients had a regular menstrual cycle before androgen treatment, according to their medical history, and none of the patients were diagnosed with PCOS. As a control group, we examined 10 individuals, matched for age and BMI, who had undergone pelvic surgery for gynecologic malignancies. All 10 control women had a regular menstrual cycle prior to their surgery, and magnetic resonance imaging and transvaginal ultrasonography indicated that there was no ovarian disease or polycystic ovarian morphology. None of the androgen-exposed ovaries or control ovaries showed polycystic ovarian morphology macroscopically. Compared with the control group, the mean thickness of the tunica albuginea and the collagenous layer of the tunica were significantly greater in the FTM-TS group. Diffuse stromal hyperplasia was observed significantly more frequently in the FTM-TS group than in the control group. The mean density of the healthy follicles did not differ significantly between the FTM-TS and control groups. However, we found that there were significantly greater numbers of atretic follicles in the FTM-TS group. These findings in androgen-exposed ovaries are slightly different from those in the ovaries of PCOS patients, which did not have an increase in atretic follicles, but had an accumulation of small viable antral follicles [50].

DISCUSSION

Several previous researchers suggested that the pathogenesis of transsexualism is multidimensional, and there are several etiological hypotheses: congenital origins, such as genetic predisposition and impaired brain development; and acquired environmental factors, such as social attitude and nurture. We have demonstrated an important fact that PCOS is common in FTM-TS patients and that both disorders are associated with excessive exposure to androgen during the prenatal period. That is, hyperandrogenemia is thought to stimulate a process of developing FTM-TS and PCOS. Epigenetic mechanisms are also considered to be one of the pathogeneses of FTM-TS.

Current Understandings Regarding the Pathogenesis of Transsexualism: Nature or Nurture?

Until now, many researchers have reported and debated the development of gender identity and transsexualism, and the interpretation of the findings is complex and confusing. John Money, who is a pioneering transgender researcher, reported a male case of a gender identity problem related to gender change surgery in childhood. The patient, a monozygotic twin, accidentally injured his external genitalia during circumcision and the twins' parents and Money decided to raise the child as female, and gender change surgery was performed. Unfortunately, the child came to feel gender dysphoria against the reared gender [51]. From this case, we came to learn that gender identity could not be changed by social influences. It is well-known that the desire for a gender change is one of the symptoms of schizophrenia. Borras et al. reported that 20% of all schizophrenic patients experienced sexual delusions, and some of them felt their gender identity was the opposite sex [52]. This finding may suggest that neurodevelopmental problems such as schizophrenia are key factors for GID. Following this idea, research has found that brain morphology in GID cases is somewhat different compared with that of their biological sex. The bed nucleus of the stria terminalis (BNST), which is sexually dimorphic, having a larger number of neurons in natal male individuals than female individuals, is similar in number between MTF-TS patients and natal females [53]. BNST is involved in sexual behavior, anxiety, stress responses, and gonadotropin secretion in animals [54]. The human BNST is presumed to be involved in the same functions, although there is not definitive evidence. The expression of neurokinin B in the human infundibular nucleus, which regulates gonadotropin-releasing hormone secretion, is female dominant and female-stereotyped expression is also observed in MTF-TS [55]. Sex difference in the interstitial nucleus of the anterior hypothalamus 3, which is related to sexual orientation, is reversed in transsexualism [56]. Conversely, some reports imply postnatal episodes in the development of transsexualism. It was reported that only 10–27% of children diagnosed with GID had a persistent desire for a gender change [57]. The famous report of the male cases with 5α-reductase deficiency, by Imperato-McGinley, suggested that postnatal testosterone exposure can cause gender change [58]. Male patients with 5α-reductase deficiency show ambiguous external genitalia owing to diminished dihydrotestosterone levels, have female gender identity, and are raised as female. However, they recognize their gender identity as male and feel gender dysphoria against the reared gender in association with the pubertal testosterone surge. At present, arguments regarding whether nature or nurture is a determinant of GID remain inconclusive.

Androgen Exposure and Brain Development

Brain masculinization may be part of the pathogenesis of GID. So what causes brain masculinization? It is known that 46,XY patients with complete androgen insensitivity syndrome have a female gender identity and phenotype owing to deficient androgen receptor functioning. This indicates that androgen and its receptors have important roles in brain masculinization, and feminization may be a passive process unless androgen affects the brain. Similarly, there are certainly some data that show that excessive androgen exposure in female individuals results in brain masculinization, as evidenced by a relatively greater incidence of male-stereotyped behavior and male gender identity [59]. However, we do not know the precise causes of when or how masculinization of the human brain occurs.

Androgens influence patterns of cell death and survival, neural connectivity, and neurochemical characterization. It is difficult to analyze the process of in-vivo brain development in humans, so animal models and cultured nerve cells are used. Animal studies demonstrated that prenatal exposure to testosterone cause neural and behavioral sexual differentiation [59]. Gamma-aminobutyric acid (GABA), glutamate, and aspartate are the predominant amino acid neurotransmitters in the mammalian brain, and their expression levels are different between the sexes. Davis et al. showed that treating female rats with testosterone propionate on the day of birth increased their GABA levels to the levels of male rats, suggesting that sex differences may be the result of hormone exposure during brain development [60]. The above-mentioned findings indicate that the prenatal period is critical for brain masculinization.

Future Perspectives on Revealing Pathophysiology

Judging from a comprehensive review of previous studies, it is postulated that putative genetic factors, which are related to receptors and converting enzymes of sex steroids, potentiate prenatal androgen activity, that subsequently produce brain masculinization, and finally cause FTM-TS and program various organs to develop PCOS (Figure 3). If androgen activity does not occur, brain feminization may proceed.

The hypothesis of excess androgen exposure raises questions about the resource of excess androgens during the fetal period. Two mechanisms are presumed to solve this question; 1) the transport of maternal androgens to the baby's circulation via the placenta, and 2) hypersecretion of androgens by the fetal ovaries and adrenal glands. Previous research suggests that pregnant women with PCOS have high serum androgen levels, and that the serum androgen levels of the fetus are positively correlated with those of their mothers [61]. Moreover, the placentas of women with PCOS have diminished aromatase activity compared with the placentas of control women, by which to abnormally transfer maternal androgensto fetus [62]. However, the very low prevalence of FTM-TS is unexplainable, because pregnant women with hyperandrogenemia (pregnant PCOS patients) should be relatively common. Hence, maternal hyperandrogenemia does not necessarily cause FTM-TS.

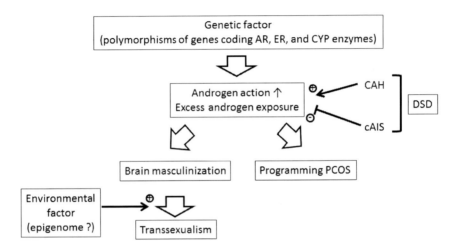

Figure 3. Hypothetical etiology of transsexualism and PCOS. Putative genetic factors, that are related to sex hormone receptors and converting enzymes, potentiate prenatal androgen actions, subsequent brain masculinization, and finally cause FTM-TS and programming various organs to develop PCOS. AR, androgen receptor; ER, estrogen receptor; CYP, cytochrome P 450; DSD, disorders of sex development; CAH, congenital adrenal hyperplasia; cAIS, complete androgen insensitivity syndrome; PCOS, polycystic ovary syndrome.

Sex difference in testosterone levels is maximal between 8 and 24 weeks of gestation [63]. Temporarily increased testosterone in the male fetus tends to decrease before birth. Conversely, fetal ovaries seem to be inactive until late fetal development because they only release a small amount of estrogen prenatally. Fetuses are also exposed to small amounts of androgen from their own adrenal glands. We speculate that certain mechanisms, such as genetic factors, activate fetal ovaries and adrenal glands to secrete androgens as male fetuses do.

CONCLUSION

It is time to determine the relationship between potentiated androgen actions and transsexualism thoroughly. Research is needed to measure and analyze the associations among: (a) maternal and fetal levels of serum androgens; (b) the genotypes encoding the metabolic enzymes of sex steroids and sex steroid receptors; and (c) in-vivo brain function and morphology. A human prospective study measuring the associations among these variables (i.e., serum androgens, genotypes, and brain morphology) would clarify the pathophysiology of gender identity disorder. Interventional studies using pregnant non-human primates exposed to excess androgens can also provide needed evidence about these relationships.

ACKNOWLEDGMENT

The authors thank the members of the GID clinic in Sapporo Medical University for providing the data and comments.

REFERENCES

[1]   Baba T, Endo T, Ikeda K, Shimizu A, Honnma H, Ikeda H, Masumori N, Ohmura T, Kiya T, Fujimoto T, Koizumi M, Saito T. Distinctive features of female-to-male transsexualism and prevalence of gender identity disorder in Japan. *J. Sex Med.* 2011;8:1686-93.

[2]   Olyslager F, Conway L. On the calculation of the prevalence of transsexualism. WPATH 20th International Symposium, Chicago, Illinois, September 6, 2007, URL:http://ai.eecs.umich.edu/people/conway/TS/Prevalence/Reports/Prevalence%20of %20Transsexualism.pdf

[3]   Vujovic S, Popovic S, Sbutega-Milosevic G, Djordjevic M, Gooren L. Transsexualism in Serbia: a twenty-year follow-up study. *J. Sex Med.* 2009;6:1018-23.

[4]   Simon L, Kozák LR, Simon V, Czobor P, Unoka Z, Szabó Á, Csukly G. Regional grey matter structure differences between transsexuals and healthy controls - a voxel based morphometry study. *PLoS One.* 2013;8(12):e83947.

[5]   Luders E, Sánchez FJ, Tosun D, Shattuck DW, Gaser C, Vilain E, Toga AW. Increased Cortical Thickness in Male-to-Female Transsexualism. *J. Behav. Brain Sci.* 2012;2:357-62.

[6]   Santarnecchi E, Vatti G, Déttore D, Rossi A. Intrinsic cerebral connectivity analysis in an untreated female-to-male transsexual subject: a first attempt using resting-state fMRI. *Neuroendocrinology.* 2012;96:188-93.

[7]   Dessens AB, Slijper FM, Drop SL. Gender dysphoria and gender change in chromosomal females with congenital adrenal hyperplasia. *Arch. Sex Behav.* 2005;34:389-97.

[8]   Dittmann RW, Kappes MH, Kappes ME, Börger D, Stegner H, Willig RH, Wallis H. Congenital adrenal hyperplasia. I: Gender-related behavior and attitudes in female patients and sisters. Psychoneuroendocrinology. 1990;15(5-6):401-20. Erratum in: *Psychoneuroendocrinology* 1991;16(4):369-71.

[9]   Stein IF, Leventhal ML. Amenorrhea associated with bilateral polycystic ovaries. *Am. J. Obstet Gynecol.* 1935;29:181–91.

[10] Zawadski JK, Dunaif A. Diagnostic criteria for polycystic ovary syndrome: towards a rational approach. In: Dunaif A, Givens JR, Haseltine FP, Merriam GR, editors. *Polycystic Ovary Syndrome.* Boston: Blackwell Scientific Publications; 1992. pp. 377-84.

[11] Rotterdam ESHRE/ASRM-Sponsored PCOS Consensus Workshop Group. Revised 2003 consensus on diagnostic criteria and long-term health risks related to polycystic ovary syndrome. Hum. Reprod. 2004;19:41-7. */Fertil. Steril.* 2004;81:19–25.

[12] Azziz R, Carmina E, Dewailly D, Diamanti-Kandarakis E, Escobar-Morreale HF, Futterweit W, Janssen OE, Legro RS, Norman RJ, Taylor AE, Witchel SF.; Task Force on the Phenotype of the Polycystic Ovary Syndrome of The Androgen Excess and PCOS Society. The Androgen Excess and PCOS Society criteria for the polycystic ovary syndrome: the complete task force report. *Fertil. Steril.* 2009;91:456-88.

[13] Kubota T. Update in polycystic ovary syndrome: new criteria of diagnosis and treatment in Japan. *Reprod. Med. Biol.* 2013;12:71-7.

[14] Diamanti-Kandarakis E, Kouli CR, Bergiele AT, Filandra FA, Tsianateli TC, Spina GG, Zapanti ED, Bartzis MI. A survey of the polycystic ovary syndrome in the Greek island of Lesbos: hormonal and metabolic profile. *J. Clin. Endocrinol. Metab.* 1999 Nov;84(11):4006-11.

[15] Azziz R, Woods KS, Reyna R, Key TJ, Knochenhauer ES, Yildiz BO. The prevalence and features of the polycystic ovary syndrome in an unselected population. *J. Clin. Endocrinol. Metab.* 2004 Jun;89(6):2745-9.

[16] Abbott DH, Barnett DK, Bruns CM, Dumesic DA. Androgen excess fetal programming of female reproduction: a developmental aetiology for polycystic ovary syndrome? *Hum. Reprod. Update* 2005;11:357-74.

[17] Muraleedharan V, Marsh H, Kapoor D, Channer KS, Jones TH. Testosterone deficiency is associated with increased risk of mortality and testosterone replacement improves survival in men with type 2 diabetes. *Eur. J. Endocrinol.* 2013;169:725-33.

[18] Francomano D, Lenzi A, Aversa A. Effects of five-year treatment with testosterone undecanoate on metabolic and hormonal parameters in ageing men with metabolic syndrome. *Int. J. Endocrinol.* 2014;2014:527470.

[19] Kravariti M, Naka KK, Kalantaridou SN, Kazakos N, Katsouras CS, Makrigiannakis A, Paraskevaidis EA, Chrousos GP, Tsatsoulis A, Michalis LK. Predictors of endothelial dysfunction in young women with polycystic ovary syndrome. *J. Clin. Endocrinol. Metab.* 2005;90:5088–95.

[20] O'Reilly MW, Taylor AE, Crabtree NJ, Hughes BA, Capper F, Crowley RK, Stewart PM, Tomlinson JW, Arlt W. Hyperandrogenemia predicts metabolic phenotype in polycystic ovary syndrome: the utility of serum androstenedione. *J. Clin. Endocrinol. Metab.*2014, in press.

[21] Inoubli A, De Cuypere G, Rubens R, Heylens G, Elaut E, Van Caenegem E, Menten B, T'Sjoen G. Karyotyping, is it worthwhile in transsexualism? *J. Sex Med.* 2011;8:475-8.

[22] Auer MK, Fuss J, Stalla GK, Athanasoulia AP. Twenty years of endocrinologic treatment in transsexualism: analyzing the role of chromosomal analysis and hormonal profiling in the diagnostic work-up. *Fertil. Steril.* 2013;100:1103-10.

[23] Zucker KJ, Bradley SJ, Oliver G, Blake J, Fleming S, Hood J. Psychosexual development of women with congenital adrenal hyperplasia. *Horm. Behav.* 1996;30:300-18.

[24] Berenbaum SA, Bailey JM. Effects on gender identity of prenatal androgens and genital appearance: evidence from girls with congenital adrenal hyperplasia. *J. Clin. Endocrinol. Metab.* 2003;88:1102-6.

[25] Hall CM, Jones JA, Meyer-Bahlburg HF, Dolezal C, Coleman M, Foster P, Price DA, Clayton PE. Behavioral and physical masculinization are related to genotype in girls with congenital adrenal hyperplasia. *J. Clin. Endocrinol. Metab.* 2004;89:419-24.

[26] Meyer-Bahlburg HF, Dolezal C, Baker SW, Ehrhardt AA, New MI. Gender development in women with congenital adrenal hyperplasia as a function of disorder severity. *Arch. Sex Behav.* 2006;35:667-84.

[27] Meyer-Bahlburg HF, Dolezal C, Baker SW, Carlson AD, Obeid JS, New MI. Prenatal androgenization affects gender-related behavior but not gender identity in 5–12-year-old girls with congenital adrenal hyperplasia. *Arch. Sex Behav.* 2004;33:97-104

[28] Krone N, Rose IT, Willis DS, Hodson J, Wild SH, Doherty EJ, Hahner S, Parajes S, Stimson RH, Han TS, Carroll PV, Conway GS, Walker BR, MacDonald F, Ross RJ, Arlt W; United Kingdom Congenital adrenal Hyperplasia Adult Study Executive (CaHASE). Genotype-phenotype correlation in 153 adult patients with congenital adrenal hyperplasia due to 21-hydroxylase deficiency: analysis of the United Kingdom Congenital adrenal Hyperplasia Adult Study Executive (CaHASE) cohort. *J. Clin. Endocrinol. Metab.* 2013;98:E346-54.

[29] Balen AH, Schachter ME, Montgomery D, Reid RW, Jacobs HS. Polycystic ovaries are a common finding in untreated female to male transsexuals. *Clin. Endocrinol.* (Oxf). 1993;38:325-9.

[30] Bosinski HA, Peter M, Bonatz G, Arndt R, Heidenreich M, Sippell WG, Wille R. A higher rate of hyperandrogenic disorders in female-to-male transsexuals. *Psychoneuroendocrinology.* 1997;22:361-80.

[31] Baba T, Endo T, Honnma H, Kitajima Y, Hayashi T, Ikeda H, Masumori N, Kamiya H, Moriwaka O, Saito T. Association between polycystic ovary syndrome and female-to-male transsexuality. *Hum. Reprod.* 2007;22:1011-6.

[32] Barnes RB, Rosenfield RL, Ehrmann DA, Cara JF, Cuttler L, Levitsky LL, Rosenthal IM. Ovarian hyperandrogynism as a result of congenital adrenal virilizing disorders: evidence for perinatal masculinization of neuroendocrine function in women. *J. Clin. Endocrinol. Metab.* 1994;79:1328-33.

[33] Moran C, Azziz R, Carmina E, Dewailly D, Fruzzetti F, Ibañez L, Knochenhauer ES, Marcondes JA, Mendonca BB, Pignatelli D, Pugeat M, Rohmer V, Speiser PW, Witchel SF. 21-Hydroxylase-deficient nonclassic adrenal hyperplasia is a progressive disorder: a multicenter study. *Am. J. Obstet. Gynecol.* 2000;183:1468-74.

[34] Carmina E, Rosato F, Jannì A, Rizzo M, Longo RA. Extensive clinical experience: relative prevalence of different androgen excess disorders in 950 women referred because of clinical hyperandrogenism. *J. Clin. Endocrinol. Metab.* 2006;91:2-6.

[35] Hu X, Wang J, Dong W, Fang Q, Hu L, Liu C. A meta-analysis of polycystic ovary syndrome in women taking valproate for epilepsy. *Epilepsy Res.* 2011;97:73-82.

[36] Baron-Cohen S, Lombardo MV, Auyeung B, Ashwin E, Chakrabarti B, Knickmeyer R. Why are autism spectrum conditions more prevalent in males? *PLoS Biol.* 2011; 9: e1001081.

[37] Schneider T, Przewłocki R. Behavioral alterations in rats prenatally exposed to valproic acid: animal model of autism. *Neuropsychopharmacology.* 2005;30:80-9.

[38] Rasalam AD, Hailey H, Williams JH, Moore SJ, Turnpenny PD, Lloyd DJ, Dean JC. Characteristics of fetal anticonvulsant syndrome associated autistic disorder. *Dev. Med. Child. Neurol.* 2005;47:551-5.

[39] De Cuypere G, Van Hemelrijck M, Michel A, Carael B, Heylens G, Rubens R, Hoebeke P, Monstrey S. Prevalence and demography of transsexualism in Belgium. *Eur. Psychiatry.* 2007;22:137-41.

[40] Coolidge FL, Thede LL, Young SE. The heritability of gender identity disorder in a child and adolescent twin sample.*Behav. Genet.* 2002;32:251-7.

[41] Heylens G, De Cuypere G, Zucker KJ, Schelfaut C, Elaut E, VandenBossche H, De Baere E, T'Sjoen G. Gender identity disorder in twins: a review of the case report literature. *J. Sex Med.* 2012;9:751-7.

[42] Gómez-Gil E, Esteva I, Almaraz MC, Pasaro E, Segovia S, Guillamon A. Familiality of gender identity disorder in non-twin siblings. *Arch. Sex Behav.* 2010;39:546-52.

[43] Bentz EK, Hefler LA, Kaufmann U, Huber JC, Kolbus A, Tempfer CB. A polymorphism of the CYP17 gene related to sex steroid metabolism is associated with female-to-male but not male-to-female transsexualism. *Fertil. Steril.* 2008;90:56-9.

[44] Fernández R, Esteva I, Gómez-Gil E, Rumbo T, Almaraz MC, Roda E, Haro-Mora JJ, Guillamón A, Pásaro E. The (CA)n Polymorphism of ERβ Gene is associated with FtM transsexualism. *J. Sex Med.* 2014;11:720-8.

[45] Hare L, Bernard P, Sánchez FJ, Baird PN, Vilain E, Kennedy T, Harley VR. Androgen receptor repeat length polymorphism associated with male-to-female transsexualism. *Biol. Psychiatry.* 2009;65:93-6.

[46] Moran LJ, Misso ML, Wild RA, Norman RJ. Impaired glucose tolerance, type 2 diabetes and metabolic syndrome in polycystic ovary syndrome: a systematic review and meta-analysis. *Hum Reprod* Update. 2010;16:347-63.

[47] Schmidt J, Landin-Wilhelmsen K, Brännström M, Dahlgren E. Cardiovascular disease and risk factors in PCOS women of postmenopausal age: a 21-year controlled follow-up study. *J. Clin. Endocrinol. Metab.* 2011;96:3794-803.

[48] Azziz R, Marin C, Hoq L, Badamgarav E, Song P. Health care-related economic burden of the polycystic ovary syndrome during the reproductive life span. *J. Clin. Endocrinol. Metab.* 2005;90:4650-8.

[49] Ikeda K, Baba T, Noguchi H, Nagasawa K, Endo T, Kiya T, Saito T. Excessive androgen exposure in female-to-male transsexual persons of reproductive age induces hyperplasia of the ovarian cortex and stroma but not polycystic ovary morphology. *Hum. Reprod.* 2013;28:453-61.

[50] Jonard S, Dewailly D. The follicular excess in polycystic ovaries, due to intra-ovarian hyperandrogenism, may be the main culprit for the follicular arrest. *Hum. Reprod.* Update. 2004;10:107-17.

[51] Diamond M, Sigmundson HK. Sex reassignment at birth.Long-term review and clinical implications. *Arch. Pediatr. Adolesc. Med.* 1997;151:298-304.

[52] Borras L, Huguelet P, Eytan A. Delusional "pseudotranssexualism" in schizophrenia. *Psychiatry.* 2007;70:175-9.

[53] Kruijver FP, Zhou JN, Pool CW, Hofman MA, Gooren LJ, Swaab DF. Male-to-female transsexuals have female neuron numbers in a limbic nucleus. *J. Clin. Endocrinol. Metab.* 2000;85:2034-41.

[54] Aste N, Balthazart J, Absil P, Grossmann R, Mülhbauer E, Viglietti-Panzica C, Panzica GC. Anatomical and neurochemical definition of the nucleus of the stria terminalis in Japanese quail (Coturnix japonica). *J. Comp. Neurol.* 1998;396:141-57.

[55] Taziaux M, Swaab DF, Bakker J. Sex differences in the neurokinin B system in the human infundibular nucleus. *J. Clin. Endocrinol. Metab.* 2012;97:E2210-20.

[56] Garcia-Falgueras A, Swaab DF. A sex difference in the hypothalamic uncinate nucleus: relationship to gender identity. *Brain. 2008*;131(Pt 12):3132-46.

[57] Shumer DE, Spack NP. Current management of gender identity disorder in childhood and adolescence: guidelines, barriers and areas of controversy. *Curr. Opin. Endocrinol. Diabetes Obes.* 2013;20:69-73.

[58] Imperato-McGinley J, Peterson RE, Gautier T, Sturla E. Androgens and the evolution of male-gender identity among male pseudohermaphrodites with 5alpha-reductase deficiency. *N. Engl. J. Med.* 1979;300:1233-7.

[59] Hines M. Prenatal testosterone and gender-related behaviour. *Eur. J. Endocrinol.* 2006;155 Suppl 1:S115-21.

[60] Davis AM, Ward SC, Selmanoff M, Herbison AE, McCarthy MM. Developmental sex differences in amino acid neurotransmitter levels in hypothalamic and limbic areas of rat brain. *Neuroscience.* 1999;90:1471-82.

[61] Sir-Petermann T, Maliqueo M, Angel B, Lara HE, Pérez-Bravo F, Recabarren SE. Maternal serum androgens in pregnant women with polycystic ovarian syndrome: possible implications in prenatal androgenization. *Hum. Reprod.* 2002;17:2573-9.

[62] Maliqueo M, Lara HE, Sánchez F, Echiburú B, Crisosto N, Sir-Petermann T. Placental steroidogenesis in pregnant women with polycystic ovary syndrome. *Eur. J. Obstet. Gynecol. Reprod. Biol.* 2013;166:151-5.

[63] Hines M. Sex-related variation in human behavior and the brain. *Trends Cogn. Sci.* 2010;14:448-56.

In: Gender Identity   ISBN: 978-1-63321-488-0
Editor: Beverly L. Miller   © 2014 Nova Science Publishers, Inc.

Chapter 14

GOD AND THE TRANSGENDER PERSON

Trista L. Carr[1],*, Psy.D. and Mark A. Yarhouse[2],†, Psy.D.
[1]Private Practice and CSATF-SP at Corcoran
[2]Regent University

ABSTRACT

Transgender (TG) individuals who believe in the God of the three major faith traditions, Judiasm, Islam, and Christianity, and have an internal conflict surrounding their gender identity often say to themselves, "Where is God in all of this?" (Yarhouse & Carr, 2012). For the many people who wonder, "Why do I have these experiences?" there is no consensus for how to best answer that question. Experiencing these questions or conflicts and not having many solid answers may make lead TG persons of faith to feel confusion, frustration, or anger—this negative affect can be directed inward (toward themselves) or outward (toward their parents, their religious institutions and leaders, and even to God). In this chapter we present some questions and results from preliminary research with TG persons of faith that might help clinicians and religious persons explore this area and find their own answers. Topics that are explored include the etiology of Gender Dysphoria and the potential conflict with any of the three major Abrahamic religions (Judaism, Christianity, and Islam), the pursuit of God for meaning and purpose for the TG individual, how TG persons of faith can live in the tension, and lastly, we give specific recommendations for both clinicians and TG individuals based on the limited existing research in this area.

Transgender (TG) individuals who are or have been part of a religious faith tradition can struggle with what it means to navigate gender identity questions in light of their religious identity. In this chapter we consider this question with reference to God, which, for the sake of this discussion, we are refer to in relation to the three major faith traditions, Judaism, Islam, and Christianity. There are other major world religions, of course (e.g., Hinduism, Buddhism), and many transgender individuals will benefit from a more focused analysis of

---

* E-mail: Dr.Carr@tristacarr.com.
† E-mail: markyar@regent.edu.

gender identity in relation to those world religious. For our purposes, we recognize and consider those who report an internal conflict surrounding their gender identity and often say to themselves, "Where is God in all of this?" (Yarhouse & Carr, 2012).

Also, we understand that for many TG persons, the topic of a conflict with God could be a minor (or nonexistent) question or issue, as they simply do not identify with an organized religion. However, for the sake of people of faith, we want to explore some questions that might help clinicians and religious persons explore this area and find their own answers. Though we speak in generalities to "people of faith" who relate to God, we focus primarily on the experiences of the Christian population with which the authors most closely identify and have garnered research.

ETIOLOGY: GENDER DYSPHORIA AND THE CONFLICT

Questions about causation can be a point of concern for people of faith who experience gender identity concerns. There may be many different reasons why transgender persons feel that their sense of themselves as either male or female is at odds with their biological/birth-sex. The research on the etiology of gender dysphoria is mixed to say the least.

The most prominent theory of causation is the brain-sex theory, which suggests that the brain develops differently for transgender individuals than cisgender people. The brain-sex theory is based on the understanding that male/female differentiation of the genitals occurs at a different stage of prenatal development than the male/female differentiation of the brain. The theory posits that male-to-female (MtF) transsexual persons experience differentiation of the genitals in one direction (male) and brain differentiation in the other direction (female). Proponents believe that they way to test this theory is to study regions of the brain of MtF transsexual persons to see if they are more like that of cisgender females than cisgender males, which has been reported in some studies (e.g., Zhou, Hofman, Gooren, & Swaab, 1995). Likewise, in the brain-sex theory, the brain development of a female-to-male (FtM) transgender individual would be more like the development of the brain of a cisgender male. The research regarding the brain-sex theory is limited and subject to criticism.

Other models of etiology are multifactorial and also draw on learning theory and social environment. For example, Meyer-Bahlburg (2002) identified several risk factors thought to be associated with the development of gender dysphoria. These include (for biological males who are gender dysphoric) feminine appearance, inhibited/shy temperament, separation anxiety, late in birth order, sensory reactivity, sexual abuse. Other risk factors include parental preference for a girl, parental indifference to cross-gender behavior, and reinforcement of cross-gender behavior.

Given the range of experiences under the transgender umbrella, it is unlikely that there is one unifying theory that will account for every expression. However, it is common for people who experience gender dysphoria to wonder how it developed and where God is in reference to their concerns. Thus for the many people who wonder, "Why do I have these experiences?" there is no consensus for how to best answer that question. Experiencing these questions or conflicts and not having many solid answers may make lead TG persons of faith to feel confusion, frustration, or anger—this negative affect can be directed inward (toward themselves) or outward (toward their parents, their religious institutions and leaders, and even to God).

Individuals who have grown up in religious institutions of the three major faith traditions have typically been taught what is "right" and what is "wrong". Some religious institutions can be very black and white when it concerns various topics of morality and ways of being. As such, some individuals are taught that "gender dysphoria is wrong" and that it is a "sin" or a reflection of willful disobedience. In other cases, people are taught that gender dysphoria may be the result of a world that is "fallen" or steeped in sin but there is an appreciation that the individual who experiences gender dysphoria did not choose to have these experiences. From this perspective, experiencing gender dysphoria is not right or wrong, but *what you do with it* may be right or wrong. A third, but less often espoused teaching, more notably within Christianity, is the belief that being transgender is a reflection of God's diverse creation. The notion is that these individuals represent a more complete reflection of the person of God as compared to how cisgender males and females reflect the person of God. This third theological stance will not be addressed here in short due to the fact that transgender individuals espousing this belief are less likely to present to therapy due to a feeling of incongruence or religious/spiritual conflicts.

The first statement—gender dysphoria is wrong—can be really confusing to someone who experiences gender identity questions or conflicts. After all, individuals with gender dysphoria did not choose to experience these conflicts. They merely found themselves with this experience frequently starting at a young age. Thus, the question for the TG person might be, "How can something that just happened be 'wrong' or a 'sin'?"

When people hear that gender dysphoria is wrong in their places of worship, it may make them feel as though there is something "wrong," "bad," or "sinful" about them. The general tone and approach of the religious institution may even make these individuals feel as if they are bad as persons. Either way, transgender people of faith might feel a lot of shame and guilt from hearing this message.

For example, in our qualitative research with 32 MtF transgender Christians (Carr, Yarhouse, & Thomas, 2013; Yarhouse & Carr, 2012), many of our participants indicated that their religion/faith was hurtful to them personally and inflicted psychological harm or emotional distress; thus, indicating to our participants that there was something wrong with them. One 55-year-old participant wrote: "The negative messages from the Church did irreparable harm to my self-esteem that took most of my life to recover from."

In addition, derogatory or insulting comments about transgender people are hurtful when they are from people who are important to the person (i.e., parents, friends, teachers, coaches, and religious leaders). These comments may be especially hurtful in religious settings, or when God or sacred texts are used to insult or condemn the way the individual has always felt. This type of shame induced in the name of God can become equated with God's view of the person, making the person feel as if God could never love him or her because of the experience of gender dysphoria—something this individual has no control over feeling or not feeling.

One of our Christian participants noted: "My faith in God has been shaken only in trying to sift out the truth and understanding of my relationship that is authentic and not based on teaching which I now question because of the attitudes and actions of those who were teaching. I miss being able to freely embrace my faith without feeling like I am not accepted as a real person or welcomed genuinely."

Hearing the second statement—gender dysphoria is neither right nor wrong, but *what you do with it* may be right or wrong—can be confusing to someone who wishes to ask questions and explore options. The question of what exactly would be right or wrong to do can be a concern for a faith community, not to mention the person sorting out these issues. For others, it might be helpful to discuss this with trusted and mature persons in one's faith community, particularly if living a life in keeping with one's faith community's expectations is intrinsically important to the individual.

For instance, in some faith communities, the option of hormonal treatment or surgical interventions to address feelings of gender dysphoria are not condoned. It is seen as a sin to alter the body that God gave to the individual to inhabit. It is almost perceived as an affront to God—essentially saying to God that a mistake was made, or that God somehow made a mistake at the point of the creation of that person. Thus, the question of what to do with the internal experiences of conflict for individuals from these type of faith traditions may be either (a) helping the transgender person find non-invasive ways to manage the gender dysphoria or (b) helping the individual to manage the religious disonnance should the person choose to utilize hormonal or surgical procedures.

Ultimately, this is the overarching challenge: To help the TG individual know that having experiences of gender dysphoria does not mean he or she is "bad." Does struggling with gender identity questions or conflicts make that individual a "bad" person? Most religions recognize that everyone struggles with different issues and questions, and sometimes even with the answers that they find. For example, some people may wrestle with feelings of envy, jealousy, anxiety, or depression. Other struggles feel different than that and also resonate with us: some may struggle finding their voices as artists; a lover may struggle to express his love; another person may wrestle against an adversary. Internal conflict takes many shapes and sizes—and struggles, in and of themselves, *do not* make anyone a bad person.

PURSUING GOD FOR MEANING AND PURPOSE

In spite of the encouragement that struggling with gender dysphoria does not make someone a "bad" person, the transgender individual may still feel like these larger questions loom overhead: "Where's God in all of this? If He thinks this is wrong, then why did He let me experience this? And why doesn't He help me deal with it?"

It can surely be confusing. Being taught that God does not approve of gender dysphoria may make the transgender person feel torn. The individual may feel as though it is impossible to make sense of his or her faith and gender identity. However, this is a key point: *the transgender person does not have to choose one or the other.*

For individuals who believe in a personal God, it may be helpful for them to invite Him into the process of sorting out what the feelings and experiences mean and what to do in response. By including God in this process, people feel comforted, less isolated and alone, and may have more clarity about who they are. Take for example, this Christian's experience:

> At first, my own loathing of myself and the way I was treated held me back. Then as
> I began to accept my gender diversity I felt the walls lift. Then the doubts returned and I
> wondered if God was really with me or I was fooling myself. At the moment, I am
> realizing that God is not as hung up on my gender as I am and that I am worried more

about what other people think rather than on spreading the truth about Jesus. All in all, though, my faith is growing and my relationship with Him is growing as I learn to lean on Him...He will lead me where he wants me, because he called me. I am never alone because he promised never to leave me nor forsake me. And nothing this workd [*sic*] throws ar [*sic*] me can hurt me because for me, too, to live is Christ and to die is gain, absent from the body is Present with the lord [*sic*].

In addition to praying and inviting God on the journey, the individual can pose other internal questions, "What else can I do?" or "What does this look like?" or "So, where do my experiences of gender dysphoria fit into God's intention for gender and gender identity?" These questions raise the topic of meaning and purpose.

For the Abrahamic faith traditions, and more specifically within Christianity, the conventional understanding is that the creation story tells us something about God's intent for people to be either male or female. The story does not end there, however. Within most Christian traditions, one quickly learns that creation has been affected by *the fall*—that is to say that the original sin of Adam and Eve negatively impacts all of the created order, including one's gender and sexuality, to some extent.

Some transgender persons of faith view their dysphoria as a result of *the fall*. Others would see their psychological sense of their gender as a more accurate reflection of who they really are. Neither group blames themselves for their experiences of gender dysphoria (they are not morally responsible for having gender dysphoria—it's not their fault), and both would say they have decisions to make about how they will live and respond to their dysphoria. The former group might identify the least invasive ways to manage their dysphoria in light of their biological sex, while the latter group may be more likely to explore expressing their sense of themselves through cross-sex behavior, dress, and possibly other, more invasive, avenues.

Part of the journey may involve learning how to deal with difficult things and learning not to give up in the midst of pain. Not only Christianity, but also Judaism and Islam have a robust understanding of this concept of "suffering well". In a traditional Christian framework, this reflects redemption, which includes the process of sanctification. It is the process of life that people go through—the trials, the difficult times, the moments when one feels like there is nothing left to give—that molds people more and more into the image and likeness of Christ. Both Judaism and Islam have similar tenants.

In keeping with the question of how to live and manage gender dysphoria, transgender people of faith might also ask how God could use experiences of gender dysphoria in their lives. To answer this question, it may be helpful for these individuals to reflect on how these experiences fit within a larger understanding of the world based on their religious faith traditions.

Many people of faith often consider any experience that is an ongoing and enduring difficulty as an opportunity to grow closer to God through reliance on God in ways that are not experienced when they are not faced with such difficulties. Furthermore, such experiences are often seen as ways to build one's strength and turn the individual into a better person.

As such, another helpful question for the person to ask may be something along these lines: "Is there an opportunity here (in the midst of experiences of gender dysphoria) to experience God in a more real and intimate way?" From this perspective, the individual can possibly rely on God differently through the most enduring and ongoing challenges being faced.

Here are some additional questions that can be posed to the transgender person: "Can you think of any times God has used your ongoing and enduring difficulties to make you stronger or to help others in some way?" "How has God used your experiences of gender dysphoria to help you become a better person?" These answers are not always obvious, and so much of this can remain a mystery. Yet, it is helpful to have people of faith consider the different ways God has potentially used their struggles to make this world a little better.

It is often through pondering questions like these, and others triggered by one's responses to these, that the search for meaning and purpose can be facilitated.

LIVING IN THE TENSION

Questions about what it means to trust God with experiences of gender dysphoria are also common. This may be especially hard for individuals depending on whether or not they believe God is to blame for their dysphoria, or if they believe God can but has chosen not to bring about resolution.

Additionally, it can be helpful for the individual to think about God's intention for him or her as a person. That is, what is the big picture when it comes to who that person is—not just for that person as someone who experiences gender dysphoria—for his or her identity as a whole.

A transgender person of faith may say something like, "My experience of the other gender may be just as satisfying and real *to me* as what others experience when their psychological and emotional sense of themselves lines up with their sexual anatomy and biology. But what does God intend, and what would God have *me* do?"

At this point, TG persons of faith may be feeling different emotions, such as frustration, discouragement, confusion, anger, or sadness because their feelings of gender dysphoria seem to contrast with what they believe is, or perceive as God's intention, for their gender identity. We believe it is important to ask these questions and to acknowledge how the person feels.

Also know that we are not trying to place pressure on a person of faith to have a change of gender identity, or to bring the outward physical person into conformity with one's perceived inward gender. If the person feels that kind of pressure at this point, what is being perceived is most likely internal—it is coming from somewhere inside of that individual and usually based on some element of shame or of being "not good enough."

We know of people who have said they experienced gender dysphoria, and have changed their outward physical person to conform to their inner sense of their gender identity, though this does not appear to be a common experience. We know of other people whose birth sex was either male or female who still experience gender dysphoria and who have created tailored paths and journeys that allow them many options for managing their dysphoria (e.g., taking hormones, part-time cross dressing, having some but not all of the sex-reassignment surgeries, etc.).

We think it would be a mistake to talk about or expect any sort of specific change that a religious TG person should experience. Many people have wished the feelings of gender dysphoria would just "go away." And many people have prayed for a long time that God would just "take away" those feelings and experiences. However, the feelings and experiences still remain. This leaves some TG persons of faith in a state of frustration and anxiety, and they may wonder if they are "praying enough" or "working hard enough". Because of this, they can end up feeling badly about themselves.

Other TG persons of faith in this state of frustration and anxiety feel angry with God because they feel like He has not heard their prayers. Or worse, they feel as though God did hear their prayers but that He is ignoring them and there is some reason why He has chosen not to intervene. Because of this anger, these people may end up changing religious traditions, or abandoning their faith or trust in God. For example, Fitzgerald, Meier, Hughes, Teo, Nguyen, & Carnew (2013) found that nearly 73% of their transgender population moved away from their childhood religious identification as adults.

Maybe a TG person of faith who presents to therapy has had similar reactions. If so, we hope to encourage that person with the idea that this is a process: how this individual experiences and understands his or her gender dysphoria now will likely be different years down the road. In the same way, how this individual experiences his or her faith and religious beliefs now could change over time.

There are many things we go through as we mature and grow older that help us to become the people we have been created to be. Part of this journey involves knowing that it is fairly normal for people to question their faith, or have doubts about God. Another part of the journey is learning how to deal with difficult things and learning not to give up in the midst of very painful parts and intense doubt. It is important to reiterate that even though life can be especially challenging at times for TG persons of faith, they do not have to give up their spirituality in light of their gender identity—nor do they have to prescriptively change their inner sense of gender in order to retain a relationship with God.

SPECIFIC RECOMMENDATIONS

With that said, let us move into some practical recommendations of how to clinically work with TG individuals who present to therapy due to an internal struggle with the experience of gender dysphoria in light of their faith values. First and foremost, clinicians should strive to create a climate of safety and non-judgment. Additionally, they would be wise to assume a posture of humility and curiosity as each TG person who presents to therapy has unique concerns and experiences of not only a sense of gender but of religion, spirituality, and the faith tradition in question. In addition to the graceful posture of the clinician and the safe therapeutic milieu, the client needs to be informed that the experience of gender dysphoria will not suddenly disappear one day after any specific number of sessions of therapy, just like it did not suddenly appear one day. It is helpful to use the metaphor of being on a journey, and specifically a journey that the client is taking at his or her own pace. Moreover, a potential outcome of this journey is that the retelling of the journey could be a resource to others in the future. Another powerful intervention is to ask the client to invite God into his or her experience. As noted previously, inviting God into the process has the potential of reducing the experiences of anxiety, fear, and of being alone. Some people have found the following prayer helpful:

> I would like to invite You into my experience. I do experience gender identity questions or concerns, and I want to ask you to be with me in what I am experiencing. Please guide me as I search for ways to respond to my gender dysphoria.

I do not want to pretend that it is not there, and I do not want to box this up. I want what I feel, my thoughts, my actions, my experiences, and my intentions to be used by you, and so I ask for your guidance and direction. Amen.

As clinicians we are often in the position of helping our clients tap into resources that they might not otherwise have access to or be able to easily find. This is no different when working with TG persons. For religiously-oriented TG individuals, it could be extremely beneficial to find a safe place of worship that can support them as they ask questions and explore their options. If clients do not have the insight or ability to find such places of worship, clinicians will hopefully have contacts in the community to which clients can be directed.

In addition to physical places of worship, it is often helpful for TG persons of faith to find support via the Internet. There are multiple support networks online for TG individuals of various faith traditions. These avenues of support may be instrumental in helping clients find and express their voices. They can learn from the experiences of other TG persons of faith. Clinicians need to be aware of and help guide their clients to on-line groups that are productive and open to various TG presentations and resolutions in order to help the clients have a range of experiences to evaluate. It is often in the interactions with people at varying stages of transition who have struggled with different aspects of their faith traditions that clients can gain a sense of the multiple pathways to resolution that can occur for TG persons of faith.

CONCLUSION

The degree and scope of resolution or transition for TG persons of faith who have an internal struggle due to their understanding of their faith traditions can vary greatly. In the same vein, individuals who espouse one of the faith traditions from the three major Abrahamic religions (Judaism, Islam, & Christianity) and experience gender dysphoria may choose to disavow their faith or belief in God, or choose to change their beliefs in order to accommodate their TG experiences. Although we focused primarily on Christianity, we see value in developing resources for navigating religious identity and gender identity conflicts in these three world religions and, of course, other religions, such as Hinduism and Buddhism.

Mental health clinicians are held to ethical standards that promote the value of each client's diverse ways of being, including religious and gendered ways of being. It remains an important point to note that TG individuals do not need to give up their religious or spiritual ways of being in order to resolve any internal conflict regarding their gender dysphoria and faith. Both aspects of their being can be valued and respected while being explored in the process of helping them come to manageable resolutions.

It is helpful to think of this process as a journey, as we noted above. Any transition process for a TG individual takes time. It also takes time to explore and evaluate one's faith and spiritual beliefs to come to a solid sense of oneself as being a beloved child of the Almighty. As clinicians we have the honor of sojourning with our clients through these waters that can be very choppy and overwhelming. It is our privilege to provide the safe space needed to traverse the uncharted territory for each individual.

REFERENCES

Carr, T. L., Yarhouse, M. A., & Thomas, R. L. (2013). MTF transgender Christians: An exploratory study with milestone events. *Poster presented at the National Transgender Health Summit.* Oakland, CA. May 17-18, 2013.

Fitzgerald, K. M., Meier, S., Hughes, L. C., Teo, L., Nguyen, C., & Carnew, M. (2013). Religiosity in the female to male transgender community. *Poster presented at the National Transgender Health Summit.* Oakland, CA. May 17-18, 2013.

Meyer-Bahlburg, H. F. L. (2002). Gender Identity Disorder in young boys: A parent- and peer-based treatment protocol. *Clinical Child Psychology and Psychiatry*, 7 (3), 360-376.

Yarhouse, M. A. & Carr, T. L. (2012). MTF transgender Christians' experiences: A qualitative study. *Journal of LGBT Issues in Counseling*, 6(1), 18-33. doi: 10.1080/15538605.2012.649405.

Yarhouse, M. A. & Tan, E. S. N. (2014). *Sexuality and sex therapy: A comprehensive Christian appraisal.* Downers Grove, IL: InterVarsity Academic.

Zhou, J. N., Hofman, M. A., Gooren, L. J. G., & Swaab, D. F.. (1995). A sex difference in the human brain and its relation to transsexuality. *Nature,* 378, pp. 68-70.

In: Gender Identity
Editor: Beverly L. Miller

ISBN: 978-1-63321-488-0
© 2014 Nova Science Publishers, Inc.

Chapter 15

REPORT ON TG CHRISTIANS' MILESTONE EVENTS

Trista L. Carr[1], Psy.D., Mark A. Yarhouse[2], Psy.D. and Rebecca Thomas[2], M.A.
[1]Private Practice, California
[2]Regent University, Virginia

This report presents the findings from an exploratory study of the experiences of 34 male-to-female transgender persons of faith. These findings are from a larger study on the experiences of transgender (TG) Christians (Yarhouse & Carr, 2012). Some of the items discussed are ages/timeframes in which people begin to acknowledge for themselves that there is an apparent conflict between their birth sex and their sense of gender; when and what types of attributions are made to these experiences; when and with whom they disclosed their inner conflict; and if/when they began to transition. Additionally, questions are asked about the participants' experiences within their faith traditions, including such areas as church life, relationship with God, and understanding of Scripture. Granted this study is retrospective and subject to all the limitations of recall, but prior research on children whose gender dysphoria persists and desists (Steensma, Biemond, deBoer, & Cohen-Kettenis, 2010), as well as milestone events in identify formation in other areas of study (e.g., lesbian, gay and bisexual [LGB] studies; e.g., Dube&Savin-Williams, 1999) warrants some examination of typical timelines in which some of common life events generally occur.

When considering milestone events in gender identity development among TG Christians, we see that the average age of awareness of a gender identity conflict was 8 years old. The conflict itself was indicated via interest in cross-dressing behaviors. It is interesting that this is not necessarily confusing to a child; however, initial internal confusion was reported at an average age of 11 years old. This subjective experience of confusion most typically stemmed from either gender-variant behaviors or the consequences arising from such behaviors or interests. This may have to do with increased exposure to peers and evaluations of interests and mannerisms with reference to a larger peer group.

The average age for making initial attributions about their experiences of internal conflict was approximately 18.5 years old. Attributions in the context refer to how a person makes sense or establishes meaning with reference to their experience of internal conflict. The most frequent initial attribution participants made was that "something is wrong with me." This was followed closely by a compelling need to educate themselves about their experiences and a deep desire to be a woman. It would be interesting to see if attributions and meaning-making occurred later in the teen years with this sample and if that is a reflection of the average age of participants. Given remarkable social changes over the past 20 years, perhaps a younger sample would make attributions at a younger age.

The average age for initial disclosure of gender dysphoria to others was 34 years, 9 months, with the overwhelming majority disclosing to their spouse or significant other. This particular piece of data may also be reflective of an age cohort effect. Although milestone events are not typically a point of study (as there would be among those who study sexual identity development), there does appear to be much more focus today on recognizing TG issues at a younger age and finding appropriate support for such persons.

In regards to attempting to address the conflict between their birth sex and inner gender identity, some participants indicated that it was a complex and ongoing process. However, for those that indicated an age, they typically started trying to sort out their experiences at an average of nearly 27 years old and did so by both seeking out a professional counselor or expert and by engaging in cross-dressing behaviors. It seems as though initial attempts to make meaning of their experiences came before disclosing their conflict to another. This means that these attempts to work through conflict were probably completed in isolation unless a therapist was indeed invited into the process.

When asked about gender identity resolution as a milestone, the majority of participants either indicated that they are still in process, or they did not give an age of when the internal conflict was resolved. However, for those who did indicate an age, it was slightly over 46.5 years old, and even more frequently around the age of 58. Thus, it seems that resolution for this sub-population of MTF individuals occurred at a later age if at all. It will be interesting to see if a younger sample of TG persons experience resolution at an earlier age or whether there are those who are unable to experience resolution even in the most supportive environments. Again, this is an area for further research.

The average age for identifying as a Christian was approximately 23. The meaning associate with being a Christian was discussed in our previous analysis (Yarhouse & Carr, 2012) but referenced a personal relationship with Jesus, recognizing Jesus as savior, and so on. The majority of participants denoted starting a personal relationship with Jesus through being saved by grace through faith. Thus, the majority of the participants seem to claim a conversion experience that is consistent with truth claims that are central tenets of Christianity. At the same time, the participants described themselves as highly spiritual and moderately religious overall. Some of the participants indicated that they were not at all religious but considered themselves highly spiritual. This may reflect the experiences they had with organized religion, which was frequently negative, and contrasts sharply with the experiences they have reported in their relationship with God (Yarhouse & Carr, 2012).

Responses about the etiology of gender dysphoria reflected by the incongruence between their inner gender identity and their assigned birth sex ranged from it being purely genetics to it being a part of God's will and plan for their lives. A sizable group ($n = 5$) felt as though there are multiple causes for their conflict that include things such as genetics/epigenetics, one's childhood experiences, God's plan, and/or environmental factors. Although researchers today are not clear on the etiology, this may be an important issue for both counseling and pastoral care. Because there are different ways of understanding etiology—different explanatory frameworks—that reside between differing opinions on how to respond to internal conflicts, it may be helpful to explore attributions and meaning-making, particularly in light of what a church teaches about sexuality, gender, gender identity, and gender expression.

Many participants also indicated that transgender issues are generally not discussed in Scripture. This is an important consideration for church leaders. From the perspective of those who are navigating these concerns, many do not feel that the Bible explicitly addresses this area, which is a perspective those in leadership might benefit from understanding, despite possible disagreements surrounding the topic.

Many individuals ($n = 10$) in the study had not yet found resolution between their biological sex and inner gender identity, recognizing it as an ongoing struggle. Those who did indicated achieving resolution reported that it occurred through sex reassignment surgery (SRS). Assistance from others was another key theme, as they recognized the need for support from friends and loved ones in addition to professionals such as counselors and psychologists.

In perhaps one of the more poignant areas for discussion, TG Christians offered suggestions to the church. These included offering acceptance, not forcing individuals to change, and learning from the TG population. These themes reinforce the idea that within churches, open discussion about transgender issues needs to happen, at least from the perspective of TG Christians. Even in terms of advice individuals in the study would give other TG individuals, seeking out trustworthy people was the most common response. There seems to be a great need for dialogue and for supportive others.

It is important to note that this is a relatively small study of MTF Christian transgender individuals; thus, the results are not generalizable to all individuals who are transgender and Christian. Additionally, results do not include those who do not espouse a Christian identity or those with an FTM transgender identity. Furthermore, the participants are older, with an average age of 55; as such the data may not be representative of the experiences of younger MTF transgender Christians. Unfortunately, researchers inadvertently did not ask the participants about their racial/ethnic identities or their educational or socioeconomic status; thus the data needs to be understood in light of this oversight.

REFERENCES

Dube, E. M., &Savin-Williams, R. C. (1999). Sexual identity development among ethnic sexual-minority male youths. *Developmental Psychology*, 35(6), 1389.

Steensma, T. D., Biemond, R., deBoer, F., & Cohen-Kettenis, P. T. (2010). Desisting and persisting gender dysphoria after childhood: A qualitative study. *Clinical Child Psychologyand Psychiatry*, 1-18. Doi: 10.1177/1359104510378303.

Yarhouse, M.A. & Carr, T.L. (2012). MTF transgender Christians' experiences: A qualitative study. *Journal of LGBT Issues in Counseling*, 6(1), 18-33. doi: 10.1080/15538605. 2012.649405.

INDEX

B

C

E

H

N

O

Q

R

S